John Flavel, American Tract Society

Christ Knocking at the Door of Sinners' Hearts

a solemn entreaty to receive the Saviour and his gospel in the day of mercy

John Flavel, American Tract Society

Christ Knocking at the Door of Sinners' Hearts
a solemn entreaty to receive the Saviour and his gospel in the day of mercy

ISBN/EAN: 9783337285135

Printed in Europe, USA, Canada, Australia, Japan

Cover: Foto ©Lupo / pixelio.de

More available books at **www.hansebooks.com**

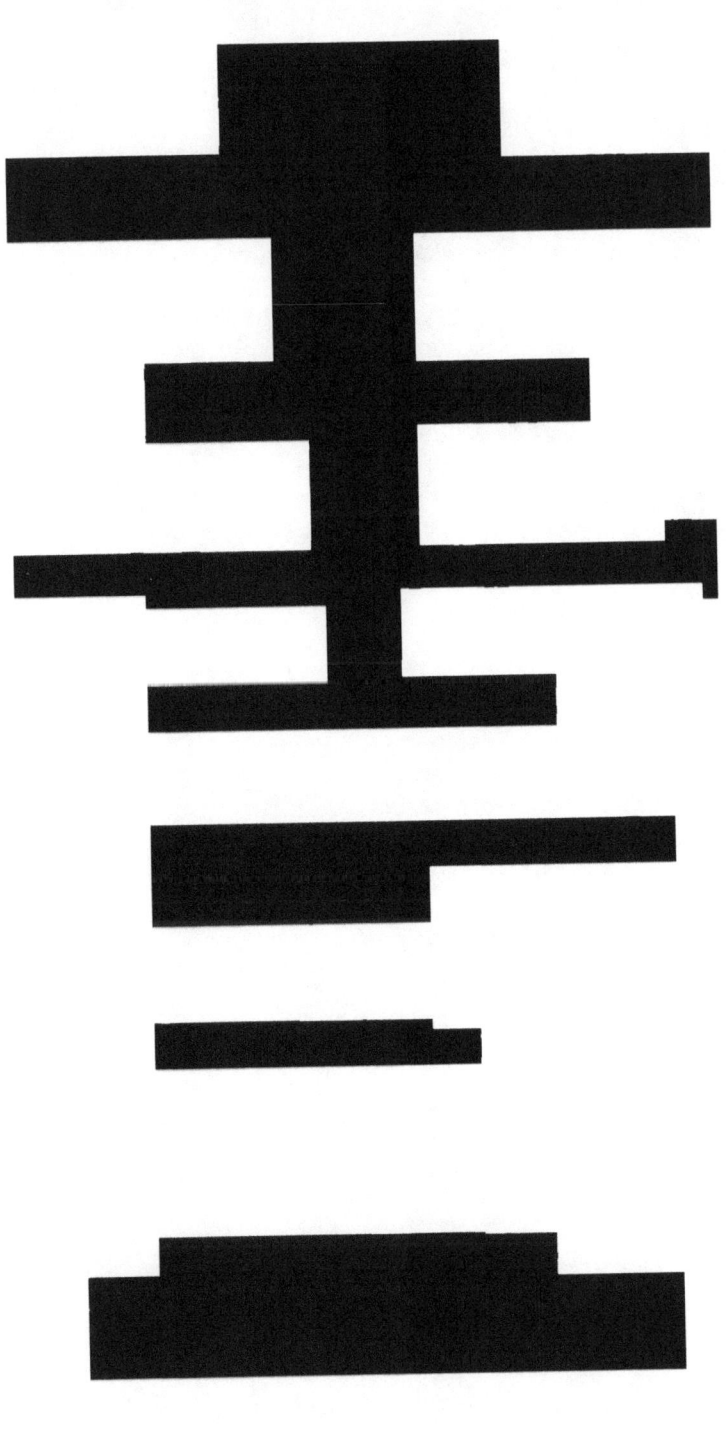

PREFATORY NOTICE.

THE following is a revised edition of an admirable treatise by the author of "The Fountain of Life" and "The Method of Grace."

It appeared originally under the title of "England's Duty;" and consisted of twelve sermons, preached, under the rich effusions of the Spirit, to the author's congregation, in the years 1688–9, about two years before his death, on the restoration of religious freedom, through the revolution that virtually annulled the Act of Uniformity, by which the author for twenty-five years had been restrained from the free and public exercise of his ministry.

In this edition the treatise has been arranged in the form of chapters, and while considerable liberty has been taken with the language, in changing obscure phraseology, substituting modern for obsolete words, and omitting repetitious passages, the spirit of the writer and his views of Christian doctrine have been carefully preserved, and every scriptural quotation has been verified. A new title has likewise been adopted, more significant of the subject-matter of the work. It is believed, that in its present form, it will be esteemed a worthy companion to those already named, and, under the divine blessing, add greatly to the usefulness of the estimable author.

FROM THE

AUTHOR'S EPISTLE TO THE READER.

CANDID READER—The following discourse comes to thy hand in the native plainness in which it was preached. I was conscientiously unwilling to alter it, because I found by experience the Lord had blessed and prospered it in that dress, far beyond any other composures on which I had bestowed more pains. Let it not be censured as vanity or ostentation, that I here acknowledge the goodness of God in leading me to, and blessing my poor labors on this subject. Who and what am I, that I should be continued and again employed in the Lord's harvest, and that with success and encouragement, when so many of my brethren, with much richer gifts and graces, have in my time been called out of the vineyard, and are now silent in the grave. It is true, they enjoy what I do not; and it is as true, I am capable of doing some service for God which they are not. In preaching these sermons, I had many occasions to reflect upon the sense of that scripture, "The ploughman shall overtake the reaper, and the treader of grapes him that soweth seed." Amos 9:13. Sowing and reaping times trod so close upon each other, that, in all humility I speak it to the praise of God, it was the busiest and most blessed time I ever saw since I first preached the gospel.

We have now a day of special mercy: there is a wide door of religious opportunity opened to us. O that it may prove an effectual door. It is wonderful, that after all our sinful provocations this sweet voice is still heard, "Behold, I stand at the door and knock." Our mercies and liberties are obtained for us by our potent Advocate in the heavens: if we bring forth fruit, well; if not, the axe lieth at the root of the tree. Let us not feel secure. Jerusalem was the city of the great King; the seat of his worship and the symbols of his presence were fixed there; it was the joy of the whole earth, the house of prayer for all nations; thither the tribes went up to worship, the tribes of the Lord unto the testimony of Israel. For there were set thrones of judgment, the thrones of the house of David. Psa. 122:4, 5. These privileges she enjoyed through the succession of many ages, and she had remained the glory of all nations to this day, had she known and improved in that day the things that belonged to her peace; but her people neglected their season, rejected their mercies, and miserably perished in their sins: for there ever was and will be found to be an inseparable connection between the final rejection of Christ, and the destruction of the rejecters, Matt. 22:5–7, the contemplation of which drew compassionate tears from the Redeemer's eyes, when he beheld it in his descent from the mount of Olives. Luke 19:41, 42.

As to this treatise, thou wilt find it a persuasive to open thy heart to Christ. Thy soul, reader, is a magnificent structure built by Christ; such stately rooms as thy understanding, will, conscience, and affections, are too good for any other to inhabit. If thou art in thy unregenerate state, he solemnly demands in this treatise admission into the soul he made, by the consent of the will; which, if thou refuse to give him, then witness is taken that Christ once more demanded entrance into thy soul, which he made, and was denied it. If thou hast opened thy heart to him, thou wilt, I hope, meet somewhat in this treatise that will clear thy evidences and cheer thy heart. Pray, read, ponder, and apply. I am

                Thine and the church's servant,

                            JOHN FLAVEL.

CONTENTS.

From the Author's Epistle to the Reader, ... 5

CHAPTER I.
THE OFFERS OF MERCY RECORDED AND WITNESSED FOR THE JUDGMENT-DAY.

"Behold, I stand at the door and knock: if any man hear my voice, and open the door, I will come in to him, and will sup with him, and he with me." Rev. 3:20 9

CHAPTER II.
THE PRESENCE OF CHRIST IN HIS ORDINANCES.

"Behold, *I* stand at the door and knock," 27

CHAPTER III.
THE HEART BARRED AGAINST CHRIST.

"Behold, *I stand at the door* and knock," 43

CHAPTER IV.
CHRIST'S PATIENCE IN WAITING UPON OBSTINATE SINNERS.

"Behold, *I stand* at the door and knock, ... 73

CHAPTER V.
EVERY CONVICTION OF CONSCIENCE AND MOTION OF THE SPIRIT A KNOCK FROM CHRIST.

"Behold, I stand at the door *and knock*, ... 107

CHAPTER VI.
CHRIST'S EARNEST ENTREATY FOR UNION AND COMMUNION WITH SINNERS.

"Behold, *I stand at the door and knock*," 141

CHAPTER VII.
CHRIST REJECTS NONE WHO OPEN TO HIM.

"*If any man* hear my voice, and open the door, I will come in to him," 181

CHAPTER VIII.

NONE RECEIVE CHRIST UNTIL HIS SPIRITUAL QUICKENING VOICE IS HEARD.

"If any man *hear my voice*, and open the door, I will come in to him,"· 216

CHAPTER IX.

THE OPENING OF THE HEART TO CHRIST BY FAITH THE GREAT DESIGN OF THE GOSPEL.

"If any man hear my voice, *and open the door*, I will come in to him," 248

CHAPTER X.

CHRIST BRINGS GREAT BLESSINGS TO THE SOUL THAT OPENS TO HIM.

"If any man hear my voice, and open the door, *I will come in to him, and will sup with him, and he with me,*" 271

CHAPTER XI.

COMMUNION BETWEEN CHRIST AND BELIEVERS ON EARTH.

"I will come in to him, *and will sup with him, and he with me,*"··· 304

CHAPTER XII.

COMMUNION BETWEEN CHRIST AND BELIEVERS ON EARTH—CONTINUED

"I will come in to him, and will sup with him, *and he with me,*"····· 324

CHAPTER XIII.

THE TRUTH HELD IN UNRIGHTEOUSNESS.

"The wrath of God is revealed from heaven against all ungodliness and unrighteousness of men, who hold the truth in unrighteousness." Rom. 1:18, ... 349

CHAPTER XIV.

THE TRUTH HELD IN UNRIGHTEOUSNESS—CONTINUED.

"The wrath of God is revealed from heaven against all ungodliness and unrighteousness of men, who hold the truth in unrighteousness." Rom. 1:18, ... 376

CHRIST KNOCKING AT THE DOOR.

CHAPTER I.

THE OFFERS OF MERCY RECORDED AND WITNESSED FOR THE JUDGMENT-DAY.

"*BEHOLD*, I STAND AT THE DOOR AND KNOCK: IF ANY MAN HEAR MY VOICE, AND OPEN THE DOOR, I WILL COME IN TO HIM, AND WILL SUP WITH HIM, AND HE WITH ME." Rev. 3:20.

This day hath our compassionate Redeemer opened unto us a door of liberty—liberty to us to preach, and liberty for you to hear the glad tidings of the gospel. This is a day few looked for; how often have I said in the years that are past, God hath no more work for me to do, and I shall have no more strength and opportunities to work for God. And how often have you said in your hearts, we have sinned our ministers out of their pulpits, and our eyes shall no more behold these our teachers. But lo, beyond the thoughts of most hearts, a wide and, I hope, an effectual door is now opened in the midst of us. O that it may be to us as the valley of Achor was to Israel, "for a door of hope," Hosea 2:15; not only making the troubles they met with in that valley an inlet to their mercies, as ours have been to us, but giving them that valley as a pledge of greater mercies intended for them. Upon the first appearance of this mercy, my thoughts were how to make the most fruitful improvement of it among you, lest we should sin ourselves back again into bondage.

In the contemplation of this matter, the Lord directed me to this scripture, wherein the same hand that opened to you the door of liberty, knocks importunately at the doors of your hearts for entrance into them, and for union and communion with them. It will be sad indeed if he who hath let you into all these mercies, should himself be shut out of your hearts; but if the Lord help you to open your hearts now to Christ, I doubt not this door of liberty will be kept open to you, how many soever the adversaries be that will do their utmost to shut it up. Ezek. 39 : 29. The mercies you enjoy this day are the fruits of Christ's intercession with the Father for one trial more: if we bring forth fruit, well; if not, the axe lieth at the root of the tree. Under this consideration I desire to speak, and even so the Lord help you to hear what shall be spoken from this precious scripture, "Behold, I stand at the door and knock: if any man hear my voice and open the door, I will come in to him, and will sup with him, and he with me."

These words are a branch of that excellent epistle dictated by Christ, and sent by his servant John to the church of Laodicea, the most formal and degenerate of all the seven churches; yet the great Physician will try his skill upon them, both by the rebukes of the rod and by the persuasive power of the word, "Behold, I stand at the door and knock," etc.

This text is Christ's wooing voice, full of heavenly rhetoric to win and gain the hearts of sinners to himself; wherein we have these two general parts.

1. Christ's suit for a sinner's heart.
2. The powerful arguments enforcing his suit.

1. *Christ's suit for a sinner's heart*, in which is, (1,) *the solemn preface*, ushering it in, "*Behold.*" The preface is exceedingly solemn; for besides the common use of this word *behold* in other places, to excite attention or put weight into an affirmation, it stands here, as a judicious

expositor says, as a term of notification or public record, wherein Christ takes witnesses of the most gracious offer he was now about to make to their souls, and will have it stand for a perpetual memorial of this offer, as a testimony for or against their souls to all eternity, to cut off all excuses and pretences for time to come.

(2.) *The suitor*, Christ himself, "*I* stand;" I who have a right of sovereignty over you; I who have shed my invaluable blood to purchase you, and might justly condemn you upon the first denial or demur, "behold, I stand:" this is the suitor.

(3.) *His posture and action*, "I stand at the door and knock:" the word is fitly translated, "I stand," yet so as that it notes a continual action. I have stood, and do still stand with unwearied patience; I once stood personally and bodily among you in the days of my flesh, and I still stand spiritually and representatively in my ambassadors at the door, that is, the mind and conscience, the faculties and powers which are introductory to the whole soul.

The word "door" is here properly put to signify those introductory faculties of the soul, which are of like use to it, as the door is to the house. This is the Redeemer's posture, his action is *knocking*, that is, his powerful and gracious attempts to open the heart to give him admission. The word "knock" signifies a strong and powerful knock; he stands patiently, and knocks powerfully by the word outwardly, by the convictions, motions, impulses, and strivings of his Spirit inwardly.

(4.) *The design and end of the suit;* it is for "opening" to him, that is, consenting, receiving, and heartily accepting him by faith. The Lord opened the heart of Lydia, Acts 16 : 14; that is, persuaded her soul to believe; implying that the heart by nature is strongly barred and locked up against Christ, and that nothing but a power from him can open it.

2. *The powerful arguments and motives used by Christ to obtain his suit* in the sinner's heart; and they are drawn from two inestimable benefits which accrue to the opening or believing soul.

(1.) *Union:* "I will come in to him;" that is, I will unite myself with the opening, believing soul; he shall be mystically one with me, and I with him.

(2.) *Communion:* "I will sup with him, and he with me;" that is, I will feast the believing soul with the delicacies of heaven; such comforts, joys, and pleasures as none but believers are capable of.

And, to set home all, these special benefits are proposed by Christ to all sorts of sinners, great and small, old and young: "*If any man* hear my voice, and open the door:" that so no soul might be discouraged from believing by the greatness or multitude of his sins, but the vilest of sinners may see free grace triumphing over all their unworthiness, on their consent to take Christ according to the gracious offers of the gospel.

The words thus opened afford many great and useful points of doctrine, comprehending in them the very substance of the gospel. The first which arises from the solemn and remarkable preface, "BEHOLD," will be this:

That every offer of Christ to the souls of sinners is recorded and witnessed with respect to the day of account and reckoning.

Here we shall inquire into three things: Who are God's witnesses to all the offers of the gospel; what they witness to; and why God records every offer of Christ, and takes a witness thereof.

I. WHO ARE GOD'S WITNESSES to all the tenders and offers made of Christ by the gospel? and they will be found to be more than a strict legal number; for,

1. *His ministers,* by whom he makes them, are all wit-

nesses as well as officers of Christ to the people. "I have appeared unto thee for this purpose, to make thee a minister and a witness." Acts 26 : 16. Here you see ministers have a double office, to propose and offer Christ, and then to bear witness for or against those to whom he is thus offered; they are expressly called God's witnesses. Rev. 11 : 7. Their labors witness, their sufferings witness, their solemn appeals to God witness, yea, the very dust of their feet shaken off against the refusers of Christ, turns to a testimony against them. Mark 6 : 11. Every sigh, every drop of sweat, much more of blood, are placed in God's book along with all their sermons and prayers, and will be produced and read in the great day against all the refusers and despisers of Christ.

2. *The gospel itself*, which is preached to you, is a testimony or witness for God against every one who rejects it. "He that rejecteth me, and receiveth not my words, hath one that judgeth him; the word that I have spoken, the same shall judge him in the last day." John 12 : 48. And this is the sense of Christ's word, Matt. 24 : 14, "And this gospel of the kingdom shall be preached in all the world, for a witness unto all nations; and then shall the end come." Ah, what a solemn record is here; every sermon you hear, yea, every reproof, persuasion, and conviction is a witness for God to condemn every soul in judgment that complies not immediately with the calls of the gospel: so many sermons, so many witnesses.

3. *Every man's conscience* is a witness for God, that he has a fair offer made him; the very consciences of the heathen who never saw a Bible, who had no other preachers but the sun, moon, and stars and other works of nature; yet of them the apostle says, that they "show the work of the law written in their hearts, their conscience also bearing witness, and their thoughts the mean while accusing or else excusing one another." Rom. 2 : 15. Certainly if such vigor and activity was put into the consciences of

heathen, who could only read the will of God by the dim moonlight of natural reason, how much more vigorous and active will conscience be in its accusing office against all who live under the bright beams of gospel light. Their consciences will be swift witnesses, and will ring sad peals in their ears another day. They "shall know that there hath been a prophet among them." Ezek. 2 : 5. This single witness is instead of a thousand other witnesses for God.

4. *The examples of all who believe and obey the gospel*, are so many witnesses for God against the despisers and neglecters of the great salvation. Every mourning, trembling soul among you is a witness against all the dead-hearted, unbelieving, disobedient ones that sit with them under the same ordinances. Hence it is said, "Do ye not know that the saints shall judge the world?" 1 Cor. 6 : 2. They shall be assessors with Christ in the great day, and condemn the world by their examples, as Noah did the old world. Thus, "John came unto you in the way of righteousness, and ye believed him not: but the publicans and the harlots believed him; and ye, when ye had seen it, repented not afterward, that ye might believe him." Matt. 21 : 32. As if he had said, What shift do you make to quiet your consciences and stifle your convictions, when you see publicans, the worst of men, and harlots, the worst of women, repenting, believing, and hungering after Christ; their examples shall be your judges. These are God's witnesses.

II. Next let us consider what is the OBJECT MATTER unto which they give their testimony, and that will be found twofold, according to the twofold effect the gospel has upon them who hear it: of both which the apostle gives this account, "To the one we are the savor of death unto death; and to the other the savor of life unto life." 2 Cor. 2 : 16. Accordingly a double record is made.

1. *Of the obedience and faith of some*, which record

will be produced to their joy and comfort in the day of the Lord; "when he shall come to be glorified in his saints, and to be admired in all them that believe (because our testimony among you was believed) in that day." 2 Thess. 1 : 10. Ministers are instruments of espousing souls to Christ, and witnesses to those espousals between him and them. 2 Cor. 11 : 2. Both these offices are exceedingly grateful and pleasant to every faithful minister.

2. A record is made, and witness taken *of all the refusals, disobedience, and slightings of Christ by others.* Thus Moses will be the accuser of the Jews. "Do not think that I will accuse you to the Father: there is one that accuseth you, even Moses, in whom ye trust." John 5 : 45. This is the saddest part of a minister's work; the forethoughts of it are more afflictive than all our labors and sufferings. There is a threefold record made in this case.

(1.) Of the time men have enjoyed under the means of salvation, how many years they have sat barren and coldhearted under the labors of God's faithful ministers. "Behold, these three years I come seeking fruit on this fig-tree, and find none." Luke 13 : 7. "Behold," the same term of notification with that in the text, applied to the time of God's patience towards them. And again, "From the thirteenth year of Josiah the son of Amon king of Judah, even unto this day, that is the three and twentieth year, the word of the Lord hath come unto me, and I have spoken unto you, rising early and speaking; but ye have not hearkened." Jer. 25 : 3. O consider, all the years and days you have spent under the gospel are upon your doomsday-book.

(2.) Records are also made of all the instruments God has employed for the conversion and salvation of your souls. So many ministers, whether fixed or transient, as have spent their labors upon you, are upon the book of your account. "The Lord hath sent unto you all his servants the prophets, rising early and sending them; but ye have not hearkened nor inclined your ear to hear." Jer. 25 : 4. They have wasted their health, dropped their compassionate tears, and burnt down one after another like candles, to direct you to Christ and salvation, but all in vain.

(3.) Every call, persuasion, and argument used by them to espouse you to Christ, is likewise upon the book of account. "Because I have called, and ye refused; I have stretched out my hand, and no man regarded; but ye have set at naught all my counsel, and would none of my reproof." Prov. 1 : 24, 25. These calls and counsels are of too great value with God, though of none with you, to be lost and left out of your account.

III. We shall inquire into THE GROUNDS AND REASONS of these judicial procedures of God: why he will have every man's obedience and disobedience registered and witnessed for or against him, under gospel administrations; and there are two weighty reasons thereof.

1. That *wherever the end of the gospel is attained in the conversion of a soul, that soul, and all who were instrumentally employed about the salvation of it, may have the proper reward and comfort in the great day.* "As also ye have acknowledged us in part, that we are your rejoicing, even as ye also are ours in the day of the Lord Jesus." 2 Cor. 1 : 14. This will be matter of joy unspeakable, both to you that shall receive, and to them that shall give such a comfortable testimony for you. O the joyful congratulations of that day between laborious, faithful ministers, and their believing, obedient hearers. "Lord, this was the blessed instrument of my happy illumination and conversion; though I might have ten thousand instructors in Christ, yet not many fathers; for by the blessing of thy Spirit on this man's ministry, my soul was begotten to Christ." And, on the other side, "Lord, these are the souls for whom I travailed, as in birth, until Christ was formed in them." It is a glorious thing to say, as the prophet, "Here am I, and the

children God hath given me." Nay, those who were but collaterally useful to help on the work of God begun by others, must not lose their reward in that day. "And he that reapeth receiveth wages, and gathereth fruit unto life eternal, that both he that soweth and he that reapeth may rejoice together." John 4 : 36.

2. Records are now made, and witness taken, *that thereby the judicial sentence of Jesus Christ in the last day may be made clear to all the world;* that every mouth may be stopped, and no plea left in the mouth of any condemned sinner. For Christ in that day cometh "to convince all that are ungodly," Jude 15; to convince by demonstration, that all that are Christless now may be found speechless then. Matt. 22 : 12. Hence it is said, "The ungodly shall not stand in the judgment." Psalm 1 : 5. And no wonder, when so many full testimonies and unexceptionable witnesses shall come point blank against them : the ministers that preached, the word they preached, their own consciences, and the example of all believers will be produced against them.

INFERENCE 1. *The undoubted certainty of a day of judgment is hence evinced.* To what purpose else are records made, and witness taken, but with respect to an audit-day? This is a truth sealed on the conscience of the very heathen; their consciences bear witness. Rom. 2 : 15. But in vain are all these records made, unless there be a day to produce and plead them; and of that day the prophet Daniel speaks, "The judgment was set, and the books were opened." Daniel 7 : 10. And again, "I saw the dead, small and great, stand before God; and the books were opened; and another book was opened, which is the book of life; and the dead were judged out of those things which were written in the book, according to their works." Rev 20 : 12.

Believe it, friends, these are no cunningly devised fables,

but awful and infallible truths. If the gospel now produces saving effects, it will then be a time of refreshing to our souls, Acts 3 : 19 ; but to all who reject it, it will be a day of terror, wrath, and amazement. It will be the day in which the Lord Jesus shall be revealed from heaven with his mighty angels, in flaming fire taking vengeance on them that know not God, and that obey not the gospel of our Lord Jesus Christ. 2 Thess. 1 : 7, 8.

2. *What a motive is here to ministerial diligence and faithfulness.* It is an awful work that is under our hands; the effects of the gospel which we preach will be the savor of life or death to them that hear us. If the Lord prosper it in our hands, we shall be witnesses for you ; it will be an addition to our glory in heaven. "They that be wise, shall shine as the brightness of the firmament; and they that turn many to righteousness, as the stars for ever and ever." Dan. 12 : 3. But if we are ignorant, lazy, or men-pleasers, our people will come in as swift witnesses against us, and their blood will be required at our hands ; it will be an intolerable aggravation to our misery in hell, to have any that sat under our ministry thus upbraiding us: "O cruel man, thou sawest my soul in danger, and never didst deal faithfully and plainly with me; the time and breath that was spent in idle and worldly discourse, might have been instrumental to save me from this place of torment." Let ministers consider themselves as witnesses for God, and their people as witnesses for or against them; and under that consideration, let them so study, preach, and pray, that they may with Paul take God to record that they are free from the blood of all men : no men on earth have more motives to diligence and faithfulness than we have.

3. *What an argument is this to banish formality from all who hear us.* Every Sabbath, every sermon, is recorded in heaven for or against your souls : in what way soever you attend to the word, all that you hear is set down in the

book of your account; think not you shall return as you came; the word will have its effect; it shall not return in vain, but shall accomplish the end for which it is sent. Isa. 55 : 11. The decrees of heaven are executed by the gospel; some souls shall be quickened, and others shall be slain by the word of God's mouth. The gospel is a river of the water of life, which quickens and refreshes every thing that lives; but the miry and marshy places shall not be healed. Ezek. 47 : 11. How weighty, therefore, is that caution of our Lord, "Take heed how ye hear." Luke 8 : 18. When you come under an ordinance, you are sowing seed for eternity, which will spring up in the world to come. Preaching and hearing may be considered two ways, physically and morally; in the former respect, these acts are quickly over and pass away. I shall by and by have done preaching, and you hearing; but the consequences thereof will abide for ever. Therefore, for the Lord's sake, away with formality; no more drowsy eyes or wandering thoughts. Oh, when you come to attend upon the ministry of the gospel, that such thoughts as these may prepare your minds: The word I am going to hear will quicken or kill, save or condemn my soul; if I sit dead under it, and return barren from it, I shall wish one day that I had never seen the face nor heard the voice of the minister who preached it.

4. *What a dreadful condition are all those in who are enemies to the gospel and those who preach it:* who, instead of embracing and obeying the message of the gospel, reject and despise it; instead of opening their hearts to receive it, open their blasphemous mouths to deride it, and hiss it, if it were possible, out of the world. Ah, what a book of remembrance is written for such men. I fear that never, since Christianity blessed this nation, was there an age more deeply drenched in the guilt of this sin than the present. How are the messengers of the gospel slighted and rejected! What have we done to deserve it? Is not our

case this day much like that of the prophet? "Shall evil be recompensed for good? for they have digged a pit for my soul. Remember that I stood before thee to speak good for them, and to turn away thy wrath from them." Jer. 18 : 20. What brutish madness hath possessed the souls of these men! But alas, it is not so much they, as Satan acting in them; he is a jealous prince, the gospel alarms him, his subjects are in danger of revolting from him: no wonder, therefore, he makes an outcry at the preaching of the gospel, as is usually made when an enemy invades a kingdom. In this case Christ directs his ministers to shake off the dust of their feet for a testimony against them. Mark 6 : 11. The meaning of which is this, that as you shake off the dust of your feet, even so Jesus Christ will shake off those men who despise the gospel and abuse his messengers.

5. Hence it likewise follows, *that the case of the heathen world will be easier in the day of judgment, than theirs who live and die unregenerate and disobedient under the gospel of Christ.* There are more witnesses prepared, and records filed against the day of your account, than can possibly be against them: they have abused but one talent, the light of nature; but we thousands, even as many as we have had opportunities and calls under the gospel. Upon this account Christ saith, "Whosoever shall not receive you, nor hear your words, when ye depart out of that house or city, shake off the dust of your feet. Verily, I say unto you, it shall be more tolerable for the land of Sodom and Gomorrah, in the day of judgment, than for that city." Matt. 10 : 14, 15.

Ah, what a fearful aggravation does it put on our sin and misery, that we are not only accountable for all the light we had, but for all that we might have had in the gospel-day. Capernaum was lifted up to heaven in the enjoyment of means and precious opportunities, Matt. 11 : 23; and had an answerable downfall into the depth of misery from that height of mercy; as the higher any one is lifted up upon a rack, the more terrible is the injury he receives by the fall.

6. We may also infer, *that the day of judgment must take up a vast space of time.* God will bring every thing into judgment, Eccl. 12 : 14 : not only sinful actions, but words, Matt. 12 : 36; not only words, but heart-secrets. Rom. 2 : 16. If all the records and registers now made shall then be opened and read, all the witnesses for or against every man examined and heard, judge then what a vast space of time will that great day take up. This is sure, things will not be huddled up, nor shuffled over in haste; you have taken your time for sinning, and God will take his time for judging.

Consider the multitudes, multitudes without number, who are to be judged in that day, even all the posterity of Adam, which are as the sand upon the sea-shore; that not only so many persons, but all that they have done, must come into judgment, even the very thoughts of their hearts which never came to the knowledge of men; their consciences to be interrogated, and all other witnesses fully heard: how great a day must this day of the Lord be.

But the main use of this point will be for EXHORTATION, that seeing all the offers of Christ are recorded and witnessed, with respect to a day of account, every one of you would immediately embrace the present gracious tender of Christ in the gospel, as you hope to be acquitted in that great day: take heed of denials, nay, even of delays; "for if the word spoken by angels was steadfast, and every transgression and disobedience received a just recompense of reward: how shall we escape if we neglect so great salvation?" Heb. 2 : 2, 3. The question is put, but no answer made: "How shall we escape?" The wisdom of men and angels cannot tell how. To enforce this exhortation, I shall present you with ten weighty considerations, which may the Lord follow home, by the blessing of his Spirit on all your hearts.

7. *Consider how invaluable a mercy it is that you are yet within the reach of offered grace.* The mercies set before you this day, were never set before the angels who fell; no *Mediator* was ever appointed for them. O astonishing mercy! that those vessels of gold should be cast into everlasting fire, and that such clay vessels as we are, should be thus put into a capacity of greater happiness than ever they fell from; nay, the mercy offered to you is not only denied to the angels that fell, but to the greatest part of your fellow-creatures of the same rank and dignity with you: " He showeth his word unto Jacob, his statutes and his judgments unto Israel. He hath not dealt so with any nation: and as for his judgments, they have not known them. Praise ye the Lord." Psalm 147 : 19, 20. A mercy deservedly celebrated with a joyful Alleluia. What vast tracts are there in the world where the name of Christ is unknown; it is your special mercy to be born in a land of Bibles and ministers, where it is as difficult for you to avoid the light, as it is for others to behold and enjoy it.

8. *Consider the nature, weight, and worth of the mercies which are this day freely offered you.* Certainly they are mercies of the first rank, the most precious and necessary among all the mercies of God. Christ the first-born of mercies, and in him pardon, peace, and eternal salvation are set before you: it would be surprising to see a starving man refuse offered bread, or a condemned man a gracious pardon. Lord, what a compound of sloth and stupidity are we, that we should need so many entreaties to be happy.

9. *Consider who it is that makes these gracious tenders of pardon, peace, and salvation, to you;* even that God whom you have so deeply wronged, whose laws you have violated, whose mercies you have spurned, and whose wrath

you have justly incensed. His patience groans under the burden of your daily provocations: he loses nothing if you are lost, and receives no benefit if you are saved; yet the first motions of mercy and salvation to you freely arise out of his grace and good pleasure. God entreats you to be reconciled. 2 Cor. 5:20. The blessed Lord Jesus, whose blood thy sins have shed, now freely offers that blood for thy reconciliation, justification, and salvation, if thou wilt but sincerely accept him ere it be too late.

10. *Reflect seriously upon your own vileness, to whom such gracious offers of peace and mercy are made.* Thy sins have set thee at as great a distance from the hope of pardon, as any sinner in the world. Consider, man, what thou hast been, what thou hast done, and what vast heaps of guilt thou hast contracted by a life of sin; and yet, that unto thee pardon and peace should be offered in Christ after such a life of rebellion, how astonishing is the mercy. The Lord is ready to pass by all thy former rebellions, thy deep-dyed transgressions, and to sign an act of oblivion for all that is past, if now at last thy heart relents for sin, and thy will bows in obedience to the great commands and calls of the gospel. Isa. 55:2; 1:18.

11. *Consider how many offers of mercy you have already refused, and that every refusal is recorded against you;* how long you have tried, and even tired the patience of God already, and that this may be the last overture of grace that ever God will make to your soul. Certainly there is an offer that will be the last offer, a striving of the Spirit which will be his last striving; and after that, no more offers without you, no more motions or strivings within you for evermore. The treaty is then ended, and your last neglect or rejection of Christ recorded against the day of your account; and what if this should prove to be that last tender of grace which must conclude the treaty between Christ and you? what an undone wretch must you then be,

with whom so gracious a treaty breaks off upon such dreadful terms.

12. *Consider well the reasonable and gracious nature of the gospel-terms on which life and pardon are offered to you.* Acts 20 : 21. The gospel requires of you repentance and faith. Can you think it hard when a prince pardons a rebel, to require him to fall on his knees, and stretch forth a willing and thankful hand to receive his pardon? Your repentance and faith are much of the same nature. Here is no legal satisfaction required at your hands, no reparation of the injured law by your doings or sufferings; but a hearty sorrow for sins committed, sincere purposes and endeavors after new obedience, and a hearty, thankful acceptance of Christ your Saviour; and for your encouragement herein, his Spirit stands ready to work in you all that you need. "Turn you at my reproof: behold, I will pour out my Spirit unto you, I will make known my words unto you." Prov. 1 : 23. "Thou also hast wrought all our works in us." Isa. 26 : 12.

13. *Consider how your way to Christ, by repentance and faith, has been travelled before you by thousands of sinners for your encouragement.* You are not the first that ever ventured his soul in this path; multitudes have gone before you, and that under as much guilt, fear, and discouragement as you can pretend to; and not a man among them was repulsed or discouraged: here they have found rest and peace to their weary souls. Heb. 4 : 3; Acts 13 : 39. Here the greatest sinners have been set forth for an ensample to you that should afterwards believe on his name. 1 Tim. 1 : 16. You see, if you will not, others will joyfully accept the offers of Christ. What discouragements have you that they had not; or what greater encouragements had they which God has not given you this day? therefore they shall be your judges.

14. *Consider the great hazard of the precious seasons you now enjoy.* Opportunity is the golden spot of time, but

it is a very slippery and uncertain thing: great and manifold are the hazards attending it. Your life is uncertain, your breath continually going in your nostrils; and that which is every moment going, will be gone at last. The gospel is as uncertain as your life; God hath made no such settlement of it, but that he may at pleasure remove it, and will certainly do so if we thus trifle under it: it is but a candlestick, though a golden one, Rev. 2:5, and that you all know is a movable thing. Not only your life, and the means of your eternal life, I mean the gospel, are uncertain; but even the motions and strivings of the Spirit with your soul are as uncertain as either. "Work out your own salvation with fear and trembling; for it is God which worketh in you both to will and to do of his good pleasure." Phil. 2:12, 13. That God now works with you is matter of great encouragement to your work; but that he works at his own pleasure, as a free agent who can cease when he pleases and never give one knock at your heart more, should make you work with fear and trembling.

15. *Think what a fearful aggravation it will be both of your sin and misery, to perish in the sight of an offered remedy;* to sink into hell between the outstretched arms of a compassionate Redeemer, that would have gathered you, but you would not. Heathens, yea, devils will upbraid you in hell for such unaccountable folly and desperate madness; heathens will say, "Alas, we had but the dim light of nature, which did indeed discover sin, but not Christ the remedy. Ah, had your preachers and your Bibles been sent among us, how gladly would we have embraced them." God said to Ezekiel, "Surely, had I sent thee to them, they would have hearkened unto thee." Ezek. 3:6. See also Matt. 11:21. The very devils will upbraid you: "O if God had sent a Mediator in our nature, we would not have rejected him as you have done;" but "he took not on him the nature of angels."

16. *How just, as well as sure, will your condemnation be in the great day, against whom such a cloud of witnesses will appear.* O how manifest will the righteousness of God be; men and angels shall applaud the sentence, and your own consciences shall acknowledge the equity of it. You that are *Christless* now, will be *speechless* then. Matt. 22 : 12. "Knowing therefore the terror of the Lord, we persuade men." 2 Cor. 5 : 11. I tremble to think of being summoned as a witness against any of your souls. O that I may be your rejoicing, and you mine in the day of our Lord Jesus Christ.

CHAPTER II.

THE PRESENCE OF CHRIST IN HIS ORDINANCES.

"BEHOLD, *I* STAND AT THE DOOR AND KNOCK." Rev. 3:20.

Having pondered Christ's solemn preface to his earnest suit, the next thing which comes under our consideration, is *the person soliciting* and pleading for admission into the hearts of sinners, which is Christ himself.

"Behold; *I* stand." The only difficulty here is rightly to apprehend the manner of Christ's presence in gospel administrations; for it is manifest that the person of Christ was at this time in heaven: his bodily presence was removed from this lower world above sixty years before this epistle was written to the Laodiceans. John's banishment into Patmos is, by Eusebius, out of Irenæus and Clemens Alexandrinus, placed in the fourteenth year of the reign of the emperor Domitian, and under his second persecution, which was about the ninety-seventh year from the birth of Christ.

Yet here he saith, "Behold, I stand;" not my messengers and ministers only, but I by my spiritual presence among you; I your sovereign Lord and owner, who have all right and authority by creation and redemption to possess and dispose of your souls; it is I that stand at the door and knock, I by my Spirit, soliciting and moving by the ministry of men. You see none but men; but believe it, I am really and truly, though spiritually and invisibly, present in all those administrations: all those knocks, motions, and solicitations, are truly mine; they are my acts, and I own them, and so I would have you to conceive and apprehend them. Hence the second doctrine is this:

Jesus Christ is truly present with men in his ordinances, and hath to do with them, and they with him, though he be not visible to their carnal eyes.

Thus runs the promise: "Where two or three are gathered together in my name, there am I in the midst of them." Matt. 18 : 20. The middle place in the Jewish assemblies, was the seat of the *president*, where he might equally hear and be heard of all. So, saith Jesus, will I be in the midst of the assemblies of the faithful, met together in my name and by my authority, to bless, guide, and protect them. Hence the church is called the place of his feet, Isaiah 60 : 13; a manifest allusion to the ark, called God's footstool. Psalm 99 : 5. And agreeably hereunto, Christ is said to walk among the seven golden candlesticks. Rev. 2 : 1. There are the spiritual walks of Christ; there he converses and communes with men. And this presence of Christ was not the peculiar privilege of the first churches, but is common to all the churches of the saints to the end of the world, as appears by that glorious promise so comfortably extended to the church from first to last: "Lo, I am with you always, even to the end of the world." Matt. 28 : 20. This promise is the ground of all our faith and expectation of benefit from ordinances; and the subjects of it are not here considered personally, but officially; to you, and all that succeed you in the same work and office; not to you only as extraordinary, but to all the succeeding ordinary standing officers in my church. As for the apostles, neither their life nor their extraordinary office was to continue long, but this promise was to continue "to the end of the world."

Nor is this promise made absolutely, but conditionally; the connection of the promise with the command enforces this qualified sense: "The Lord is with you, while ye be with him." 2 Chron. 15 : 2. Ignorant, idle, unqualified persons cannot claim the benefit of this gracious grant.

Once more, this promise is made to every hour and minute of time. I am with you "all the days," as it is in the Greek text; in dark and dangerous, as well as peaceable and encouraging days: and it is closed with a solemn amen, so be it, or so it shall be.

To open this point distinctly, we are to consider that there is a threefold presence of Christ.

1. *There is a corporeal presence of Christ*, which the church once enjoyed on earth, when he went in and out among his people, Acts 1 : 21 ; when their eyes saw him, and their hands handled him. 1 John, 1 : 1. This presence was a great consolation to the disciples, and therefore they were much dejected when it was about to be removed from them. But after his work was finished on earth, this bodily presence was no longer necessary to be continued in this world, but to be removed to heaven, John 16 : 7 ; as indeed it was, and must there abide until the time of the restitution of all things. Acts 3 : 21. And in this respect he tells the disciples, "I leave the world, and go to the Father." John 16 : 28.

2. There is *a represented presence* of Christ in ordinances. As the person of a king is represented in another country by his ambassadors, so is Christ in this world by his ministers: "We are ambassadors for Christ, as though God did beseech you by us; we pray you in Christ's stead, be ye reconciled to God." 2 Cor. 5 : 20. Christ is engaged in other work for us in heaven, but we stand in his stead on earth. And this shows the great dignity of the ministerial office: whatever abuse or contempt is cast on ministers, it reflects upon Christ: "He that despiseth you, despiseth me." Luke 10 : 16. It also teaches us whence is the validity of gospel administrations. Christ ratifies and confirms them with his own authority. It also instructs us how wise, spiritual, and holy, ministers should be, who represent Christ to the world. A drunkard, a persecutor, a sensual world-

ling, is but an ill representative of the blessed and holy Jesus.

3. Besides these two, there is *a spiritual presence* of Christ in the churches and ordinances; and this presence of Christ by his Spirit, who is his vicegerent or representative, is to be considered as that from which all gospel ordinances derive their beauty and glory, their power and efficacy, their awful solemnity, and their continuance and stability.

(1.) From the presence of Christ by his Spirit, the ordinances and churches derive their *beauty and glory:* "To see thy power and thy glory, so as I have seen thee in the sanctuary." Psalm 63 : 2.

As the beauty of the body results from the soul which animates it; and when the soul is gone, the beauty of the body is gone also; so the beauty and glory of all ordinances come and go with the Spirit of Christ, which is the very soul of them. The churches are indeed golden candlesticks, but the candlestick has no light but what the candle gives it; hence that magnificent description of the new temple is closed up in this expression: "The name of the city from that day shall be, The Lord is there." Ezek. 48 : 35.

(2.) From this spiritual presence of Christ, gospel-ordinances derive all the *power and efficacy* which is by them exerted upon the souls of men, either in their conversion or edification. This power is not inherent in them, nor do they act as natural, necessary agents, but as instituted means, which are successful or unsuccessful according as Christ by his Spirit coöperates with them: "So then, neither is he that planteth any thing, neither he that watereth; but God that giveth the increase." 1 Cor. 3 : 7. That is, they are nothing to the accomplishment of men's salvation, without the concurrence of the Spirit of Christ. For when the apostle makes himself and Apollos, with all other ministers, nothing, we must understand him as speaking comparatively and relatively; they are necessary in their places, and sufficient in their kind for what they are appointed to, else it would be a reflection on the wisdom of God that instituted them: but in themselves they are nothing; as a trumpet or wind instrument is nothing as to its use, except breath be inspired into it, and that breath modulated by the skill of the inspirer; like Ezekiel's wheels, that moved not but as the Spirit that was in them moved and directed their motions. If ordinances wrought upon souls naturally and necessarily, as the fire burns, they could not fail of success on all that come under them. But it is with them as with the waters of the pool at Bethesda, whose healing virtue was only found at the season when the angel descended and troubled them.

(3.) This spiritual presence of Christ gives the ordinances of the gospel the *awful solemnity* which is due upon that account to them. The presence of Christ in them commands reverence from all that are about him. "God is greatly to be feared in the assembly of the saints, and to be had in reverence of all them that are about him," Psalm 89:7; hence is that solemn caution or threatening, "If ye will not be reformed by me by these things, but will walk contrary unto me, then will I also walk contrary unto you." Lev. 26:23, 24. The Hebrew word signifies to walk rashly with God, without considering with whom we have to do, and what an awful majesty we stand before. And the punishment is suitable to the sin: I also will walk at an adventure with you, making no discrimination in my judgments between your persons and the persons of the worst of men. O that this were duly considered by all that have to do with God in gospel-institutions.

(4.) It is the spiritual presence of Christ in his churches and ordinances which gives them their *continuance and stability*. Whenever the Spirit of Christ departs from them, it will not be long before they depart from us; or if they should not, their continuance will be little to our advantage. When the glory of the Lord descended from between the cherubims, when that sad voice was heard in the temple, "Let us go hence," how soon were both city and temple made a desolation; and truly Christ's presence is not so fixed to any place or ordinances, but the sins of the people may banish it away. Rev. 2 : 5. Who will tarry in any place longer than he is welcome, if he have anywhere else to go?

But more particularly, let us here discuss these two points : How it appears Christ is thus spiritually present with his churches and ordinances; and why it is necessary he should be so.

I. BY WHAT EVIDENCE does it appear that there is such a presence of Christ with his churches and ordinances? And this will appear by two undeniable evidences.

1. *From their wonderful preservation;* for it is wholly inconceivable, how the churches, ministers, and ordinances should be supported and preserved without it, amidst such hosts of powerful and enraged enemies. If Christ were not among them, they had certainly been swallowed up long ago. It is he who holds the stars in his right hand. Rev. 2 : 1. His walking among the seven golden candlesticks is their best security. The burning bush is a rare emblem to open this mystery; the bush burned with fire, but was not consumed. Exod. 3 : 3. The bush was a resemblance of the church of God in Egypt, the flames upon it were their terrible persecution; the wonder, that no ashes appeared as the effects of those terrible flames; the reason whereof was, God was in the bush—Jesus Christ was in the midst of his people.

By virtue of his presence we are here this day, in the enjoyment of gospel liberty, no society of men in the world have such security as the church has on this account. The mightiest monarchies have been overturned, no policies nor human power could preserve them; but the church and ordinances are still preserved, and shall ever be, by virtue of that gracious promise, "For I am with thee, saith the LORD, to save thee: though I make a full end of all nations whither I have scattered thee, yet will I not make a full end of thee." Jer. 30 : 11. Babylonian, Persian, and Grecian monarchies have destroyed and ruined one another, but still the church of Christ lifts up its head, and beholds their ruins.

2. This presence of Christ in and with his ordinances, is undeniably evinced from *their supernatural effects upon the souls of men.* "The weapons of our warfare are not carnal, but mighty through God to the pulling down of strong holds." 2 Cor. 10 : 4. The Spirit of Christ gives them their success and efficacy; the sword of the gospel has its point and edge, but it is impossible that the heart of a stupid, hardened sinner should ever be wounded by it, if the Spirit of Christ do not direct it. When sinners fall down convinced under the authority of the word, they feel and readily acknowledge that God is in it of a truth. 1 Cor. 14 : 25. Ruffinus reports, that at the council of Nice, a godly man of no great learning was the instrument of converting a learned philosopher, whom the bishops, with all their arguments, could not persuade; of which the philosopher himself gave this remarkable account: "While you reasoned with me," said he, "against words I opposed words, and what was spoken I overthrew by the art of speaking; but when instead of words power came out of the mouth of the speaker, words could no longer withstand truth, nor man resist the power of God."

And this, indeed, is the true and just account of all those marvellous and gracious changes made on the souls of men by the preaching of the gospel. Can the vanishing breath of a dying man, think you, inspire spiritual and eternal life into the souls of other men? Can he search the conscience, break the heart, and bow the will at this rate? No, this is the power and operation of Christ; and of that presence, says Mr. Burgess, we must say as Martha did to her Saviour concerning the death of her brother Lazarus, "Lord, if thou hadst been here, my brother had not died." John 11 : 21. So say I, if that presence and power of Christ were felt by all, which has been certainly experienced by many, they would not remain in the state of spiritual death as they do. But though there are thousands under ordinances who never felt this power of Christ upon them, yet, blessed be God, there are also multitudes of witnesses and evidences of this truth, that there is a real, spiritual, energetic presence of Christ in his own appointments; which was the first thing to be evinced.

II. We inquire into THE REASONS, OR THE USES AND ENDS which make such a presence of Christ necessary. And they are,

1. *To preserve and support his ministers and churches amidst such hosts of powerful and enraged enemies.* This presence of Christ is as a wall of fire round about them. The divine presence with Jeremiah was as a life-guard to him against the rage of the princes and nobles of Israel: "I will make thee unto this people a fenced brazen wall; and they shall fight against thee, but they shall not prevail against thee: for I am with thee to save thee and to deliver thee, saith the Lord. And I will deliver thee out of the hand of the wicked, and I will redeem thee out of the hand of the terrible." Jer. 15 : 20, 21.

It was easier for the Roman army to scale the walls and batter down the towers of Jerusalem, than for all the enemies in that city to destroy the prophet of God, thus guarded by the divine presence. Athanasius and Luther had the power of the empire engaged against them, yet the presence of Christ was their security. The witnesses could not be slain till they had finished their testimony. Rev. 11 : 7. To this presence alone the faithful witnesses of Christ owe their marvellous preservation at this day; had not Christ said, "Lo, I am with you," you had not said at this day, " Behold, our ministers are still with us."

2. The presence of Christ is necessary *to assist his ministers in their work*, for it is a work quite above their own strength. It is well that we are workers together with God, else we should soon faint under our labors. When Moses objected, "I am not eloquent," the Lord told him, "I will be with thy mouth." Exod. 4 : 10, 12. When God guides the tongue, how powerful and persuasive must the language be. When the apostles, illiterate men, were sent out to convert the world, Christ promised to give them " a mouth and wisdom," Luke 21 : 15—a mouth to speak, and wisdom to guide that mouth ; and then their words were demonstrations; all their adversaries could not resist the spirit and power by which they spoke. Empires and kingdoms full of enemies received the gospel ; but the reason of this wonderful success is given us: "They went forth and preached everywhere, the Lord working with them." Mark 16 : 20. It is sweet and prosperous working in fellowship with Christ ; the Spirit of Christ gives a manifold assistance to his ministers in their work ; it is he who directs their mind in the choice of those subjects wherein they labor with such success to their hearers. He dictates the matter, influences their affections, guides their lips, and follows home their doctrine with success. This is a special use and end of Christ's presence with his ministers and ordinances.

3. The spiritual presence of Christ is necessary for *the preparation and opening of the people's heart to receive and embrace the gospel to salvation*. Not a heart will open to receive Christ till the Spirit of Christ unlock it. Paul and Timothy were extraordinarily called to preach the gospel at Philippi, and there Lydia was converted. But how? Not by their skill or eloquence, but by the Spirit's influence ; the Lord opened the heart of Lydia. Acts 16 : 14. The church could not be increased without conversion ; conver-

sion could never be wrought without Christ's influence and spiritual presence. So that this presence is of absolute necessity; the church cannot subsist, nor the great ends of ordinances be attained without it.

INFERENCE 1. Is Christ really present in all gospel administrations? *how awfully solemn, then, is every part of gospel worship.* We have to do with Christ himself, and not with men only, in gospel ordinances. Happy were it if, under this consideration, all our people received the word we preach as the Thessalonians did, not as the word of man but as the word of God. 1 Thess. 2:13. Then it would work effectually in us as it did in them. But alas, we have low apprehensions of the word; we come to judge the gifts of the speaker, not to have our minds informed, our consciences searched, our lusts mortified, and our lives regulated. But O that men would realize the presence of Christ in ordinances, and seriously consider that word of his, "All the churches shall know that I am he which searcheth the reins and hearts; and I will give unto every one of you according to your works." Rev. 2:23.

How would this lead vain and wandering hearts to holy seriousness. O if men would consider that they are before the Lord Jesus Christ, as Cornelius and his family did: "Now therefore are we all here present before God, to hear all things that are commanded thee of God," Acts 10:33; if they would consider the word as the executioner of God's eternal decrees, which returns not in vain, but accomplishes that whereunto God sends it, Isa. 55:11, and eventually proves the savor of life or death eternal to them who sit under it, 2 Cor. 2:16; in a word, were it but considered as the rule by which its hearers shall be judged in the great day, John 12:48, then how would men tremble at the word. What mighty effects would it have on their hearts. How would it run and be glorified. But alas, as Job speaks, "He goeth by me, and I see him not: he passeth on also, but I perceive him not." Job 9 : 11. Few realize the spiritual presence of Christ in ordinances.

2. If Christ be really present with his churches and ordinances, *how vain are all attempts of enemies to subvert and destroy them.* That promise, Matt. 28 : 20, supposes the continuance of a gospel and church-ministry to the end of the world, else there would be a promise without a subject: as there *ought* to be a church, so there *shall* be a church with ministers and ordinances, let Satan and antichrist do their worst. I do not say this promise secures this or that particular church or nation, for the presence of Christ may cease to be realized in any one place; but still, the church is safe. And there are three things which secure it against all hazards.

(1.) *The invaluable treasures God has lodged in the church,* namely, his truths, his worship, and his elect; such a precious cargo secures the vessel which carries it, whatever storms or tempests may befall it.

(2.) *The covenant and promise of God with the church* is its abundant security: "Upon this rock will I build my church; and the gates of hell shall not prevail against it." Matt. 16 : 18. The faithfulness of God is pledged for his people's security. If the church fail, his faithfulness must fail with it.

(3.) But above all, *the presence of Christ in the midst of the church,* puts it out of all danger of failure. In that promise, "Lo, I am with you always," are found all munitions and fortifications whatsoever. Here we have his eye of providence, his hand of power, and whatever else is needful to support and secure it. God accounts his presence our safety. Isa. 41 : 10. The enemies of God and his people account it so too, Exod. 14 : 25; and shall it not be so in our account? Provoke not the Lord Jesus to withdraw his presence, and fear not the consultations and oppositions of hell or earth.

3. From this spiritual presence of Christ all his faithful ministers should *draw encouragement, amidst the manifold difficulties and discouragements they daily encounter in his service.* Christ is with them, and they work in fellowship with him; let them not be dismayed. The difficulties and discouragements which the ministers of Christ meet are great and manifold; and the more faithful and successful any of them are in their Master's work, the fiercer opposition they must expect. Besides all the discouragements rising out of their own hearts, which are not a few, they must encounter the opposition of enemies from abroad, and the stubbornness of the hearts they work upon. Satan is a jealous prince, and will raise all manner of outcries and opposition against those heavenly heralds who come to proclaim a new prince in his dominions, and withdraw his miserable subjects from their cursed allegiance to him. What is it to preach the gospel, saith Luther, but to drive the fury of the world upon the head of the preacher? But this would be easily supportable, did our work but prosper upon the hearts of our hearers. But this, alas, is the killing consideration of all; we know the worth of souls, and how great a service it is to save them from death. James 5 : 20. We also know the terrors of the Lord, which excite our utmost endeavors to persuade men. 2 Cor. 5 : 11. We feel the compassions of Christ stirring within us, which makes us long after their salvation. Phil. 1 : 8. We preach, we pray, yea, we travail again, as it were, in birth until Christ be formed in them. Gal. 4 : 19. And when we have done all, we find their hearts as iron and brass. Jer. 6 : 28. We mourn in secret when we cannot prevail, and often our hands hang down with discouragement, and we are ready to say with the prophet, "I will not make mention of him, nor speak any more in his name." Jer. 20 : 9. But here is our relief, under all discouragements: the work is Christ's, the power is his, he is with us, and we are workers together

with him. There was a time when three thousand souls were born to Christ during one sermon; it may be now, three thousand sermons may be preached, and not one soul be converted: yet, let us not be discouraged; a time of eminent conversion is promised, and to be expected in these latter days, when the living waters of the gospel shall make every thing to live whither they come, Ezek. 47 : 9; and when the fishers, that is, the ministers of Christ, shall not fish with hooks as they now do, taking now one, then another single convert, but shall spread forth their nets, and inclose multitudes at a draught—when they shall "fly as a cloud, and as the doves to their windows." Isa. 60 : 8. God now opens a door of opportunity beyond our expectation; O that the hearts of ministers and people were suitably enlarged, and the people made willing in the day of his power.

4. Hence, we also infer *the great dignity of the ministerial office, and the suitable respect due to all Christ's faithful ministers.* The Lord Jesus himself is represented by them, they stand in his stead, 2 Cor. 5 : 20; his authority is put upon them: the honor and dishonor given them redound to the person of Christ. The Galatians received Paul as an angel of God, even as Christ Jesus. Gal. 4 : 14. Yet how have their persons and office been vilified and despised in this degenerate age; how many learned, pious, laborious, peaceful ministers of Christ have, in this age, been hunted up and down in the world as wild beasts, and been made the filth and offscouring of all things. 1 Cor. 4 : 13. The word signifies the filth which scavengers rake together in the streets, to be carried to the dunghill. No doubt but Satan designs in this to invalidate their ministry, discourage their labors, and break their hearts; but Jesus Christ will support us under all these abuses, wipe off the dirt thrown at us for his name's sake, and reserve some of us for better days.

5. Is Christ present in his ordinances? *what a strong*

engagement then lies upon you all to wait assiduously upon the ministry of the word, and to bring all that are capable to wait upon Christ with you. We read in the days of Christ's flesh, when he performed his miraculous cures upon the sick, what thronging there was after him; how parents brought their children, masters their servants, pressing in multitudes, uncovering the house to let down their sick to him. Luke 5 : 19 ; 12 : 1. Ah, shall men be so earnest for a cure for their bodies, and so indifferent for their souls? It is true, the Spirit of Christ is not laid under any necessity to act always with the word : he acts as a free agent, "The wind bloweth where it listeth," John 3 : 8 ; but it is encouragement enough to wait continually upon his ordinances, that he sometimes graciously and effectually works with them. It is good to lie in the path of the Spirit; and there is a blessing pronounced upon them who wait continually at his gates. Prov. 8 : 34. O therefore neglect no opportunity within your reach ; for who knows but it may be the season of life to thy soul.

6. *What an unspeakable loss is the loss of the gospel,* seeing the presence of Christ comes and goes with it. When the gospel departs, the Spirit of Christ departs with it from among men; no more conversions, in God's ordinary way, are then to be expected : well therefore might the Lord say, "Woe also to them when I depart from them." Hosea 9 : 12. The Spirit may, in some sense, depart, while the ordinances are left standing for a time among the people ; but we can then expect no benefit from them. But when God takes away ordinances and the Spirit too, woe indeed to that people. Where then are the fruits answerable to our precious means? The gospel is a golden lamp, and the graces of the Spirit communicated by it are golden oil, as in that stately vision, Zech. 4. Will God maintain such a lamp, fed with such precious oil, for men to trifle and play by? And no less ominous and portentous is that bitter

enmity to the gospel and the serious professors of it, which is too often found among us; this great hatred brings on the days of visitation and the days of recompense with a swift and dreadful motion upon any people. Hosea 9 : 7.

7. If Christ be present by his Spirit and energy in his ordinances, *there is no reason to despair of the conversion and salvation of the greatest sinners that yet lie dead under the gospel.* What though their hearts be hard, their understandings dark, and their wills never so perverse and obstinate? all must give way, and open in the day of Christ's power, when his Spirit joins himself with the word. This makes it an irresistible word; it is glorious to observe the hearts of publicans and harlots opening and yielding to the voice of Christ. Matt. 21 : 31. Who were those three thousand persons, pricked to the heart by Peter's sermon, Acts 2 : 36, but the very men that, with wicked hands, had crucified the Lord Jesus? And what were the converted Corinthians but idolaters, turned from dumb idols, whoremongers, adulterers, effeminate, and such like persons? 1 Cor. 12 : 2; 6 : 11. God has his elect among the vilest of men: the gospel will find them out, and draw them home to Christ, when the Spirit animates and blesses it. Well might the apostle therefore say, that the gospel preached with the Holy Ghost sent down from heaven, is an object worthy for angels to behold with admiration. 1 Pet. 1 : 12. What though Satan has strongly fortified their souls against Christ with ignorance, prejudice, and enmity, the weapons of our warfare are mighty through God, to pull down these strong holds. Despair not therefore of your sinful and dead-hearted relatives; bring them to the gospel on the encouragement of these words of Christ, "The hour is coming, and now is, when the dead shall hear the voice of the Son of God; and they that hear shall live." John 5 : 25.

8. Is Christ spiritually present in his ordinances? O then *what an endeared affection should every gracious soul*

bear to the ordinances of God. They are the walks of Christ and of his Spirit, the appointed times and places for your meeting and communion with him; there your souls first met with Christ; there you began your acquaintance with him; there you have had many sweet interviews with him since that day; they were the means of your regeneration, 1 Pet. 1 : 23, the bread of life by which your souls have been sustained ever since, and therefore to be more esteemed by you than your necessary food. Job 23 : 12. Here you have found the richest cordials to revive your drooping spirits, when ready to faint under sin within you and afflictions upon you. No wonder David's soul even fainted for the courts of God, Psalm 84 : 2, and that Hezekiah desired a sign on his sick-bed, that he should go up to the house of the Lord. Isa. 38 : 22. Here are the choicest comforts of the saints upon earth; all our fresh springs are in Zion. Psalm 88 : 7. What a dungeon, what a barren wilderness were this world without them. Prize the ordinances, love the ordinances, wait assiduously on the ordinances, and pray for the liberty and efficacy of the gospel, that it may continue and increase in your days and in the days of your posterity.

CHAPTER III.

THE HEART BARRED AGAINST CHRIST.

"BEHOLD, *I STAND AT THE DOOR* AND KNOCK." REV. 3:20.

HAVING finished Christ's solemn preface, and shown the manner of his presence in his churches and ordinances, I now come to a third doctrine which is necessarily implied in these words, "Behold, I stand at the door and knock;" and the sad truth therein implied is this:

The hearts of men are naturally locked, and fast barred against Jesus Christ their only Saviour.

If it were not so, what need were there of all the pains and patience exercised by Christ in waiting and knocking importunately for entrance into the hearts of men? To keep a clear method in this point, three things must be stated in the doctrinal part: How it appears that the hearts of men are thus shut up; what are those locks and bars that shut them up; and that no power of man can remove these bars. Let us consider,

I. How IT APPEARS that the hearts of men are thus shut up. That all hearts are naturally shut and made fast against Christ, is a sad but certain truth; we read, John 1:11, "He came unto his own, and his own received him not." He came unto his own people, from whose stock he sprung—a people to whom he had been prefigured in all the sacrifices and types of the law, and who might in him clearly discern the accomplishment of them all. His doctrines and his miracles plainly told them who he was, and whence he came; yet few discerned and received him as the Son of God. Christ found the doors of men's hearts generally shut against him, save only a few whose hearts were opened by the almighty power of God, in the way of faith. John 1:12. These indeed received him, but all the rest excluded and denied entrance to the Son of God. So again, John 5 : 33–40, Christ reasons with them, and gives undeniable demonstrations that he was the Messiah come to save them. He proves it from the testimony of John, verse 33, "Ye sent unto John, and he bare witness unto the truth;" he tells them the design of his coming among them was their salvation, verse 34; shows them the great seal of heaven, his uncontrollable miracles, verse 36, "The works that I do, bear witness of me, that the Father hath sent me." And if that were not enough, he reminds them of the immediate testimony given of him from heaven, "The Father himself which hath sent me, hath borne witness of me." He did so at his baptism: "And lo, a voice from heaven, saying, This is my beloved Son, in whom I am well pleased." Matt. 3 : 17. And so again at his transfiguration on the holy mount, "While he yet spake, behold, a bright cloud overshadowed them: and behold, a voice out of the cloud, which said, This is my beloved Son, in whom I am well pleased; hear ye him." Matt. 17 : 5. He bids them search the Scriptures, and critically examine his perfect correspondence with them. John 5 : 39. This was enough, one would think, to open the door of every man's understanding and heart to receive him with full satisfaction; and yet, after all, behold the unreasonable obstinacy and resistance of their hearts against him: "Ye will not come to me, that ye might have life." Ver. 40.

Not a soul will open, with all the reasons and demonstrations in the world, till the almighty power of God be put forth to that end. "If another come in his own name," saith he, verse 43, "*him will ye receive;*" any one rather than the Son of God. Every impostor can easily deceive you; it is to me only your hearts have such a strong aversion. Now there is a twofold shutting up of the heart against Jesus Christ.

1. *Natural.* Every soul comes into this world shut up

THE HEART CLOSED. 45

and fast closed against the Lord Jesus. The will of man, which is the freest faculty, comes into the world barred and bolted against Christ. "The carnal mind is enmity against God; for it is not subject to the law of God, neither indeed can be." Rom. 8 : 7. "It is God which worketh in you both to will and to do of his good pleasure." Phil. 2 : 13. This is a dismal effect of the fall. Who does not feel strong aversions and obstinate resistances in his own heart, when moving towards Christ in the first weak and trembling acts of faith?

2. There is a *judicial* shutting up of the heart against Christ. This is a sore and tremendous stroke of God, punishing former rebellions: "Israel would none of me, so I gave them up unto their own hearts' lusts." Psalm 81 : 11, 12. This looks like a prelude of damnation, a very near preparation to ruin. "Israel would none of me;" there is the *natural* shutting up of the heart: "so I gave them up;" there is the *judicial* shutting up of the heart: they *would* not hear, they *shall* not hear. O fearful judgment! Thus the Lord gave up the heathen, Rom. 1 : 26; they had abused their natural light, and now their minds are *judicially* darkened; given up to a sottish and injudicious mind, not able to distinguish duty from sin, safety from danger—a mind that should choose the worst things, and reject the best. This was the reprobate mind unto which God gave them up; what sadder word can the Lord speak than this, unless it be, "Take him, Satan!" It is true, those whom God shuts up he can open, and those whom justice shuts up, mercy can set free; but it is beyond all the power of angels and men to do it. "He shutteth up a man, and there can be no opening." Job 12 : 14. These two closings of the heart are not always found together in the same person; and blessed be God that they are not. Christ meets with many a repulse, and endures with much patience the gainsaying of sinners, before he pronounces the

dreadful sentence upon them, "Go, and tell this people, hear ye indeed, but understand not; and see ye indeed, but perceive not. Make the heart of this people fat, and make their ears heavy, and shut their eyes; lest they see with their eyes, and hear with their ears, and understand with their heart, and convert, and be healed." Isa. 6 : 9, 10.

But when it comes to this, dreadful is the case of such souls; and none are in greater danger of this judicial stroke of God, than those who have sat long under the light, rebelling against it. That is the first thing, the hearts of men by nature are locked and shut up against Christ.

II. Let us examine WHAT THOSE LOCKS AND BARS ARE, *which oppose and forbid Christ's entrance into the hearts of sinners.* And they will be found to be, ignorance, unbelief, pride, custom in sin, presumption, and prejudices against the ways of holiness. Bars enough to secure the soul in Satan's possession, and frustrate all the designs of mercy, except an almighty Power from heaven break them asunder.

1. The first bar making fast the soul of man against Christ, is *ignorance.* If knowledge is a key that opens the heart to Christ, as is plain from Luke 11 : 52, where Christ denounceth a woe on them that took away "the key of knowledge," then ignorance must needs be the lock that makes fast the door of the heart against Christ. On this ground Christ told the woman of Samaria, that her unbelief grew upon the root of her ignorance. "If thou knewest the gift of God, and who it is that saith to thee, Give me to drink, thou wouldest have asked of him and he would have given thee living water." John 4 : 10. Ah, sinners, did you but know what a Christ he is that is offered to your souls in the gospel; did you see his beauty, fulness, and suitableness, and feel your own need of him, all the world could not keep you from him: you would break through all reproaches, all sufferings, all self-denials, to come to the enjoyment of him. But alas, it is with you as it was

with those who said to the church, "What is thy beloved more than another beloved, that thou dost so charge us?" Sol. Songs, 5 : 9. Unknown excellences attract not: ignorance is Satan's sceptre which he sways over all his kingdom of darkness, and by which he holds his vassals in miserable bondage to him; hence the devils are called, "The rulers of the darkness of this world." Eph. 6 : 12. Alas, were the eyes of sinners opened to see their woful state and their remedy in Christ, he could never hold them in subjection one day longer; they would break away from under his cruel government and run by thousands to Christ; for so they do as soon as God opens their eyes: in the same hour that they are "turned from darkness to light," they are also turned "from the power of Satan unto God." Acts 26 : 16. O that you did but know the worth of your souls, the dreadful danger they are in, and the fearful wrath that hangs over them, with the willingness and ability of Christ to save them; you could not sleep one night longer in the state you are: your next cry would be, "What shall I do to be saved?" Who will show me the way to Christ? Help, ministers! help, Christians! yea, help, Lord! These would be the lamentations and cries of those who are now secure and quiet. But "the god of this world hath blinded the eyes of them which believe not," 2 Cor. 4 : 4: no cries for a physician, because they have no consciousness how their souls are wounded by sins of commission and by sins of omission. O that the great Physician would apply his excellent eye-salve to your understandings, which are yet darkened with gross ignorance both of your misery and remedy.

2. The second bar or lock which shuts Christ out of men's souls, is the sin of *unbelief*. This is one of the strongest holds of Satan wherein he trusteth; this is a sin that not only locks up the heart of a sinner, but also binds up the hand of a Saviour. "He did not many mighty works there, because of their unbelief." Matt. 13 : 58.

Unbelief obstructed his miraculous works when he was on earth, and it obstructs his gracious work now he is in heaven. A Saviour is come into the world, but, poor unbeliever, thy soul can neither have union nor communion with him till this bar of thy unbelief be removed. The gospel is come among us with mighty arguments to convince and powerful motives to persuade, but little saving effect follows: its main design is to many frustrated, and all this through unbelief, shutting up and hardening men's hearts under it. "The word preached did not profit them, not being mixed with faith in them that heard it." Heb. 4:2. Ah, cursed bar! which shuts up thy heart, shuts out thy Saviour, and will effectually shut thee out of heaven, except the almighty power of God break it asunder. They could not enter in because of unbelief. Heb. 4:6. The ruin of souls is laid at the door of unbelief; it is the damning sin, Mark 16:16, and truly called so, because no other sin could condemn but in virtue of this sin.

3. The third bar denying entrance to Christ into the hearts of sinners, is *pride* and stoutness of spirit. The natural heart is a proud heart; it lives upon its own stock, it cannot stoop to a sincere and universal renunciation of its own righteousness: "Being ignorant of God's righteousness, and going about to establish their own righteousness, they have not submitted themselves to the righteousness of God." Rom. 10:3. Pride stiffens the will that it cannot stoop or condescend to declare their own emptiness, discover their own shame, and live wholly upon the righteousness of another. Proud nature chooses the way of destruction, rather than to deny itself in such a point as this. This makes faith so exceedingly difficult, because it involves such deep points of self-denial in it. To give up all to Christ, to draw all from Christ, and to be willing to part with all for Christ—what will can be brought to a deliberate consent to such things as these, unless an omnipotent power bow it? It is

natural to men rather to eat a brown crust, or wear a coarse, ragged garment which they can call their own, than to feed on the richest dainties, or wear the costliest garments which they must receive as alms or a gift from another. O how hard is it to subdue this pride of the heart, even after light and convictions are come into the soul—to convince men of their undone condition, and the absolute necessity of another and higher righteousness than their own. When souls are in treaty with Christ, this sin makes the last opposition. Fain would they come to Christ, ten thousand worlds for Christ; but they think they must not approach him without some qualifications which are yet wanting. But, soul, if ever Christ and thou conclude a union, thou must deny self even in this the most refined form of it, and come as Abraham did, naked and empty-handed, to Him who justifieth the ungodly. Down with this house-idol, thy self, thy righteous self, dressed up, like another Agag, with such specious pretences of humility.

4. The fourth bar forbidding Christ's entrance into the soul, is *custom in sin*. Sin has so fixed itself by long continuance in the soul, and the soul is so settled and confirmed in its course, that all arguments and persuasions to change our path are swept away by the power of custom, as straws and feathers are by the rapid course of a mighty torrent. "Can the Ethiopian change his skin, or the leopard his spots? then may ye also do good, that are accustomed to do evil." Jer. 13 : 23. Soap and nitre may as soon make an Ethiopian white, or take the spots out of the leopard's skin, as the reasonings of men remove the mighty power of customary sin. Physicians find it a hard thing to cure an ill habit of body. It is a great matter to be accustomed this way or that from our childhood; every repeated act of sin confirms and strengthens the habit; and hence it is that we see so few conversions in old age. It was a wonder in the primitive times, that Marcus Caius Victorius embraced

Christianity in the sixtieth year of his age. Take an habitual drunkard, a self-righteous moralist, and lay before them the necessity of a change, and you will find it as easy to stop the course of a river with the breath of your mouth, as to stop them in an accustomed course of sinning.

5. The fifth bar resisting Christ's entrance into the soul, is the sin of *presumption:* this sin parts Christ and thousands of souls in the world; presuming, they hope; and hoping, they perish. When men presume that their condition is safe already, their souls never go out after a Saviour. This was the ruin of Laodicea: "Because thou sayest, I am rich, and increased with goods, and have need of nothing; and knowest not that thou art wretched, and miserable, and poor, and blind, and naked." Rev. 3:17. This damning presumption is discovered in three things: 1. Many think they have that grace which they have not, mistaking the *similar* for the *saving* works of the Spirit; a fatal mistake, never rectified with many thousands till it be too late. 2. They presume to find that mercy in God, which they will never find; for all the saving mercies of God are dispensed to men through Christ, in the way of regeneration and faith. Jude, ver. 21. 3. They presume upon the time for repentance and faith hereafter, which their eyes shall never see. And thus presumption locks up the heart against Christ, and leaves sinners perishing even in the presence of a Saviour. They make a bridge of their own shadow, and so perish in the waters.

6. The sixth and last sin barring the heart against Christ, is a strong *prejudice against holiness,* and the strict duties of religion. Thus, in the very infancy of Christianity, the world was driven off from religion by the common prejudices which lay upon the professors of it: "As concerning this sect, we know that everywhere it is spoken against." Acts 28:22.

Thus Justin Martyr complains that Christians were

everywhere condemned by common fame; and on this account Christ pronounces a woe upon the world, because of offences. Matt. 18 : 7. Alas, it will be the ruin of thousands; some have imbibed such prejudiced opinions and unjust notions of religion and its professors, as to make them irreconcilable enemies to it. Satan has dressed it up in their fancies in such an odious form, as to make them loathe both the name and the thing. These prejudices are drawn from various things; sometimes from the necessary duties of Christianity, which are laid as crimes on the people of God: "When I wept, and chastened my soul with fasting, that was to my reproach." Psalm 69 : 10. Sometimes the groundless and malicious slanders and inventions of the enemies of Christianity are the occasion of real prejudices to the world: "Come, and let us devise devices against Jeremiah, and let us smite him with the tongue." Jer. 18 : 18. Sometimes innocent and serious professors of godliness are censured and condemned on account of hypocritical professors, who never heartily espoused religion. And lastly, the ways of holiness suffer from the infirmities of weak Christians, who give too many occasions to prejudice the world against the ways of God.

By these things multitudes are kept from attendance on the means of grace, and multitudes more have their hearts shut up from receiving any saving benefit under them.

These are the common bars and locks by which the strong man armed secures his possession in the souls of sinners; and,

III. These bars are too strong for any but THE ALMIGHTY POWER OF GOD to remove or break. It is said that the Lord opened a door of faith to the Gentiles. Acts 14 : 27. The arm of the Lord must be revealed, or none will open to Christ by faith. Isa. 53 : 1.

1. The iron bar of *the divine law*, that thundering, terrible law, cannot force open the heart of an unbeliever; all

the dreadful curses flying out of its fiery mouth, make no more impression than a tennis-ball against a wall of marble. You read of them who hear the words of this curse, yet bless themselves in their heart, saying, they shall have peace, though they walk in the imaginations of their hearts, to add drunkenness to thirst. Deut. 29:19.

They play with hell and eternal torments, rush into iniquity as the horse rusheth into the battle, act as men in love with their own death, and as those who are at an agreement with hell. O the besotting, hardening, infatuating power of sin!

2. The golden key of *free-grace* cannot, in itself, remove these bars and open men's hearts to Christ: "We have piped unto you, and ye have not danced." Matt. 11:17. The melodious sounds of grace, mercy, peace, and pardon, affect not the dead hearts of unbelievers: like deaf adders, they stop their ears at the voice of the charmer, charm he never so wisely. These gospel melodies only dispose them to a more quiet sleep in sin.

3. No *works of providence* are in themselves sufficient to open the hearts of men to Christ.

The *judgments* of God cannot do it; thousands have been sick with smiting, that yet cannot be made sick for sin. "Thou hast consumed them, but they have refused to receive correction: they have made their faces harder than a rock; they have refused to return." Jer. 5:3. Messengers of judgment are abroad, smiting some in their estates, scattering in one day the labor of many years; and therein giving a warning to the conscience to make sure of Christ and the world to come, since their comfort and happiness are scattered in this world. Some are smitten in their dearest relatives; death knocks at their door, and carries out the delight of their eyes, and admonishes their souls to place their happiness in more durable comforts: some are smitten with disease, giving warning of the near approach of their latter end, and bidding them prepare for another habitation; but all in vain.

No *mercies* of God are in themselves sufficient to open the obdurate hearts of sinners to Christ. God has heaped up mercies by multitudes upon many of you; all these mercies of God should lead you to repentance. Rom. 2:4. They take you in a friendly way by the hand, and thus talk with you: "Ah, sinner, how canst thou grieve and dishonor the God who thus feedeth, clotheth, and comforteth thee on every side? Do you thus requite the Lord, O foolish people and unwise?" Yet all will not do, neither judgments nor mercies can fright or allure the carnal heart to Jesus Christ. It is his Spirit, his almighty power alone, that opens these everlasting gates, and makes these strong bars give way and fly at his voice.

INFERENCE 1. *Behold here the dismal state of nature, and the woful condition of all unregenerate souls;* Christ the Redeemer shut out, sin and Satan shut in. This is the horrid state of nature shut up in unbelief. Rom. 11:32. Ah, Lord, what a condition is this; we should certainly account it an unspeakable misery to be shut up in a house haunted by the devil, where we should be continually frightened with dreadful noises and apparitions; but alas, what is an apparition of the devil without us, to the inhabitation of the devil within us? Nay, what is the possession of a body, to Satan's possession of the soul? Yet this is the very case of the unregenerate. Luke 11:21. The strong man armed keepeth the palace, till Christ dispossesses him by sovereign victorious grace. Poor wretch, canst thou start at a supposed vision of a spirit, and not tremble to think that thy soul is the habitation of devils? There is a twofold misery lying upon all Christless, unregenerated persons.

Satan is their *ruler* in this world, "the spirit that now worketh in the children of disobedience." Eph. 2:2.

As the Holy Spirit of God dwells and rules in sanctified souls, walks in them as in hallowed temples, guiding and comforting them; so Satan dwells in unregenerate hearts, inflaming them with his temptations, and using their faculties and members as instruments of unrighteousness. And then,

He will be their *tormentor* in the world to come: he that *tempts* now, will *torment* then. "Depart from me, ye cursed, into everlasting fire, prepared for the devil and his angels." Matt. 25:41. Flee, therefore, and escape for your lives, sleep not quietly another night in so dismal and dreadful a state. "If the Son make you free, ye shall be free indeed." John 8:36.

2. *What a glorious work of sovereign, omnipotent grace is the effectual conversion of a sinner unto God.* If every heart by nature be secured for Satan under so many locks and bars, the opening of any heart to Christ is deservedly marvellous in our eyes. You all acknowledge that the opening of the graves at the resurrection will be a glorious display of Almighty power, and so it will: it will be a wonderful thing to see the graves opened and the dead raised at the voice of the archangel and the trump of God; but give me leave to say that the opening of thy heart, poor sinner, to receive Christ, is a more glorious work than that of raising the dead; it is therefore deservedly put in the first rank of the great mysteries of godliness, that Christ is "believed on in the world." 1 Tim. 3:16. He that well considers Christ, may justly wonder that all the hearts in the enlightened world do not stand wide open to embrace him; yet he that shall consider the frame and temper of the natural heart, and how strongly Satan has intrenched and fortified himself in it, may justly wonder to hear of a work of conversion in an age. O brethren, consider the marvels of conversion, the wonderful works of God upon the soul that opens unto Christ by faith.

There is *a new eye created in the mind:* "The Son of God is come, and hath given us an understanding, that we may know him that is true." 1 John, 5 : 20. O that precious eye of faith, which shows the soul as it were a new world, a world of new and ravishing objects. Eph. 5 : 8. All the angels in heaven, all the ministers and libraries upon earth, cannot create such an eye and give such an illumination; it is only He who "commanded the light to shine out of darkness, that" thus "shineth in our hearts, to give the light of the knowledge of the glory of God in the face of Jesus Christ." 2 Cor. 4 : 6.

And what a glorious supernatural work is *the conviction of the conscience* by the saving beams of light upon it. Now the conscience, which lay in a dead sleep, begins to startle and look about it with fear and horror. Life and feeling have got into it, and now it cries, "Ah, sick, sick at the heart for sin, sick for a Saviour."

And no less marvellous an effect of the Almighty power is the *bowing of the stubborn will* so efficaciously, so congruously, and so determinately and fixedly to the Lord Jesus. The will is efficaciously determined, so as no power of hell or nature can resist or frustrate that mighty power which worketh effectually in all them that believe. 1 Thess. 2 : 13. Yet it works not by way of compulsion, but in harmony with and agreeably to the nature of the will : "I drew them with cords of a man, with bands of love." Hosea 11 : 4. Satan bids for the soul, but Christ infinitely outbids all his offers ; eternal, spiritual, and unsearchable riches, instead of sensual, perishing enjoyments, which determine the choice of the will in its own natural method, by the sight of the excelling glory of spiritual things. And thus the mighty, supernatural power of God opens the heart which Satan had secured so many ways against Christ.

3. Hence it also follows, *that man has no will of his own to supernatural good.* The will cannot, by its own

power, open itself to receive Christ by faith. When it does open to him, it is not by its natural power, but by the power of God upon it. The admirers of nature talk much of the sovereignty of the will, as if it alone had escaped the fall, and that no more than moral suasion is needed to open it to Christ; that is, that God needs do no more to save men than the devil does to damn them. But if ever God makes you sensible what the work of saving conversion is, you will quickly find that your will is lame to spiritual things ; you will cry out of a wounded will, as well as of a dark head and a hard heart. You will quickly find that "it is God which worketh in you both to will and to do of his own good pleasure." Phil. 2 : 13. The birth of the new creature is not of the will of man, but of God. John 1 : 13.

4. Learn, hence, *the necessity of conversion in order to salvation.* Christ and heaven are shut up against you till your hearts are savingly opened unto him. "Marvel not that I said unto thee, ye must be born again." John 3 : 7. O sinner, that hard heart of thine must be humbled ; thy stubborn and refractory will must be bowed ; all the powers of thy soul must be unlocked and opened to Christ ; he must come into thy soul, or thou canst never see the face of God in peace. It is Christ in you that is "the hope of glory." Col. 1 : 27. Till thy heart is opened, Christ, with all the hopes of glory, stands without thee. If hope from the death of Christ, without the application of his Spirit, be enough to save men, then why are any damned ? See 1 Cor. 1 : 30. Adam's sin damns none but only such as are in him ; and Christ's righteousness saves none but those that are by faith in him: the eternal purpose of the Father, the meritorious death of the Son, put no man into the state of salvation and happiness till both are brought home by the Spirit's powerful application in the work of saving conversion. It is good news indeed, that Christ died for sinners ; it is good news that Christ is brought to our very doors in the tenders of the

gospel, and that the Spirit knocks at the door of our hearts, by many convictions and persuasions to open to him and enjoy the unspeakable benefits of his death : these things bring us nigh to Christ and salvation ; and yet all this may be, eventually, but a dreadful aggravation of our damnation, and will certainly be so to them whose hearts are but almost opened to Christ.

5. See, hence, *the necessity of fervent prayer to accompany the preaching of the gospel.* Without the Spirit and power of God accompanying the word, no heart can ever be opened to Christ : alas, such bars as these are too strong for the breath of man to break ; let ministers pray, and the people pray, that the gospel may be preached "with the Holy Ghost sent down from heaven." 1 Pet. 1 : 12. It greatly concerns us who preach the gospel, to wrestle with God upon our knees for help in the dispensation of it unto the people—to steep that seed we sow among you in tears and prayers before you hear it. And I beseech you, brethren, let us not strive alone ; join your cries to heaven with ours, for the blessing of the Spirit upon the word. How does Paul beg of the people, as a beggar would for alms, for their assistance in prayer : "I beseech you, brethren, for the Lord Jesus Christ's sake, and for the love of the Spirit, that ye strive together with me in your prayers to God for me." Rom. 15 : 30.

For want of such wrestlings with God in prayer, there is so little efficacy in ordinances. Martha told her Saviour, "Lord, if thou hadst been here, my brother had not died," John 11 : 21 ; and I may tell you, that if the Spirit had been here, your souls had not remained dead under the word as they do this day. O when the Sabbath draws near, let fervent cries ascend from every family to heaven. Lord, pour out thy Spirit with thy word ; make it mighty through thy power to open these gates of iron and break asunder these bars of brass.

The subject supplies us with matter for EXHORTATION to duty. Seeing the case stands thus, that all hearts by nature are barred and shut up against Christ, let every soul strive to its uttermost to get the heart and will opened to Christ: "Strive to enter in at the strait gate." Luke 13 : 24. Christ is at the door; O strive with yourselves as well as with God now to get it opened, now that salvation is come so near your souls.

OBJECTION. But have you not told us that no sinner can open his own heart, nor bow his own will to Christ?

ANSWER. True, he cannot convert himself, but he may do many things in order to it, and which have a tendency to it, which he does not do; and so he perishes, not because he cannot, but because he will not open his heart to Christ.

Many things may be done by sinners which are not done; and though in themselves they are insufficient, yet being the way in which the Spirit of God usually works, we are bound to do them. As for example, 1. If it be not in your power to open your heart to Christ, it is in your power to forbear the external acts of sin, which set your heart the more against Christ. Who forces thine hands to steal, or thy tongue to swear or lie? Who forces the cup of excess down your throat? 2. If you cannot open your heart under the word, it is in your power to attend upon the external duties and ordinances of the gospel. Why cannot those feet carry thee to the assemblies of the saints, as well as to a tavern? 3. And if you cannot admit the word effectually into your heart, certainly you can apply your mind with more attention and consideration to it than you do. Who forces thine eyes to wander, or closes them with sleep, when the awful matters of eternal life and death are sounding in thine ears? 4. If you cannot open your heart to embrace Christ, certainly you can reflect when the obvious characters of a Christless state are plainly held forth before your eyes. God has given you a self-reflecting power: the spirit of man knoweth the things of a man. 1 Cor. 2 : 11. When you hear of convictions of sin, compunction of heart for sin, deep concern of the soul about its eternal state, hungering and thirsting after Christ, anxious days and nights about salvation, which others have felt, you can certainly examine whether it were ever so with you; and if not, methinks it might conduce to the prevention of your misery, to bemoan yourself, saying, " Ah, my poor soul, canst thou endure everlasting burnings? What will become of thee if Christ pass thee by, and his Spirit strive no more with thee?" Why cannot you throw yourself at the feet of God, and cry for mercy? Prayer is a part of natural worship; distress usually puts men upon it who have no grace. Jonah 1 : 5. Do this towards the opening and saving of your soul, which though it be not in itself sufficient, nor puts God under any obligation or necessity to show you mercy, yet it puts you in the way of the Spirit. And is not thy soul, sinner, worth as much as this? Have you not taken a great deal more pains for the trifles of this world? And will it not be a dreadful aggravation of sin and misery to all eternity, that you perished so easily? Do not you see many round about you striving for Christ and salvation, while you sit still with folded arms as if you had nothing to do for another world? "The kingdom of heaven suffereth violence, and the violent take it by force." Matt. 11 : 12.

Why should other men's souls be dearer to them than yours to you? What discouragements have you which other men have not; or what encouragements have they which you have not?

OBJECTION. Say not, We have no assurance that our pains shall prosper, or our strivings be made effectual to conversion: if there were any promise in the gospel that such endeavors should be seconded from heaven and made available to salvation, then we would strive as long as breath and life should last; but all this may be to no purpose, we may be Christless and hopeless when all is done.

ANSWER. But yet remember, God may bless these weak endeavors, and give you his Almighty Spirit with them: nay, it is highly probable that he will do so; and is a strong probability nothing with you? Do you perform no actions about your civil callings without an assurance of success? When the merchant ventures his life or property at sea, is he sure of a good return; or does he not venture upon the mere probabilities of a gainful voyage? When the husbandman plows his land, and empties his bags and purse upon it, is he sure of a good harvest? May not a blight defeat all his hopes? Yet he ploweth and soweth in hope, and ordinarily God makes him partake of his hope; but without such industry his expectations would be in vain. Away then with vain excuses; up and be doing in the use of all appointed means, and the Lord be with you.

Before I dismiss this point, let us TRY ourselves by it, whether God has opened our hearts to Christ, broken these bars of ignorance, unbelief, custom, and prejudice—whether we are ready to receive Christ Jesus the Lord.

This is a solemn application of the subject, and the consequences of it may be great: O that our faithfulness and seriousness in the trial may be answerable. Try yourselves by these following MARKS:

MARK 1. If your eyes be not opened *to see sin in its vileness, and Christ in his glory, suitableness, and necessity*, then your hearts were never yet effectually opened by the gospel. Men's eyes may be opened to see sin, and their hearts at the same time be shut up by unbelief against Christ; but no man's heart can be opened to Christ while his eyes are shut: "This is the will of him that sent me, that every one which seeth the Son and believeth on him, may have everlasting life." John 6:40. The work of faith is always wrought in the light of conviction; the cure of the heart begins at the eye of the mind, Acts 26 : 18, "to open their eyes, and to turn them from darkness to light, and from the power of Satan unto God." God opens men's hearts by shining into them. 2 Cor. 4 : 6. If, therefore, any man's eyes be still blinded with ignorance and prejudice, so that he sees not his own guilt and misery, nor the worth and necessity of a Saviour, that man's heart is still under Satan's lock and bar, sin is shut in and Christ is shut out of his soul.

MARK 2. No heart opens to Christ by faith till it be first *wounded by compunction and humiliation;* this heart-wounding work is always antecedent to the work of faith. I doubt not but your thoughts forerun my discourse, and are directed to that scripture where Peter, preaching to those who had crucified Christ, and bringing his discourse close to their consciences in the application of that sermon, convinces them not only what an atrocious crime the crucifying of the Son of God was in itself, but also charges it home upon them: "Him, being delivered by the determinate counsel and foreknowledge of God, ye have taken, and by wicked hands have crucified and slain. When they heard this, they were pricked in their heart, and said unto Peter and to the rest of the apostles, Men and brethren, what shall we do?" Acts 2 : 23, 37. Upon this outcry three thousand souls opened in one hour to Christ. Now consider whether your hearts have been thus wounded; has sorrow for sin pierced thy soul? Vain sinner, that frothy heart of thine must bleed under compunctions for sin, or there will be no room for Christ in it. Come, soul, it is in vain to flatter yourself in your own eyes: reflect upon the frame of your heart, call back the days that are past, and say, when was the time, and where was the place when thou layedst at the foot of God, mourning on account of thy sins. Did ever God hear such a cry as this from thy soul? "Ah, Lord, my soul is distressed; I roll hither and thither for ease and comfort, but find none. O the insupportable weight of guilt; O the bitterness of sin. My soul fails under it; Lord, undertake for me." I do not say the degrees of compunction and humiliation are equal in all converts, neither are their sins or their ability to bear sorrows for them equal; but this I say, thy heart must ache for sin, or it will never open to Christ: he binds up none but broken hearts. Isa. 61 : 1.

MARK 3. If Christ is come into thy heart, *the love and delight of every sin is gone out of it.* Christ and the love of sin cannot dwell together: what he said to the soldiers that apprehended him in the garden, he says to every soul that comes to apprehend him by faith, "If ye seek me, let these go their way," John 18 : 8; away with the sin thou most delightest in. Christ cannot come in till this be gone. "Seek ye the Lord while he may be found, call ye upon him while he is near: let the wicked forsake his way, and the unrighteous man his thoughts: and let him return unto the Lord, and he will have mercy upon him; and to our God, for he will abundantly pardon." Isa. 55 : 6, 7. Here are the terms of your acceptance and salvation plainly laid down, forsake thy ways and thoughts: the way means the external acts of sin, and the thoughts the internal acts of contrivance and delight in sin; both these must be forsaken; and that is not all, for this makes but a negative holiness, "Let him return to the Lord, and he will have mercy." It is in vain for men to make the door of salvation wider than God has made it; we cannot bring down Christ's terms lower than he has set them: if we will not come up to them, Christ and we must part. And this makes the great struggle in the souls of converts. O it is hard to give up pleasant and profitable lusts; but away they must go, a bill of divorce must be signed for them, or you cannot be espoused to the Lord Jesus. This will be found to be much harder than to part with all external things for Christ's sake.

MARK 4. No heart can open truly to Christ, that is not *made willing upon due deliberation to receive him, with his cross of sufferings and his yoke of obedience.* Matt. 16 : 24 ; 11 : 29. Any exception against either of these is an effectual bar to union with Christ; he looks upon that soul as not worthy of him, that puts in such an exception. Matt. 10 : 38. If thou judgest not Christ to be worth all sufferings, all losses, all reproaches, he judges thee unworthy to bear the name of his disciple. So for the duties of obedience, called his yoke ; he that will not receive Christ's yoke can never receive his person, nor any benefit by his blood.

MARK 5. Every heart that opens sincerely and evangelically to Christ, opens to him *in deep humility and sense of its emptiness and unworthiness;* all self-righteousness is given up as dung and dross. Phil. 3 : 8. Thus Abraham came to him as to one that justifieth the ungodly. "To him that worketh not, but believeth on him that justifieth the ungodly, his faith is counted for righteousness." Rom. 4 : 5. Yea, here is the true way of justification indeed ; where the imputed righteousness of Christ comes, all self-righteousness vanishes before it. By "him that worketh not," understand not an idle, lazy believer, who takes no care of the duties of obedience ; an idle faith can never be a saving faith. But the meaning is, he worketh not to meet the demands of the first covenant—to make up a righteousness for himself by his own working, to cover himself with a robe of righteousness of his own weaving. Thou must receive Christ into a naked, unworthy soul, or not receive him at all. Paul heartily rejected all his own righteousness, cast down that *house-idol* to the ground, that he might be found in the righteousness of Christ. Phil. 3 : 9. Cast that idol out of doors, it stands in the way of a better righteousness. There are divers ways wherein sinners maintain their own righteousness to their ruin. There is a gross and a more refined self-righteousness ; the one more palpable and easily liable to conviction, the other much harder to be discovered and cured. Ask some men on what their hopes of salvation are grounded, and they will tell you they are just in their dealings with men and constant in their prayers to God; that is all, and therefore they doubt not of their salvation. Thus they substitute a righteousness of their own in the place of Christ's blood, and are their own *destroyers* by seeking in this way to be their own *saviours*. But there is a more refined way of self-righteousness, dressed up in such pretences of humility that men are hard to be convinced of it. I pity many souls on this account who stand off from Christ, and dare not believe because they want such and such qualifications to fit them for Christ. O, saith one, could I find so much brokenness of heart for sin, so much reformation and power over corruptions, then I could come to Christ; the meaning of which is, if I could bring a price in my hand to purchase him, then I should be encouraged to go to him. Here now is horrible pride covered over with a veil of humility. Poor sinner, either come naked and empty-handed, according to Isa. 55 : 1, and Rom. 4 : 5, or expect a repulse; for Christ is not the sale, but the gift of God.

MARK 6. Whatever soul opens to Christ, *opens finally and everlastingly to him;* the heart once opened to Christ, must stand open for ever to him, never to shut him out any more. And here is a very observable difference between a man who comes to Christ in a sudden fright of conscience, and parts from him again when that fright is over, and a man who receives Christ to dwell in his heart by faith. Eph. 3 : 17. When Christ comes into the heart, he saith, "Here will I dwell for ever;" and, "Lord," saith the soul, "so I receive thee; this is the day of union, O let me never know a day of separation; let it never be in the power of life or death, angels, principalities or powers, things present or to come, to make a separation between thee and me." "Soul," saith Christ, "thou shalt be mine while I am in heaven;" and, "Lord," saith the soul, "I will be thine while I am on earth." "I will never leave thee nor forsake thee," saith Christ; "O, my Lord," saith the soul, "hold me fast in thy hand, that I may never leave nor forsake thee; my estate, liberty, and life may and must go, but it is the fixed purpose of my heart never, never to let thee go." The espousals between Christ and the soul are for ever: "I will betroth thee unto me for ever," yea, *for ever*. Hos. 2 : 19. And here lies another great difference between the hypocrite who takes Christ with a politic reserve, that will venture with Christ at sea no further than he can see the shore, and the upright heart that embarks itself with Christ without reserve, come what will; that saith to him, as Ittai to David, when entreated to go back in a time of danger, "Nay, where my Lord Jesus Christ is, whether it be in liberty or in prison, in life or in death, there also will I be." Flesh may persuade to a retreat; but, saith the soul, I cannot retreat: wherever the truths, the interest and glory of Christ are, there also must I be; for upon these terms I first received him, and opened the door of my heart to him. These things are no matters of surprise to me, Christ and I have debated them long ago; he dealt fairly with me, and I must deal faithfully with him.

Now, brethren, view over these six trials; have your eyes been opened to see sin in its vileness, and Christ in his beauty and necessity? Have your hearts been wounded with compunction and sorrow for sin? Are the love and delight of sin gone out of your souls? Have you no exceptions either to the cross or yoke of Christ? Have you given up all your own righteousness, whether gross or refined, for dung and dross, and received Christ for ever? Then thy heart is savingly opened to him.

The last improvement of this doctrine will be, to draw from it CONSOLATION to all whose hearts the Lord has thus opened to receive Christ at his knocks and calls of the gospel.

Has God indeed opened your heart, and made you sincerely willing to receive Christ? then there are ten sweet consolations, like so many boxes of precious ointment, to be poured forth in the close of this discourse, upon every such soul.

Consolation 1. The opening of any man's heart to receive Christ, is *a clear, scriptural evidence of the Lord's love to and setting apart that man for himself from eternity.* I do not say that every man whose heart is opened by faith, is thereupon immediately assured and satisfied that God has chosen him to salvation. But whether he apprehend it or not, the thing in itself is certain. "Knowing, brethren beloved, your election of God. For our gospel came not unto you in word only, but also in power, and in the Holy Ghost, and in much assurance." 1 Thess. 1 : 4, 5. Their election of God was the thing to be proved; but alas, might they say, Who can know that but God alone? it is among the divine secrets. Yes, saith the apostle, we know it, and by this we know it; for our gospel came not unto you in an empty sound, but in mighty efficacy, effectually opening your hearts to believe. A more clear and certain evidence of your election cannot be given in this world.

Again, look into Rom. 8 : 30 : "Moreover, whom he did predestinate, them he also called; and whom he called, them he also justified; and whom he justified, them he also glorified." There are two great and ravishing truths cleared in this scripture: the one is, that the whole number of the called upon earth were predestinated to life before the world was; the other is, that as the whole number of the glorified saints in heaven is made up of souls called and justified on earth, so the called soul, that is, the soul that savingly opens to Christ by faith, may, from that work of the Spirit upon him, solidly reason backward to God's electing love before all time, and forward to his glorification with God when time shall be no more. O how strong is the consolation flowing out of this glorious work of the Spirit on our hearts.

CONSOLATION 2. The opening of the heart to receive Christ, is *the peculiar effect of the almighty power of God.* The arm of an angel is too weak to break those strong bars before-mentioned; therefore the exceeding greatness of his power is applied unto this work of believing: "The exceeding greatness of his power to us-ward who believe, according to the working of his mighty power which he wrought in Christ when he raised him from the dead." Eph. 1 : 19, 20. Here is power, the power of God, the greatness of his power, the exceeding greatness of his power, the very same power which wrought in Christ when he raised him from the dead; and all this is needed to make the heart of man open by faith to receive Christ. The only key that fits the cross wards of man's will and effectually opens his heart, is in the hand of Christ: "He hath the key of David; he openeth, and no man shutteth." Rev. 3 : 7.

How long some of you sat under able ministers, searching sermons, and alarming providences; yet to no purpose, till this almighty power came with the word, and then the work was done. "Thy people shall be willing in the day of thy power." Psalm 110 : 3. What a glorious power was that which opened Christ's grave, when he lay in the heart of the earth, with a weighty stone rolled upon his sepulchre. And how mighty a power was that which broke asunder all those bars which kept thy soul in the state of sin and death. None feel this power but those whom God intends for salvation; and having once wrought this, it is engaged to go through with all the rest which yet remains to be done to perfect thy salvation.

CONSOLATION 3. The opening of thy heart to Christ is not only an effect of almighty power, but an effect *without which all that Christ has done and suffered had been of no avail to thy salvation;* neither the eternal decrees of God, nor the meritorious sufferings of Christ, are effectual to any man's salvation, until this work of the Spirit be wrought upon his heart. The offering of Christ is sufficient to purchase our redemption, but the receiving of Christ by faith brings home salvation to our souls. Where there are many causes to produce one effect, that effect is not produced until the last cause has wrought. Thus it is here: the moving cause, namely, the free-grace of God, has wrought; and the meritorious cause, the death of Christ, has also wrought; but still the heart, even of an elect man, remains under guilt and condemnation, till the Spirit, who is the applying agent, has also wrought the blessed effect we now speak of. It is Christ in us, that is, in union with our souls, which is to us the hope of glory. Col. 1 : 27 ; 1 Cor. 1 : 30. Behold, then, the last stroke given in this opening of the heart by faith; herein electing love has brought home Christ, with all the purchases and benefits of his death, into the actual possession of thy soul. O how transporting a consideration is this.

CONSOLATION 4. In this work, the opening of the heart by faith, *the great design of the gospel is also accomplished.* You behold in the church a glorious frame of ordinances set up by divine institution, ministers appointed to preach, sacraments, prayers, singing—a variety of ordinances set up and excellent gifts bestowed on men, as the fruit of Christ's ascension into heaven. Now, what was the design of God in the institution of all these things, but that by them, as instruments in his hand, our ignorant, dead, unbelieving hearts might be opened to Christ in acts of repentance and faith, and built up to a perfect man ? Ministers are sent to open your eyes, to turn you from darkness to light, and from the power of Satan to God. Acts 26 : 18. They are not sent by Christ into this world to get a living, to pursue a trade for themselves, but to bring you to faith. 1 Cor. 3 : 5.

When God's elect are thus brought in and built up in Christ, you shall see this glorious frame of ordinances taken down; there will be no more preaching nor hearing, the end of all these things being accomplished: "Then cometh the end, when he shall have delivered up the kingdom to God, even the Father." 1 Cor. 15:24. The consideration of the accomplishment of the great and principal design of the gospel thus far upon thy heart, is matter of transporting joy. Ministers may and must die, ordinances may be removed, but this blessed effect of them upon thy soul shall never die: God will perfect what he hath begun.

CONSOLATION 5. *That day wherein thy heart is savingly opened to receive Christ, that very day is salvation come to thy soul.* When the heart of Zaccheus was opened to Christ, he tells him, "This day is salvation come to thy house." Luke 19:9. Salvation was come into the world before thou wast born; yea, salvation was come to thy door in the tenders of the gospel before; but it never came into thy soul till the day wherein thy heart opened to Christ by faith. And is not this matter of singular consolation? If salvation be not, what is? No wonder that the eunuch went home rejoicing, when he had received Christ by faith, Acts 8:39; that the jailer rejoiced with all his house. Acts 16:34. Neither blame nor wonder at such men for rejoicing, for it is the day of their salvation. It is true their salvation was not finished that day, there were many things yet to be done and suffered by them before the completion of it; but it was begun that day, the foundation was laid in the soul that day, and the top-stone shall be set up with shouting in due time, crying, Grace, grace unto it.

CONSOLATION 6. The opening of a sinner's heart to Christ makes *joy in heaven, a triumph in the city of our God above.* "I say unto you, that likewise joy shall be in heaven over one sinner that repenteth, more than over ninety and nine just persons which need no repentance."

Luke 15 : 7. As when a young prince is born, all the kingdom rejoices, and there is a demonstration of joy and thankfulness in every city and town; it is much more so in heaven, when a soul is born to Christ under the gospel. It is a satisfaction to the heart of the Lord Jesus, who now beholds more of the travail of his soul; and to all the angels and saints, that another soul is espoused to him.

When the gospel is effectually brought home by the Spirit to the heart of a sinner, and wounds him for sin, and sends him home, crying, O sick, sick of sin, and sick for Christ! the news thereof is presently in heaven, and sets the whole city of God rejoicing. Christ never rejoiced over thee before; thou hast wounded him and grieved him a thousand times, but he never rejoiced in thee till now; and that which gives joy to Christ may well be matter of joy to thee.

CONSOLATION 7. The day thy heart is unlocked, unbarred, and savingly opened by faith, that very day *an intimate, spiritual, and everlasting union is made between Christ and thy soul; from that day Christ is thine, and thou art his.* Christ is a great and glorious person; but how great and glorious soever he be, the feeble arms of thy faith may surround and embrace him, and thou mayest say with the church, "My beloved is mine, and I am his." Sol. Song, 2 : 16. For mark what he says in the text, "If any man open to me, I will come in to him." That soul shall be my habitation, there will I dwell for ever. Thus will Christ dwell in your heart by faith. What soul feels not itself advanced by this union with the Son of God? Hereby the believer becomes a member of his body, of his flesh and of his bones: this is an honor bestowed upon thy soul, above all that ever God bestowed upon any angel in heaven; to them Christ is a head by way of dominion, but to thee by way of vital influence. Angels are as the nobles of his kingdom, but the believer his bride, and all the angels of heaven are ministering spirits unto such.

CONSOLATION 8. The opening of thy heart to Christ brings thee not only into union with his person, but into the state of sweet, soul-enriching communion with him. So he speaks in the text, "If any man open the door, I will come in to him, and will sup with him, and he with me." Thou hast lived many years in the world, and never hadst any communion with God till this day. Christ and thy soul have been strangers till now. Thou mayest have had communion with ordinances, and even external communion with saints, but for communion with Christ thou couldst know nothing of it, till thou receivedst him into thy soul by faith. Now thou mayest say, "Truly my fellowship is with the Father, and with his Son Jesus Christ." 1 John, 1:3. And thenceforth thy communion with men is pleasant and desirable.

CONSOLATION 9. The opening of a man's soul to Christ by faith, is *a special and peculiar mercy.* God has done that for thee which he has not done to millions: "Who hath believed our report; and to whom is the arm of the Lord revealed?" that is, to how small a remnant in the world. Isa. 53:1. And the apostle puts the work of faith among the great mysteries of godliness, the wonders of religion: "Preached unto the Gentiles, believed on in the world.", 1 Tim. 3:16. The sound of the gospel is gone forth into the world: "Many are called, but few are chosen." Matt. 22:14. There were many widows in Israel in the days of Elias, but to none of them was Elias sent, save unto Sarepta, a city of Sidon, unto a woman that was a widow. Luke 4:25, 26. There may have been hundreds who sat under the same sermon which opened thy heart to Christ, but it may be to none of them was the Spirit of God sent that day, to open their hearts by faith, but to thee; thou wilt freely acknowledge thyself as unlikely and unworthy as the vilest sinner there. O astonishing mercy!

CONSOLATION 10. And lastly, in the same day thy heart

opens by faith to Christ, *all the treasures of Christ are unlocked and opened to thee.* In the same hour in which God turns the key of regeneration to open thy soul, the key of free-grace is also turned to open to thee the unsearchable riches of Christ; then the righteousness of Christ becomes thine to justify thee, the wisdom of Christ to guide thee, the holiness of Christ to sanctify thee; in a word, he is that day made of God to thee, "wisdom, and righteousness, and sanctification, and redemption." 1 Cor. 1:30. "All are yours; and ye are Christ's, and Christ is God's." 1 Cor. 3:22, 23. Thus I have showed you some of the great things God does for those souls who open their hearts to receive Christ on the terms of the gospel.

CHAPTER IV.

CHRIST'S PATIENCE IN WAITING UPON OBSTINATE SINNERS.

"BEHOLD, *I STAND* AT THE DOOR AND KNOCK." REV. 3:20.

THE verb here rendered "I stand," would strictly be rendered "I have stood," but being joined with a verb of the *present tense*, is here translated "I do stand," a frequent Hebraism in Scripture. It intimates the continued patience and long-suffering of Christ; I have stood and still do stand, exercising wonderful patience towards obstinate sinners. Which gives us this fourth doctrine:

Great and admirable is the patience of Christ, in waiting on trifling and obstinate sinners.

Thus Wisdom, that is, Christ, expresses himself: "I have called, and ye refused; I have stretched out my hand, and no man regarded." Prov. 1:24. Here you have not only Christ's earnest calls, but suitable gestures also, to gain attention. The stretching forth of the hand was a signal given to procure attention. Acts 21:40. Yet none regards; and this the Lord does not once or twice only, but all the day long, Isa. 65:2, showing forth all long-suffering, as the apostle speaks, 1 Tim. 1:16. In opening this point, I will show what divine patience is; wherein it is evidenced; and why it is exercised towards sinners.

I. WHAT DIVINE PATIENCE IS. It is an ability in God not only to delay the execution of his wrath for a time towards some, but to delay it in order to the eternal salvation of others.

1. *It is an effect of power* in God, not the effect of inability or want of opportunity. All sinners are continually within the reach of the arm of his justice, and he can strike when and where he will. Esau had a revengeful mind

against Jacob, but wanted opportunity, and therefore was forced to delay the execution of his wrath until the days of mourning for his father were ended, and then, saith he, "will I slay my brother Jacob." Gen. 27 : 41. But in God it is a glorious effect of power. "The Lord is slow to anger and great in power." Nah. 1 : 3. The greatness of his patience flows from the greatness of his power. So the apostle speaks, Rom. 9 : 22 : "What if God, willing to show his wrath, and to make his power known, endured with much long-suffering the vessels of wrath fitted," or made up, "to destruction?" And therefore when Moses prays for the exercise of divine patience towards the provoking Israelites, he does it in this form: "And now, I beseech thee, let the power of my Lord be great, according as thou hast spoken, saying, the Lord is long-suffering, and of great mercy, forgiving iniquity and transgression." Numbers, 14 : 17, 18. He could exercise this almighty power upon thee, and crush thee by it as a moth is crushed; but behold, he exercises it upon himself in staying the execution of his own justice. It is the power of God over his wrath, restraining it from day to day.

2. This patience *is exercised towards such as perish, in a delay of their damnation;* and though this be but a suspension of his wrath for a time, yet it is a glorious act of patience in him, as Rom. 9 : 22 shows. Is it nothing for a sinner condemned as soon as born, to be reprieved so many years out of hell? Thou hast been provoking him daily and hourly to cut thee off, and send thee to thy own place; and yet to be on this side the everlasting burnings, this is wholly owing to the riches of his forbearance. Ah, how is God to be admired in this his glorious power over his own wrath! When we look abroad into the world, and see everywhere sinners ripe for destruction, daring the God of heaven to his face, yet forborne, how admirable is this power of God!

3. God not only exercises this power in a suspension of

his wrath against some, who, alas, must feel it at last; but *he delays the execution of his wrath in a design of mercy towards others, that they may never feel it.* Isa. 48 : 8, 9. Thus he bears with his own elect all the years of their lives wherein they lie in the state of nature, and go on in a course of rebellion against God; and this long-suffering of God towards them proves their salvation, as you have it in 2 Pet. 3 : 15; "And account that the long-suffering of our Lord is salvation." What is the meaning of that? Ah, Christian, thou mayest easily know the meaning of it, without turning over many Commentaries. Thou art now in Christ, safely escaped from the danger of wrath to come; but thou owest this thy salvation to the patience and long-suffering of God towards thee. For what if he had cut thee off in the days of thy ignorance and rebellion against him, and thou knowest that thou didst give him millions of provocations so to do, where hadst thou now been? Thou hadst never seen Christ, nor the least dawning hope of salvation by him. Remember how oft you lay in those days upon the bed of sickness and upon the brink of the grave; and what was it that saved thee from eternal wrath but this admirable patience of Christ? Well, therefore, may the apostle say, "Account that the long-suffering of our Lord is salvation."

This patience of God seems to spring out of his mercy; only it differs from mercy in this, that man as *miserable* is the object of mercy, but man as *criminal* is the object of patience. Such is the nature of divine patience, a power of God over his own wrath, not only to suspend it for a time towards them that perish, but to delay the execution of it in a design of salvation towards others.

II. THE EVIDENCES of this divine patience, or wherein it appears in its glorious manifestations towards provoking sinners; and there are seven full evidences and discoveries of it, which should make the hearts of sinners melt within them, while they are sounding in their ears. Ah, methinks such as these should melt down your hard hearts before the Lord:

1. The first evidence shall be taken *from the multitude of sins which men are guilty of before him*, the least of which is a burden too heavy for any creature to bear; the Psalmist says, "Innumerable evils have compassed me about." Psalm 40:12. It was true, as applied to the person of David; and though it be there also applied to the person of Christ, yet none of them were his own sins, but ours—called his, by God's reckoning or imputing them to him. Men can number vast sums, millions of millions; but no man can number his own sins, they exceed all account. There is not a member of the body, though never so small, but has been the instrument of innumerable evils. For instance, the tongue, the apostle tells us, is a world of iniquity. Jas. 3:6. And if there be a world of sin in one member, what then are the sins of all? How many idle, vain words, has thy tongue uttered. And yet for them, Christ says, men shall give an account in the day of judgment. Matt. 12:36. And what have the sins of thy thoughts been? Solomon says, "The thought of foolishness is sin." Prov. 24:9. O who can understand his errors? Yet the patience of God has not failed under such innumerable evils. O glorious patience! well may it be ushered in in the text with a term of admiration, "Behold, I stand!"

2. The second evidence of the divine patience shall be taken from *the heinous nature of some sins above others, whereby sinners fly, as it were, in the very face of God;* and yet he bears with long-suffering, restraining his hands from cutting them off. All sins are not of equal magnitude; some have a slighter hue, and some are deeper; called upon that account scarlet and crimson sins, Isaiah 1:18, double-dyed abominations; such are sins against knowledge, or sins committed after convictions, and cove-

nants, and rebukes of providence. I do not only speak of outward gross acts of sin; for though they are of greater infamy, yet inward sins may be of greater guilt, even those sins that never defamed thee in the world; but whatever they are, reader, whether outward or inward, thy conscience is privy to them, and thy soul may stand amazed at the patience of God in forbearing all this while under such provocations against him; especially, considering how many are this day in hell that never provoked God by sinning with such a high hand as thou hast done.

3. There is a yet greater evidence of the patience of God in his bearing with us under the guilt of *the special sin of slighting and neglecting Jesus Christ.* Here is a sin that goes to the very heart of Jesus Christ. He can bear any sin rather than that; and yet this has Christ borne from every one of you. You have spurned the yearnings of his mercy, slighted his grace, trampled his precious blood under foot, and yet he has borne with you to this day. Let thy conscience answer, whether thou art not equally deep in the guilt of making light of Christ with those upon whom this sin was charged by the Lord Jesus. Matt. 22:2-6. Christ suffered the wrath of God in thy stead, and brought home salvation in gospel-offers to thy door; and then to be slighted! No patience but his own could bear it. Every sermon and prayer you have sat under with a dead heart, every motion of his Spirit which you have quenched, what is this but making light of Christ and the great salvation? Here the deepest project of infinite wisdom, and the richest gift of free-grace, wherein God commends his love to men, are undervalued as small things: thus have you done days without number; and yet his hand is not stretched out to cut thee off in thy rebellion. "Who is a God like unto thee?" Micah 7:18. What patience is like the patience of Christ?

4. *The length of time the patience of Christ has borne with thee* speaks its perfection and riches. Consider, sin-

ner, what age thou art of, how many years thou canst number, and that all this hath been a time of patience, for thou wast a transgressor from the womb; yet, for his name's sake hath he deferred his anger and hath not cut thee off. Isa. 48 : 8, 9. How soon did the wrath of God break forth upon the angels when they sinned in heaven; and how long has it borne with thee, while thou hast been provoking him on earth. Was there ever patience like the patience of God? Many thousands have been sent away to hell since the beginning of thy day, but thou art yet spared. O that the long-suffering of God might be salvation to thee.

5. A great evidence of the power of divine patience may be drawn from *the grievousness of our sins against God, during the whole time of his forbearance.* It is true there is no passion in the divine nature, no perturbation; his anger is a mild and holy flame; yet the contrariety of sin to the holiness of his nature is what makes his patience wonderful in the eyes of men. The Scripture, speaking in language fitted to the understanding of the creature, represents God as wounded to the heart by the sins of men : "I am broken with their whorish heart, which hath departed from me," Ezek. 6 : 9; "Behold, I am pressed under you, as a cart is pressed that is full of sheaves," Amos 2 : 13, when the axle-tree is ready to crack under the load. It is said, " They mocked the messengers of God, and despised his words, and misused his prophets, until the wrath of the Lord arose against his people, till there was no remedy," 2 Chron. 36 : 16; his patience would endure no longer, and therefore, when he executed his wrath upon provoking sinners, that execution is represented in the nature of an ease or relief to his burdened patience and justice : " Ah, I will ease me of mine adversaries, and avenge me of mine enemies." Isa. 1 : 24. Yet observe, it comes in with an Ah, a kind of regret and reluctance ; so Isa. 10 : 25, " Yet a very little while and the indignation shall cease, and mine anger

in their destruction." God could have given ease and rest this way to his anger long ago, but he chooses rather still to bear with thee, than on these terms to ease himself of thee.

6. *The vast expense of his riches and bounty upon us, during the whole time of his forbearance and patience towards us*, speaks him infinite in his long-suffering towards us. "Despisest thou the riches of his goodness and forbearance and long-suffering, not knowing that the goodness of God leadeth thee to repentance?" Rom. 2 : 4. As if he had said, "Vile sinner, canst thou compute the treasures of mercy thou hast been riotously wasting all this while? Dost thou know what vast sums Christ has spent upon thee to preserve thee so long out of hell?" There are two treasures spending upon sinners, all the time of God's forbearance with them : there is the precious treasure of thy time wasted, and the invaluable streams of gospel-grace running all this while to waste. Thy time is precious ; the whole of thy time between thee and eternity is but little, and the most of it has been wasted in sin and upon vanity. But that is not all, the treasures of gospel-grace have been wasting all this while upon thee. It is compared to golden oil, maintaining the lamps of ordinances. Zech. 4 : 12. Who would maintain a lamp with golden oil for careless children to play by? Yet this has God done while thy soul has trifled with him. The witnesses and ministers of Christ, in Rev. 11 : 3, 4, are compared to those olive-trees that drop their precious oil, their gifts, graces, yea, and their natural spirits with them, into this lamp, to keep it burning. All this while the blood of Christ has been running in vain, the ministers of Christ preaching and beseeching in vain, the Spirit of Christ striving with you in vain. You burn away golden oil, and yet your lamp is not gone out. O marvellous patience! O the riches of God's forbearance!

7. The riches of divine patience towards you are greatly

heightened *by the quick destruction the Lord has sent on other sinners, while he has spared and passed over you.* This comparative consideration calls upon you in the apostle's language, "Behold, therefore, the goodness and severity of God: on them which fell, severity; but toward thee, goodness, if thou continue in his goodness: otherwise thou also shalt be cut off." Rom. 11:22. Some sinners have been cut off in the beginning of their days, many in the very acts of sin, and those not greater than thy sins; they are gone to their own place, and thou art still left a monument of the patience and forbearance of God. The sin of Achan was not a greater sin than thy covetousness and earthliness of heart is; the sin of Nadab and Abihu, in offering up strange fire, was not greater than thy superstition in offering up uncommanded services to God: yet the hand of God fell on them, and smote them dead—in the day and place wherein they sinned, they perished; they were taken away in their iniquities, but thou art reserved. O that it may be for an instance and example of the riches of divine patience, which may at last lead thee to repentance.

Thus I have given you seven evidences of the wonderful patience of Christ, who hath stood and still doth stand at the door, knocking.

III. Next, we will inquire into the REASONS of this marvellous patience of Christ, this astonishing long-suffering of God towards sinners.

1. The exercise of his patience is *a standing testimony of his reconcilable and merciful nature towards sinful man.* This he showed forth in his patience towards Paul, a great example of his merciful nature, for a pattern to them who should hereafter believe on him. 1 Tim. 1:16. The long-suffering of God is a special part of his revealed glory; and therefore when Moses desired a sight of his glory, he proclaims his name, "The LORD, the LORD God, merciful and gracious, long-suffering, and abundant in goodness and

truth." Exod. 34 : 6. He would have sinners look towards him as a God willing to be reconciled, a God that retains not his anger for ever; but if sinners will take hold of his strength and make peace with him, they may have peace. Isa. 27 : 5. This long-suffering is an attribute very expressive of the divine nature; he is willing sinners should know, whatever their provocations have been, that there is room for pardon and peace, if they will yet come in to accept the terms. This patience is a diadem belonging to the imperial crown of heaven; the Lord glories in it, as peculiar to himself: "I will not execute the fierceness of mine anger; for I am God, and not man." Hos. 11 : 9. As though he had said, "Had I been as man, the holiest, meekest, and most mortified upon earth, I had consumed them long ago; but 'I am God, and not man :' my patience is above all created patience; no husband can bear with his wife, no parent with his child, as I have borne with you." This is one reason of Christ's waiting upon trifling sinners, to give proof of his gracious, merciful, and reconcilable nature towards the worst of men.

2. The Lord exercises this patience towards sinners, *thereby to lead them to repentance;* this is the direct intention of it. The Lord desires and delights to see ingenuous relentings and brokenness of heart for sin; and there is nothing like his forbearance and patience in promoting such an evangelical repentance. All the terrors of the law will not break the heart of a sinner, as the patience and long-suffering of God will; therefore it is said that the goodness, forbearance, and long-suffering of God, lead men to repentance. Rom. 2 : 4. These are fitted to work upon all the principles of humanity which incline men to repentance; reason, conscience, gratitude, feel the influences of the goodness of God herein, and melt under it. Thus Saul's heart relented: "Is this thy voice, my son David? and Saul lifted up his voice and wept. And he said to David, Thou art more

righteous than I; for thou hast rewarded me good, whereas I have rewarded thee evil." 1 Sam. 24: 16, 17. Thus the goodness and forbearance of God doth, as it were, take a sinner by the hand, lead him into a corner, and say, "Come, let us talk together; thus and thus vile hast thou been, and thus and thus long-suffering and merciful has God been to thee; thy heart has been full of sin, the heart of thy God has been full of pity and mercy." This dissolves the sinner into tears, and breaks his heart in pieces. If any thing will melt a hard heart, this will do it. O how good has God been to me. How have I tried his patience to the uttermost, and still he waits to be gracious, and is exalted that he may have compassion. The sobs and tears, the ingenuous relentings of a sinner's heart, under the apprehensions of the sparing mercy and goodness of God, are the music of heaven.

3. The Lord exercises this *long-suffering towards sinners, to clear his justice in the damnation of all obstinate refusers of Christ and mercy.* Christ waits at our doors now, that he may be clear in his sentence against us hereafter. This patience of Christ takes away all pleas out of the mouths of impenitent sinners; the more Christ's patience has been, the less defence they will have for themselves.

Think with thyself, sinner, what wilt thou answer in the great day, when Christ shall say, "Did I not stand at thy door from day to day, from Sabbath to Sabbath, from year to year, calling and persuading thee to be reconciled and accept pardon and mercy in the proper season of them, and thou wouldest not? " I gave her space to repent, and she repented not." Rev. 2: 21. The Lord gives you time now, a space for repentance, such a space as millions of souls, gone into a miserable eternity, never had. With whomsoever Christ has been quick and severe, surely he hath not been so with you. This time of Christ's patience will be evidence enough to clear him and condemn you; men and angels shall applaud the sentence, dreadful as it is, and say, "Righteous art thou, O Lord, in judging thus."

4. The Lord exercises his admirable patience towards sinners *for the continuation and increase of the church.* The church must be continued and enlarged from age to age; and if God should cut off sinners as soon as they provoke him, whence should the elect of God rise in this world? Many that will heartily embrace Christ, must be the descendants of such as reject him. If God should cut off these in the beginning of their provocations, how would the church be continued? Where had good Abijah and Hezekiah been, if wicked Jeroboam and Ahaz had been cut off in their first transgressions? The Lord suffers many wicked parents to stand for a time under his patience, because children are to spring from them who will obey and embrace Christ whom their wicked parents rejected. Yea, the wicked not only propagate the church, but are useful to preserve and defend it; as the chaff is a defence to the wheat: "The earth helped the woman." Rev. 12 : 16.

5. The Lord exercises this long-suffering towards sinners, in gracious condescension to *the prayers of his people.* Except the Lord of hosts had left unto us a very small remnant, we should have been as Sodom, and we should have been like unto Gomorrah. Isa. 1 : 9. The prayers and intercessions of the saints are a screen between wicked men and the wrath of God for a time. The innocent preserve the island. Job 22 : 30. The world stands by the prayers of the saints; what multitudes of rebellious, Christ-despising sinners swarm in every part of this nation! Such declare, by their open practice, that they will not have Christ to reign over them; they now contemn his offers, and despise his messengers; but blessed be God, yea, and let them bless him too, there are others praying to the Lord for them, beseeching his forbearance towards them. Little do the wicked know how much they are beholden to the prayers of the

saints. These and such like reasons prevail with the Lord Jesus to stand in a waiting posture at the door of sinners' hearts. Ah, how loath is he to give them up. We now proceed to the uses of this doctrine.

And first, this point will be very fruitful for INFORMATION of our understandings in several great and useful points, both doctrinal and practical, wherein every soul is deeply concerned; and therefore, I beseech you, let them be heard and pondered with an answerable attention and seriousness of spirit.

INFERENCE 1. If the Lord Jesus exercises such admirable patience, *then how much better is it for sinners to be in the hands of Christ, than in the hands of the holiest man in the world.* O sinner, it is better for thee to fall into the hands of the meek and merciful Jesus, than into the hands of the dearest friend thou hast on earth: no creature can bear what Christ bears—no patience is like the patience of Christ. It is said of Moses, "Now the man Moses was very meek, above all the men which were upon the face of the earth." Numb. 12:3. There was never such a man born into the world, for patience, meekness, and long-suffering, as Moses was; and yet this mirror of meekness could not bear the provocations of Israel: "Ye rebels," saith he, "must we fetch water out of this rock?" Numb. 20:10. Thus was his spirit ruffled with the provocations of Israel, and this lost him the land of Canaan. Jonah was a good man, a prophet of the Lord; yet because the Lord would not be so quick and severe with Nineveh as Jonah had predicted, in what uncomely language does his angry soul speak to his God: "O Lord, was not this my saying, when I was yet in my country? Therefore I fled before unto Tarshish; for I knew that thou art a gracious God, and merciful, slow to anger, and of great kindness, and repentest thee of the evil. Therefore now, O Lord, take, I beseech thee, my life from me; for it is better for me to die than to live." Jonah

4 : 2, 3. As if he had said, "Ah, Lord, I knew it would come to this; I knew thy gracious nature, how inclined thou art to mercy, and that upon the first appearance of their repentance thou wouldst repent of the evil, and so free-grace would make me seem as a deceiver among them."

Give me leave to speak a higher word than all this, and let it not seem strange, that the patience of the glorified saints in heaven is nothing to the patience of Christ towards provoking sinners upon earth. Those glorified souls, though they have patience among other graces, perfected in its kind, still it is but finite patience and cannot bear what Christ's patience bears. Take an instance of it out of Rev. 6 : 9, 10, 11 : "I saw under the altar the souls of them that were slain for the word of God, and for the testimony which they held; and they cried with a loud voice, saying, How long, O Lord, holy and true, dost thou not judge and avenge our blood on them that dwell on the earth? And it was said unto them, that they should rest for a little season." Here you see glorified souls less able to bear the slow pace of justice towards their enemies, than Christ was. There was no sinful impatience, but yet a patience short of Christ's infinite patience. Ah, if you were to depend on the patience of any creature in heaven or earth, you had worn it out long ago. "I will not execute the fierceness of mine anger; for I am God, and not man." It is well that we have to do with God : "If a man find his enemy, will he let him go well away?" 1 Sam. 24 : 19. No, he will reckon with him before he parts with him. Sinner, the Lord finds thee daily in thy sins, and yet allows thee to go; yet beware thou try not his patience too far, lest vengeance overtake thee at last, and pay the justice of God with all the arrears due to his patience.

2. Hence it follows, *that convinced and broken-hearted sinners need not be discouraged in going to Jesus Christ for mercy, seeing he exercises such wonderful patience*

towards obstinate and refusing sinners. This inference breathes the pure gospel; it is a cordial to cheer the heart that is moving towards Christ with fear and trembling. It is a great artifice of Satan, to daunt and discourage poor convinced sinners by telling them there is no hope of mercy for them; that they shall find the arms of mercy closed; that the time of mercy is now past, and they come too late. O how busy is Satan with such suggestions as these in many of your souls. But I am instructed to tell you that these are but the artifices of the enemy: you are going to the fountain of mercy, patience, goodness, and long-suffering; go on, and you shall find abundantly more than you expect. He will not cast off a soul that comes mourning and panting towards him, and is willing to subscribe the gospel-articles of reconciliation. No, he will not shut out such a soul, whatever its rebellions and provocations have been. Sinner, thou art going to the meek and merciful Jesus, who has said, "Come unto me, all ye that labor and are heavy laden, and I will give you rest. Take my yoke upon you, and learn of me; for I am meek and lowly in heart." Matt. 11:28, 29. You are going to meekness and mercy itself: he is "the Lamb of God," that is his name. Go on then, trembling sinner; do not stand any longer inquiring, shall I, shall I? but make a bold and necessary venture of faith; try him once, and then report what you find him to be. Certainly, if he exercises such patience as he does towards the vessels of wrath while they are fitting for destruction, Rom. 9:22, he will not want patience for a vessel of mercy, preparing by humiliation and faith for Christ and glory. Does he bear with those that stand in defiance, and will he fall on those that are mourning before him upon the knee of submission? Shall a condemned sinner, who is preparing for hell, find so much forbearance, and a poor broken-hearted sinner none? It cannot be. If Jesus Christ bore with thee when thy heart was hard as a rock, and would not shed one tear for sin, will he execute his wrath upon thee, and show thee no mercy, when thy heart is broken to pieces with sorrow, and filled with loathing and detestation against sin, and thyself for sin? Did he bear with thee when sin was thy delight; and will he destroy thee now it is thy burden? It cannot be.

Moreover, if the Lord Jesus were not willing to show mercy to thy soul, now that thine eyes are opened and thy heart touched to the quick, why has he foreborne the execution of his wrath so long? He might have taken his own time to cut thee off; he might have made any day the execution-day. But among all the days of thy life, the day of thy humiliation, the day of thy faith, is not likely to prove that day.

Again, as great and vile sinners as thyself have ventured upon the grace of Christ, and found it infinitely beyond their expectation. These the Lord Jesus has set forth as encouraging examples to all broken-hearted sinners coming after; that they, seeing how it fared with those who went before them to Christ, may be encouraged to go to him with more confidence. "I obtained mercy, that in me first Jesus Christ might show forth all long-suffering, for a pattern to them which should hereafter believe on him to life everlasting." 1 Tim. 1:16. Then shut your ears against all the whispers of Satan: entertain no evil reports of Christ. Satan loves to draw a false picture of Christ, and represent him in the most discouraging form to trembling sinners; but you will not find him so. What can Christ say more to convince and satisfy souls than he has done? He has left the bosom of the Father, he has entered into union with thy nature, he has poured out his soul unto death; he has told us, that he will in nowise cast out those that come unto him. Thousands have gone before us in the paths of repentance and faith, and found it according to his word; you have been spared all your life to this day of mercy. O do not stand off now upon such weak objections.

3. *The long-suffering of Christ towards sinners teaches his ministers to imitate their Lord in patience and long-suffering.* Christ is our pattern of patience; if he wait, much more may we. We think it much to stand from Sabbath to Sabbath, pleading and inviting, and are apt to be discouraged when we see no fruit follow. The want of success is apt to cast us under Jeremiah's temptation, to speak no more in his name, and make us lament with Isaiah that we have labored in vain. It is a hard case to study, pray, and preach, and see all our labors without fruit. It is not so much the toil as the returning of our labors upon us in vain, that discourages our hearts. Ministers would not die so fast, says Mr. Lockyer on Colossians, nor be grey-headed so soon, did they see the fruits of their labors upon their people. But let us look to our Pattern in the text, "Behold, I stand at the door and knock." If the master wait, let not the servant be weary: "The servant of the Lord must not strive; but be gentle unto all men, apt to teach, patient; in meekness instructing those that oppose themselves; if God peradventure will give them repentance to the acknowledging of the truth." 2 Tim. 2:24, 25.

Though the beginning be small, our latter end may greatly increase. Though we now fish with hooks, and take but now one and then another, the time may come, and we hope it is at the door, when we shall spread our nets and inclose multitudes. Aretius, a pious divine, comforteth himself thus, under the unsuccessfulness of his labors: "Perhaps future days will afford more tractable spirits and easier tempers of mind than our present times give." Besides, the fruit of our labors may spring up to a blessed harvest when we are gone: "One soweth, and another reapeth," John 4:37; but if not, our reward will not be measured by the success, but by the sincerity of our designs and labors. Our zeal for the conversion of souls to Christ will be accepted, but our discouragement in his service will certainly displease him. If Israel be not gathered, yet shall we be glorious in the eyes of the Lord. However, let this be a caution to you that hear, that you cast not our souls under such discouragements. If I may speak the sense of others from my own experience, I can assure you that the fixedness of your hearts in the ways of sin, and your untractableness to the calls of God, are a greater burden and discouragement to ministers than all the sufferings they meet with from the world; yet are they contented to pray and preach in hope, encouraging themselves—the Lord grant it be not without ground—that a crop shall yet spring up, which shall make the harvest-men rejoice.

4. *From the patience and long-suffering of Christ, we may learn the invaluable preciousness of souls, and the high esteem Christ has for them.* Though your souls be cheap in your own eyes, and you are contented to sell them for a trifle, for a little sensual pleasure and ease, yet certainly Jesus Christ has a high estimate of them, else he would never stand knocking with such importunity, and waiting with such wonderful patience for their salvation. Christ knows their worth, though you do not; he accounts, and so should you, one of your souls of more worth than the whole world. Matt. 16:26. The soul of the poorest child or meanest servant is of greater value in Christ's eye, than the whole world; and he has given three great evidences of it.

(1.) That he thought it worth his blood to redeem and save it. "Ye were not redeemed with corruptible things, as silver and gold; but with the precious blood of Christ." 1 Pet. 1:18, 19. Had they not been precious in his eyes, he would never have shed his most precious blood to ransom them.

(2.) Were they not highly valuable in his eyes, he would never wait with such unwearied patience to save them. He has borne thousands of repulses and unreasonable denials from you. Sinner, Christ has knocked at thy door in many a sermon, in many a prayer, in many a sickness—in all which thou hast denied him or delayed him; yet still he continues knocking and waiting. Thou couldst not have made the poorest beggar in the world wait at thy door so long as thy Redeemer has been made to wait, and yet he is not gone; at this day his voice sounds in thine ears, "Behold, I stand at the door and knock." Here is clear demonstration of the preciousness of thy soul in the Redeemer's eyes. And then,

(3.) When Christ ends the treaty, and gives up the souls of men for lost, with what sorrow does he part with them. Never did one friend part from another with such demonstrations of sorrow as Christ parts with the souls of sinners. The bowels of his compassion roll together; for he knows what is coming upon them, and what that eternal misery is into which their wilful rejection of him will cast them. You read of the Redeemer's tears shed over the obstinate inhabitants of Jerusalem: "And when he was come near, he beheld the city and wept over it, saying, If thou hadst known, even thou, at least in this thy day, the things which belong unto thy peace! but now they are hid from thine eyes." Luke 19:41, 42. Like unto this is that expression, Isa. 1:24, "Ah, I will ease me of mine adversaries, and avenge me of mine enemies." Though it be an case to his justice, yet he cannot give them up without an "Ah," an interjection of sorrow; so in Hos. 11:8, "How shall I give thee up, Ephraim? How shall I deliver thee, Israel?" I must do it, but how shall I go about it? All these expressions show the great value God has for your souls; and did you know it also, you would not make Christ wait one hour longer.

5. Hence it follows, *that greater is the sin, and severer will be the condemnation of them that perish under the gospel, than of all others.* Let me speak freely to you of this. Jesus Christ has spent more of the riches of his

patience upon you in one year, yea, in this very day, than he has spent upon the heathen in all their lives. They never heard of Christ and the great salvation—they have had no calls to faith and repentance as you have had; do not think God has dealt in this way with other nations. You have his Sabbaths, ministers, calls; "He hath not dealt so with any nation; and as for his judgments, they have not known them." Psalm 147 : 20. God has dealt in a peculiar way with us, and these special favors will make dreadful accounts. He told the Jews, among whom he had preached and wrought his miracles, it would be more tolerable for Sodom and Gomorrah, in the day of judgment, than for them; and in his name I will tell you this day, that barbarous Indians will have a milder hell than you. The Lord told Ezekiel, "Thou art not sent to a people of a strange speech and of a hard language, whose words thou canst not understand. Surely, had I sent thee to them, they would have hearkened unto thee. But the house of Israel will not hearken unto thee; for they will not hearken unto me : for all the house of Israel are impudent and hard-hearted." Ezek. 3 : 5–7.

Ah, had a heathen people had your Sabbaths, your ministers, and Bibles, they would not have dealt by Christ as you have done. But look you to it, for certainly the severity of his justice will at last recompense the expense of his patience. There are two glasses turned up this day, and both are almost run down : the glass of the gospel running down on earth, and the glass of Christ's patience running down in heaven. Be sure of it, that for every sand of mercy, every drop of love that runs down in vain in this world, a drop of wrath runs into the vial of wrath which is filling up in heaven.

6. *If Christ hath exercised such wonderful patience and long-suffering towards you, before he could gain entrance into your hearts, then you have reason to exercise*

your patience for Christ, and account all long-suffering to be your unquestionable duty. Christ was not weary in waiting upon you, be not you weary in waiting upon him, or for him. There are three things wherein the people of God will have much occasion to exercise their patience with respect to Christ.

(1.) You will need patience to wait for *the answers of your prayers:* you knock and wait at the door of mercy, and no answer comes; hereupon discouragement and weariness seize your spirits. Possibly some of you have prayers many years gone upon the file in heaven, some upon spiritual accounts and some upon temporal; and because the answer is not sent, your eyes are ready to fail with waiting: for the Lord may bear long with his own elect. Luke 18:7. The seed of prayer lies under the clods, and will at last spring up. He never said to the seed of Jacob, Seek ye me in vain. Isa. 45:19. None seek God in vain, but those who seek him vainly. You should not be too short-breathed in waiting on God for the returns of prayer, considering how long you made Christ wait on you.

(2.) You will have occasion to exercise your patience *in bearing the burden of reproaches and sufferings for Christ.* "For unto you it is given in the behalf of Christ, not only to believe on him, but also to suffer for his sake." Phil. 1:29. Sufferings, you see, are the gift of Christ; the comfort of suffering is his gift, and so is the ability to suffer also; and that which will increase your suffering ability, will be the consideration of Christ's long suffering towards you, and the hard things he endured for you and from you.

(3.) You will have occasion to exercise your patience *for the day of your complete redemption and salvation.* If you love Christ fervently, the time of your separation from him will be borne with difficulty; vehement love needs the allay of patience. "The Lord direct your hearts into the love of God, and into the patient waiting for Christ."

2 Thess. 3 : 5. Others need patience to die, but you will need as much patience to live; but wherever the exercise of your patience shall be, whether in waiting for the returns of your prayers, in bearing the cross of Christ, or in waiting for the day of your complete redemption and enjoyment of Christ, this single consideration, that Christ stood and waited so long on you, is enough to fortify your patience against all the difficulties it can encounter.

7. *If Christ thus patiently wait upon trifling and obstinate sinners, then let no godly persons be discouraged because their unregenerate relatives have not yet made their first step towards Christ, in the way of repentance and faith.* It may be you have laid up a stock of prayers for them: the believing husband has prayed for his unbelieving wife, and the believing wife for her unbelieving husband; godly parents for their ungodly children, and the pious child for his ungodly parents; and yet no returns of prayer appear. Many cries are gone up to heaven like that of Abraham, "O that Ishmael might live before thee." Gen. 17:18. Be not discouraged, Christ waits, and therefore well may you. Those cries of parents, "Lord, my poor child is in the state of nature, look in mercy upon him, open his eyes, break his heart for sin, draw his will to Christ," may not be lost, though the fruit of them yet appear not. Consider how long Christ waited on you. There are three things that encourage hope.

(1.) That your hearts and theirs were of the same natural character; and the same power which opened your hearts, can open theirs: thy understanding was once as dark, thy heart as hard, and thy will as inflexible as thy relatives' now are. The same hand that opened thy heart can open theirs. Do not think Christ had an easier task to win thy heart than he will have to win theirs. Almighty power wrought upon you, and the same power can work effectually upon them; "the Lord's hand is not shortened, that it cannot save; neither his ear heavy, that it cannot hear." Isa. 59 : 1.

(2.) You have reason to wait, as it is probable you yourselves have put stumbling-blocks in the way of their souls to Christ, and hindered the answers to your own prayers for the conversion of your relatives. O Christians, there is more due to them than your prayers—prayers must be accompanied with example; had they not only heard your cries to God for them, but seen your suitable encouraging example set before them also, you and they might have rejoiced together long ago. But,

(3.) Consider that God many times makes the fruit of such prayers to spring up after those that sowed them are dead and gone. The Lord may give life to your prayers when you are dead: certainly your prayers die not with you. It is the opinion of some that Paul's conversion was the return of Stephen's prayer, "Lord, lay not this sin to their charge." Acts 7 : 60. Stephen died, but his prayers lived, and were answered upon one that stood by and consented to his death. But however it be, wait still upon God; if your prayers come not into their bosoms, they will certainly return into your own. Here is duty discharged, and love to Christ and their souls manifested, which will be your comfort, however God dispose the event.

But further, the doctrine of Christ's patience puts a great and serious EXHORTATION into my mouth, to press one of the greatest duties. And could I deliver this exhortation to you upon my knees, with tears of blood mingled with my words, might that prevail, I would surely do it.

8. My exhortation is to all that are in an unregenerate state, that they *presume not to try the patience of Christ any longer*. If you have any regard to your eternal happiness, exercise not his patience another hour. O that this hour might put an end to Christ's waiting and your dan-

ger! Hitherto you have wearied men, but will you weary God also? Christ has called, but you have refused; he has stretched out his hands, but you have not regarded. Prov. 1 : 24. Your thoughts have been wandering after vanity while the voice of the gospel has been sounding in your ears: some of you have been sottish, and incapable of apprehending spiritual truths; others of you sensual, given up to the pleasures of the world, and abandoning all serious thoughts about the world to come. Some of you have been buried alive in the cares of the world, and others settled upon a dead formality in religion; and to this day Christ hath called upon you in vain. Now that which I exhort you to is, that you venture not to try the patience of Christ one day longer; if you have any regard to the everlasting happiness of your souls, come not under the guilt and danger of one denial or delay more. If you ask me, Why may we not venture a little longer? Christ has borne with us all this while, and will he not bear a little longer? May we not take a little more pleasure in sin? May we not hazard one sermon or Sabbath more? I answer, No. If your souls are precious in your eyes, let there be no more denials, nor delays to Christ's suit. For,

(1.) How patient and long-suffering soever Christ has been, yet *there will be an end of the day of his patience*— a time when he will wait no longer, when his Spirit shall strive no more with you. There will be a knock of Christ at the heart, which will be the last knock that ever he will give—a time when the master of the house will rise up, and the door be shut. Matt. 25 : 10. You have had to do with a meek and patient Saviour; but believe it, sinners, there is a day of "*the wrath of the Lamb*," and that day will be dreadful. Then will sinners cry "to the mountains and rocks, Fall on us, and hide us from the face of him that sitteth on the throne, and from the wrath of the Lamb." Rev. 6 : 16. O if this wrath be once kindled, though but a little! Blessed are they that trust in him, that have finished their agreement with him. The day of Christ's patience towards Jerusalem was a long day, but it had an end, and it ended in their desolation, Matt. 23 : 37; therefore try the patience of Christ no further: you know not the limits of it; it may end with your next refusal, and then where are you?

(2.) The longer Christ has exercised his patience already towards you, the more terribly will he avenge the abuse of it upon you in hell. It is past doubt with me, that there are different degrees of torment in hell: the Scriptures are plain and clear on this point. Now, among all the aggravations of the torments of hell, none can be greater than the reflections of damned souls upon the abused patience and grace of Christ. Those who had the best means, the loudest calls, and the longest day under the gospel, will certainly have the hottest place in hell, if the goodness and long-suffering of Christ do not now lead them to repentance. The cries of such souls will be heard above the cries of all other miserable wretches who are cast away. It shall be more tolerable for Sodom and Gomorrah than for Capernaum. Matt. 11 : 23. O friends, you little know the reflections of conscience in hell upon such hours as you now enjoy—such wooing, charming voices and allurements to Christ as you now hear. There are many thousands of souls in hell from the dark, heathenish parts of the world, where they never heard of Christ; but your misery will be far beyond theirs, your reflections more sharp and bitter: therefore delay no longer, lest you perish with peculiar aggravation of misery.

(3.) Try the patience of Christ no further, I beseech you, forasmuch as you see every day the patience of Christ ending towards others—patience retiring, and justice arising to triumph over the abusers of mercy. You not only read in Scripture the ending of God's patience with men, but you may see it every day. If you look into scripture, you may find the patience of God ended towards multitudes of sinners, who possibly had the same presumptions and vain hopes for the continuance of it that you now have. If you look into 1 Peter, 3 : 19, 20, you there find that Christ "went and preached unto the spirits in prison; which sometime were disobedient, when once the long-suffering of God waited in the days of Noah." The meaning of which is, that in the days before the flood, Christ by his Spirit strove with the disobedient and rebellious sinners in the ministry of Noah, who then were living men and women as we are, but now are "spirits in prison," that is, damned souls in hell, for their disobedience: and truly, brethren, you may frequently behold the glass of patience run down, the very last sand in it spent upon others. Whenever you see a wicked, Christless man or woman die, you see the end of God's patience with that man or woman; and all this for a warning to you, that you venture not to trifle and dally with it as they did.

(4.) Do not try God's patience any longer, if you love your souls, for this reason: because when men grow bold, and encourage themselves in sin on account of God's forbearance and long-suffering towards them, there cannot be a more certain sign that his patience is very near its end towards them. It is time for God to put an end to his patience, when it is made an encouragement to sin. He cannot suffer so vile an abuse of his patience, nor endure to see it turned into wantonness. This quickly brings up sin to its finishing act, and then patience is just finishing also. That patience is thus abused, appears from Eccl. 8 : 11 : "Because sentence against an evil work is not executed speedily, therefore the heart of the sons of men is fully set in them to do evil." When divine patience is thus abused, look for a sudden change. O therefore beware of provoking God, for now the day of patience is certainly near its end with sinners. "Because I have called, and ye refused; I have stretched out my hand, and no man regarded: but ye have set at naught all my counsel, and would none of my reproof: I also will laugh at your calamity; I will mock when your fear cometh: when your fear cometh as desolation, and your destruction cometh as a whirlwind." Prov. 1 : 24–27. Ah, when sinners scoff and mock at the threatenings of God, and bear themselves up on his patience, as that which will never break under them, then look out for a whirlwind, a sudden tempest of wrath, which will hurry such souls into hell. Then misery comes like a storm blowing furiously from all quarters. The heavens are yet clear over you, but a storm is nigh, and may certainly be presaged from such vile abuses of the glorious patience of Christ towards you. This is the first exhortation, try not the patience of Christ by any further delays.

9. *Again, admire Christ's patience and forbearance until now*, that he has not cut you off in sin, but brought about your salvation by his long-suffering towards you. Here now I must change my voice, and turn it to those whose hearts the Lord hath opened. Stand amazed at the riches of his grace towards you, and see that you account this long-suffering of God to be your salvation; for in plain truth it is so: your salvation was bound up in Christ's forbearance. If Christ had not borne with you as he did, you had not been where you are. I could heartily wish, that all the time you can redeem from the necessary employments you have in the world, may be spent in a humble, thankful admiration of this wonderful grace and patience of Christ, and in duties answerable to the intentions and ends thereof. To this end I shall subjoin divers weighty *considerations*, which, methinks, should melt every heart wherein the least degree of saving grace is found.

(1.) Bethink yourselves of *the great and manifold provocations you have given the Lord to put an end to all further patience towards you;* not only in the days of your unregeneracy, but even since your reconciliation to him. Do you not believe thousands of sinners are now in the depths of hell, who never provoked the Lord more than you have done? Were you not once among the vilest of sinners? "And such were some of you," 1 Cor. 6:11—as vile as the vilest among them; yet you are washed in the blood of Christ, while your companions are in the lowest hell: or if your lives were more clean, sure your hearts were as filthy as theirs. And certainly your sins, since the time of your reconciliation, have had special aggravations enough to put an end to all further mercies towards you. Light and love have aggravated these sins, and yet the Lord has not cast you off.

(2.) *How often have you been on the very brink of hell, in the days of your unregeneracy.* Every sickness and every danger to life which you have escaped in those days, was a marvellous escape from the everlasting wrath of God. Had thy disease prevailed one degree further, thou hadst been past hope and out of the reach of mercy's arm now. Doubtless some of you can remember, when in such and such a disease, you were like a ship riding in a furious storm by one cable, and two or three of the strands even of that cable were snapped asunder. So it has been with you: the thread of life, how weak soever, has held till the bonds of union between Christ and your souls were fastened, and the eternal hazard over. This is admirable grace.

(3.) *How often has death entered into your houses and taken away your nearest relatives,* but had no commission to carry you out with them, because the Lord had a design of mercy upon your soul. This cannot but affect a gracious heart, that God should smite so near, and yet spare you.

(4.) This also is affecting, *that God has not only given you time beyond others, but in that time the precious opportunities and means of your salvation,* both external and internal. There is the very marrow and kernel of the mercy. Had God lengthened out his patience for a while, but given you no means of salvation, or afforded you the means but denied you the blessing and efficacy of them, at the most it could have been but a reprieve from hell; but for the Lord to give you the gospel, and with the gospel to send down his Spirit to persuade and open thy heart to Christ, here is the riches of his goodness as well as forbearance.

10. This doctrine of the patience of Christ exhorts all who have felt it, *to exercise a Christlike patience towards others.* As you have found the benefit of divine patience yourselves, see that you exercise the meekness and long-suffering of Christians towards those who have wronged and injured you. Who should show patience more than those who have found it? Do not be severe, short, and quick with others, who have lived yourselves so many years upon the long-suffering of God. We are poor, hasty creatures, quick to revenge injuries; but O, had God been so to us, miserable had our condition been. Christ has made this duty the scope of that excellent parable, Matt. 18, from verse 23 onward, where the king takes an account of his servants, reckoning with them one by one, and among them finds one who owed him ten thousand talents; and having nothing wherewith to pay, his lord commands him, his wife and children, and all he had, to be sold, and payment to be made; but the servant falling down and begging patience, his lord was moved with compassion, and loosed him, and not only forbore, but forgave the debt. One would think the heart of this man would have been a fountain of compassion towards others; but see the deep corruption of nature: the same servant finding one of his fellow-servants who owed him but a hundred pence, laid hands on him, and took him by the throat. Alas, the wrongs done to us are but trifles, compared with the injuries we have done to God; where others have wronged you once, you have wronged God

a thousand times. Methinks the patience of Christ towards you should melt your hearts into an ingenuous readiness to forgive others; especially, considering that an unforgiving spirit is a dreadful sign of an unforgiven person.

11. *Burden not the patience of Christ after your reconciliation to him.* Let it suffice that you tried his patience long enough before. Give him no new trials of it, now he is come to dwell in and with you for ever. There are two ways wherein God's own people do greatly provoke him after their reconciliation.

(1.) *By sluggishness and deadness of spirit in duty;* turning a deaf ear to the calls and motions of Christ's Spirit exciting them to the sweet and pleasant duties of religion. We have a sad instance of this in the bride: "It is the voice of my beloved that knocketh, saying, Open to me, my sister, my love, my dove, my undefiled; for my head is filled with dew, and my locks with the drops of the night." Sol. Songs, 5 : 2. One would think that Christ might have opened the heart of his own spouse with less solicitation and importunate arguments than he here uses. What wife could shut the door upon her own husband, and bar him out of his own house? And yet see the idle excuse she makes. "I have put off my coat; how shall I put it on? I have washed my feet; how shall I defile them?" Ver. 3.

O the sluggishness of even regenerate persons! Those who have opened the door to Christ by regeneration, even they do often shut it against him in the hours and seasons of communion with him. Strange, that Christ should be put off while calling to such pleasant and heavenly exercises as communion with him; but flesh will be flesh, even in the most spiritual Christians. Little do we know what a grief this is to Christ, and what a loss to us.

(2.) Many grieve Christ's Spirit, and sorely try his patience, even after reconciliation, *by sinning against light and love.* That caution, Eph. 4:30, is not without weighty cause: "Grieve not the Holy Spirit of God, whereby ye are sealed unto the day of redemption."

Do we thus requite the Lord? Is this the return we make for all his kindness and unparalleled love towards us? Certainly, Christ can bear a thousand injuries from his enemies, easier than such affronts from his own people. Did you not promise him better obedience? Did you not engage to more holiness and watchfulness, in the day that you sued out your pardon and made your peace with him? Are all those vows and covenants forgotten? If you have forgotten them, God hath not.

12. *Improve the time that remains in this world with double diligence,* because you made Christ wait so long, and cast away so great a part of your life, before you opened your hearts to receive him. The morning of your life, which was certainly the freshest and freest part of it, was no better than time lost with many of you; all the days of your unregeneracy Christ was shut out, and vanity shut into your hearts. You never began to live till Christ gave you life, and that was late in the day with many of you. How should this provoke to extraordinary diligence in the short remains of time we have yet to enjoy. It was Augustine's lamentation, "O Lord, it repents me that I loved thee so late." This consideration excited Paul to extraordinary diligence for Christ. It made him fly up and down the world like a seraph, in a flame of holy zeal for Christ. Those who have much to write, and are almost come to the end of their paper, had need write close. Friends, you have something to do for God on earth, which you cannot do for him in heaven. Isa. 38 : 18, 19. You who have ungodly relatives, have something to do for them here which you cannot do in heaven. You can now counsel, exhort, and pray, in order to their conversion and salvation; but when you are gone down to the grave, these opportunities of service are cut off.

13. *Let us all be ashamed and humbled for the baseness of our hearts, which made Christ wait at the door so long before we opened to him.* O what wretched hearts have we. They are no more affected with the groans of Christ's heart than with those of a beast; nor so much, if that beast were our own. O the vileness of nature, to make the Prince of the kings of the earth, bringing pardon and salvation with him, stand so long unanswered. Let who will cry up the goodness of human nature, I am sure we have reason to look upon the vileness of it with amazement and horror.

14. *Let us bless the Lord Jesus for the continuation of his patience,* both to ourselves and to the nation in which we live. The merciful and long-suffering Redeemer continues among us the ambassadors of his mercy, who proclaim his readiness to pardon; and with infinite compassion speaks to us this day, as he did to Ephraim of old, "How shall I deliver thee?" Look upon this day of mercy as the fruit of the intercession of your great Advocate in heaven. Luke 13 : 7–9. God has put us upon one trial more: if now we bring forth fruit, well; if not, the axe lies at the root of the tree. Once more Christ knocks at our door; the voice of the bridegroom is heard—those sweet voices, "Come unto me," "Open to me." Your opening to Christ now, will be unto you as the valley of Achor, for a door of hope. Hosea 2 : 15. But what if all this should be turned into wantonness and formality! What if your obstinacy and infidelity should wear out the remains of that little strength and time left you, and that former labors and sorrows have left your ministers! Then we are ruined for ever: then farewell gospel, ministers, reformation, because we knew not the time of our visitation. What was the awful sentence of God on the fruitless vineyard? "I will take away the hedge thereof, and it shall be eaten up; and break down the wall thereof, and it shall be trodden down; and I will

lay it waste: I will also command the clouds that they rain not upon it." Isa. 5:5, 6. The hedge and the wall are the spiritual and providential presence of God; these are the defence and safety of his people: the clouds and the rain are the sweet influences of gospel-ordinances. If the hedge be broken down, God's pleasant plants will soon be eaten up; and if the clouds rain not upon them, their root will be rottenness and their blossom will go up as dust; our churches will soon become as the mountains of Gilboa; therefore see that you know and improve the time of your visitation.

I shall conclude this fourth doctrine by a few words of CONSOLATION to those who have answered, and are now preparing to answer, the design of Jesus Christ in all his patience towards them, by their compliance with his great design and end therein. O blessed be God, and let his high praises be for ever in our mouths, that at last Christ is like to obtain his end upon some of us, and that all do not receive the grace of God in vain. And there are three considerations which will raise your hearts to the height of praise, if the Lord has made them indeed willing to open to the Lord Jesus.

15. *The faith and obedience of your hearts make it evident, that the Lord's waiting on you hitherto has been in pursuance of his design of electing love.* What was the reason God did not take you away by death, though you passed so often upon the very brink of it, in the days of your unregeneracy? Surely this was the reason: that you, and such as you, might be brought to Christ at last. Therefore, though the Lord allowed you to run on so long in sin, still he continued your lives and the means of your salvation, because he had a design of mercy and grace upon you. And now the time of mercy, even the set time, is come. "Praise ye the Lord."

16. *You may also see the sovereignty and freeness of divine grace in your vocation.* Your hearts resisted all along the most powerful means, and the importunate calls of Christ; and would have resisted still, had not free and sovereign grace prevailed when the time of love was come. Ah, it was not the tractableness of thine own will, or the easy temper of thy heart to be wrought upon; the Lord let thee stand long enough in the state of nature to prove that there was nothing in thy nature but obstinacy and enmity. Thou didst hear as many powerful sermons and melting prayers, and didst see as many awakening providences, before thy heart was opened to Christ, as thou hast since, yet thy heart never opened till now; and why did it open now? Because now the Spirit of God joined himself to the word; victorious grace went forth in the word to break the hardness and conquer the rebellions of thy heart. The gospel was now preached with the Holy Ghost sent down from heaven; "which things," says the apostle, "the angels desire to look into." 1 Pet. 1 : 12. Ah, friends, it is a glorious sight, worthy of angelic observation and admiration, to behold the effects of the gospel preached with the Holy Ghost sent down from heaven; to see, when the Spirit is present with the word, the blind eyes of sinners are opened, and they are brought into a new world of ravishing objects; to behold fountains of tears flowing for sin, out of hearts lately as hard as rocks; to see all the bars of ignorance, prejudice, custom, and unbelief fly open at the voice of the gospel; to see rebels against Christ laying down their arms at his feet, and on the knees of submission crying, "Lord, I will rebel no more;" to see the proud heart, hitherto wrapt up in its own righteousness, now stripping itself naked, and made willing that its own shame should add to the Redeemer's glory. These are sights which angels desire to look into.

Certainly your hearts were more tender, and your wills more ready to yield and bend in the days of your youth, than they were when sin had so hardened them, and long-continued custom riveted and fixed them; yet then they did not, and now they do yield to the calls and invitations of the gospel. Ascribe all to sovereign grace, and say, "Not unto us, O Lord, not unto us, but unto thy name give glory." Psa. 115:1. The experience of our own hearts will furnish us with arguments enough to resist all temptations to self-glory. Certainly you "were born not of blood, nor of the will of the flesh, nor of the will of man, but of God." John 1:13.

17. This is a comfortable consideration, that *he who waited on you so long, and won your hearts at last, will not now forsake you.* I question not but there are many fears and jealousies within you that all this will come to nothing, and that you will perish at last. Divers things foment these jealousies within your hearts: the weakness of your own graces, which, alas, are but in their infancy; the sense you have of your remaining corruptions, and the great strength they still retain; the subtlety of Satan, who employs all his temptations to reduce you, sometimes roaring after his escaped prey with hideous suggestions, which make your souls tremble; sometimes the discouraging apprehensions of the difficulties of religion, feeling the spirituality of active obedience and the difficulty of passive obedience to be above your strength; sometimes feeling within yourselves the hiding of God's face, and the withdrawment of sweet and sensible communion with him. These, and such things as these, cause many a sorrow in your hearts; but cheer up, Christ will not lose at last what he pursued so long: he that waited so many years for thy soul, will never cast it away now that he has the possession of it.

CHAPTER V.

EVERY CONVICTION OF CONSCIENCE AND MOTION OF THE HOLY SPIRIT A KNOCK FROM CHRIST.

"BEHOLD, I STAND AT THE DOOR *AND KNOCK.*" Rev. 3:20.

In the former chapter, we have seen the Redeemer's posture, a posture of condescending humility—rather the posture of a servant than of the Lord of all : "Behold, I stand at the door." We now come to consider his action or motion for entrance : I stand "*and knock.*" This metaphorical action of knocking, signifies nothing else but the motions made by Christ for entrance into the souls of sinners ; and affords us this fifth doctrine :

That every conviction of conscience and motion on the hearts of sinners is a knock of Christ for entrance into their souls.

This action of knocking is sometimes ascribed to the soul, and is expressive of its desire to come into the gracious presence and communion of God : so Matt. 7 : 7, " To him that knocketh, it shall be opened ;" that is, to him that seeks by importunate prayer, fellowship and communion with the Lord, it shall be granted. But here it is applied to Christ, and is expressive of his importunate desire to come into union and communion with the souls of sinners. Here I shall show what are the doors of the soul at which Christ knocks ; what his knocking at these doors implies ; by what instruments he knocks at them ; and in what manner he performs this action.

I. What are THE DOORS OF THE SOUL at which Christ knocks. You all know that the term Christ here used cannot be literal, but metaphorical. It is a figurative speech ; a "door" is introductory to the house, and whatever introduces into the soul is the door of the soul. In the soul of man there are many powers and faculties that have this use, to introduce things into the soul. Some are more outward, as we may speak comparatively; and some more inward, as the doors of our houses are. Christ knocks orderly at them all, one after another, for the operations of the Spirit disturb not the order of nature.

1. The first door that opens into the soul is the *understanding*. Nothing passes into the soul but it first comes through this door of the understanding; nothing can touch the heart or move the affections, but what has first touched the understanding. Hence we read so often in Scripture of the opening of the understanding, that being, as it were, the front door of the soul.

2. Within this is the royal gate of the soul, namely, *the will*, that noble and imperial power. Many things may pass into the mind or understanding of a man, and yet be able to get no further; the door of the will may be shut against them. There were many precious truths of God let into the understandings of the heathen by the light of nature, but they could get no further; their hearts and wills were locked and shut up against them. They held the truths of God in unrighteousness, Rom. 1:18; that is, they bound and imprisoned the common notices which the law of nature impressed upon their minds concerning the being and nature of God, and the duties of both tables of the law. These truths could get no further into their souls: and, which is a sad and dreadful consideration, Christ himself stands between these two doors, in the souls of many persons; he has got into their understandings and consciences, and they are convinced of the necessity of receiving Jesus Christ, but still the door of their will is barred against him, which drew from him the sad complaint, "Ye will not come unto me, that ye might have life." John 5:40. When this door of the will is once effectually opened, then all the inner doors of the affections

are quickly set open to receive and welcome him—desire, joy, delight, and all the rest, stand open to him. These are the doors at which the Redeemer knocks.

II. We must consider WHAT IS MEANT BY CHRIST'S KNOCKING at the door, and what that action implies. In the general, knocking is an action significant of the desire of one who is without, to come in; it is a sign appointed to that end. And what is Christ's knocking, but a signification to the soul of his earnest desire to come into it—a notice given to the soul of Christ's willingness to possess it for his own habitation? It is as if Christ should say, "Soul, thou art the house that was built by my hand, purchased and redeemed by my blood; I have an unquestionable right to it, and now demand entrance." More particularly, there are divers great things implied in this gracious act of Christ's knocking at the door of the soul.

1. It implies *the special favor and distinguishing grace and goodness of Jesus Christ,* that he will stand and knock at our doors when he passes by so great a part of the world, never giving one such knock or call at other men's doors. It is certainly the most admirable condescension and favor of heaven; and shows a man to be highly favored of God. O amazing! that when Christ passes by the souls of thousands and millions, and gives not one effectual knock or call at their doors all the days of their life, he will please to turn aside to thy soul, and wait and knock there for entrance. Here is one of the greatest acts of favor that can be shown to the soul of a sinner. How many souls there are in the world equal in natural dignity to yours, and of sweeter natural tempers, whom yet the Lord Jesus lets alone in the quiet possession of Satan. Luke 11:21. There is a deep silence and stillness in their consciences, no stirrings nor disturbances by convictions, but, through a dreadful judgment of God, they are left in a deep sleep; and if their consciences at any time begin to disturb them, how soon are they hushed

and quieted again by Satan! What the condition of the world was in former ages we know from the Scriptures, where we learn that God in times past suffered all nations to walk in their own ways. Acts 14:16. It is the greatest mercy for the sleepy conscience of a sinner to be roused by convictions, because it is introductory to all other spiritual mercies. This act of grace is little appreciated by the sons and daughters of men: much rather would poor sinners be let alone, than be thus disturbed by troublesome convictions; and when Christ disturbs their rest, how do they startle at the knocks of his word and Spirit. How angry are they that they cannot be let alone to enjoy their quiet sleep in sin till the flames of hell awaken them! Mr. Fenner, that great and eminent instrument of God in this work, tells us in one of his sermons how it fared with a certain man that came to hear him preach. It seems the word had got entrance into his conscience and gave it a terrible alarm, and as he was going home, some that followed him heard him thus blaming and bemoaning himself: "O what a fool, what a beast was I to come under this sermon to-day! I shall never have peace and quietness any more." And what is the reason that smooth and general preaching is so much applauded in the world, and close convincing doctrine so much shunned and hated, but this, that sinners are very loath to be disquieted and have their consciences thoroughly awakened? Whatever your apprehensions be, certainly it is an unspeakable mercy for Christ to knock, and disquiet the souls of sinners by his calls.

2. The next thing implied in this action of Christ is, *that the first motions towards the recovery and salvation of sinners begin not in themselves, but in Christ.* We never knock at heaven's door by prayer till Christ has first knocked at our door by his Spirit. Did not Christ move first, there would be no motions after him in our hearts: we move towards him, because he hath first moved upon our souls.

Christ would ever be unsought and undesired, did he not make the first motion. All our motions are secondary and consequential motions. "I am found of them that sought me not." Isa. 65:1. As "we love him because he first loved us," 1 John, 4:19, so we seek him because he first sought us. Alas, poor sinners are well satisfied to lie fast asleep in the devil's arms. When the Spirit of God goes forth with the word of conviction, he finds the souls of men in the same posture which the angels who had surveyed the world reported the whole earth to be in: "Behold, all the earth sitteth still, and is at rest." Zech. 1:11. Every man was settled and satisfied in his own way. What a strange stillness and midnight silence is there among sinners. Not a sigh, not a cry to be heard for sin. So the psalmist represents the case of sinners: "The Lord looked down from heaven upon the children of men, to see if there were any that did understand and seek God. They are all gone aside, they are all together become filthy: there is none that doeth good, no, not one." Psalm 14:2, 3. There is one thing peculiarly strange in this case: that even those whose earthly pleasures and delights, which brought them into this sleep and security, are taken away from them by the hand of Providence, I mean their estates, health, and children, even they awake not; they have no stirrings after God. O what a dead sleep hath sin cast the souls of sinners into. You have a notable scripture to this purpose in Job 35:9, 10; they are the words of Elihu concerning those under grievous oppression from the cruel hands of wicked men: "By reason of the multitude of oppressions they make the oppressed to cry; they cry out by reason of the arm of the mighty. But none saith, Where is God my Maker, who giveth songs in the night?" that is, comfort and refreshment to the afflicted. Here are men turned out of their estates, thrown into prison, cast on all extremities and miseries, and what do these poor creatures do? Why, they cry by reason of their oppression: O my father, my mother, my wife, my child, my estate, my liberty! But none saith, Where is my God? O my sin, or my misery by reason of sin! "Where is he who giveth songs in the night?" The people of God when they lie musing upon their beds under affliction, have their "songs in the night;" in the midst of the multitude of their troubled thoughts within them, the comforts of God delight their souls. These are their songs in the night, but no such words or thoughts have carnal men. How plain is it, that all the first motions of salvation have their spring and rise in God, and not in us.

3. Christ's knocking at the door of the heart *shows the method of the Spirit in conversion to be in harmony with the nature of man's soul.* Mark Christ's expression in the text; he does not say, Behold, I come to the door and break it open by violence. Christ makes no forcible entries, whether sinners will or not; he will come in by consent of the will, or not at all. "I stand and knock; if any man open the door, I will come in to him." There is a great difference between a friendly admission by consent, and a forcible entrance: in a forcible entrance, bars of iron are brought to break open the door; but in a friendly admission, one knocks and the other opens. Forcible actions are unsuitable to the nature of the will, whose motions are free and spontaneous; therefore it is said, "Thy people shall be willing in the day of thy power." Psalm 110:3. It is true, the power of God is upon the will of man in the day of his conversion, or else it would never open to Christ; but yet that power of God doth not act against the freedom of man's will; God makes it willing, taking away the obstinacy and reluctance of the will by the efficacy of his grace—a sweet and pleasant victory; and so the door of the will still opens freely: "I drew them with cords of a man, with bands of love." Hos. 11:4. "I drew them," there is almighty power; but how did this power draw them? "With cords of

a man," that is, with rational arguments convincing the judgment. Beasts are driven and forced, but men are drawn by reason. It must be confessed that when the day of God's power is come for bringing home a poor sinner to Christ, the power of God's Spirit draws him effectually : " Every man that hath heard, and hath learned of the Father, cometh unto me," John 6 : 45 ; yet the soul comes freely by the consent of his will, for this is the method of Christ in drawing souls to him. There is in the day of a sinner's conversion an offer made for the will, both by Satan and by Christ ; Satan bids riches, honors, and pleasures, with ease and quietness to the flesh in the enjoyment of them. Abide where thou art, saith Satan ; remain with me, and thou shalt escape all the persecutions, losses, and troubles in which conscience entangles other men ; thou shalt draw thy life through peace and pleasure to thy dying day. O, saith the flesh, this is good ; what can be better for me ? But then, saith Christ, dost thou not consider that all these enjoyments will quickly be at an end ! and what shall become of thee then ? Behold, I offer thee the free, full, and final pardon of thy sins ; peace and reconciliation with God ; treasures in heaven ; all these shall be thine, with troubles, reproaches, and persecutions in this world. The understanding and conscience of a sinner being convinced of the vanity of earthly things, and the indispensable necessity of pardon and peace with God—I say, when a convinced judgment hath duly balanced these things, and laid them before the will, and the Spirit of God puts forth his power in the renovation of it, it moves towards Christ freely, and yet cannot, according to its natural order, act otherwise than it doth. And doubtless this is the true meaning of that expression so often mistaken and abused in Luke 14 : 23, " Compel them to come in." What, by forcing men against the light of their consciences ? No ; to the shame of many Protestants let us hear the explanation of Stella, a popish commentator upon this passage : " Christ compels men to come in, by showing to their will such an excelling good as it cannot but embrace ;" for the will is naturally carried to the best good. And thus the Spirit works upon the soul harmoniously and agreeably to its nature.

4. Christ's knocking at the door of the soul implies *the immediate access of the Spirit of God to the soul of man.* He can come to the very innermost door of the soul at his pleasure, and make what impression upon it he pleases. Instruments used in this work have no such privilege or power. Ministers can but knock at the external door of the senses. "Thine eyes shall see thy teachers." We can see their persons and hear their voices—we can reason with sinners, and plead with their souls; but awaken them we cannot, open their hearts we cannot ; we can only lodge our message in their ears, and leave it to the Spirit of God to make it effectual. This is a work belonging to the Spirit of God, incommunicable to angels or men. If an angel from heaven were the preacher, he could not give one effectual stroke to the conscience : much less can man ; we have no dominion over your consciences. The keys of the doors of your souls hang not at our girdles, but are in the hands of Christ. He hath the key of David ; he openeth, and no man shutteth; and he shutteth, and no man openeth. Rev. 3 : 7. The conscience and all the faculties of the mind lie naked and open to the stroke of God's Spirit ; he can wound them and heal them, and make what impression he pleases upon them. Learn hence, what need there is both for ministers and people, before they enter upon the solemn ordinances of God, to lift up their hearts by prayer for the blessing and power of the Spirit upon them. Lord, send forth thy Spirit; pour it forth upon and with thy word. Ah, how many sermons have we preached and you heard, and yet there is no opening. In the next place let us consider,

III. BY WHAT INSTRUMENTS Christ knocks at the doors ; that is, the judgment, conscience, and will of a sinner. And here my work will be to show how the Spirit of God makes use both of the *word* and *works* of God to rouse the consciences and open the hearts of sinners. These are the two hammers or instruments of the Spirit, by which he knocks at the door of the heart.

1. *The word written or preached,* but especially preached. To this Christ gives the preference above all other instruments employed about this work; and hence the word is called God's hammer: "Is not my word like as a fire? saith the Lord; and like a hammer that breaketh the rock in pieces?" Jer. 23 : 29. By this hammer Christ knocks at the door of a sinner's soul, to give warning that he is there. The Spirit of God can open the heart immediately, if he pleases; but he will honor his word in this work. And therefore, when Lydia's heart was to be opened, Paul the great gospel-preacher must be invited, even by an angel, to come over to Macedonia and assist in that blessed work. Acts 16 : 9. Lydia was to be converted, her heart must be opened to Christ; the angel could not do it, but calls for the help of the apostle, God's appointed instrument to carry on that work. So saith God to Paul, "I have appeared unto thee for this purpose, to make thee a minister and a witness both of these things which thou hast seen, and of those things in the which I will appear unto thee; delivering thee from the people and from the Gentiles, unto whom now I send thee to open their eyes, and to turn them from darkness to light and from the power of Satan unto God." Acts 26 : 16–18. There are three ways in which the Holy Spirit uses the word as his hammer in knocking at the door of the soul.

(1.) He knocks by particular *convictions of the word on the conscience:* this knock by conviction rings and sounds through all the rooms and chambers of the soul; particular and effectual conviction wounds to the very centre of the soul. When the word comes home by the Spirit's application, like that of Nathan to David, "Thou art the man," then all the powers of the soul are roused and alarmed; now it pierces as a two-edged sword, Heb. 4:12, and divides the soul and spirit, the superior and inferior faculties of it—lays open the secret guilt and inmost thoughts of a man's heart, before which the sinner cannot stand. The secrets of his heart are made manifest; and falling down on his face, he must acknowledge that God is in the word of a truth. 1 Cor. 14:24. O these convictions of the word are such a knock at the door of the conscience as will never be forgotten, no, not in heaven to all eternity.

(2.) Christ knocks in the word by *its awful threatenings*, menacing the soul that opens not with eternal ruin; these are dreadful knocks. O, sinner, saith Christ, wilt thou not open? Shall all the tenders of my grace made to thee be in vain? Know then, that this thy obstinacy shall be thy damnation. Thus the word denounces ruin, in the name of the great and terrible God, to all impenitent and obstinate unbelievers, John 3:36: "He that believeth not the Son shall not see life; but the wrath of God abideth on him." O dreadful sound! like unto which is that in John 8:24, "If ye believe not that I am he, ye shall die in your sins." As if he had said, "Thy *mittimus* for hell shall be made and signed. Will you not come to me, that you may have life? Then you shall even die in your sins. O it were better for thee to die any kind of death than to die in thy sins." These are loud knocks of the word, terrible sounds, yet no more than are needed to startle the drowsy consciences of sinners. And then,

(3.) The Spirit knocks by *the gracious invitations of the word;* and without this, no heart would ever open to Christ. It is not frosts and snow, storms and thunder, but the gentle distilling dews and cherishing sunbeams that make the flowers open in the spring. The terrors of the law may be preparatory, but only the grace of the gospel is that which effectually opens the sinner's heart. The obdurate flint will sooner break when smitten upon the soft pillow, than upon the anvil. Now the gospel abounds with alluring invitations to draw the will and open the heart of a sinner; such as that, Matt. 11 : 28, "Come unto me, all ye that labor and are heavy laden, and I will give you rest." What a charming voice is here; he that considers it, may well wonder what heart in the world can resist it. Like unto this is Isaiah 55 : 1, "Ho, every one that thirsteth, come ye to the waters, and he that hath no money; come ye, buy, and eat; yea, come, buy wine and milk without money and without price." Come, sinner, come; though thou hast no qualifications nor worthiness, nor righteousness of thy own—though thou art but a heap of sin and vileness, yet come; grace is a *gift*, not a *sale*. And such is John 7 : 37, "In the last day, that great day of the feast, Jesus stood and cried, saying, If any man thirst, let him come to me and drink." As if he had said, My grace is not a sealed fountain; it is free and open to the greatest of sinners; if they thirst, they are invited to come and drink. This is that oil of the gospel-grace which makes the key turn so pleasantly and effectually among all the cross-wards of man's will. Thus you see how the word preached becomes an instrument in the Spirit's hand to open the door of a sinner's heart, at which it knocks by its mighty convictions, dreadful threatenings, and gracious invitations.

2. We now come to the second hammer by which the Spirit knocks at the sinner's heart, and that is *the providential works of God*. These, in subserviency to the word, are of excellent use to awaken sinners and make them open their hearts to Christ. God hath magnified his word above all his name, yet there are some of the providential works of God greatly serviceable in this case; the word sanctifies providences, and providences assist the word and make it work. There are two sorts of providential dispensations

which the Lord Jesus makes use of to gain entrance for him into the hearts of men, namely, judgments and mercies.

(1.) *Judgments and afflictions:* the word of God many times works not till some stroke of God come to quicken and assist it. Thus did the Lord open the heart of that monster of wickedness, Manasseh; the word could not work alone, but a smart rod quickened its operation. "And the Lord spake to Manasseh, and to his people; but they would not hearken. Wherefore the Lord brought upon them the captains of the host of the king of Assyria, which took Manasseh among the thorns, and bound him with fetters, and carried him to Babylon. And when he was in affliction he besought the Lord his God, and humbled himself greatly before the God of his fathers." 2 Chron. 33 : 10–12. Thus the heart of this man relented under the word, assisted by the rod. It is good that God takes such a course with some sinners, else the word would do them no good: and to this purpose is Job 36 : 8–10 : "If they be bound in fetters and be holden in cords of affliction, then he showeth them their work and their transgressions that they have exceeded. He openeth also their ear to discipline." This is the rough course which the obstinacy of men's hearts makes necessary for their recovery; and therefore it is observable, that some words of God have lain dead in sinners' hearts for years together, and at last have begun to work under some smart rod. Alas, while all things are pleasant and prosperous about us, the word has but little effect: "I spake unto thee in thy prosperity; but thou saidst, I will not hear. This hath been thy manner from thy youth, that thou obeyedst not my voice. The wind shall eat up all thy pastures, and thy lovers shall go into captivity; surely then shalt thou be ashamed and confounded for all thy wickedness." Jer. 22 : 21, 22. As though he had said, Your eyes are so dazzled with the beautiful flowers, and your ears so charmed with the syren songs of earthly delights, that my word can take no effect upon you. Let an east-wind blow, and wither up these flowers; then the word shall work, and conscience deeply feel the concerns of eternity. This course God takes with many of you; you sit from Sabbath to Sabbath under the word, and nothing takes effect on your hearts. Will you not hear the voice of my word? saith God; go, death, smite that man's child, I will try what that will do; go, poverty, and blast his estate, and see what that will do; go, sickness, and smite his body, and shake him over the grave's mouth, I will see what that will do. Thus God sends to sinners, as Absalom sent to Joab—who refused to come near him, till he set fire to his field of corn, and then away comes Joab. 2 Sam. 14:29-31. And thus the Lord opened the heart of the jailer, by putting him into a fright, a panic fear of death. Acts 16:27. Thus does the Lord devise means to bring back his banished.

(2.) As God makes use of the hammer of judgments, so *he makes use of mercies* to make way for Christ into the hearts of men. Every mercy is a call, a knock of God: and truly if there were any ingenuousness left unextinguished in the heart, one would think mercy would prevail more than all judgments. Knowest thou not that the goodness of God leadeth thee to repentance? Rom. 2:4. Or in other words, Dost thou not see the hand of mercy stretched out to lead thee into a corner, there to mourn over thy sins committed against so gracious and merciful a God? By every mercy you receive, Christ doth, as it were, sue you to open your hearts to him; they are so many gifts sent from heaven to make way for Christ into your hearts. It would be an endless task to enumerate all the mercies bestowed to this end upon the unregenerate: but surely this is the errand of them all; and the Lord takes it ill when his end is not answered in them: hence is that complaint, Jer. 5:24; "Neither say they in their heart, Let us now fear the Lord our God, that giveth rain, both the former and the latter, in his season." Some of you have been marvellously preserved in times of common contagion and death, when thousands have fallen at your right hand and left: then have you been preserved or recovered, according to Exod. 15 : 26, " I will put none of these diseases upon thee, for I am the Lord that healeth thee." I am *Jehovah Rophe*, the Lord the physician: many of you have been at the grave's mouth in diseases, others upon the deep; yet the hand of mercy pulled you back, and suffered you not to drop into the grave and hell in the same moment. O what a knock was here given by the hand of mercy at thy hard heart. Certainly, if men would but observe, they might see a marvellous working and moulding of things by the hand of providence, for the production of thousands of mercies for them: and if mercy would do the work and win you over to Christ, many rods had been spared which your obstinacy has made necessary. O ungrateful sinners, doth your Redeemer thus woo you by so many gifts of mercy, and yet will you shut him out? " Do ye thus requite the Lord, O foolish people and unwise?" For which of all his benefits do your ungrateful souls shut the doors upon him?

You have seen what Christ's knocking at the soul of a sinner implies, and by what instruments it is performed.

IV. We will now consider THE MANNER IN WHICH THIS ACTION IS PERFORMED in the ten following particulars, wherein much of the mystery of conversion will be opened; the Lord grant that your experience may answer to them. We cannot indeed exactly describe and mark all the footsteps of the Spirit, in this work upon the souls of men; yet these things seem eminently observable.

1. The knocks of Christ at the sinner's heart are *silent and secret* to all persons in the world, except the soul itself at whose door he knocks. Here are many hundreds this day under the word: if the Lord shall this day knock by conviction at any man's heart, none will hear that knock, but that

man only; for it is a knock without sound or noise to any but the particular soul concerned in it. It was foretold of our Redeemer, and of this very act of his, "He shall not cry, nor lift up, nor cause his voice to be heard in the street." Isa. 42:2. The kingdom of God cometh not into the souls of men with public observation. Luke 17:20. "What man knoweth the things of a man, save the spirit of man which is in him?" 1 Cor. 2:11. None knows what convictions another man's conscience feels, until he himself shall discover them; you hear the same sound of the gospel, but you hear not the inward strokes it gives to another man's conscience. Christ's approaches to the soul make no noise; little do we know what the Spirit of Christ whispers in the ear of him who sits next to us. It is said of the inward comforts of the Spirit, "To him that overcometh will I give to eat of the hidden manna." Rev. 2:17. This is true also of inward terrors and troubles. Christ's knocks by conviction are but a secret whisper of his Spirit in the ear of a sinner, saying, "Thou art the man;" this is thy case. This is the first thing in the manner of Christ's knocking, it is a silent knock without public sound.

2. These silent, inward knocks of the Spirit of Christ *greatly differ as to the terror or mildness of them in different persons.* Some hear them with terror and astonishment, others in a milder and more gentle manner. When the Lord knocked at the jailer's conscience, it was a terrible stroke; he called for a light, and sprang in like a man distracted; and trembling and astonished, fell down at the apostles' feet, crying, "Sirs, what must I do to be saved?" Acts 16:29, 30. Here was a terrible knock indeed, which almost affrighted his soul out of his body: it is as if he had said, Tell me, in God's name, and tell me quickly, whether there is any way of salvation, and where it lies; for I am a lost man, an undone soul. But when the Lord opened the heart of Lydia, there were no such terrors. He spoke to her

in a more mild and gentle voice, as you see, Acts 16:14. The Spirit of God varies his method according to the temper of the soul he works on. Knotty pieces need greater wedges and harder blows to rive them asunder. As God directs his ministers to make a difference, to deal tenderly and compassionately with some, but others to "save with fear," Jude 22, so he himself observes like different methods.

3. Some knocks of Christ are *successful*, and obtain the desired effect. He knocks, and the soul opens. But others are *unsuccessful;* he knocks once and again by convictions, which may cause the conscience to startle a little, but there is no opening to Christ by faith. O friends, this is a dreadful word to consider: "I have called, and ye refused; I have stretched out my hand, and no man regarded." Prov. 1:24. There is a call without an answer, a knock and no opening; and these things are very common, especially among the unconverted who live under a lively, rousing gospel-ministry. Of this Christ complains, Matt. 16:17: "Whereunto shall I liken this generation? It is like unto children sitting in the markets, and calling unto their fellows, and saying, We have piped unto you, and ye have not danced; we have mourned unto you, and ye have not lamented." Neither the delightful melody of gospel-grace, nor the mournful and dreadful threats of perdition to unbelievers, avail to open your hearts to embrace me; no voices from mount Gerizim or mount Ebal will prevail with you. How many witnesses to this truth have we seen! God forbid it should be thus with you. There are some souls who hear and open, even every one who hath heard and learned of the Father. John 6:45. When the Spirit of God puts forth his power with the word, then, and not till then, it becomes successful.

4. Sometimes Christ knocks with *a succession of convictions, a quick repetition of his calls.* Some men have had thousands of convictions in a few years; for in this case the Lord saith, as in Exod. 4:8, "If they will not hearken to

the voice of the first sign," yet they may "believe the voice of the latter sign." And yet sometimes neither the former nor the latter avail any thing. "How often would I have gathered thy children together, even as a hen gathereth her chickens under her wings, and ye would not!" Matt. 23:37. "How often!" intimating the many calls Christ gave Jerusalem to come unto him, yet all in vain. Obstinate sinners, Christ has been knocking and calling at some of your consciences from your very childhood; thousands of convictions have been tried upon some of you, and yet to this day your souls are shut fast against him. The Lord hath waited from year to year for your answer, by this signifying how loath he is to part with you: at such a time thou wast upon a sick-bed, nigh unto death; at such a time under such a sermon, and then Christ knocked at thy soul: if all this is in vain, as many convictions as you have stifled, so many fagots you carry with you to hell, to increase your flames and torments. Yet commonly those quick repetitions and redoublings of the strokes of convictions end well; and it is a good sign when one conviction revives another, and the Lord keeps the soul still waiting. But O, take heed and try not his patience too long, lest the next stroke be more dreadful than all the former—not to open your hearts, but smite dead your hopes of heaven.

5. Sometimes Christ knocks *intermittingly*, knocking and stopping, and that at a considerable distance of time; a conviction this day, and, it may be, not another for many months. . There are some aged sinners that have not had more than one or two remarkable awakenings of conscience in fifty or sixty years, and then no more. Do not think that the Spirit will always strive with men. Gen. 6:3. There is a time when God says to the word, Convict the conscience of that man or woman no more, but henceforth be thou not to open but to shut him up. Isa. 6:10. Reader, bethink thyself, how long is it since thy conscience was roused and

awakened? O, saith one, seven or eight years ago I heard such a sermon, which tore my conscience to pieces; I fell under such a providence, which roused and awakened all my fears; but since that time, all has been still and quiet. May the Lord give you a second awakening, lest you awake with the flames of God's wrath about you. I observe it is usual, when God works upon any very early in life, he knocks thus intermittingly: now the conscience is active, and full of trouble, then the vanities of youth extinguish these convictions again; but the Lord follows his design, and at last the conviction settles and ends in conversion.

6. *Christ sometimes knocks with both hands at once,* with the word and the rod together; the latter in subserviency to the former; and if ever the soul is likely to open, it will open then, when ordinances and afflictions work together. The word smites the conscience with conviction, and at or about the same time Providence smites the outward man with some affliction, to make the word effectual; or, under some smart affliction, a suitable word is seasonably directed to the conscience; and thus the one assists the other, and both together produce the desired effect. Thus the Lord wrought upon the Thessalonians: "And ye became followers of us and of the Lord, having received the word in much affliction." 1 Thess. 1:6. A child dies, an estate is lost, or sickness seizes you at the time when conscience is prepared by a conviction from the word, or afflictions have prepared it for the word. The rod upon the back helps the word to work upon the heart; and if both these working in fellowship will not do the work, there is little hope that any thing will do it.

7. *Every knock of Christ disturbs the sinful rest of the soul;* it rouses guilt in the conscience, and puts the inner man into great distress and trouble. Before Christ comes and knocks at the door of the heart, all is still and quiet within: the soul is in a quiet sleep of sinful security,

no fears or troubles molest its rest. "When a strong man armed keepeth his palace, his goods are in peace; but when a stronger than he shall come upon him and overcome him, he taketh from him all his armor wherein he trusted." Luke 11 : 21, 22. The armor which Satan puts into the hands of sinners, to defend themselves against the convictive strokes of the word, are the general mercy of God, the outward duties of religion, partial reformations, etc. But when Christ comes by effectual conviction, he disarms the sinner of all these pleas, and then the soul sees what broken reeds it has leaned upon. "When the commandment came, sin revived, and I died," Rom. 7 : 9; all my vain hopes expired. No artifice of Satan can any longer quiet the sinner's conscience; he sees himself in a miserable condition, and meditates an escape; farewell now to sound and quiet sleep: no peace till out of danger.

8. *Every effectual knock of Christ gives an alarm to hell*, and puts Satan to all his shifts and arts to secure the possession of the convinced sinner. The devil is a jealous spirit, and when his interest is in danger he bestirs himself to purpose; the time of conviction is an hour of temptation. "We wrestle not against flesh and blood, but against principalities, against powers, against the rulers of the darkness of this world, against spiritual wickedness in high places." Eph. 6 : 12. The strife between Satan and the soul is now for nothing less than the prize of eternal life; it is now for all or none, for life or death, for heaven or hell. The powers of hell are now all in arms to destroy convictions, and secure the possession of the soul against Christ; as when a grenade falls into a garrison, the first care of the defendant is to stifle it before it break. While Christ is speaking by his Spirit in one ear, the devil is whispering in the other; and the things he whispers to quench convictions are usually such as these: There is time enough yet, why such haste? Enjoy thy pleasures a little longer, thou mayest come to

Christ and be saved at last. If that will not do, then he changes his voice: To what purpose wilt thou go to Christ? It is now too late, the time of grace is over; hadst thou come to him in thy youth, and obeyed his first call, you had been saved; but now it is to no purpose. If this will not quiet the soul, then he says, Thy sins are too great to be pardoned; there is no hope for such a prodigious sinner as thou art. If the Lord help the soul to overcome this by discovering to it the riches of mercy, pardoning the greatest of sinners, then he represents the multitudes who are in the same case with the convinced sinner: Come, fear not; if it go ill with thee, it will be as bad for millions of others; if thou go to hell, thousands will go with thee. But if the soul be unwilling to be lost, even with so many others, then he bids it look upon the train of troubles and afflictions that come along with Christ, and will certainly follow him, if the door be open to let him in: If Christ come in, reproaches, losses, and sufferings will come in with him; troops of miseries follow him: he himself has told thee so; and art thou mad to ruin all thy comforts in the world, and plunge thyself into a sea of trouble for what thine eyes never saw? But if the soul reply, These are more tolerable than damnation; better that my flesh suffer for a time, than my soul be cast away for ever; then he represents the insuperable difficulties of religion: What a hard thing it is to be saved; how many painful duties and acts of mortification the soul must pass through. Thus you see what an alarm conviction gives to the powers of hell.

9. *Every effectual knock of Christ is continued;* new convictions revive former ones, and the Lord never ceases to knock till the door is opened. If one sermon will not do, another shall; if one wound be healed by the art of Satan, a fresh wound shall be made; if a former conviction vanish, the next shall be sealed upon the soul: and when the Spirit of the Lord sealeth a conviction upon the conscience, raze it

out who can. And here is the difference between special and common convictions: common convictions come and go; they put the soul in a fright for a day or a month, and then trouble it no more for ever; but special convictions will be continued, one thing following another, for Christ is in pursuit of the soul, and will pursue it, till at last he overtake it.

10. *All the knocks of Christ cease when the sinner's day of grace is ended.* This is a dreadful consideration—when the time of mercy is over, no more strivings of the Spirit. Christ says to the drowsy sinner, as to the drowsy disciples in the garden, "Sleep on now, and take your rest." Matt. 26:45. I called thee in such a sermon, but thou heardest not; by such a providence, but thou obeyedst not: sleep on now, and take thy rest. "My people would not hearken to my voice, and Israel would none of me. So I gave them up to their own hearts' lust, and they walked in their own counsels." Psa. 81:11, 12. I have done with them, the treaty is ended; I will make no more essays towards their conversion and salvation. "So I gave them up." Methinks it sounds as much as this: Take them, sin—take them, Satan, I will have no more to do with them. "Ephraim is joined to idols: let him alone." Hosea 4:17. His heart is glued fast to sin, he is enamoured with other lovers, let him alone. O beloved, it is a dreadful thing for God to say, Let this man alone in his formality, and that man in his carnal security. Let not this be misapplied by trembling souls under conviction. I know the fear of this judgment is upon their hearts; nothing makes them tremble more than lest the day of grace be ended with them. But there is no ground for this fear, while the Spirit continues convincing and the soul trembling lest his convictions should prove ineffectual. Thus much of the nature, instruments, and manner of Christ's knocking at the door of a sinner's heart. Our way is now opened to an application of this point, which I will present in several particulars.

INFERENCE 1. *Into how deep a sleep hath sin cast the souls of sinners, that Christ must stand so long, and give such loud repeated knocks, before it will awake and open to him!* There is the spirit of a deep sleep fallen upon men, like that into which God cast Adam. God speaks once, yea, twice, but man regards it not; it is the hardest thing in the world to rouse and awaken a man out of his carnal security. Look over Satan's kingdom, and you find a general stillness and quietness among his subjects: there is no trouble for sin, no strivings after salvation, no crying out, "What must I do to be saved?" Acts 16:30. Go into the crowds of worldly men and women, and you find them all intent and busy about other matters. How long will you be in their company before you hear one groan for sin, or see one tear fall from their eyes on that account. O what a marvellous thing is here! Do not their consciences know the guilt that lies upon them? Are they not aware of a day of reckoning which approaches? Yes, yes, these things are not hid from their consciences. What art, then, is used to keep them so still and quiet? Why, there are divers means used to still the consciences of sinners, and they do it effectually. There are four causes and occasions of this wonderful stillness in the souls of sinners.

(1.) *Ignorance of the nature of regenerating grace*—taking that for regeneration which is not such: thus did the Jews confidently affirm God to be their God, yet they did not know him. John 8:54. How many poor ignorant creatures think there is no need of any other work of regeneration, but what passed upon them in baptism. They were born and baptized Christians, and that is enough, they think, to save them. "We have Abraham to our father." Matt. 3:9. They thought it sufficient that Abraham's blood ran in their veins, though there were not a spark of Abraham's faith kindled in their souls. The Lord forgive the sin of those men who lead souls into such fatal mistakes.

O if men were but aware of the necessity of a greater and further work to pass on their souls than their baptism, powerless profession, or the similar works which appear in formal hypocrites, heaven and earth would ring with their cries. But ignorance of the nature and necessity of special regenerating grace, like a dose of opium, casts the consciences of many into this deep sleep.

(2.) *Freedom from grosser sins and pollutions of the world* stills and quiets the consciences of thousands: they have had a sober and fair education; and though there is no grace and regeneration, yet what saints do they seem to themselves, being adorned with sobriety and civility. This stilled the conscience of the Pharisee: "God, I thank thee that I am not as other men are, extortioners, unjust, adulterers, or even as this publican." Luke 18:11. Thus, like delicate Agag, they pride themselves in moral and social virtues, wherein many thousands of the heathen were better than themselves; but justice will hew them to pieces, as Agag was, notwithstanding all their moral ornaments and endowments.

(3.) *The strict performance of the external duties of religion* quiets the consciences of many. They question not but those who do so well shall fare well, and flatter themselves that God will never damn men and women who keep their church and say their prayers as they do. Thus the carnal Jews deluded themselves, crying, "The temple of the Lord, the temple of the Lord, are these." Jer. 7:4. As malefactors, in some countries, flee to the church from the hand of justice, so do these; but God will pluck them from the horns of the altar, and convince them that the empty name of religion is no security from damnation.

(4.) Many consciences are quieted in a natural, sinful state, *by misinterpreting the voice of providence.* It may be that God prospers your earthly affairs, succeeds and smiles upon your undertakings; and this you conclude must be a token of his love and favor. But alas, this is a great mistake: may the Lord give you better evidences of his love than these; for who prosper more in the world than wicked men? And who are more crossed than the people of God? Read Job 21, and Psalm 73, and compare both with Eccl. 9:1, and you will quickly see the vanity of all hopes built on such a foundation. But by such things as these the god of this world blinds the eyes of multitudes.

2. *If every conviction be a knock of Christ, how deeply are we all concerned in the success of convictions.* Conviction is an embryo of the new creature: if it come to a perfect new birth, it brings forth salvation to your souls; if it fails, you are finally lost. It is of infinite moment, therefore, to every one, to be tender of these convictions of conscience. It is true, conviction and conversion are two things: there may be conviction without conversion, though there can be no conversion without conviction. The blossoms on the trees in the spring of the year cannot properly be called fruit, but are rather the rudiments of fruit, or something in order to fruit. If they open kindly, and knit or set firmly, perfect fruit follows them; but if a blight or a frosty morning kill them, no fruit is to be expected. Thus it is here. Great care, therefore, ought to be taken about the preservation and success of convictions, both by the soul itself that is under them, and by all others who are concerned about them.

(1.) *What care should the soul itself have, on whom convictions are wrought.* Beware, friends, how you quench them or hinder their operations, lest you hinder, as much as in you lies, the formation of Christ in your souls. The life of your souls is bound up in the life of your convictions. I know it is hard for men to dwell with their own convictions: guilt and wrath are sad subjects for men's thoughts to dwell upon; but it is far better to dwell with the thoughts of sin and wrath here, than to lie under them in hell for ever. You may be freed from your convictions and your salvation together. Be not too eager after peace—a good trouble is better than a false peace. And on the other hand, beware that your convictions turn not into discouragements to faith; this will cross the proper intention of them: they are Christ's knocks for entrance, and were never intended to be bars or stumbling-blocks, but steps in your way to Christ.

(2.) *Let all that are concerned about convinced souls, beware what counsels they give and what rules they prescribe,* lest they destroy all in the bud.

There are two errors too commonly committed: one in *excess,* persuading souls under trouble of conscience that there is no coming to Christ for them, unless they are so and so prepared, humbled just to such a degree: this is dangerous counsel; it overheats the troubles of conscience, and keeps the soul from its proper present duty and remedy. I am sure Paul and Silas took no such course with the convinced jailer, Acts 16:31, nor Peter with the three thousand wounded consciences, Acts 2:38. Nor do I find where God has stated the time and degree of spiritual troubles, so that there must be no approaches to Christ in the way of faith, until they have suffered them so long and to such a height. If they have imbittered sin to the soul, and made it see the necessity of a Saviour, it cannot move too soon after Christ in the way of faith. Let no man set bounds where God sets none.

There is another error committed in *defect;* when promises and comforts are applied before the nature of faith is known, or one act of reliance put forth towards Christ. These hasty comforts come to nothing; they will not, they cannot stand. It is a dangerous thing to apply gospel-cordials, and pour out the precious ointment of the promises upon them who were never heart-sick for sin—to address to such persons upon every slight trouble, which is but as an early dew, the peculiar consolations of penitent and believing souls. How many such unskilful empirics are there in every place! Such as the prophet Jeremiah complains of: "They have healed the hurt of the daughter of my people slightly, saying, Peace, peace; when there is no peace." Jer. 6:14. Remember, that the foundation is now laying for eternity, and that this is the time of deep consideration; men must ponder the terms and count the cost, and deliberately accept and close with Christ, before the consolations of the promises can properly be administered to them.

3. *What a blessing is a rousing, faithful ministry among a people.* By such a ministry Christ knocks powerfully: this is one of the greatest blessings God can bestow upon a people, when he sends among them powerful and judicious preachers of the gospel, under whose ministry their consciences cannot sleep quietly. These are the instruments by which Christ knocks at men's hearts; and as for those that sew pillows for drowsy sinners to sleep quietly upon, the Lord owns them not as his. "Thy prophets have seen vain and foolish things for thee: and they have not discovered thine iniquity." Lam. 2:14.

It is true that those ministers that give men no rest and quietness in their sins, must expect but little rest and quietness themselves. What is it for ministers to preach home to the consciences of others, but to pull down the rage of the world upon their own heads? But certainly you will have cause to bless God to eternity, for casting your lot under such a ministry; and the Lord accounts such a mercy sufficient to recompense any outward affliction that lies upon you. You fare richly under such doctrine, though the Lord should feed you with the bread of affliction, and give you the waters of adversity to drink; this makes amends for all. Thine eyes shall behold thy teachers, and they shall be driven no more into corners. Isa. 30:20. O blessed be God that England's corners are this day emptied, that its pulpits may be filled with laborious, faithful ministers. O that the knocks of Christ may be heard in all the cities, towns, and villages of this nation. The kingdom of God is come nigh unto us; this mercy is invaluable: pray that the Lord may continue it, and make all your ministers and means, whether public or private, successful.

4. *Let all men beware of whatever may deafen their ears and drown the sound of Christ's knocks and calls in the gospel.* What pernicious enemies to the souls of men are those persons who turn away men's ears from attending to the knocks and calls of Christ in his word. Such are, 1. Profane, wicked men, who, like Elymas the sorcerer, make it their business by wicked insinuations and jeers to turn away men's ears from the gospel. "O full of all subtlety and all mischief, thou child of the devil, thou enemy of all righteousness, wilt thou not cease to pervert the right ways of the Lord?" Acts 13:10. All opposition to godliness has a spice of devilishness, and no child more resembles his father than a scoffing enemy resembles his father the devil. But blessed be God for the good providence which, in a great measure, has stopped the mouths both of the father and his children. 2. Take heed of carnal and ungodly relations, who discourage and threaten their servants, and all who depend on them, from attending upon the means, or giving way to the convictions which God has awakened in their hearts. Cruel parents, who had rather see their children turned into their graves, than turning to the ways of serious godliness! O that any should dare to quench the beginnings of spiritual life in those to whom they were instruments to convey natural life. 3. Take heed of the world, its distracting cares and pleasures; what a din and noise do these things make in the ears of men. "The cares of this world, and the deceitfulness of riches, and the lusts of other things entering in, choke the word, and it becometh unfruitful." Mark 4:19. Tell not them of getting Christ, they must study how to get bread. These are some of the distracting and diverting sounds which drown the voice of

Christ's knocks and calls in the gospel. As you value your souls, beware of them.

Christ is now come near us in the gospel. Behold, he stands at the door and knocks: and I this day demand your answer—in his name I do solemnly demand it; what shall I return to him who sent me? What sayest thou, sinner? Wilt thou open to Christ, or wilt thou shut him out, and with him thy own pardon, peace, and salvation? Once more, let me try the force of a few more arguments upon your hearts, and refute your vain pleas to the contrary. Methinks no heart should be able to resist such MOTIVES and rational persuasions as these following will be found to be.

MOTIVE 1. *You are in extreme need of Christ;* you want him more than bread or breath. Many things are convenient for your bodies, but Christ is the "one thing needful" for your souls. Luke 10 : 42. Necessity is an engine that will open any thing that can be opened: necessity will make all fly before it. Now there is a plain, present, absolute necessity lying on every one of you to open your heart to Christ, and that without delay. Necessity goes before the face of Christ, to open the way for him into the heart. Thou must have him, or be lost for ever. Christ and faith are not the may-be, but the must-be, to the happiness of thy soul. A man may be poor, and happy; reproached, and blessed; but he cannot be Christless and safe, nor Christless and comfortable. You must have Christ, or you cannot have life, John 3 : 36; you must have Christ, or you can have no hope, Col. 1 : 27. Christ and life, Christ and hope, go together: no Christ, no life; no Christ, no hope. Sinner, thou must have Christ, or thou canst have no pardon; for Christ and pardon are undivided. Eph. 1 : 7. In a word, you must have Christ, or you can have no salvation. Acts 4 : 12. Well, then, if thou canst have no life nor hope, no pardon nor salvation, without Christ, then a plain necessity goes before Christ to open his way into thy heart: methinks thou shouldst now say, Then will I open to Christ, whatever the terms are. Come sufferings, losses, reproaches, yea, death itself, all is one; Christ I must have, and Christ I will have: necessity is laid upon me, and my heart is opened to Christ by it. Woe to me for ever, if I miss of Christ.

MOTIVE 2. *The Lord Jesus is this day come nigh to your souls.* I may say to you as Christ did to the Jews, "The kingdom of God is come nigh unto you." Luke 10 : 9. The Lord grant he be not as nigh to some of you as ever he shall be; for he must come nearer, or else you are lost for ever. It is not Christ among you in the means of grace, but Christ within you by the work of grace, which must be unto you "the hope of glory." Col. 1 : 27. He is not only among you in external means, but he is come into your understandings and consciences; yea, some motions of his you feel upon your affections: there wants but a little more to make you eternally happy. O what would one effectual touch upon your wills be worth now! The head-work is done; O that the heart-work were done too. You are *almost saved;* but to be almost saved, is to be wholly and eternally lost, if it go no further. It is a sad thing for a man who hath one foot in heaven, to slide from thence into hell; it is sad to be shipwrecked at the harbor's mouth.

MOTIVE 3. *Jesus Christ has an unquestionable right to enter into and possess* every one of your souls. Satan is but an usurper: Christ is your lawful owner and proprietor; thy soul, sinner, hath not so full a title to thy body, as Christ hath to thy soul. Satan keeps Christ out of his right. Christ knocks at the door of his own house; he built it, and therefore may well claim admission into it: it is his own creature. "By him were all things created that are in heaven and that are in earth, visible and invisible;" bodies or souls.

Col. 1 : 16. The invisible part, thy soul, is his workmanship—a stately structure of his own raising. He has also a right by redemption; Christ hath bought thy soul, and that at the invaluable price of his own blood. Who then can dispute the right of Christ to enter into his own house? But, alas, he cometh to his own and his own receive him not. John 1 : 11.

Motive 4. Open the door to Christ, for *a train of blessings and mercies come in with him*—a troop of privileges follow him. In the same day and hour that Christ comes into thine heart by a full and deliberate choice, a pardon comes with him of all the sins that ever thou hast committed, in thought, word, or action. Will such a pardon be welcome to thy soul? Then let Christ be welcome, for where Christ comes, pardon comes. Eph. 1 : 7. If you open to Christ, you open to peace, and who would shut the door of his soul against peace? If peace be welcome, let Christ be welcome; for peace follows faith in Christ. Rom. 5 : 1. Where Christ comes, liberty comes. "If the Son therefore shall make you free, ye shall be free indeed." John 8 : 36. Are you in love with bonds and fetters? Satan's laws are written in blood. Christ's yoke is easy, and his commands not grievous. If you love liberty, love Christ. In a word, where Christ comes, salvation comes; for he is "the author of eternal salvation to all them that obey him." Heb. 5 : 9. If therefore you love pardon, peace, liberty, and salvation, shut not the door against Christ; for all these follow him wherever he goes.

Motive 5. *Christ this day solemnly demands entrance into thy soul;* he begs thee to open to him, 2 Cor. 5 : 20; he commands thee to open unto him, 1 John 3 : 23; he denounces eternal ruin to those who refuse him entrance. Now consider well—here is entrance demanded under pain of the eternal wrath of God: this demand is recorded in heaven; at your own peril be it, if you shut the door against him. Only this will I say in my Redeemer's behalf; if you refuse, bear witness heaven and earth this day that Christ solemnly demanded entrance into thy soul, and was refused; bear witness that the door was shut against the only Redeemer, who intreated, commanded, and threatened eternal damnation to the rejecters of him. Oh, methinks that scripture, Prov. 1 : 24–31, should strike terror into the very centre of the soul that refuses the offers of Christ!

MOTIVE 6. And so I have done my master's errand: *if you now refuse the knock of Christ at your hearts, he may never knock more;* and where are you then? There is a knock which will be the last knock, a call which will be his last call; and after that no more knocks or calls, but an eternal silence as to any overture of mercy.

OBJECTION 1. But if I do open to Christ, he will never come in to such a filthy, polluted, sinful soul as mine is.

ANSWER. Who saith so? Who dare affirm so impudent a falsehood in the very face of the text, "If any man open to me, I will come in to him?"

OBJECTION 2. If I open to Christ, I must bid farewell to rest in this world; reproaches, sufferings, and losses follow him.

ANSWER. If Christ, pardon, and salvation are, in thy estimation, not worth the enduring and suffering these small things, sure thou valuest Christ and thy soul at a low rate. O who can sufficiently bewail the ignorance and folly of unbelievers, who will sell their souls and hopes of heaven for such trifles! And if Christ and thy soul must part on these terms, then hear me, sinner, and let it sink into thine heart:

Thy damnation will be just; for thou hadst thine own choice, and hast deliberately preferred the insignificant trifles of this world before Christ and salvation. It was plainly told thee what the issue of thy rejecting Christ would be; and yet, after sufficient warning, thou hast ventured upon it. Whatever other sinners will plead, I know not, but as for thee, thou must be speechless. Matt. 22:12. If thou die Christless, thou must appear at his bar speechless; and the day of judgment will be the day of the revelation of the righteous judgment of God. Rom. 2:5.

It will also be unavoidable, for there is no other way to salvation but this. Acts 4:12. No Christ, no heaven; no faith, no Christ. "How shall we escape, if we neglect so great salvation?" Heb. 2:3. Mercy itself cannot save thee out of Christ, for all the saving mercy of God is dispensed to men through him. Jude 21. It is to no purpose to cry for mercy, when Christ, in whom all the mercies of God are dispensed to men, is rejected by thee.

This doctrine winds up in CONSOLATION to all such as, hearing the knocks of Christ, have opened or are now resolved to open their hearts to him; and that nothing, henceforth, may keep Christ and their souls asunder, to such I shall address the following grounds of comfort.

1. *An opening heart to Christ is a work wholly and altogether supernatural;* a special work of the Spirit of God, never found upon any but an elect soul. There are common gifts of the Spirit, such as knowledge, vanishing convictions, etc., but the opening of the heart by faith is the special, saving, and peculiar work of the Spirit. "This is the work of God, that ye believe on him whom He hath sent." John 6:29. Yea, the almighty power of God, the exceeding greatness of his power, is exerted in the work of faith. Eph. 1:19. It rises not out of nature, as common gifts do; but of this it is expressly said, "Not of yourselves, it is the gift of God." Eph. 2:8. Where this work is effectually wrought, we may reason as solidly as comfortably from it, both backward to the electing love of God, and forward to our eternal glorification with him. Rom. 8:30.

2. *The opening of thy heart to Christ by saving faith, gives thee an interest in Christ the very same hour.* The

relation is then constituted, the conjugal bond is fastened between him and thy soul. "As many as received him, to them gave he power," right or privilege, "to become the sons of God, even to them that believe on his name." John 1 : 12. You neither need nor may expect an extraordinary messenger or voice from heaven, to tell you that Christ is yours and you are his; you have a better foundation in this word and work of faith. For my part, if God will give me the clear and satisfying experience of this work upon my heart, I would never desire more satisfaction on this side heaven. I know not but the devil may counterfeit an extraordinary voice, and cheat the soul by a lying oracle; but if I really feel my heart and will sincerely opening to Christ upon gospel terms, I am sure there is no deceit in that.

3. *The opening of thy heart to Christ by faith is a good assurance that heaven shall be opened to thy soul hereafter.* Heaven is shut against none but those who shut their hearts against Christ by unbelief. Will you bar Christ out of your souls by ignorance and unbelief, and then cry, Lord, open to us? God will open to none but them that open to Christ. Eternity itself shall but suffice to bless God for this opening act of faith. "He that believeth shall be saved." Mark 16 : 16.

4. *The opening of thy soul to Christ by faith makes it Christ's habitation for ever:* in that hour out go sin and Satan, and in come Christ and grace. "If any man open unto me, I will come in to him," saith the text. Of such a soul Christ saith, as it was said of the temple, "The Lord hath chosen Zion; he hath desired it for his habitation. This is my rest for ever; here will I dwell, for I have desired it." Psa. 132 : 13, 14. The soul now becomes a hallowed temple to the Lord; as he hath said, "I will dwell in them, and walk in them; and I will be their God, and they shall be my people." 2 Cor. 6 : 16. O what a heaven on earth is here! Christ dwelling in the soul is the glory of the

soul, as God's dwelling in the temple was the glory of the temple.

5. In a word, *the opening of the heart to Christ is the work which answers the great design of the gospel.* Wherefore has God set up ordinances and ministers, yea, wherefore is the Spirit sent forth, but to open the hearts of sinners to Christ by faith? When this is done, the main intention of the gospel is attained; the union is effected between Christ and the soul; it is now put out of hazard. The whole work of the gospel after that, is but to build up, confirm, and comfort the soul, ripen its implanted graces, and make it meet for glory.

CHAPTER VI.

CHRIST'S EARNEST ENTREATY FOR UNION AND COMMUNION WITH SINNERS.

"BEHOLD, *I STAND AT THE DOOR AND KNOCK.*" REV. 3:20.

HERE are pains and patience, all means used by Christ to gain entrance into the souls of sinners. The language speaks the earnestness of his suit, and the vehemency of his desire to be in union with the souls of men. The sixth doctrine, therefore, will be,

Jesus Christ is an earnest suitor for union and communion with the souls of sinners.

This doctrine lies directly and fully in the intention of the text. In opening it, two things must be spoken to, in the doctrinal part: the demonstration of this truth, that he is so; and the marvellous grace and condescension of Christ, that he should be so.

The DEMONSTRATION of this truth, that Christ is an earnest suitor *for union and communion with the souls of sinners*, I shall draw from a view and consideration of the dispositions and actions of the Lord Jesus towards sinners from first to last. And when you have compared them all together, and by them seen the temper of his heart, how great and clear a light will shine upon this point. That his heart hath still inclined towards union and communion with sinful man, will appear by considering him before his incarnation; in the days of his flesh; at his death; and since his ascension into heaven.

I. Consider him BEFORE HIS INCARNATION, and you will find two things in that state which plainly speak his desire after union with us.

1. *In the covenant of redemption he made with God concerning us before this world had a being;* for such a

covenant and promise did really pass between him and the Father before all time, or else I know not how to understand this scripture: "In hope of eternal life, which God, that cannot lie, promised before the world began." Titus 1:2. To whom could that promise be made, which bears date before the creation, but unto Christ? What else can this mean but the covenant of redemption made between the Father and the Son? the terms whereof are set down in Isa. 53:10, 11, where you find what Christ was to do, namely, "to make his soul an offering for sin"—and what should be his reward for pouring out his soul unto death, namely, "To see his seed; to see the travail of his soul," even a church purchased with his own blood. Whether this be not a great demonstration of the inclination of Christ's heart towards union and communion with sinners, let all men judge. O what a value did Christ set upon our souls, that upon such costly terms he would consent to redeem them! Unto this agreement God the Father held him: "God spared not his own Son." Rom. 8:32. And this very covenant Christ pleaded with the Father: "I have manifested thy name unto the men which thou gavest me out of the world: thine they were, and thou gavest them me." John 17:6. This plainly shows the vehement desire of Christ's heart to be in union with men; according to Prov. 8:31: "Rejoicing in the habitable part of his earth, and my delights were with the sons of men." Blessed Jesus, nothing but the strength of thine own desire and love could have drawn thee out of that bosom of delights to suffer so many things for the sake of sinners.

II. Let us consider Christ's disposition towards union and communion with sinners, IN THE DAYS OF HIS FLESH; and every thing done by Christ carries and confirms this conclusion.

1. *Christ's assumption of our nature* manifested his desire after union with us. Herein he gave two incomparable proofs of his transcendent love to us, and desire after us

(1.) *In passing by a superior and more excellent nature.* "Verily he took not on him the nature of angels." Heb. 2:16. Angels were excellent creatures, but behold those vessels of gold cast into the fire, and earthen potsherds fitted for glory. It is true, the angels who kept their first estate are members of Christ's kingdom; he is a head to them by way of dominion, but unto us by way of vital union. Christ takes the believer into a nearer union with himself than any angel in heaven. For the multitudes of apostate angels he never designed recovery, but left them as they were before, bound in chains of darkness unto the judgment of the great day. Jude 6.

(2.) *In uniting our nature to himself, and that after sin had blasted its beauty,* and let in so many direful calamities upon it. He was found in the likeness of sinful flesh, Rom. 8:3; that is, he was subject to weariness, pains, and death, which, though there is no sin in them, are the effects and consequences of sin: such a nature he took into personal union with himself, not to experience any new pleasure in it, but to enable him to suffer and satisfy for us; and thus to give a convincing proof of the strength of his love, and the vehemency of his desire to us. His personal union with our nature shows his desire after a mystical union with our persons. He would never have been the Son of man, but to make us the sons and daughters of the living God; he came in our likeness, that we, by sanctification, might be conformed to his likeness. Behold how near Christ comes to us by his incarnation. O what a stoop did he make therein to recover us. Rather than lose us, he was contented to lose his manifested glory for a time; for his incarnation made him "of no reputation." Phil. 2:7. Behold the desire of the Saviour after union with sinners.

2. *The whole life of Christ upon earth* was an evident proof and demonstration of the desire of his heart to be in union and communion with us: "For their sakes I sanctify

myself." John 17 : 19. The life of Christ was wholly set apart for us; therefore it is said, " Unto us a child is born, unto us a son is given." Isa. 9 : 6. What was the errand upon which Christ came into this world, but to " seek and to save that which was lost?" Luke 19 : 10.

All the miracles he wrought on earth were so many works of mercy. He could have wrought miracles to destroy and ruin such as received him not; but his almighty power was employed to heal and to save the bodies of men, that thereby he might win their souls unto himself. " God anointed Jesus of Nazareth with the Holy Ghost and with power; who went about doing good, and healing all that were oppressed of the devil; for God was with him." Acts 10 : 38. When the apostles desired a commission from him to command fire from heaven to destroy the Samaritans, he rebuked them, saying, " Ye know not what manner of spirit ye are of. For the Son of man is not come to destroy men's lives, but to save them." Luke 9 : 55, 56. The whole life of Christ in this world was nothing else but a wooing, drawing motive to the hearts of sinners; he rejected not the vilest of sinners. Luke 7 : 39. He rejected none that came to him; he would not have even little children forbidden to be brought unto him. Mark 10 : 14. What his winning compassion should be, was long before predicted by the prophet: " A bruised reed shall he not break, and the smoking flax shall he not quench." Isa. 42 : 3. Christ was in the world as a magnet drawing all men to him; his deportment was every way suitable to his commission, which was to preach good tidings unto the meek, to bind up the broken-hearted, to proclaim liberty to the captive, and the opening of the prison to them that are bound. Isa. 61 : 1.

3. *As his life, so his doctrine was a most pathetic invitation unto sinners.* " Never man spake like this man." John 7 : 46. Whenever he opened his lips, heaven opened, the very heart of God was opened to sinners; the whole

stream and current of his doctrine was one continued powerful persuasive to draw sinners to him. This was his language: "Come unto me, all ye that labor and are heavy laden, and I will give you rest." Matt. 11 : 28. " In the last day, that great day of the feast, Jesus stood and cried, If any man thirst, let him come unto me and drink." John 7 : 37. He compares his invitations to the call of a hen, to gather her chickens under her wings: " O Jerusalem, Jerusalem, how often would I have gathered thy children together, as a hen doth gather her brood under her wings!" Luke 13 : 34. Certainly the whole gospel is nothing but the charming voice of the heavenly bridegroom.

4. *The joy he always expressed for the success of the gospel*, shows him to be an earnest suitor for the hearts of sinners. It is very remarkable that all the evangelists who have recorded the life of Christ, never mention one laugh or smile from him, for he was "a man of sorrows." Yet once we read that he rejoiced in spirit; and you shall see the occasion of it in Luke 10 : 21 : "In that hour Jesus rejoiced in spirit." And what was it that gladdened his heart but the report brought him by the seventy, who returned with joy, saying, "Lord, even the devils are subject to us through thy name!" And he said unto them, "I beheld Satan as lightning fall from heaven." Ver. 17, 18. Satan's kingdom was going down in the world, and the mysteries of salvation were revealed unto babes ; this made his holy heart leap with joy, to behold the success of the gospel destroying Satan's kingdom, and the poorest, meanest among men enlightened and converted by it. This was a cordial to his very soul, and showed the earnestness of his desire after union and communion with sinners.

5. *His sorrows and mourning upon account of the obstinacy and unbelief of sinners*, speak the vehemence of his desire after union with them. It is said, Mark 3 : 5, " When he had looked round about on them with anger,

being grieved for the hardness of their hearts." You see that a hard heart is a grief to Jesus Christ. O how tenderly did Christ mourn over Jerusalem, when it rejected him. It is said that when Jesus came nigh to the city, he wept over it. Luke 19:41. The Redeemer's tears wept over obstinate Jerusalem spoke the zeal and fervor of his concern for their salvation; how loath Christ is to give up sinners. What a mournful voice is that in John 5:40: "Ye will not come to me, that ye might have life." How ready would I be to give you life; but you would rather die than come to me for it. What can Christ do more to express his willingness? All the sorrows that ever touched the heart of Christ from men, were on this account, that they would not yield to his calls and invitations.

6. This appears to be the great design of Christ, by *the labors he underwent day and night to accomplish it.* Many weary journeys Christ took, many sermons and prayers he preached and poured out, and all with the design to open the hearts of sinners to him, and win the consent of their wills to become his. This was the work which he preferred to his necessary food: "My meat is to do the will of him that sent me, and to finish his work." John 4:34. As if he had said, My bringing home the elect of God and saving them from the wrath to come, is more to me than meat and drink. So vehement and intense were his desires after the winning of sinners, that he would lose no occasion to accomplish it. If he were never so weary with his travels and labors, and an occasion offered to save a lost soul, he would be sure to improve it. You have an instance of this in John 4: Then cometh he to a city of Samaria, called Sychar. Now Jacob's well was there. Jesus therefore being weary with his journey, sat thus on the well. Christ was weary with his journey, and sat on the well for a little rest and refreshment in the heat of the day. At the same time comes a woman of Samaria, to draw water; a great sinner she was: Christ

compassionately beholding this miserable object, forgets his own weariness, and presently preaches repentance to this sinner and opens her heart; a greater refreshment to him than that well could afford by giving him a seat to sit on or water to drink.

7. *The great encouragements Christ always gave to coming and willing souls*, plainly show the earnest desire of his heart after union with them. Never were such encouragements given as Christ gave to draw the souls of men to him. It is remarkable in what general terms and forms of expression he delivered them, that none might be discouraged, but come in hope to him : " Come unto me, all ye that labor." Matt. 11 : 28. "If any man thirst." John 7 : 37. All the terms of invitation are exceeding large, which shows the desire of his heart to be so also ; and his practice was answerable to his invitation ; his mercies and compassions never failed when the vilest sinners came to him in repentance and faith. You read that when Christ sat at meat in the house of Simon the Pharisee, there came in a poor convinced sinner, who had guilt enough upon her to sink ten thousand souls to hell; this poor woman comes with great humility unto Christ, not presuming to come before his face, but falls down behind him, kisses his feet, washes them with tears, and wipes them with the hair of her head—all demonstrations of a broken heart. And how did the merciful Jesus welcome this poor sinner ? He seals her pardon, commends the fervor of her affections, and sends her away a joyful soul, Luke 7 : 37–50 ; herein making good that gracious promise, "Him that cometh to me I will in no wise cast out." John 6 : 37.

8. *The dreadful threatenings of Christ against all who refuse him* and shut the doors of their hearts against him, show his vehement desire to prevent the loss and ruin of souls. The threatenings of Christ are not intended to discourage any from coming to him, to fright away

souls from him; no, that is not their intention: but to bring them under a blessed necessity of compliance with his terms. O the dreadful threatenings which, like claps of thunder, come from the mouth of Christ against all who refuse or delay to come unto him: "If ye believe not that I am he, ye shall die in your sins." John 8:24. "He that believeth not the Son shall not see life." John 3:36. What a terrible thunder-clap is that against all unbelievers. "He that believeth not, shall be damned." Mark 16:16. All these and many more warnings are given from heaven to prevent the ruin of men; the very threatenings of the gospel carry a design of mercy in them: damnation is threatened, that it may be prevented.

9. And then, in the last place, herein appears the earnestness of Christ after union with sinners, that when he could be no longer a preacher to this world in his own person, *he ordained a succession of ministers, in his bodily absence from us, to gather and build the church,* and to continue to the end of the world—to carry on the suit that Christ had begun, as long as there was one elect soul in the world lying in the state of sin and nature.

Christ could not always abide here; he must die, or we could not live; he must rise again, or we could not be justified; our interests called him to another place and state. Now when Christ was to ascend to heaven, he chooses and calls men, men like ourselves, whose presence and appearance should not affright or discourage us—who should treat with us in a familiar way about the great concerns of our salvation in his name and stead. "We are ambassadors for Christ, as though God did beseech you by us: we pray you in Christ's stead, be ye reconciled to God." 2 Cor. 5:20. He did not commission angels to be his legates, their presence would confound and terrify us; but men cast in the same mould with yourselves, who may say to you as Elihu said to Job, "Behold, I am according to thy wish in

God's stead: I also am formed out of the clay. Behold, my terror shall not make thee afraid, neither shall my hand be heavy upon thee." Job 33:6, 7. Upon these commissioned officers of Christ he poured forth excellent gifts, in great and useful variety, to fit the capacities and various dispositions of men's souls. When he ascended up on high he gave gifts unto men, Psalm 68:18; this ministerial office is by him established in the church, "till we all come in the unity of the faith and of the knowledge of the Son of God, unto a perfect man, unto the measure of the stature of the fulness of Christ." Eph. 4:13. Unto these his ministers he gives the highest encouragements to quicken them in their labors. If one do one part of the work and another the other—if one soweth and another reapeth, he tells them both, "He that reapeth receiveth wages, and gathereth fruit unto life eternal; that both he that soweth and he that reapeth may rejoice together." John 4:36. He tells them that every soul they win to him shall be as a jewel in their crown of glory. "They that be wise shall shine as the brightness of the firmament; and they that turn many to righteousness, as the stars for ever and ever." Dan. 12:3. What is Christ's intention in all these encouragements to his ministers? Surely, it is as if he should say to his servants, Study hard, pray earnestly, plead with sinners affectionately; every soul you win to me shall make an addition to your glory in heaven.

. Weigh now the force of this second demonstration from the life of Christ. Will you have a proof of Christ's earnestness to gain the hearts of sinners? his whole life on earth was a proof of it; his doctrine, so full of pathetic invitations, proves it; the joy of his heart at the success of the gospel—his tears and sorrows for the obstinacy of unbelievers—his labors and travels to gather sinners to him—his admirable encouragements put into general invitations—his dreadful threatenings to all who reject his invitations—his commissioning and qualifying, continuing and encouraging his ministers to carry on his suit in his name—all these things make a full demonstration that Jesus Christ is an earnest suitor for union and communion with the souls of sinners.

III. THE DEATH OF CHRIST is the fullest demonstration that ever was or can be given of his love to sinners, and desire after union and communion with them. His doctrine and life discovered much, but his sufferings and death abundantly more. In his doctrine he spent his *breath*, but upon the cross he spent his *blood*. Here he comes suing to the souls of sinners in his scarlet robes, his red garments—garments dipt in his own blood. You may now propound the same admiring question the church propounded, Isa. 63 : 1, 2 : " Who is this that cometh from Edom, with dyed garments from Bozrah; this that is glorious in his apparel, travelling in the greatness of his strength? Wherefore art thou red in thine apparel, and thy garments like him that treadeth in the wine-fat ?" Wilt thou know, sinner, why he comes to thee in red garments? It is to give thee such a demonstration of his love as may draw forth all the love of thy heart to him; by this blood he has purchased thy soul as a spouse for himself. Acts 20 : 28. There are two things in the death of Christ which prove the fervor of his desires after us : the greatness of the sufferings which he endured, and the end to which they were designed; both of which show how the heart of Christ is heated with the vehemency of his own desires after union with our poor souls.

1. *The greatness of the sufferings of Christ* shows the ardor of his affection. Christ's sufferings are twofold, external in his body, and internal in his soul; both together making up the fulness of his sufferings. When you shall see what Christ has endured to purchase you to himself, then you may learn what a value he placed upon you, and what desire he has after you.

(1.) The *external* sufferings of Christ in his body were

exceedingly great, for the death he died was not a natural, but a violent death. This death was not in accordance with his nature; for he was not a sinner, and no punishment was due to him. His body was intended for a sacrifice to God, and as a sacrifice it died; therefore it is said, he was "put to death in the flesh," 1 Pet. 3:18—his soul and body were violently rent asunder in the fulness of his strength and vigor. And this violent death was also a cursed death: he was "made a curse for us; for it is written, Cursed is every one that hangeth on a tree." Gal. 3:13. A ceremonial curse was affixed to the death of the cross; he that is hanged is accursed of God, saith the law: the intention of that death was to show that the person who died was so vile that he was not worthy to touch heaven or earth, and therefore was hanged between both. Moreover, the violent death Christ died was a most painful death—full of torture, slow and lingering; the cross was a rack to the body of Christ: "I may tell all my bones; they look and stare upon me." Psalm 22:17. But yet,

(2.) The sufferings of his body were but the body of his sufferings; the sufferings *of his soul* were the very soul of his sufferings. These inward sufferings of Christ may likewise be considered two ways. 1. In his bitter sufferings in the garden. O what agonies and conflicts, what sharp encounters and distresses his soul there met with from the wrath of God endured for your sakes. Once and again he cried out, Abba, Father, all things are possible, let this cup pass; Father, if it be possible, let this cup pass: thrice he returned to the same place, falling on his face to the ground. The sufferings of his soul threw his blessed body into a bloody agony: "His sweat was as it were great drops of blood falling down to the ground." Luke 22:44. 2. In the fulness of his sufferings on the cross. There was his soul for a time deserted of the Father, as to any communications of joy and comfort from him, which occasioned the bitter outcry, "My God, my God, why hast thou forsaken me?" Matt. 27 : 46. Never was such a cry heard since the heavens were spread over the earth; never had Christ seen a frown in his Father's face, from eternity, before this time; but now the smiling face of God was hid, and a strong impression of his wrath made upon his Son. And now, brethren, you see what Christ hath endured both in his body and in his soul; and all for the sake of sinners. What think you now; is not Christ an earnest suitor? Does not all this fully and plainly speak the ardor of his love, the fervor of his desire after union and communion with us? If this do not, then nothing can demonstrate love and desire.

2. Let us next consider *the intention of these sufferings of Christ*, and how this also demonstrates the earnestness of his desire after union with us. There was a double use and end of the sufferings of Christ.

(1.) One end of Christ's death was *to purchase our freedom*, that we might be capable of being espoused to him; for we were not in a capacity, while under the curse of the law, to be married unto Christ. The apostle compares the law to a husband, to whom the wife is bound as long as he liveth, and not capable of a second marriage until her husband be dead. Rom. 7 : 2, 3. The death of Christ was the death of the law, as a covenant of works holding us under its curse; and so it gave us a manumission or freedom from that bond, and a capacity of espousals to Christ: "Wherefore, my brethren, ye also are become dead to the law by the body of Christ; that ye should be married to another, even to him who is raised from the dead." Verse 4. A slave to another is not capable of being disposed of in marriage until made free: you were in bondage to the law—the slaves of sin and Satan; Christ bought your liberty, for his blood is called a ransom, Matt. 20 : 28, and so put you into a capacity of being espoused to himself. Here you see Christ loved you not for any advantage he could receive from you, for you had nothing to bring him; nay, he must purchase you, and that with his own blood, before he could be united to you. O incomparable love; O fervent desires!

(2.) Another design of the death of Christ was to gain our hearts and affections to himself by *the arguments of his death;* this he himself has declared to be the intention of it: " I, if I be lifted up from the earth, will draw all men unto me. This he said, signifying what death he should die." John 12 : 32, 33. Christ endured all that you have heard, and infinitely more than the tongue or pen of man can express; and all to draw thy soul, and win thy consent to come unto him.

The Lord Jesus, by his sufferings, casts a threefold cord over the souls of sinners to draw them to himself.

The death of Christ *obtains complete righteousness for guilty sinners;* and if any thing will draw the heart of a sinner to Christ, this will. The anxious search and inquiry of a convinced sinner is after a perfect righteousness to justify him before God. This is what the sinner wants; conscience says, Thou hast broken all the laws of God, and art therefore condemned : the law sentences thee to hell. Now what would a poor sinner give for a release from this sentence of the law? O, ten thousand worlds for a pardon! Why, here it is, saith Christ; come unto me, and thou shalt receive a free, full, and final pardon; my blood cleanseth from all sin, my righteousness answers all the demands of the law. I have taken away the handwriting that was against thee, and nailed it to my cross. Col. 2 : 14. Come unto me, and take up thy cancelled bonds; come unto me, and divine justice shall never fright thy conscience more; nay, thou shalt build thy hope upon it. You read that God hath set forth Christ " to be a propitiation through faith in his blood, to declare his righteousness for the remission of sins that are past, through the forbearance of God; to declare, I say, at this time his righteousness; that he might be just, and the justifier of him which believeth in Jesus." Rom. 3:25, 26. Here you see the justification and pardon of a sinner built upon that very attribute which was so dreadful to him before. Well then, sinner, is there guilt upon thy conscience, and does thy soul shake and quiver to think how it shall stand before the just and terrible God in the great day? Hearken to the voice of Christ crucified, who calls thee to receive thy discharge; which if thou refuse, the law still stands in its full force against thy soul. This is one cord Christ casts from the cross over the souls of guilty sinners, to draw them to him.

The death of Christ *procures perfect cleansing from the pollution of sin, and washes the souls of sinners from all their uncleanness.* For, "this is he that came by water and blood, even Jesus Christ; not by water only, but by water and blood." 1 John, 5:6. He comes by sanctification, as well as by justification. Lord, saith the convinced sinner, what an unclean nature, heart, and life have I? Oh, I am nothing but uncleanness, an abhorrence to God and myself. How shall such a heart as mine be cleansed? Come unto me, saith Christ; I came by water as well as blood; in me thou shalt find a fountain for sanctification as well as justification: come unto me, my Spirit shall cleanse thy heart; he shall take away the pollutions of sin, so that it shall be presented to God without spot.

The transcendent love of Christ shines out in its full strength upon the souls of sinners from the cross; and there is nothing like love to attract love. When Christ was lifted up upon the cross, he gave such a glorious demonstration of the strength of his love to sinners, as one would think should draw love from the hardest heart that ever lodged in a sinner's breast. "Herein is love, not that we loved God, but that he loved us, and sent his Son to be the propitiation for our sins." 1 John, 4:10. Here is the triumph, the riches and glory of divine love; never was such love manifested in the world. There is much of God's love in temporal providences, but all is as nothing to this; this is love in its highest elevation, its meridian glory; before it was none like it, and after it shall none appear like it. Thus you see Christ casting forth from the cross a threefold cord, which is not easily broken, to draw the hearts of sinners to him.

IV. What a mighty demonstration of the desire of his heart towards us, did our Redeemer give AT HIS ASCENSION INTO HEAVEN. As the whole life of Christ upon earth was a persuasive argument to draw sinners to him, so his ascension to heaven has many mighty attractives for the hearts of men. I will only mention two.

1. *The gifts he bestowed on men at his ascension, for this very purpose;* whereof the Psalmist gives this account: "Thou hast ascended on high, thou hast led captivity captive: thou hast received gifts for men; yea, for the rebellious also, that the Lord God might dwell among them." Psalm 68:18. He alludes to the Roman conquerors, who in the day of their triumph, scattered their gifts among the people. Thus Christ at his ascension shed forth the gifts of the Spirit in various kinds, qualifying men for the work of the ministry, to enable them to plead with your souls and carry on his suit when he should be in heaven. These gifts were extraordinary in the first age, as the gifts of tongues and miracles; and ordinary, to continue to the end of the world. Eph. 4:8, 13. To some he gives depth of learning and judgment, to others pathos, a melting influence upon the affections; but all are designed to win your hearts to Christ. This shows what care he took, and what provision he made for the success of his great design to draw the hearts of sinners to him.

2. *The ends of his ascension,* as they are declared in Scripture, plainly show the vehemency of Christ's desire to draw souls to him. The declared ends of his ascension were,

(1.) To make way for the *Spirit's coming* to convince, convert, and comfort all that come unto him: "Nevertheless I tell you the truth; it is expedient for you that I go away; for if I go not away, the Comforter will not come unto you; but if I depart, I will send him unto you. And when he is come, he will reprove the world of sin, and of righteousness, and of judgment." John 16:7, 8. Without the conviction of these things, no man can come to Christ; and no such convictions can be wrought upon the conscience of any man, without the Spirit; and the Spirit could not have come to effect these things upon men's hearts, if Christ had not ascended: "But this spake he of the Spirit, which they that believe on him should receive, for the Holy Ghost was not yet given, because that Jesus was not yet glorified." John 7:39. Thus Christ provided for carrying on his great design upon your hearts when he was entering into his own glory: the thoughts of that glory made him not to forget his great design upon earth.

(2.) Another end of Christ's ascension was, to make *intercession* with the Father for every soul that should come unto him; that their future sins might make no breach of the covenant between God and them: a privilege that should draw the hearts of all sinners to him. "My little children, these things I write unto you that ye sin not." Mark it, the intercession of Christ must encourage no man to sin; that would be a vile abuse of the grace of God. But "if any man sin, we have an Advocate with the Father, Jesus Christ the righteous: and he is the propitiation for our sins." 1 John, 2:1, 2. That is, if sin surprise and deceive a regenerate soul, the bent of whose heart is against it, let him not be discouraged; he has a potent Advocate ascended into the heavens, to continue the peace between God and that soul. O what an encouragement is here to gain the consent of a sinner's heart to embrace Jesus Christ.

(3.) Another declared end of Christ's ascension was, to lead *captivity captive*, as in the forecited place, Psalm 68 : 18; that is, to lead captive and triumph over Satan as a conquered enemy, who lead us captive in the days of our vanity. He conquered Satan upon the cross, Col. 2 : 15, and he triumphed over him at his ascension; and without such a conquest and triumph no soul could come to Christ.

(4.) In a word, Christ ascended into heaven to prepare *mansions* of rest and glory for every soul that should embrace him by repentance and faith in this world. "In my Father's house are many mansions: if it were not so, I would have told you. I go to prepare a place for you." John 14 : 2. As if he had said, It satisfies me not to enjoy my glory in heaven alone; all that come unto me by faith, shall be with me where I am; let them know, for their encouragement, that the glory which God hath given me, I have given them. John 17 : 22. All these things loudly speak the fervent desire of Christ's soul after union and communion with sinners; which was the thing to be demonstrated.

Having proved the point that Christ is an earnest suitor for union and communion with the souls of sinners, we next come to show THE MARVELLOUS GRACE AND CONDESCENSION OF CHRIST that it should be so. And this will appear five ways, to the astonishment of every considering soul.

1. Though Christ be thus intent and earnest in his suit for your consent, *yet he gains nothing by you when you do consent;* the gain is to yourselves, and not to him : He "is over all, God blessed for ever," Rom. 9 : 5—above all accessions from the creature. What does the sun gain by enlightening and animating the world? Or what does a fountain gain when men drink and are refreshed by its waters? If any soul that hears me this day should resolve henceforth to break asunder all the ties and engagements between him and sin—to subscribe the articles of the gospel—to give away

himself, soul and body, to Christ—to live henceforth as a dedicated servant to the Lord Jesus—this would turn to the infinite and everlasting advantage of such a soul; but Christ cannot be profited thereby.

2. And that which still increases the wonder is, that though Christ make no profit by our conversion, *yet has he impoverished himself to gain such unprofitable creatures as we are to him.* He hath made himself poor to make us rich; so speaks the apostle: "For ye know the grace of our Lord Jesus Christ, that though he was rich, yet for your sakes he became poor, that ye through his poverty might be rich." 2 Cor. 8:9. He expends his riches, but gains no advantage to himself. His incarnation impoverished his reputation. Phil. 2:7. How poor was Christ when he said, "But I am a worm, and no man; a reproach of men, and despised of the people." Psalm 22:6. How poor in temporal comforts, when he said, "The foxes have holes, and the birds of the air have nests; but the Son of man hath not where to lay his head." Matt. 8:20. Yea, how poor was he in spiritual comforts, when that astonishing cry broke from him upon the cross, "My God, my God, why hast thou forsaken me?" Matt. 27:46. O let it astonish us, that Christ should earnestly desire union with our souls upon terms of such deep self-denial to himself.

3. Though Christ gain nothing by you, and impoverished himself for you, yet he *endures many vile repulses, delays, and denials of his suit, and yet will not leave you.* O astonishing grace! One would think that the least delay, and much more a refusal of an overture from Christ, upon such terms as these, would make his indignation quickly rise against such a soul; and that he would say, Thou hast refused my offer, so full of self-denying and condescending grace, and never shall another offer be made to so unworthy a soul. Yet you see he is contented to wait as well as knock: "Behold, I stand at the door and knock."

4. Herein the admirable grace of this heavenly suitor appears, that *Jesus Christ passes by millions of creatures of more excellent gifts*, and never makes them one offer of himself, never turns aside to give one knock at their door; but comes to thee, the vilest of creatures, and will not go from thy door without being heard. Knowest thou not, sinner, that among the unsanctified there are multitudes of men and women of more excellent parts, strong memories, and solid judgments—yea, of purer conversation, strict morality, adorned with excellent social virtues, capable, if called, to do him abundantly more service than thou canst? yet these are passed by, and he becomes a suitor to such a poor worthless thing as thou art, yea, and rejoices in his choice. "I thank thee, O Father, Lord of heaven and earth, because thou hast hid these things from the wise and prudent, and hast revealed them unto babes." Matt. 11 : 25. Here is the triumph of free-grace.

5. This increases the wonder, *that Jesus Christ should desire and delight to dwell in such an unclean heart as thine*, which, from the beginning, has been the seat and throne of Satan, full of all uncleanness and abominations. O that Christ should make an overture of love to such a polluted soul—that he should choose to erect his throne where Satan's seat was! Look into thine own heart, sinner, and think what can Christ see there to be desired? Thou knowest thy heart has been a sink of sin, thy conscience like a sewer, into which all the filth of thy life has been cast; yet Christ passes by thee, as thou liest in thy blood and filthiness, and casts his love upon thee and his desire towards thee. Ezek. 16 : 6, 8. All these things make it astonishing in our eyes that Jesus Christ, the Lord from heaven, should become an earnest suitor for union and communion with the souls of sinners.

INFERENCE 1. If Christ is such an earnest suitor for union and communion with the souls of sinners, it follows, *that sinners can justly charge their damnation upon none but themselves.* Your blood must be upon your own heads; salvation by Christ is not only freely offered, but you are with great importunity persuaded to accept it. Christ offers you life, and you choose rather to die than accept it upon his terms; where now can your ruin be charged but upon your own wilful obstinacy? "O Israel, thou hast destroyed thyself." Hosea 13:9. Thou art the author of thine own ruin; I would have gathered thy children, said Christ to Jerusalem, but thou wouldest not; your ruin, therefore, lies upon yourselves, and upon none besides. Indeed, if the ministers of Christ are negligent in their duty, they may be accessories to your destruction; but that is poor relief to you. As for myself, I hope I may, with Paul, take God to record this day, that "I am pure from the blood of all men." Acts 10:26. Now, consider what a dismal aggravation of your destruction will this be, that you perished by your own hands: this cuts off all plea and apology.

2. Hence it also follows, *that distressed sinners have no reason to question Christ's willingness to receive them when their hearts are made willing to come unto him.* It would be little less than a blasphemous imputation of insincerity to Christ himself, to question his willingness to receive broken-hearted sinners, after so many protestations as he has made in the gospel, of his earnestness for their salvation; that scripture, John 6:37, puts it out of doubt: "Him that cometh to me I will in no wise cast out." I know guilt breeds many fears and jealousies in the hearts of sinners; will Christ ever accept and receive such a one as I? Try him, he has said he will: let him have but the deliberate consent of thy heart to his terms, and then, if thou art rejected, thou wilt be the first soul that ever met a repulse from him.

3. *By Christ's earnest suit for the souls of sinners, you may see the inestimable worth of the soul of man.* Were

not the soul of man of great value, Jesus Christ would never be so deeply concerned about winning and saving it. Sinners have a low esteem of their own souls—they will sell them for naught; but Christ knows their true worth, and his solicitude to save them is answerable to his estimation of them; he counts when he has gained a soul, that he has gained a treasure. Therefore he pleads and waits so earnestly for the salvation of them. Two things speak the great value of the soul of man.

(1.) *That it is now capable of espousals to the Son of God;* upon which account it is that Christ so earnestly seeks its love, and sues for its consent. This is a dignity beyond that of all other creatures in heaven or in earth; no angel in heaven, no other creature but the soul of man on earth, is capable of espousals to Christ. It is a dignity above that of angels, for Christ took not on him their nature, and the union of the divine and human natures is the foundation of the union between Christ and his people. Angels are members indeed of Christ's kingdom, and he is to them a head of dominion; but the honor was never conferred upon angels to be members of his body, flesh and bones, as the saints are. Eph. 5 : 30.

(2.) As the soul is capable of espousals to Christ on earth, so it is capable of *glory with Christ in heaven throughout eternity.* "Father, I will that they also whom thou hast given me, be with me where I am; that they may behold my glory which thou hast given me." John 17 : 24. The soul of man has a natural capacity of enjoying eternal blessedness which other creatures have not. And this will be the aggravation of hell-torments, that men capable of the highest happiness should, as it were, receive that capacity in vain; but that which constitutes an actual right to the everlasting enjoyment of Christ in glory, is the soul's espousals to him here by his grace. Upon these two accounts it is that Christ puts such a price upon them, courts their love so affectionately, laments their loss so pathetically, and encourages his ministers to all diligence in persuading and wooing them for him with such abundant rewards. Dan. 12 : 3. Know then your own worth and dignity; neither pawn nor sell so precious a thing as thy soul for any thing Satan can set before thee by way of exchange for it. "What shall a man give in exchange for his soul!" Mark 8 : 37.

4. Is Christ such an earnest suitor for union with sinners? *then certainly, they are the enemies of Christ and the souls of men, who any way endeavor to hinder or break off the union between Christ and them.*

Some there are who labor to create jealousies and prejudices in the souls of men against Christ and his ways—men that bring up an evil report of Christ and religion, as that which will expose them to all the miseries of the world. Instigated by Satan, they whisper into the soul's ear, whom Christ is wooing for himself, that the severity of religion will certainly extinguish all their joys and pleasures; they shall never laugh more, never be merry any more; besides, it will expose all their comforts upon earth to hazard, their estates and lives must fall a prey to their enemies, and this suffering is the estate with which Christ will endow them if they consent to his terms. And that this is no groundless jealousy of their own, but that Christ himself has openly declared as much : "He that loveth father or mother more than me, is not worthy of me ; and he that loveth son or daughter more than me, is not worthy of me. And he that taketh not his cross, and followeth after me, is not worthy of me." Matt. 10 : 37, 38. This is what they must expect as the fruit of their consent to Christ's proposals. But O, what will these men have to answer, and how will they stand before Christ another day, who are such professed enemies to his cross, and set themselves so directly in opposition to the great designs of Christ ! Is it not enough that you will not enter yourselves, but you will hinder them that would? Matt. 23 : 13. Thus ungodly parents discourage their children, and one relative another. But, to help souls under this discouragement, I will leave only this one caution with them, that such seeming friends are real enemies, their words are poison to your souls. Satan has employed them to do his work, and hired their tongues for his service. But if the serious care of salvation, and fervent love of Christ be in thy heart, thou wilt resolve, as Jerome did, "If my father and my mother should hang about my neck with tears and entreaties to keep me from Christ, I would fling off my father and my mother, to go to Christ."

To this head also belong all those scandals and offences which loose and careless professors cast in the way to discourage others from coming unto Christ: "Woe unto the world because of offences." Matt. 18 : 7. Woe to the world, this will be their ruin; for by this means such prejudices will be begotten in their souls against Christ and religion, as they will never be able to free themselves from. "Whoso shall offend one of these little ones which believe in me, it were better for him that a millstone were hanged about his neck, and that he were drowned in the depth of the sea." Matt. 18 : 6. Christians, look carefully to your conversation; for besides the evil effects of sin upon yourselves, you see the mischievous effects of it upon others. And thus we may understand those words, "I charge you, O ye daughters of Jerusalem, by the roes and by the hinds of the field, that ye stir not up nor awake my love till he please." Sol. Song 2 : 7. Roes and hinds are timid creatures, the least noise will startle and fright them away: such are those who are coming to Christ; young beginners in the ways of religion, how small a matter may discourage them. O friend, you have sins enough of your own; bring not the sin and ruin of other men upon you also.

5. *How great is the blindness and ignorance of sinners, who need so much entreaty and importunity to be made happy!* It is your ignorance, sinners, that makes all

the gospel importunity necessary; did you know your own misery, and see Christ as to his necessity, suitableness, and excellency, all these persuasions might be spared; nay, you yourselves would become importunate suitors for Christ. He would not need to be twice offered: there is a conscience in every man, set there on purpose by the Lord to give each an alarm; but the alarm is not heard for want of the knowledge of your sin and misery. Ah, soul, didst thou but know who it is that sues for thy love, and what the benefits of union with Christ are, thou wouldst answer his first call in such language as this: Lord Jesus, write down thine own terms; be they what they will, I am ready to subscribe them with the full consent of my heart and will. And then, how soon would the union be made between Christ and you. Yea, you would watch for and hang on half a word of encouragement from Christ's mouth, as Benhadad's servant did on that word of Ahab, "my brother" Benhadad. 1 Kings, 20: 32, 33. There is no need of rhetoric to persuade a condemned malefactor to accept his pardon, or a hungry man to sit down at a full table; but, alas, sin is not felt, Christ is not known; and therefore the one is not bewailed, nor the other desired.

This doctrine also naturally leads us to PERSUADE sinners to embrace Christ's offer, subscribe to his terms, and debate no more with him, but end the treaty in a cordial present consent; and so close the union between him and their souls. How long, sinner, wilt thou halt, and thy will hang undetermined between Christ and sin, and unresolved in so great and deep a concern? O that Christ's overture may bring the matter to an issue. Why will you trifle and dally with him at this rate? There is, indeed, a treaty on foot between Christ and you; but you may perish for all that; there is no conclusion or agreement made; Christ and you may yet part. The Lord help you, therefore, to consider with all seriousness the terms propounded by Christ in the gospel; to count the cost—not to be always deliberating, but to bring matters to an issue, and that with all convenient speed : in order whereunto I will lay two things before you. Ponder well what are the advantages you will gain by Christ, and what is the most you can lose by your consent to his terms; and then bring your thoughts to an issue.

6. *Ponder well the advantages* you will gain by Christ : these are so great and manifold, that it is impossible for me to enumerate or estimate them. It shall suffice in this place to show you one of those bunches of the grapes of Eshcol, that by it you may estimate the riches and fertility of the good land settled upon you by Christ as a dowry; and these are four.

(1.) The same day and hour you give your cordial consent to take Christ upon gospel-terms, that is to say, Christ with his yoke of obedience, and Christ with his cross of sufferings, *all your debts to the law are discharged and paid*. What have you been doing ever since you came into the world, but running into debt to God, deeper and deeper every day? What a vast sum owest thou to his justice! and thou art not able to pay one farthing. If thou consent not to Christ's offer, the bailiff and executioner, death and Satan, will shortly be upon thee, and hurry thee away to that prison from whence thou shalt not come until thou hast paid the last farthing. Matt. 5 : 25, 26. If thou consent to Christ's terms, thy debts are paid upon thy marriage-day, thy bonds are cancelled, and thy discharge in heaven is sealed : "There is therefore now no condemnation to them which are in Christ," Rom. 8 : 1 ; and the reason is given, The righteousness of the law is fulfilled in us that believe. Ver. 4. But how in us? Certainly the meaning is not that the act of faith doth, as a work of ours, satisfy the demands of the law and fulfil its righteousness ; but it apprehends the righteousness of Christ, applies it and makes it ours, and so "the righteousness of the law is fulfilled in us that believe." Is it an ease and a comfort to be out of debt? Then embrace the offer of Christ; for after thy espousals to him, the law cannot touch thee by an act of condemnation: it goes to the husband, Christ; thou art discharged. Then resolve what to do: shall the debt run on and increase till justice come to exact it upon you in hell-torments? Or will you accept of Christ and the riches of righteousness in him, and so be fully and finally acquitted from all your debts at once, and able to lie down in peace and enjoy your life without fear?

(2.) Your consent to Christ's terms, *will advance you to an honor above and beyond that of angels.* It is said that the children of the resurrection shall be equal to angels. Matt. 22 : 30. And it is most sure, that in some respects their union with Christ advances them far above angels; for the apostle tells us, they are ministering spirits, sent forth to minister to them that shall be heirs of salvation, Heb. 1 : 14; as the nobles in a kingdom count it no dishonor to perform their service to the heir apparent. The ministry of angels is a mystery which we little understand; but by it we receive great and manifold advantages, and it certainly puts great honor on all the members of Christ.

(3.) Christ will not only pay all your debts and exalt you to a dignity above angels, but in the day wherein you cordially consent to his terms, *he will entitle you to the most glorious inheritance purchased by his blood.* You shall be "heirs of God, and joint heirs with Christ." Rom. 8 : 17. O what an inducement is here to close the union between Christ and our souls. If I consent to take Christ upon gospel-terms, I shall be entitled to all the glory in heaven; it shall be mine as truly as it is Christ's. It is true the glory of Christ will far surpass the glory of the saints; he will shine among them as the sun compared with the stars; but the glory which God gave him, that is, the communicable glory, shall be as truly theirs, as it is his. "The glory which thou gavest me, I have given them." John 17 : 22. Tell my brethren, saith he, John 20 : 17, "I ascend unto my Father and your Father, and to my God and your God." This you shall gain by closing this treaty with a hearty consent to Christ's terms and proposals.

(4.) If you will consider and consent, *you shall be presented by Christ to the Father, pure and spotless, with exceeding joy and gladness in the great day.* This will be a presentation of your persons to God that should make your hearts leap for joy as you read what the Scriptures speak about it. This, methinks, should induce every soul without further delay to present himself, soul and body, willingly and cheerfully to Jesus Christ. For, first, Christ will bring you in the great day to his Father, in the beauty of perfect holiness, not a spot or wrinkle upon your souls. Eph. 5 : 27. The blood of Christ perfectly washes away every spot of guilt. Then the Spirit of Christ shall have perfectly cleansed the soul from all the defilement of sin; so that it shall come to God pure and beautiful out of Christ's hand. Second, This presentation will be made with the greatest honor and solemnity. We little think in what triumph Christ intends to bring the poorest believer to his Father. "With gladness and rejoicing shall they be brought: they shall enter into the king's palace." Psalm 45 : 15. They shall be presented "faultless before the presence of his glory, with exceeding joy." Jude 24. Joy running over joy, upon all hands: God himself will rejoice that he created a soul that has sincerely bestowed itself upon Christ; Jesus Christ will rejoice that he shed his blood for the soul that places his sole righteousness therein; the Holy Spirit will rejoice that he came with a commission from the Father and the Son to draw such a soul to Christ, who has obeyed his voice. The angels will rejoice with joy unspeakable. "There is joy in the presence of the angels of God over one sinner that repenteth." Luke 15 : 10. If the consent of any of your souls shall be this day gained to Christ—if the word you have heard shall send any poor soul hence to his closet there to make his covenant with Christ, for that is the way of making the union with Christ—in that hour the news of it will be in heaven and excite joy among the angels of God. Lay these and many other privileges together, which the Scriptures will abundantly furnish you, and then consider what a rich bargain Jesus Christ confers on your souls.

7. Again, on the other hand, consider *what you may lose* by your consent to be Christ's, and whether these losses are sufficient to balance the gain of such a consent, that so your choice of Christ may be deliberate and full, and you may never repent of the choice you have made. It is a rule in the civil law, *Non consentit qui non sentit*—he cannot consent that does not think, understand, and deliberate; and this is the reason of so much flinching from Christ and shameful apostasy in times of persecution: men did not think of such sufferings and losses, they are matters of surprise to them. To prevent all such occasions of offence, our Lord deals candidly and openly with us, and tells us beforehand what are the worst things that may befall us for his sake. "These things have I spoken unto you, that you should not be offended. They shall put you out of the synagogues; yea, the time cometh, that whosoever killeth you will think he doeth God service." John 16:1, 2. But he adds, "These things have I told you that, when the time shall come, ye may remember that I told you of them." Ver. 4. Remember, in times of persecution, that all these things were propounded and consented to; they were the very terms you subscribed to me; had you not liked them, you might, at the everlasting ruin of your immortal souls, have refused and rejected them. The things you are to balance with the gain of Christ may be divided into two classes.

(1.) The things that you *must* part with, namely, *your lusts and all the vicious pleasures you have had in them.*

However much profit or pleasure they have brought you, away they must go; they must be devoted to destruction and mortification, or you can have no interest in Christ; you must bid adieu for ever to all your sinful courses and companions. "His servants ye are to whom ye obey." Rom. 5:16. Be they as pleasant and profitable as your right eye or hand, they must be plucked out and cut off. Matt. 6:29, 30. Does this sound harsh and unpleasant to your ears? Does this cause you to demur? O consider what it is to part with sin; it is but to part with the disease of your souls, and the instruments of your everlasting ruin. Which of you would not be glad to part with a fever, the stone, or dropsy? What is passion, but the fever of the soul? What is a hard heart, but a stone? What is covetousness or earthly-mindedness, but the insatiable dropsy of the soul? Now, if men would be glad to be rid of such dreadful diseases in their bodies, and to be restored to soundness, ease, and health; how much more should you be glad to be rid of your corruptions, and have the rectitude, ease, and pleasure of your souls restored again? yea, instead of the impure, vicious pleasures you have taken in sin, you shall enjoy the pure, suitable, and everlasting pleasures of holiness. Consider now, and accordingly make your choice, whether you will take the pleasures of sin, which are but for a season, in exchange for the everlasting joys which are at God's right hand for ever.

(2.) There are other things which you *may* be called to part with, and give up for Christ. It is uncertain whether *God may call you to part with your liberty, estate, relations, and life for Christ.* Many are never actually called forth to such sufferings; but because many are, and every one of you may be so called, you must realize them, ponder them, and subscribe to those very terms, making full account of these things as if they were now before you, for so Christ hath propounded them. Luke 9:23. But then weigh these troubles with the advantages you shall have by them, and not alone by themselves; for so Christ has presented them to you. "And every one that hath forsaken houses, or brethren, or sisters, or father, or mother, or wife, or children, or lands, for my name's sake, shall receive a hundred-fold, and shall inherit everlasting life." Matt. 19:29.

Now, if you think such gainful troubles, such soul-enriching losses are worth accepting for Christ's sake, then close the union with Christ and bring the matter to a conclusion. Do not befool yourselves by a fond and groundless presumption that these things will never befall you. I fear many flatter themselves with such vain hopes; the Lord knows how soon these suppositions at a distance may be turned into realities before your eyes. You have much reason to expect them, and much more to embrace them, whenever Christ shall call you to them. This is the great work you have now to do, and you cannot safely demur any longer; this matter must come to a conclusion, and the sooner the better. For,

You know that *your lives* are uncertain, and it is madness to let the great concerns of your salvation lie one day at hazard; your breath is continually coming and going, and must at last be gone. James 4:14. Your souls hang over everlasting dangers by that feeble breath which plays in your nostrils, and every disease is like the flame of a candle held under that thread; and can it either be safe or comfortable to delay so great a work as this, upon which all your expectations of eternal blessedness depend?

Not only your lives are uncertain, but *the enjoyment of the gospel*, and all the opportunities and means of your conversion, are as uncertain as they. It is true, and to the glory of God be it acknowledged, we now enjoy the freedom and fulness of gospel-mercies; but where has God made any such settlement of these blessings upon you, as puts the enjoyment of them out of hazard? The rain is over, but the clouds may return after the rain. If your privileges bring forth good fruit in your conversion, well; if not, the axe lieth at the root of the tree. Matt. 3:10. And if God remove the gospel from us, as our delays and triflings may provoke him to do, then the treaty is ended, and there is little probability that any thing further will be done between Christ and you. Luke 13:25.

Bring this matter to an issue with all due speed, because you are not able to give *one sound reason for a moment's delay* of so great and weighty a concern. Can you be safe too soon? Can you be happy too soon? Certainly you cannot be out of the danger of hell too soon; and therefore why should not your closing with Christ upon his own terms be your very next work? If the main work and business of every man's life be to flee from the wrath to come, as indeed it is, Matt. 3:7, and to flee for refuge to Jesus Christ, as indeed it is, Heb. 6:18, then all delays are highly dangerous. The man-slayer, when fleeing to the city of refuge before the avenger of blood, when his heart was hot within him, did not think he could reach the city too soon. Set your reason to work upon this matter; put the case as really it is: I am fleeing from wrath to come; the justice of God and the curses of the law are closely pursuing me; is it reasonable that I should sit down in the way to gather flowers, or play with trifles? for such are all other concerns in this world, compared with our salvation.

Bring this treaty to an issue with all due speed, because *most souls that perish, perish by delays;* men think they have time enough before them and that to-morrow will be as to-day, and so Satan gets, part by part, what he had not confidence to demand in the whole lump. Most that perish under the gospel had convictions upon their consciences, and vain purposes in their hearts; but not bringing them to a speedy execution, that was their undoing. "He beholdeth himself, and goeth his way, and straightway forgetteth what manner of man he was." James 1 : 24. It is an allusion to a man that looks in the morning into a glass, where he discerns a spot upon his face, and resolves with himself soon to wash it off; but some diversion or other falls in, other matters take up his thoughts, and so the spot remains all day and he carries it to bed at night. O these delays in closing with Christ are the undoing of millions.

Delay not to close this treaty with Christ, because *all delay increases the difficulty;* and the longer you neglect, the more will your hearts "be hardened by the deceitfulness of sin." Heb. 3 : 13. Continuance in sin and quenching convictions insensibly harden the heart and make the will stubborn. Under the first convictions the heart is tender, the affections flowing; if this advantage were apprehended and pursued, how soon might the work come to a comfortable conclusion; but after a while, those soul-affecting words, sin, Christ, heaven, hell, death, and eternity, will become words of a common sound.

And lastly, beware of delays in this matter, because you *can never expect a fairer opportunity* for the dispatch of this great concern than, by the special indulgence of Heaven, you enjoy this day. "Now is the accepted time; behold, now is the day of salvation." 2 Cor. 6 : 2. You have the wind and tide with you; if you will not weigh anchor now, you may lie wind-bound to your dying day. What advantage can you reasonably expect, which God has not furnished you with at this day? You have the means of grace among you, and you have freedom to attend on those means without fear. Say not, I have such or such troubles and encumbrances in the world; for you must never expect to be without them, except you shall find the world another thing than all others find it. Have you health? O what a precious season and advantage is that. Art thou sick? O what a spur is that. What is to be done must be done quickly.

But it may be some will plead ignorance, that they know not how to transact so great a concern with Christ, and therefore set not about it; and it is likely there may be truth in that plea. For the help of such souls, I will gather up the sum of what has been spoken about this matter, in the following DIRECTIONS; so that nothing but your unwillingness shall remain to hinder you.

DIRECTION 1. If ever you bring the treaty between Christ and your souls to a happy conclusion, you must *sit down and count the cost,* Luke 14 : 28, else it will be vain to engage yourselves in the profession of religion. It is not Christ's design to draw you under a rash, inconsiderate engagement, and so to reap more dishonor by your apostasy than ever he shall have glory by your profession. He would have you foresee and seriously bethink yourselves of all the troubles and inconveniences you may afterwards meet with for his sake. You are to embark yourselves with Christ, and abide with him in storms as well as in sunshine; you must "follow the Lamb whithersoever he goeth." Rev. 14 : 4. There is no retreating after engagement to Christ: "If any man draw back, my soul shall have no pleasure in him." Heb. 10 : 38. It is eternal death by the law of heaven, to desert Christ's colors in the day of battle. Well, then, retire into the innermost closet of thy soul; sit quiet and patiently there, till thou hast debated this matter fully with thy own thoughts, and hast balanced the good and the evil, the profits and losses of religion. For want of this the church is filled with hypocrites, and hell with inconsiderate and rash professors: the more we deliberate, the better we shall conclude.

DIRECTION 2. Having debated the matter over and over in thy most serious thoughts, *let not Satan discourage thee from casting thy soul at Christ's feet, with a hearty consent to all his terms,* for want of such qualifications as thou canst not find in thy own soul. It is usual for Satan to suggest, at such a time, the want of greater sorrow and humiliation for sin—that the soul has not lain long enough under the humbling work of the law—that the aggravations of sin have been such that there is no hope of acceptance. Free thy soul from these snares of Satan by the consideration of the truth, that Christ expects from thee no more humiliation than what produces such a hearty, deliberate consent as thy will is now to give; and such a consent once gained, no aggravation of sin can be pleaded against the duty of believing.

DIRECTION 3. *Distrust not the sincerity of Christ in the gracious offers he makes to coming souls.* Be sure that he speaks his very heart in them to thee; the devil labors to sow jealousy and suspicions in the hearts of convinced sinners, that they will not find such a welcome with Christ as he seems to promise them in those encouraging scriptures, Matt. 11 : 28, 29; John 6 : 37; but that something else lies hid in such scriptures, as a mystery which they understand not, and so labors to hinder the accepting act of faith. This is a case as common as it is sad. The Lord help you to avoid this snare, lest instead of honoring Christ by resolved adherence to him, you make him a liar, and impute insincerity to the God of truth: "He that believeth not God, hath made him a liar." 1 John, 5 : 10.

DIRECTION 4. *Look up to God to enable you to come to Christ in this difficult work of faith.* Do not think faith is of the growth of thine own heart : "No man can come to me, except the Father which hath sent me draw him." John 6 : 44. There is a legal spirit working under evangelical pretences in many souls; teaching them to look within themselves to find that which is quite above them. The apostle points you to the fountain of faith, in Eph. 2 : 8 : it is "not of yourselves; it is the gift of God." If the power of God must be owned as the cause of every new degree of faith in the greatest believers, as is plain from Luke 17 : 5,

"The apostles said unto the Lord, Increase our faith;" how much more is the production of faith itself, and the first vital act thereof to be ascribed to the almighty power of God?

DIRECTION 5. *Keeping thine eye of expectation upon that almighty power, plead with the Lord importunately to exert that power upon thy soul;* and give not over thy suit till thou feel that power upon thee. The time of believing is a time of earnestly pleading thine own danger and necessity; and the Spirit of the Lord will abundantly furnish thee with pleas and arguments to enforce this suit. Such as these:

(1.) Lord, I have thy call and invitation, yea, I have thy command to encourage me to believe; it is no presumption therefore, in thy poor creature, to come after thou hast invited and commanded me: hadst thou not encouraged me, I dared not have moved towards thee. Lord, whose word is it, "that we should believe on the name of his Son Jesus Christ?" 1 John, 3 : 23. Is it not thine own? This makes my faith an act of obedience.

(2.) Yea, Lord, I have thy promise, as well as thy command, made upon no other condition but my coming to thee. Blessed Jesus, hast thou not said, "Him that cometh unto me I will in no wise cast out?" John 6 : 37. An invitation is much, but thy promise is more.

(3.) O my God, I have not only thy command, making it my duty to believe, and thy promise to encourage me to that duty, but I have the examples of other sinners who came unto thee long ago, and thou didst not reject them: nor do I abuse these examples in drawing encouragement from them; for it was thy very design, in recording them, that they might be so many patterns to all that should hereafter believe on thee. 1 Tim. 1 : 16.

(4.) O my God, I am shut up under a plain necessity; I have no other way to take; I am beaten off from all other refuges; there is no help for me in angels or in men, in duties or self-righteousness; in thee only my soul can find rest. I am shut up to thee as to the only door of hope, Gal. 3 : 23 ; here I must succeed or perish : my soul is burdened and wearied; I know not how to dispose of it, but into thy hands; nor where to lay the burden of my guilt, but upon thee. If I fail here, I am lost for ever.

(5.) Lord, I am willing to renounce all other hopes, refuges, and righteousness, and to rely upon thee only. Duties cannot justify me, tears cannot wash me, reformation cannot save me; nothing but thy righteousness can answer for me. I come to thee a poor naked creature, saying as they of old, "Asshur shall not save us; we will not ride upon horses : neither will we say any more to the work of our hands, Ye are our gods ; for in thee the fatherless findeth mercy." Hos. 14 : 3. Thus plead with God, and still remember you are pleading for life, yea, for your eternal life.

DIRECTION 6. *Labor to make a resolved adventure upon Christ, amidst all these encouragements, let the issue be what it will;* resolve to venture, though you have not the least degree of assurance that you shall be accepted and pardoned. This is that brave and noble act of faith which carries the soul to Christ: much as Esther came to the king, "So will I go in unto the king; and if I perish, I perish." Esther 4 : 16. It grieves me to think how some imagine that the fervent love of Christ will save and justify them, without any act of belief on their part; but you see that scriptural faith is very different from all this. O there are great difficulties and mighty wrestlings in the work of believing : it is a great matter for a convinced sinner, in the face of so much guilt and vileness and amidst such manifold discouragements from Satan, to cast and adventure himself upon Christ, and that upon such self-denying terms; but the pinch of necessity will bring the soul to this, for now it reasons with itself as the lepers did, If we go to the camp of the Syrians, we can but die; and if we abide here, we must certainly die. 2 Kings, 7:4. So here, if I sit still in the state of nature and continue to delay, my destruction is unavoidable—to hell I must go: and if I cast myself upon Christ, I can but be rejected. But he has said, He will not cast out those that come unto him: in this way of faith there is a possibility, yea, assurance of salvation; this therefore is my only way; to him I will go, and if I perish, I perish.

DIRECTION 7. *Never measure the grace of God, nor the mercy of Christ, by your own narrow apprehensions of him;* but believe them to be far greater than your contracted understanding represents them to you. Our idea of the pardoning power and mercy of God, cast in the mould of our own thoughts, disfigures and alters them, so that they look not like themselves, but with a very discouraging aspect upon our souls. By this, Satan keeps off many souls from coming to Christ. The Lord knows how to forgive thee, though thou scarcely knowest how to forgive thyself, for the injuries thou hast done against him. That is a striking scripture to this purpose, in Isa. 55:7-9: "Let the wicked forsake his way, and the unrighteous man his thoughts; and let him return unto the Lord, and he will have mercy upon him; and to our God, for he will abundantly pardon. For my thoughts are not your thoughts, neither are your ways my ways, saith the Lord. For as the heavens are higher than the earth, so are my ways higher than your ways, and my thoughts than your thoughts." Man lies under a double misery, one by reason of affliction, another by reason of transgression; concerning both these, God's thoughts are not as ours, but far above what we can think. We cannot think such thoughts in respect to others, under misery in themselves or under transgression against us, as God does towards us; nor can we conceive what those thoughts of God are towards us, when we are under misery or sin, as he thinks them. His thoughts will still be above ours, as the heavens are above the earth. So high is heaven that the vast body of the whole earth is but a small, inconsiderable point to it; the highest cedars, mountains, clouds cannot reach it. God's thoughts are infinite, ours finite; his thoughts are continued, ours interrupted and at a stand; his are immutable, ours changeable; his are intuitive, ours discursive: therefore never measure his by your own. The thoughts of pardoning grace in him, are rich, plenteous, and glorious; but when our unbelieving hearts practise upon them, they seem quite another thing. Thou sayest, How can such a wretch as I obtain mercy? Thou knowest not, but the Lord knoweth. O if you could take in such a proper idea and apprehension of the mercy and goodness of God, as he has given of them himself, when he passed by Moses and proclaimed himself, " The Lord, the Lord God, merciful and gracious, long suffering, and abundant in goodness and truth; keeping mercy for thousands, forgiving iniquity and transgression and sin," Exod. 34 : 6, 7, this would bring you to Christ with much encouragement.

DIRECTION 8. *Be not discouraged in the work of faith, though no comfort should come in by the first act of it;* nay, though there should be an increase of trouble for the present. The first saving act of faith certainly puts you into a state of peace, but it may not presently produce the sense of peace; after you have believed and really closed with Christ, you may meet with some discouragements which may make you question whether Christ has received you or no—whether he has any love for your souls or no? Yet persevere, whether comfort come or not; though Christ and safety are inseparable, yet Christ and the sense of comfort are not so: think not that all your troubles shall be over as soon as you believe, because it is said, " We which have believed do enter into rest." Heb. 4 : 3. That scripture speaks of a state of rest, and not of a present or continued sense of rest.

The woman of Canaan did really believe in Christ, yet met with sore trials under the first act of her faith; yet this took her not off from the work of faith, but rather quickened her the more; she was glad of a word from Christ, and she expected deeds. The words were discouraging: "It is not meet to take the children's bread, and to cast it to dogs;" yet this beats not off her faith: the dog belongs to the family, and crumbs to the dog. "O woman," saith Christ, "great is thy faith." Matt. 15: 26, 27. If you resolve for Christ, you must not be discouraged; a resolute faith overcomes all difficulties. You pray, you believe, and yet have no comfort; well, the vision of peace is for an appointed time; at the end it will speak, and not lie.

DIRECTION 9. *In your treating with Christ, beware of all secret reserves that will spoil the treaty between Christ and you.* "If I regard iniquity in my heart, the Lord will not hear me." Psa. 66: 18. If there be but a reserve of one lust, that reserve will break off the treaty: be honest with Christ, and say not of any sin, "the Lord be merciful to me in this;" and be sure there is no secret purpose or reserve in thy heart for a retreat in time of danger; but embark thyself with Christ for storms and tempests, troubles and afflictions, as well as peace and prosperity. Christ bestows himself wholly upon you, and he expects the same from you: give up all, or you will receive nothing from him.

DIRECTION 10. *Close up your treaty with Christ by a solemn covenant with him;* engage yourselves to be the Lord's. "One shall say, I am the Lord's; and another shall call himself by the name of Jacob; and another shall subscribe with his hand unto the Lord, and surname himself by the name of Israel." Isa. 44: 5. Here you have two things to do: 1. To give yourselves up to Christ, according to that expression, they "first gave their own selves to the Lord." 2 Cor. 8: 5. Make your soul and body, time and talents, henceforth, dedicated things to his service. 2. Take Christ in both his natures and in all his offices to be yours; and to this covenant you are to stand to the last breath, whatever times or troubles shall come. This consent of thy heart to be Christ's, this choice of thy will in taking him for thine, is but the echo of Christ's choice of thee; and I would rather have such an evidence of my interest in him, than a voice from heaven to assure me that Christ is mine.

CHAPTER VII.

CHRIST REJECTS NONE WHO OPEN TO HIM.

"*IF ANY MAN* HEAR MY VOICE AND OPEN THE DOOR, I WILL COME IN TO HIM." Rev. 3: 20.

This expression, " If any man," extends the gracious offer of Christ, and brings in hope to every hearer. It is a general proclamation : " If any man ;" as if Christ should say, I will have this offer of my grace go round to every particular person ; if thou, or thou, or thou, the greatest, the vilest of sinners, of what quality or condition soever, old or young, profane or hypocritical, wilt hear my voice, and open to me, I will come in to your soul. And hereby all objections are obviated : as for example, I am the greatest of sinners, says one ; I have been a self-deceiving hypocrite, says another ; I have resisted grace too long, and fear the time of mercy is past, says a third. The ground of all these, and a thousand more objections, is taken away by the gracious extent of Christ's offer in the text ; for who is he that can limit where Christ does not ? This gives us a seventh profitable and comfortable doctrine :

Jesus Christ will not refuse to come in to the soul of the vilest sinner, when once it is made willing to open to him.

" If any man hear my voice and open the door, I will come in to him." It is not unworthiness, but unwillingness, that bars any man from Christ : thousands have missed of Christ by their unwillingness, but Christ never put off one soul on account of its unworthiness; Christ is not the sale but the gift of God ; you come not to make a bargain, but to receive a free gift : faith is marriage with Christ, wherein nothing but our hearty consent is expected ; so runs the strain of the whole Scriptures. " Ho, every one that thirsteth, come ye to the waters, and he that hath no money," that is, no merit, no worthiness of his own, " come ye." Isa. 55 : 1. Behold the free-grace of Christ to the vilest and most unworthy of sinners. So Rev. 22 : 17, " Let him that is athirst come ; and whosoever will, let him take the water of life freely." And in the very phrase of my text he speaks again. And yet again, in John 7 : 37, " If any man thirst, let him come unto me and drink." It is very observable throughout the whole gospel, that Christ never made any objection against any soul that came to him, on account of its sinfulness and unworthiness ; but all the complaints of Christ are on account of men's unwillingness. So in his complaint over Jerusalem, Luke 13 : 34, " I would, but you would not ;" so again, John 5 : 40, " Ye will not come to me, that ye might have life." The complaint is still upon their unwillingness. In stating this point, I shall show what it is to be truly willing to receive Jesus Christ ; and how it appears that they who are so, shall certainly be received and graciously accepted of him.

I. WHAT IT IS TO BE TRULY WILLING TO RECEIVE JESUS CHRIST ; for this is meant by opening the heart to him. Now this implies many great and weighty things.

1. It implies and necessarily includes *the right understanding of gospel terms.* These must be known, pondered, and duly considered, before the will can savingly open, in an act of consent, to Christ's offer. I desire this may be especially observed, because multitudes are mistaken about this thing : he that does not consider, does not consent ; you must exercise your understandings upon the terms and articles of Christianity, or else your consent is rash, blindfold, and unstable. This, in Luke 14 : 31, is called consulting ; the consent of faith is the result of previous consultations and debates in the mind : the soul that comes to Christ must take up religion in his most sedate and serious thoughts; turn both sides of it, the dark as well as the bright side of religion, to the eye of his mind ; balance all the conven-

iences and inconveniences, losses as well as gains. If I open to Christ, this I shall gain, but that I must lose; I cannot separate Christ from sufferings: Christ will separate me from my sins; if I seek him, I must let them go; if I profess Christ, Providence will one time or other bring me to this dilemma, either Christ or earthly comforts must go. It is necessary, therefore, that I now propound to myself what Providence may, one time or other, propound to me. He hath set down his terms: "If any man will come after me, let him deny himself, and take up his cross and follow me." Matt. 16 : 24. This self-denial deserves serious consideration; for Christ requires that I give up my life, my liberty, my estate, my relations, and also my own righteousness, which is as hard to be parted with as any of the former. I must take up my cross, that is, the sufferings and troubles which God shall appoint for me, and which I cannot avoid without sin; and I must follow Christ whithersoever he goes. I know not what religion may cost me before I die; all this it has cost others; and there is no bringing down Christ's terms lower than he has laid them. I must come up to them, they will not come down to me: if I like them not as Christ has left them, the treaty between him and me is ended. "He that loveth father or mother more than me, is not worthy of me; and he that loveth son or daughter more than me, is not worthy of me. And he that taketh not his cross and followeth after me, is not worthy of me." Matt. 10 : 37, 38. Where, by worthiness, we are not to understand the meritoriousness of these acts, but the necessary qualification of the will, and the due preparation of one coming to Christ; these previous consultations and debates in the mind prepare the will to make a serious and well-advised choice of Christ: and for want of this, there are such swarms of hypocrites and apostates in the world.

2. It implies *such a sense of misery in us, and of the necessity and excellency of Christ, as determines the will to*

the choice of him, notwithstanding all the difficulties which have fallen or can fall under consideration in the mind. When the soul sees that in Christ which preponderates over all sufferings, all losses, and all reproaches, and then determines, I will have Christ though I sacrifice all that is dear to me in the world for him, this is to be truly willing to open to Christ. It is true, the enjoyments of this world are understood by Christians as much as other men; they have a feeling sense of the sweetness of earthly enjoyments; their souls have as much affection to the body as other men; they understand the charming language of the world and their dear relations in it, as well as others; only they see a greater necessity of Christ, and a greater worth in Christ, than they do in these things. You read that in the famine of Jerusalem they gave their pleasant things for meat to relieve their soul—jewels, bracelets, gold, silver, any thing for bread, Lam. 1:11; they understood the worth of these things, knew the cost of them, but they parted with them to preserve life. So it is here—no earthly enjoyment, of what value soever it be, has such an excellency in it, such an absolute necessity to us of enjoying it, as Christ has.

OBJECTION. But O, saith the soul, who can do this? I am willing to have Christ, and to come up to every term he has laid down in the gospel; I am willing to part with every sin, and to endure any suffering for Christ; but Oh, I tremble to think, if it should come to a prison, to a stake, to an actual separation from all the comforts and relations in the world, what shall I do for strength to go through such difficult work as this? Here is the great difficulty in the way of many souls; they find a willingness, but fear the want of strength.

ANSWER. How or where you shall find strength to endure these things for Christ, is not the question now before you. God will take care for that, and it shall be given you in that hour, and so others have found who have had the same fears you have. I say, the question is not whether you are able, but whether you are heartily willing. Christ asks but your will; he will provide ability. The greatest believer in the world cannot say, I am able to suffer this or that for Christ; but the least believer in the world must say, I am willing, the Lord assisting me, to endure and suffer all things for his sake.

3. The third thing which perfects the whole act, is *an entire choice of Jesus Christ upon all the terms prescribed by him;* the entireness of the choice, without halving or dividing, excepting or reserving, makes the consent full and effectual. There is a twofold consent of the will to Christ.

There is a *partial* consent, which is always hypocritical, defective, and ineffectual; thus the hypocrite consents to the offer of Christ. He is really willing to have the pardon of Christ, and the glory purchased by Christ; but to part with his beloved lusts, and to give up his earthly enjoyments, his will cannot consent.

There is a *full and entire consent* of the will, called, a believing with all the heart. Acts 8 : 37. Now this integrity and fulness of the will's choice, is that which closeth the union between Christ and the soul, and frees a man from the danger of hypocrisy. And there are three things which make the consent to and choice of Christ complete.

(1.) *We heartily consent to be Christ's, when we give up all we are and have to him;* so that after this choice of Christ, we look upon ourselves thenceforth as not our own, but bought with a price, to glorify God in our body and soul, which are his. 1 Cor. 6 : 19, 20. Soul and body are all that we are, and both these parts of ourselves do now pass, by an act of our own consent, into the Redeemer's right; we are not to have the disposal of them; that belongs to him who purchased them. You know that in all purchases, property is altered. You did live as your own, followed your own wills and passions, were under the dominion and at the beck of every lust; but now the case is altered. "We ourselves also were sometimes foolish, disobedient, deceived, serving divers lusts and pleasures." Tit. 3 : 3. So many lusts, so many lords. But now we have given ourselves to Christ, no more to be swayed, this way or that, against his word and the voice of our own consciences. Thus our souls and bodies are his, hallowed, dedicated to Christ, temples for God to dwell in. And then all other things follow of course: if I am the Lord's, then my time, my talents, and all that I have are his.

(2.) As you must give up all to Christ, so *you must derive and draw all you want from him;* else your choice of Christ is not entire and full. God hath stored up in Christ all that you want, a full supply for every need; and made it all communicable to you : "Who of God is made unto us wisdom and righteousness, and sanctification and redemption." 1 Cor. 1 : 30. All the believer's springs are in Christ. Have I any difficult business to do that requires counsel? then I must repair to Christ the fountain of wisdom. Am I under guilt? then I must repair to Christ for righteousness. Is my soul defiled by corruption? then must I go to Christ for sanctification. Do I groan under troubles of soul or body, temptations, or afflictions? then must I relieve myself by the faith and hope of that complete redemption and final deliverance, procured by Christ from all these. If you consent to be Christ's, you must not look for justification partly upon his righteousness and partly upon your own graces and duties, but must make mention of his righteousness, even of his only. Psalm 71 : 16. If there is but one conduit in a town, and not a drop of water to be had elsewhere, then all the inhabitants of that town repair thither for water. In the whole city of God there is but one fountain, and that is Christ; there is not one drop of righteousness, holiness, strength, or comfort, to be had elsewhere.

Then we draw all from Christ, when we live upon him, as the new-born infant doth upon the mother's breast.

(3.) Then is our consent to and choice of Christ entire and full, *when we are ready to deny ourselves and part with any thing we have for his sake;* reckoning nothing lost to us which goes to the glory of Christ. How dear soever our liberties, estates, or lives are to us, if the Lord have need of them, we must let them go. Thus you read, " They loved not their lives unto the death." Rev. 12 : 11. These three things show saving faith to be another manner of thing than the world generally understands it to be ; and it is impossible for any man's will to open to and receive Christ, upon terms of such deep self-denial as these, until there be a conviction of our sin and misery, and discovery of Christ in his glory and necessity; and the drawing power of the Spirit upon the soul.

Conviction of our sin and misery makes these terms of religion acceptable ; sinners stand debating with Christ, excepting and objecting against his terms, until the Lord has shaken them by conviction over hell, and made them see the dreadful danger they are in; and then their cry is, " Men and brethren, what shall we do?" Acts 2 : 37; prescribe any means, impose upon us the greatest difficulties ; we are willing to comply with them.

Nor will souls ever comply with these terms of the gospel, until a *discovery has been made to them of Jesus Christ in his glory and necessity.* When a man feels his wants, and sees a complete remedy, his will then complies readily and freely ; the convinced sinner sees a full and suitable supply in Christ for all his wants, a complete Saviour, in whom there is nothing defective, but in all respects according to the wants of a sinner's heart. 1 Cor. 1 : 24.

To all this must be added *the powerful drawings of the Spirit,* by which the will comes to Christ. " No man can come unto me, except the Father which hath sent me draw him." John 6 : 41. When these things are felt on the soul, it hears Christ's voice, his powerful call, which breaks asunder all the bonds between a man and his earthly enjoyments; and without these things the will is not to be persuaded to comply with the difficulties of religion.

II. We are to show HOW IT APPEARS that Jesus Christ will not refuse to come into the soul of any sinner, be his sins ever so great, when once he is made willing thus to receive Christ upon his own terms. Oh, sinner, what good tidings are these to thy soul, that Christ will not disdain to be in union and communion with thee, vile as thou art, if thy will stand open to him. The tidings are sweet, and I hope thou wilt find them as sure as they are sweet and comfortable, when thou shalt have seriously pondered the following evidences.

EVIDENCE 1. The truth of this assertion is *seen in the form and manner of gospel-invitations.* They are designedly put into large, free, and most extensive terms, to assure sinners that Christ will not reject the worst sinner in the world, thus made willing to embrace him; they are framed on purpose to anticipate or take away all objections from sinners. No other condition is put in the gospel but this only, Art thou heartily willing to take Christ upon his own terms? The offers of Christ are extended to all that desire and thirst after him, John 7 : 37, to the greatest of sinners, upon this one condition, that they be willing and obedient. Isa. 1 : 19. "Go ye into all the world, and preach the gospel to every creature. He that believeth and is baptized, shall be saved." Mark 16 : 15, 16. The invitation is extended to all nations; for in Christ Jesus "there is neither Greek nor Jew, circumcision nor uncircumcision, Barbarian, Scythian, bond nor free." Col. 3 : 11. If there is any soul of any condition whatever, under the cope of heaven, whose will is wrought to a hearty compliance with the terms of the gospel, Christ will not be unwilling to come into that soul, though it has been never so vile and abominable; the heart of Mary Magdalene, which had been a habitation of devils, and the soul of a Saul, a bloody, raging persecutor, will make as delightful habitations for Christ as the soul of the most exemplary person in the world, when once the will is thus opened.

EVIDENCE 2. The truth of this assertion further appears from the encouraging *promises made by Christ to all who are thus made willing to come unto him.* All the promises with one mouth assure the willing sinner of a welcome to Christ. Mark that glorious promise, from which so many thousand souls have drawn encouragement and help at their first coming to Christ: "All that the Father giveth me, shall come to me; and him that cometh to me I will in no wise cast out. For I came down from heaven, not to do mine own will, but the will of him that sent me." John 6 : 37, 38. Note here,

(1.) That this is not a promise made to those that are already in Christ, that they shall never be cast out by apostasy or final desertion; but a promise made to coming souls, to such as are moving towards Christ, under great discouragements, fears, and tremblings. When a sinner looks to Christ, and sees his fulness and suitableness, and his own pinching need and want of him, O, says he, that I had an interest in him, though I should beg my bread in desolate places. But looking into his own heart, and seeing so much guilt and unworthiness there, then saith he, how can I think that Jesus Christ will come into such a heart as this? These are the persons upon whom this promise casts an encouraging aspect.

(2.) And because the fears of such persons are much more than the fears that others have, Christ has put a double negative into this promise, for the soul's encouragement; I will not, in any case or at any hand, cast out such a soul as this.

(3.) And to put all beyond doubt, he not only assures the soul that he will not, but condescends to give it the reason why he will not cast it out: "I came down from heaven, not to do mine own will, but the will of him that sent me." John 6 : 38. As if he had said, This was the very errand upon which I came down from heaven; it was my great business to receive all that were made willing to come to me; for this I had my Father's commission: "The Lord hath anointed me to preach good tidings unto the meek; he hath sent me to bind up the broken-hearted, to proclaim liberty to the captives, and the opening of the prison to them that are bound; to proclaim the acceptable year of the Lord, and the day of vengeance of our God; to comfort all that mourn." Isa. 61 : 1, 2. I cannot be faithful to the trust committed to me by my Father, should I shut the door upon such souls. How can Christ comfort the soul that mourns, but by opening his arms of mercy to receive it? If he should say to the convinced sinner, Hold thy peace, I will give thee riches, honors, and pleasures in the world; but as for me, thou canst not have union with me; this would never comfort the heart of a convinced sinner: it is Christ, and none but Christ, can quiet it. Like unto this, is that testimony and promise made on purpose for the encouragement of willing souls: "To him give all the prophets witness, that through his name whosoever believeth on him shall receive remission of sins." Acts 10 : 43. This you see is a truth confirmed by the testimony of all the prophets, who foretold what his gracious readiness to receive poor broken-hearted sinners should be; and they neither did, nor could conspire to deceive the world. These gracious assurances and promises cut off all pleas against faith, from the greatness of sin; and why should we except where God has not excepted? Had Christ said, All sinners of such a degree may come unto me, but let all others stand back, the case had been otherwise; but this promise assures us, that all the sincerely willing, shall be truly welcome to Jesus Christ. Moreover, these universal promises take away all fear of presumption in coming to Christ. This is the case of many a soul. I am afraid I am running from despair into presumption; I fear I am an unbidden, and therefore shall be an unwelcome guest to Christ. All this is prevented by these sweet universal terms inserted on purpose in these promises for our encouragement.

EVIDENCE 3. The willingness of Christ to receive the willing soul, however great its sins and unworthiness, appears from the *actual grants of pardon and mercy, even to the vilest sinners on earth, when they thus come to him.* Here you see how the waters of free-grace rise higher and higher. An invitation is much; a promise of welcome is more; but the actual grant of mercy is most satisfying of all. Come on, trembling soul, be not discouraged, stretch out the weak arms of thy faith to that great and gracious Redeemer; open thy heart wide to receive him : he will not refuse to come in. He hath sealed thousands of pardons to as vile wretches as thyself; he never yet shut the door of mercy upon a willing, hungering soul. It is a great matter to have the way beaten before thee in thy way to Christ. If thou wert the first sinner that had cast his soul upon him, I confess I should want the encouragement I am now giving thee; but when so many have gone before thee, and all found a welcome beyond their expectation, what encouragement is breathed into thy trembling, discouraged heart to go on and venture thyself upon Christ as they did. What an example have we in Manasseh, 2 Chron. 33 : 3–12—an idolater, one that used enchantments, divinations, and familiar spirits, and shed innocent blood in the streets of Jerusalem. A man might rake the world, and hardly bring to sight a viler wretch, a greater monster in wickedness; yet his heart being broken and his will bowed, this man found mercy. How great a sinner was Mary, that came to Christ in the house of Simon the Pharisee, Luke 7 : 37–50 ; so notorious a sinner, that Simon took offence at Christ for suffering her to come into his presence. If this man were a prophet, said he, he would have known who and what manner of woman this is who touched him, for she is a sinner. Yet Mary's heart being broken for sin, and made willing to accept of a Saviour, received a gracious demonstration of welcome from Christ, and all other sinners are encouraged by her example. Once more, you have an eminent example in the abundant welcome of another sinner to Christ, who owned himself the greatest of sinners; a persecutor, a blasphemer, injurious; but, saith he, "I obtained mercy." 1 Tim. 1 : 16. And the example of his gracious reception with Christ is recorded as an encouragement to all that should hereafter believe. How many thousands are now in hell that never were guilty of greater enormities than the Corinthians. Fornicators, idolaters, adulterers, thieves, covetous, drunkards, revilers, extortioners, such were some of them; yet they were sanctified, washed, justified, in the name of the Lord Jesus, and by the Spirit of our God. 1 Cor. 6 : 9–11. If ever Christ would have shut the door of mercy upon any—if ever he would have been reluctant to come into any souls, certainly these were the souls he would have disdained to come near. O what a demonstration is here of that comfortable point before us : that Christ will not refuse to come into the soul of the vilest sinner, when once it is made heartily willing to open to him.

Evidence 4. A further evidence of this comfortable truth shall be taken from the *scriptural emblems of the abundant grace of God, and riches of mercy in Christ, towards all broken-hearted and willing sinners.* There are some chosen emblems which bring down the grace of God before the eyes of men; among which I will single out three glorious resemblances of free-grace, chosen by his wisdom on purpose for the encouragement of drooping sinners.

(1.) *A resemblance from the heavens* that cover and compass this earth. What an inconsiderable spot is the whole terrestrial globe, to those high and all-surrounding heavens! And yet these heavens are not at so vast a distance above the earth, as the pardoning grace of God is above the guilt, yea, and the very thoughts of poor sinners. For, of the pardoning grace of God to penitent and willing souls, that precious scripture speaks, "Let the wicked forsake his way, and the unrighteous man his thoughts; and let him return unto the Lord, and he will have mercy upon him; and to our God, for he will abundantly pardon." Isa. 55 : 7. O, saith the soul, I cannot think God will ever have mercy on such a wretch as I. Why? saith he; my thoughts are not your thoughts, and it is well they are not; for as the heavens are higher than the earth, so are my thoughts higher than your thoughts. You cannot take the height nor sound the depth of my pardoning grace.

(2.) Another emblem is taken from *the sun in the heavens*. You know, that soon this part of the world will be the throne of darkness, the sable curtains of the night will spread over all its beauties, and perhaps in the morning a thick fog or mist will cover it; thick clouds may darken the heavens. But, behold the glorious creature the sun chasing before him the darkness of the night, breaking up the mists of the morning, scattering the dark and thick clouds of heaven; they are all gone, and there is no appearance of them. Just so, saith God, shall it be with thy sins, and thy fears arising out of them. "I have blotted out as a thick cloud thy transgressions, and as a cloud thy sins." Isa. 44 : 22. Thy soul is beclouded, thy fears have been like a mist, so that thou canst not see the grounds of thy encouragement; but my grace shall rise upon thee like the sun in the heavens, and scatter all these dismal clouds, both of guilt and fear, and make a clear heaven over thee, and a clear soul within thee. "Unto you that fear my name shall the Sun of righteousness arise with healing in his wings." Malachi 4 : 2.

(3.) Another resemblance you have from *the sea*, the great abyss, that vast congregation of waters whose depth no line can fathom. Veer out as much line as you will, you cannot touch the bottom. To this unfathomable ocean the pardoning grace of God is also compared : " Who is a God like unto thee, that pardoneth iniquity and passeth by the transgression of the remnant of his heritage ? He retaineth not his anger for ever, because he delighteth in mercy. He will turn again, he will have compassion upon us ; he will subdue our iniquities; and thou wilt cast all their sins into the depths of the sea." Micah 7 : 18, 19. If the loftiest pyramid or highest mountain were cast into the depth of the sea, it would never be seen more by the eyes of men. God has chosen these emblems of his grace, to obviate the common discouragement of Satan, taken from the greatness and aggravation of sin ; and thou art to make use of them, and bless the Lord for them. He never designed them for encouragement to sin, but for encouragement to repentance and faith.

Evidence 5. The truth of this conclusion will also appear from *the character and properties of the grace and pardoning mercy of God towards penitent sinners*. There are three glorious characters of divine grace, which all assure such sinners of welcome to Christ, whatever they have been or done.

(1.) It is *superabounding* grace. Waters do not so abound in the ocean, nor light in the sun, as grace and compassion in God towards broken-hearted sinners. " Let him return unto the Lord, and he will have mercy upon him ; and to our God, for he will *abundantly* pardon." Isa. 55 : 8. The compassion of God inserted that word on purpose to relieve poor souls fainting under the sense of their abounding iniquities. Here is abundant pardon for abounding guilt; and, lest a desponding sinner should not find enough here to quiet his fears, the Lord goes yet further in the expression of his grace: "Where sin abounded, grace did much more abound." Rom. 5:20. It overflowed all the bounds, it rose quite above the high-water mark of guilt; but these overflowings of grace run only through that channel of all grace, Jesus Christ, to broken-hearted and obedient sinners.

(2.) The grace of God to such souls is *free*—every way free; it is the design of the gospel to exhibit this its glory. It costs you nothing but acceptance; it is free without merit; yea, free against merit. You can deserve nothing of God, therefore his grace is free without merit; yea, you have deserved hell as often as you have sinned against him, and so it is free against merit. If a pardon were to be purchased by us, we are wholly without means for such a purchase; neither could we borrow from men or angels a sufficient sum: blessed be God, therefore, that it flows freely to us without money and without price. Isa. 55:1.

(3.) Grace glories in another property also, which is very encouraging to the soul of a drooping sinner—*it is the attribute which God greatly delights to exercise*. The mother gives not her breast with such delight to her hungry crying child, as the Lord does his mercy to broken-hearted and hungry sinners. In this attribute his people therefore admire him: "Who is a God like unto thee, that pardoneth iniquity and passeth by the transgression of the remnant of his heritage? He retaineth not his anger for ever, because he delighteth in mercy." Micah 7:18. You cannot give Jesus Christ more delightful employment than to bind up the wounds of convinced and humbled sinners. Let every such soul come to Christ and welcome; for he greatly delights in such employments.

EVIDENCE 6. Such sinners need not doubt a welcome reception with Christ; for should he reject such as these, then none can have the benefit of his blood, and consequently it was shed in vain, as water spilt upon the ground. *The blood of Christ is invaluably precious, and it cannot be lost;* it would be an impeachment of the wisdom and goodness of God to think so; yet so it must be, if brokenhearted and willing souls are rejected and turned back from him. There are but two sorts of sinners in the world, the hardened and the broken-hearted, willing and unwilling sinners. As for impenitent and obstinate sinners, they can have no benefit by the blood of Christ; they shall die in their sins; the gospel cuts them off from all expectation of pardon and mercy. Now there is but one sort of sinners more left in the world, and they are convinced and humbled sinners, who are made heartily willing to receive Christ upon his own terms—who stretch forth the hand of desire to him, and pant after an interest in him. Should Christ reject these also, who shall receive the benefit of his blood? Did Christ die in vain; or can the counsels of heaven prove abortive? No; fear not therefore to go to Christ, thou broken-hearted sinner, thou panting, longing soul; fear not, he will not cast thee out.

EVIDENCE 7. Moreover, *for the encouragement of all such souls, mercy and pardon are designed for and bestowed upon the greatest sinners, to enhance the glory of free-grace to the highest.* God chooses such sinners as you are, on purpose to illustrate the glory of his grace in and upon you: he knows that you, to whom so much is forgiven, will love much. Luke 7 : 47. Ye that have done so much against his glory, will excel others in zeal and obedience. 1 Cor. 15 : 9, 10. You will go beyond others in service for God, as you have done in sinning against him.

INFERENCE 1. *Learn hence what an invaluable mercy it is to enjoy the gospel, which is so great a relief to the distressed consciences of sinners.* Here only is that balm that heals your spiritual wounds. The gospel hath been too little prized among us, the Lord pardon the guilt thereof to us. Ah, brethren, if you were in the heathen world with your sick and wounded consciences, what would you do? There are no Bibles, ministers, or promises, not a breath of Christ, or the blood of sprinkling, which are the true remedies of sick souls. That is a pitiful cry, Micah 6 : 6, 7, "Wherewith shall I come before the Lord, and bow myself before the high God? Shall I come before him with burnt-offerings, with calves of a year old? Will the Lord be pleased with thousands of rams, or with ten thousand rivers of oil? Shall I give my first-born for my transgression, the fruit of my body for the sin of my soul?" Behold here the anguish of a distressed, sin-burdened conscience; it would give up any thing in the world for peace; men would cast their dearest children, their first-born into the burning flames, if that might be an atonement for their sins. O the power of conscience, and the misery of an unrelieved conscience; but the gospel which you enjoy leads you to the fountain of pardon and peace. "With his stripes we are healed." Isa. 53 : 5. The voice of the gospel is peace to every one that believeth—a rational peace, founded upon the full satisfaction of Christ, "In whom we have redemption through his blood, the forgiveness of sins, according to the riches of his grace." Eph. 1 : 7. Here you see justice and mercy embracing each other; God is satisfied, and the sinner justified; for conscience demands as much to satisfy it, as God to satisfy him; if God be satisfied, conscience is satisfied. "Blessed is the people that know the joyful sound." Psalm 89 : 15. And doubtless it is a joyful sound to every convinced and humbled soul. "Beautiful upon the mountains are the feet of him that bringeth good tidings, that publisheth peace." Isa. 52 : 7. It is a gospel worthy of all acceptation. 1 Tim. 1 : 15. It brings with it a fulness of blessings among the people. Provoke not God to extinguish this blessed light. Great is our wantonness, and ominous is our barrenness and ingratitude. "Yet a little while is the light with you. Walk while ye have the light, lest darkness come upon you; for he that walketh in darkness, knoweth not whither he goeth." John 12:35. Should God put out this light, whither would ye go? Who shall pour balm into your distressed consciences?

2. *Hence it follows that the heinousness of past sins is no bar to believing and accepting Christ upon gospel-terms.* Let no sinner be dismayed by the atrocity of sins past from coming to Jesus Christ for remission and peace. I am aware what mischievous use Satan makes of former sins to discourage souls from the work of faith. By heaping them together, he raises a mountain between Christ and the distressed soul; but behold this day Christ leaping over these mountains. Could this objection be rolled out of the way, sinners would go on in hope; but certainly, if God has given thee a broken heart and a willing mind, the greatness of thy sin need not discourage thee from believing. For,

(1.) Thou hast sufficient encouragement from the sufficiency of the causes of pardon, whatever thy particular enormities have been. There is a sufficiency in the impulsive cause, the free-grace and mercy of God. Exod. 34:6, 7; Mic. 7:18, 19; Isa. 55:7–9; there is mercy enough in God to heal and cover all. And there is no less sufficiency in the meritorious cause of pardon, the blood of Jesus Christ, which taketh away all sin. 1 John, 1:7; John 1:29. And it must needs be so, because of its divine blood. Acts 20:28. Neither is there any defect in the applying cause, the Spirit of God, who has already begun to work upon thy heart, and is able to break it and bow it, and bring it fully to Christ, and to complete the work of faith upon thee with power. Thou complainest that thou canst not mourn nor believe as thou wouldst; but he wants no ability to supply all the defects of thy repentance and faith. If, then, the mercy of God be sufficient to pardon the sins of a creature— if the blood of Christ, the treasures and revenues of a king, be able to pay the debts of a beggar—if the Spirit of God, who works by an almighty power, be able to convince thee of righteousness, as well as sin, John 16 : 9, 10—if all these three causes of forgiveness be sufficient, the first to move, the second to purchase, and the third to apply; what hinders but thy trembling conscience may go to Christ, and thy discouraged soul move onward with hope in the way of believing, whatever thy former enormities have been?

(2.) If God raises glory to his name out of the greatness of the sins he pardons, then the greatness of sin can be no discouragement to believing; and this he does. "I will cleanse them from all their iniquity, whereby they have sinned against me; and I will pardon all their iniquities, whereby they have sinned and whereby they have transgressed against me. And it shall be to me a name of joy, a praise and an honor before all the nations of the earth, which shall hear all the good that I do unto them: and they shall fear and tremble for all the goodness and for all the prosperity that I procure unto it," Jer. 33 : 8, 9; as a cure performed upon a man laboring under a desperate disease honors the physician, and spreads his name far and near. Satan envies God this glory and thy soul this comfort, and therefore scares thee off from Christ by the aggravations of thy sins. David was willing to give God the glory of pardoning his great iniquities, and with that very argument entreats him for a pardon: "Pardon mine iniquity, for it is great." Psalm 25 : 11. You see there are strange ways of arguing in Scripture, which are not in use among men; this is one, Lord, pardon my sin, for it is great. He does not say, Lord, pardon it, for it is but a small offence; but pardon it because it is great; and the greater it is, the greater glory wilt thou have in pardoning it. And then there is another way of arguing for pardon in the Scripture, which is peculiar; and that is, to argue from former pardons unto new pardons. When men beg pardon one of another, they are wont to say, I never wronged you before, and therefore forgive now; but here it is quite otherwise: Lord, thou hast signed thousands of pardons heretofore, therefore pardon me again. Such is the plea in Num. 14:19, "Pardon, I beseech thee, the iniquity of this people, according to the greatness of thy mercy, and as thou hast forgiven this people from Egypt even until now."

(3.) As great sins as those that now confront thy conscience have been actually forgiven to men, upon their humiliation and closing with Christ. God forbid I should diminish and extenuate sin; but certain I am that free-grace has pardoned as great sinners as thou art, upon their repentance and faith. What think you? had you had a hand in putting Christ to death, would not that sin have been as dreadful as any that now discourages you? Yea, certainly, you would have thought that an unpardonable sin; and yet behold, that very sin was no bar to their pardon when once they were pricked in their heart, and made willing to come to Christ. Acts 2:36-38.

(4.) If it be the design and policy of Satan to object the greatness of your sins to prevent their pardon, then it is neither your duty nor interest to use it for the same end; thus entering into a confederacy with your mortal enemy in a plot against the honor of Christ, and the salvation of your own soul. Take heed what you do, seal not Satan's conclusions. Do you think it is a small matter to be confederate with the devil? Certainly this is his design; he magnifies your sins to discourage you from faith. While you were secure and carnal, he never magnified, but diminished your sins to you; but now the Lord has opened your eyes, and you are brought near to the door of hope, mercy, and pardon, he magnifies them, hoping thereby to lame and weaken thy faith, that it shall not be able to carry thee to Christ.

(5.) If thy sin is really unpardonable, then God has

somewhere excepted it in the gospel-grant. He has somewhere said, The man that has committed this sin, or continued so many years in it, shall never be forgiven: but in the whole New Testament there is but one sin that is absolutely excepted from the possibility of pardon, and that such a sin as thy sorrows and desires after Christ fully acquit thee from the guilt of. This sin indeed is excepted: " The blasphemy against the Holy Ghost shall not be forgiven unto men." Matt. 12:31. This is that which the Scripture calls " a sin unto death." 1 John, 5:16. Let apostate professors, transformed into persecutors, scoffers, and haters of godliness and the professors of it, look to themselves; the dreadful symptoms of this sin appear upon such. But the humbled soul thirsting after Christ stands clear of the guilt of that sin.

(6.) If there were no forgiveness with God for great sinners, then great sinners had never been invited to come to Christ. The invitations of the gospel are no mockeries, but things of most awful solemnity. Now, such sinners are called and invited under the encouragement of a pardon. Consult Isa. 1:10–17, and see the horrid aggravations of the people's sins; and yet, at ver. 17, 18, you may read the gracious invitations of God, with promises of a full remission. So in the third chapter of Jeremiah, what a sad catalogue of sins with their aggravations do you find? and yet it is said, "Go and proclaim these words towards the north, and say, Return, thou backsliding Israel, saith the Lord; and I will not cause mine anger to fall upon you, for I am merciful."

(7.) If thy sins had not been capable of remission, God would never have given thee conviction of sin, nor have drawn forth the desires of thy heart in this manner after Christ. He hath united remission to repentance, Acts 5:31, and a blessing to gracious desires and hungerings, Matt. 5:6. There is therefore hope, that when God has given thee one, he will not long withhold the other. This very wounding of thy heart by compunction, and drawing forth thy will by inclination, shows that remission is not only possible, but even at the door.

(8.) Let this also be thine encouragement, whatever Satan or thine own heart may suggest to discourage thee, that great sinners are moving in the way of repentance and faith to a great Saviour, who hath merit enough in his blood, and mercy enough in his heart, to save to the uttermost all that come unto God by him. Heb. 7 : 25. The Lord open to the eyes of your faith the rich treasury of free-grace, Exodus 34 : 6, 7, and give you a sight of that plenteous redemption and forgiveness which are with God, Psalm 130 : 4, 7, that you may not cast reproach on the most glorious attribute of God, undervalue the precious blood of Christ, and stab your own souls with a death-wound of desperation; which is what Satan intends, and what the gospel designs to prevent.

3. If the vilest of sinners may as readily be pardoned, on their closing with Christ by faith, as the least of sinners, *the pardon and salvation of sinners is not built upon any righteousness in themselves, but only on the free-grace of God in Jesus Christ.* Do not think God hath set the blood of Christ to sale, and that those only are capable of the benefits of it who have lived the most strict and sober lives. No; though sobriety, morality, and strictness in religious duties are commanded and commended in the gospel, yet no man by these things can purchase a pardon for the least sin. "If by grace, then it is no more of works: otherwise grace is no more grace. But if it be of works, then it is no more grace; otherwise work is no more work." Rom. 11 : 6. See how these exclude one another: thus Titus 3 : 5, "Not by works of righteousness which we have done, but according to his mercy he saved us." No man can satisfy God by any thing he can do or suffer; not by *doing,* for

all we do is mixed with sin, Job 14 : 4, and that which is sinful can be no atonement for sin. All we do or can do is a debt due to God, Luke 17 : 10, and one debt cannot satisfy for another. Nor yet by *suffering*, for the sufferings awarded by the law are everlasting ; and to be ever satisfying is never to satisfy : so then, by the works of the law shall no flesh living be justified in his sight. The saints in all generations have fled to mercy for remission. Psalm 130 : 8. Of the two debtors, Luke 7 : 41, 42, though there was a vast difference in the debts, yet of the lesser, as well as of the greater, it is said they had nothing to pay. Nothing but the satisfaction of Christ can meet the demands of God upon you.

4. If the grace of Christ be thus free to the greatest of sinners, *it is both our sin and folly to keep away from Christ, and to draw back from believing, for want of qualifications which we find not to be wrought in our hearts.* Poor convinced souls think if they had more humility, tenderness, love to God, and spirituality of mind, this would be some encouragement to believe ; but because they have no such ornaments to dress up their souls withal, they are not fit to go to Christ. Now, to correct this great mistake, let two things be considered.

(1.) *Such an idea as this crosses the very stream of the covenant of grace,* where nothing is sold, but all is freely given. This is the very spirit of the covenant of works: fain would we find something in ourselves to bring to God, to procure his favor and acceptance ; but the gospel tells us we must come naked and empty-handed, to be justified freely by his grace. Rom. 3 : 24. We must be justified as Abraham was, who believed in him that justifieth the ungodly ; " To him that worketh not, but believeth on him that justifieth the ungodly, his faith is counted for righteousness." Rom. 4 : 5. The meaning is, to him that worketh not in a law-sense, to procure pardon and acceptance by and for his works. Go then, poor sinner, unto God through Christ, and tell him thou hast nothing to bring him; that thou comest not to bring, but to receive. Lord, I am a vile sinner, I have nothing to plead but thy mercy and Christ's merit. This is the spirit of the gospel.

(2.) By delaying faith, for want of these qualifications, *you invert the settled order of the gospel.* It is as if a man should say, If I were cured of such and such disease, I would go to the physician. Alas, could you otherwise procure the healing of your corruptions, or the gracious qualifications you speak of, you would have no need to go to Christ at all. Nothing is required of us in coming to Christ, but such a sense of and sorrow for sin, as makes us heartily willing to accept Christ and subscribe the terms on which he is offered in the gospel.

5. *Behold the admirable condescension of Christ, that he comes into the heart of the vilest sinner, and takes up his abode in that soul which has been the seat of Satan, where he has ruled, and every lust has been harbored!* In two things the admirable condescension of Christ appears. First, in taking union with our nature after sin had blasted the beauty of it. This was marvellous indeed, and was justly admired by the apostle: "He made himself of no reputation, and took upon him the form of a servant, and was made in the likeness of men." Phil. 2 : 7. "Yea, God sent his own Son in the likeness of sinful flesh." Rom. 8 : 3. But, secondly, it is admirable in our eyes that Christ should become united with our persons, and take up his abode in our hearts, after Satan and sin had so long inhabited and defiled them—that he should accept these members as instruments of his service—that very tongue to praise him that had blasphemed him; yet so he is willing to do, and commands us to deliver them up to him : " As ye have yielded your members servants to uncleanness, and to iniquity unto iniquity; even so now yield your members

servants to righteousness, unto holiness." Rom. 6 : 19. One would have thought Jesus Christ would have said, Vile wretch, Satan has had the service of thy soul and body, from the beginning to this day; thy memory hath been his storehouse, thy mouth his shop, thy will his throne, and all thy members his tools and instruments to sin against me: thou hast been a creature dedicated to Satan, and to him thou shalt go. Instead of this, the merciful Lord declares his willingness, if thou wilt open thy soul to receive him, to cleanse it by his Spirit, and make it his temple to dwell in. O admirable grace!

6. *How just and inevitable will be their damnation who consent not to the necessary and reasonable terms of the gospel, which is the only point on which Christ and their souls part for ever.* The terms required by the gospel are every way equitable and reasonable. If a gracious prince will bestow a pardon upon a traitor, on the condition that he lay down his arms, acknowledge his offence, and attach himself to his prince's service, and he shall refuse so to do, how just would his destruction be. And what else does God require of thee, but this? "Let the wicked forsake his way, and the unrighteous man his thoughts: and let him return unto the Lord, and he will have mercy upon him; and to our God, for he will abundantly pardon." Isa. 55 : 7. And as the damnation of such is just, so it will be inevitable : for if there is no way to glory but by Christ, as you know there is not, from Acts 4 : 12, "Neither is there salvation in any other;" and if there is no way to Christ, but by accepting him upon these very terms, as it plainly appears, from Luke 14 : 26, there is not, what remains but inevitable destruction to all that reject the terms of the gospel? If you will not have Christ with all the sufferings and reproaches that attend him, your mouths will be stopped; no plea will be left you in the great day. You refused the gracious offer when it was seasonably made

you by the gospel, and you must expect no more such offers to eternity. Thy blood, sinner, be upon thine own head; the freeness and importunity of the tenders of grace will then only serve to illustrate and clear the righteousness of God in thy condemnation.

In the next place, the doctrine naturally leads me to an EARNEST PERSUASIVE unto all sinners, of what kind or degree soever they be, to hearken to the voice of Christ, who takes them all within the compass of his gracious invitation in the text, saying, "If any man hear my voice and open the door, I will come in." Let all sinners bless God for the extent of this invitation—that they find themselves by it within the reach of a merciful Redeemer; and that there is nothing wanting to secure their salvation, but the hearty consent of their wills to the reasonable and necessary terms of the gospel. In the whole book of God, there is but one case absolutely excepted from the possibility of forgiveness; of which Christ speaks, Matt. 12:31, 32. And what is the reason that this only is an incurable wound? It cannot be because the malignity of this sin exceeds the virtue of the blood of Christ, but because there is no sacrifice appointed by the Lord for it. God never designed that the blood of Christ should be an expiatory sacrifice for that sin, as the apostle plainly speaks, Heb. 6:4–7. All other sins and blasphemies shall be forgiven unto men, saith Christ; that is, they are capable of forgiveness, upon sincere and actual repentance and faith; yea, they have been pardoned unto many. The greater any man's sins have been, the greater need he has to hasten to Christ for pardon. There are some greater sinners than others; for though no sin be light and trivial in itself, yet, compared one with another, there is a vast difference between them in the aggravation of sins. I will labor to show you by what rules men are to estimate the greatness and aggravation of sin; and then, to convince you that the greatest of sinners may have mercy as well as the less. "Publicans and the harlots go into the kingdom of God before you," saith Christ, Matt. 22 : 31. The rules by which to estimate the aggravations and greatness of sin are these:

7. *There are sins of infirmity, committed out of weakness; and there are crying sins in the ears of the Lord.* Of sins of infirmity you read in Gal. 6 : 1, where it is called being "overtaken in a fault." Here is no deliberate consent, but a surprise : these go not to the account of gross and heinous enormities, called in Scripture, crying sins, such as the sin of oppression, Hab. 2 : 10, 11 : " The stone shall cry out of the wall, and the beam out of the timber shall answer it." The meaning is, that the injustice and oppression which men have used in raising their houses, shall cry in the ears of the Lord for vengeance. The stone in the wall shall say, I was digged out of the quarry, hewn, and laid here by the unrewarded labors of the poor mason ; and the timber out of the beam shall say, I was hewn, squared, and placed here by the unrewarded hands of the carpenter. This is a crying sin ; so also is the sin of murder, when our hands have been defiled with innocent blood. This makes a dismal cry to heaven : " The voice of thy brother's blood crieth unto me from the ground." Gen. 4 : 10. This is a sin that makes a horrid outcry in both worlds at once : to God and in the sinner's conscience. The sin of Sodom made a cry which went up to heaven. " The cry of Sodom and Gomorrah is great, and because their sin is very grievous." Gen. 18 : 20. Compare these sins with those of common infirmity, which come by way of involuntary surprise, and what a vast difference will be found in the aggravation of them.

8. You find in Scripture *a great difference put between those sins committed against the light of knowledge in the sinner's conscience, and sins of ignorance committed for want of knowledge.* Christ himself puts a great difference

between them, Luke 12 : 47, 48; and so doth the apostle: "To him that knoweth to do good, and doeth it not, to him it is sin," James 4 : 17—sin with a witness.

9. *There are single acts of sin, and continued or repeated acts of sin*—sins committed after convictions, promises, and resolutions. There is not so much guilt in a single act of sin as in a continued course of sin, adding of drunkenness to thirst, Deut. 29 : 19; described also as adding sin to sin, Isa. 30 : 1. For as it is in numbering, so in sinning: if the first figure be 1, the second is 10, the third 100, the fourth 1,000; and every addition makes a greater multiplication. O what a dreadful reckoning will there be for the consciences of sinners!

10. *Contrivers and studiers of sin are always in Scripture placed in the first rank of sinners.* The best servant God has in the world may be surprised by the deceitfulness of sin, against the bent and resolution of his soul; but the contrivance and plotting sin is quite another thing; therefore it is said of the wicked, " They conceive mischief, and bring forth vanity, and their belly prepareth deceit." Job 15 : 35. Sin has its time of conception, growth, and birth; and all this by the deliberate consent of the heart and will, which cherish it.

11. *There are ringleaders in sin, and single personal sins which spread no further than ourselves.* A ringleader in sin is in Scripture reckoned among the greatest sinners: " Thou hast there them that hold the doctrine of Balaam, who taught Balak to cast a stumbling-block before the children of Israel." Rev. 2 : 14. Thus Jeroboam the son of Nebat made Israel to sin. There is the same difference between these and single personal sins, as there is between a chain-shot and a single bullet. Mind this, you that have induced others to sin by your counsel or example.

12. *There are sins in which men take pleasure, and*

sins for which men mourn. The more pleasure any man takes in sin, the greater is the sin in its aggravation. We read of some in whose mouths wickedness is sweet, and they hide it under their tongue. Job 20 : 12. That is, they draw a great deal of contemplative delight before and after the commission of sin, as well as in the commission of it. It is bad enough to sin and sigh, to sin and weep; but to sin and boast, to sin and make a mock of sin, what prodigious sinning is this! O sinner, what a heart hast thou, that can sport with that which grieves God and crucified Christ, and which, without deep repentance, will damn thine own soul.

13. *The more bonds of restraint any man breaks asunder to commit sin, the greater that sin is in the sight of God.* There are some persons upon whom God has laid more restraints to keep them back from iniquity, than he has upon others. The more mercies he has bestowed upon you, the more restraints you have from sin. So many mercies, so many ties, Jer. 2 : 5, 6; especially spiritual mercies, as light in your minds, pardons sealed to your consciences, love manifested to your souls. Such also are your own vows and resolutions: "Thou saidst, I will not transgress." Jer. 2 : 20. Didst not thou promise me, saith God, more care and circumspection for time to come? And such are all the examples and warnings God has given us by his judgments upon others. 1 Cor. 10 : 11. These things make sin out of measure sinful. The design of all this is to show you the indispensable need of repentance and faith to carry you to Christ.

OBJECTION. But I am the person upon whom these aggravated sins are found. You speak to me of going to Christ; alas, there is no hope of mercy for such a wretch as I am.

ANSWER. Give me leave to tell you, that you have a text before you which clears the way of your duty and salvation at once: "If any man," be he what he may, and be his sins never so great, "will hear my voice and open the door, I will come in to him," saith Christ. There is mercy in Jesus Christ for thee, who art guilty of crying sins; for thee, who hast sinned against light; for thee, who "hast added drunkenness to thirst;" for thee, who hast contrived sin with deliberation; for thee, who hast induced others to sin by counsel or example; for thee, who hast taken pleasure in iniquity, and made a sport of sin; yea, and for thee, who hast broken asunder the bonds of mercies, vows, and warnings, provided thou wilt now hear the voice of Christ, and thy will open to him with a hearty consent. Isa. 55:4. You are great sinners; but I show this day a great and almighty Saviour, one who is able to save to the uttermost all that come unto God by him. Heb. 7:25. There is a sacrifice appointed for these sins. Bless God for that; they are nowhere excepted from the possibility of forgiveness. Nothing but the impenitence of thy heart, and the obstinacy of thy will, can hinder thee from a full pardon. Look round about thee to the uttermost horizon of thy guilt, and Christ can save to the uttermost point the eye of thy conscience can discern, yea, and beyond it too; but then thou must come unto him. You speak of the greatness of sin, and you have indeed cause to have sad thoughts about it; but you consider not that your unbelief, by which you stand off from Christ your only remedy, is the greatest sin that ever you were guilty of against the Lord. This is the sin that binds the guilt of all your other sins upon you. Let me therefore address myself,

(1.) *To you whose consciences are alarmed with the hideous aggravations of your sins*, by reason whereof your own misgiving hearts, assisted by the policy of Satan, discourage you from all attempts to gain Christ and pardon through repentance and faith. Let me hint three or four considerations to you, by way of encouragement.

The sparing goodness of God gives encouragement that God may have a reserve of mercy for so great a sinner as thou art. O what a mercy is it, that thy life has been spared hitherto. Many of thy companions in sin are beyond hope, while thou art left. This is no sure sign of God's gracious intention to thee, unless his goodness and forbearance lead thee to repentance. Then the gracious intention of God in prolonging thy life would appear. But it is itself a great mercy, because without it no spiritual mercy could be expected.

It is matter of encouragement, that *though your disease be dreadful, it is not incurable.* The text brings it within the compass of mercy; O bless God for those words, "If any man."

As great sinners as you have been have found mercy, 1 Tim. 1:16, and God would have it recorded for your encouragement. If the Lord shall make thy heart break and thy will bow, whatever thy sins have been they shall not bar thee from forgiveness. But if thou resolve to go on in sin, or sit down discouraged, and wilt not come at the invitation of Christ, then thy wound is incurable indeed, and thy sentence has already passed upon thee for hell. "The unrighteous shall not inherit the kingdom of God." 1 Cor. 6:9. God forbid that this should be the issue of Christ's gracious invitations to thee, and forbearance of thee. Seeing mercy is tendered to any man that will accept it on Christ's terms, exclude not thyself.

(2.) I will now address this exhortation to persons who are not of the notorious rank of profane sinners, but whose lives have been drawn more smoothly through a course of morality. These have as great need to be pressed to repentance and faith as the most notorious sinners in the world. They are a generation that bless themselves in their own eyes, and thank God with the Pharisee that they are "not as other men." Luke 18:11. They acknowledge conversion to be the duty of the profane, and that such sinners stand in need of it. But as for themselves, they scarcely know where to find matter for repentance, nor do they feel any need of Christ. Now, I would lay three considerations before such persons, to convince them that their case is as sad and hazardous, yea, in some respects, more hazardous than the state of the most notorious sinners; and that a change must also pass upon them, or else it had been good for them that they had never been born.

CONSIDERATION 1. Let the moral part of the world lay this thought to their hearts, that *though their sins are not so gross to appearance as other men's are, yet, continued in, they will prove as destructive as the greater abominations of other men.* No sin, absolutely considered, is small. Every sin is damning without Christ. "The wages of sin is death." Rom. 6:23. It is no great difference, if a man be killed, whether it be by a sword or a penknife. The least sin violates the whole law. He that offendeth in one point, is guilty of all. James 2:10. The least transgression of the law pulls down its curse upon the sinner's head. And this is your misery, that you are out of Christ and stand under the terms of the first covenant. Moreover, the law of God is violated not only externally, but internally. Thus, every unchaste thought is adultery, and the inward burning of malice and anger in the heart is murder. Now, if the Lord shall bring the spiritual sense of the law home to your consciences as he did to Paul's, Rom. 7:9, you will certainly give up the plea, that you have not so much need of conversion as other sinners have. There are sins of greater infamy, and sins of deeper guilt. There may be more guilt in sins that are stifled in thy heart, and never defamed thee, than in some others that are seen by the world.

CONSIDERATION 2. *You are guilty of one sin more heinous than any outward act, that is, your trusting to your own righteousness as the Pharisees did.* "He spake this parable unto certain which trusted in themselves that they were righteous, and despised others." Luke 18 : 9. Here is an idol set up in the room of Christ. It is true, this sin makes not so loud a noise as the sins of profane persons do; but it is as abominable in the eyes of God, as the sins that are most offensive among men. Moral persons, thus trusting to their own morality, and neglecting Jesus Christ, will be found ultimately among those who have "a portion with unbelievers." Luke 12 : 46.

CONSIDERATION 3. *It has been always found a more difficult thing to convince and bring to Christ the moral part of the world, than to convince the profane part of it.* "Publicans and harlots go into the kingdom of God before you." Matt. 21 : 31. Publicans were reckoned the vilest of men, and harlots the worst of women; yet either of these were more readily brought to Christ than self-righteous Pharisees. Away then with your idle pretensions that you are safer and better than others. By what has been said, it appears that you stand in as much need of Christ as the most infamous sinners in the world do.

This doctrine presents great ENCOURAGEMENT to every obedient soul whom the Lord shall persuade to comply with the call of the gospel, whatever his former rebellions have been. There are some whose hearts the Lord has touched with a sense of their sin and misery, and of the all-sufficient remedy in Christ, but the sense of former rebellions appalls them; they cannot hope for acceptance with him. Here is good news for such souls; Christ is at the door, and former rebellions are no bar to him, provided there is now a hearty compliance with his invitation, "I will come in to him." A glorious promise, comprising five inestimable benefits.

(1.) This is the most glorious work of God that can be

wrought upon the heart of a sinner, to open it by repentance and faith, and put Christ in full possession of it. The power of all the angels in heaven, ministers on earth, duties, and ordinances cannot effect this; this is the peculiar work of God. "Of him are ye in Christ Jesus." 1 Cor. 1 : 30. As it was the marvellous work of God to unite our nature unto Christ, so it is no less a marvellous work of God to unite our persons to Christ, to prepare the soul as a habitation for Christ, and give him the possession of it.

(2.) This coming of Christ into the soul is the very foundation of all our hopes for glory; until this be done, we are without hope. But in the same hour when Christ comes into the soul, a solid foundation of the hope of glory is laid in that soul, "which is Christ in you, the hope of glory." Col. 1 : 27. I know the unregenerate world is full of hope, but their hopes are built upon the sand. Union with Christ is the firm foundation on which the hopes of heaven are laid.

(3.) "I will come in to him;" that is, to dwell in his soul for ever, never to leave him more; therefore he is said to dwell in our hearts by faith, Eph. 3 : 17—not sojourn for a night, but abide there for ever. Nothing can separate Christ and that soul. Rom. 8 : 35. Thy soul shall never be a habitation for Satan again. When Christ comes in, he saith, as of the temple, "This is my rest for ever: here will I dwell." Psalm 132 : 14.

(4.) This coming in of Christ entitles the soul to all spiritual privileges: "He that hath the Son, hath life," 1 John, 5 : 12; and, "All are yours, and ye are Christ's." 1 Cor. 3 : 22, 23.

(5.) This is the highest honor that ever God put upon a creature, "I will come in to him." O how should the soul feel itself advanced by such an honor as this. What, to be the living temple of Jesus Christ, for him to dwell and walk in thy soul! 2 Cor. 6 : 16. I tell you, this is an honor beyond and above the honor done to angels.

And how near art thou to all these blessed privileges in the day that thy heart is wounded for sin? Thy thoughts become solicitous about union with Christ, and thy will begins to yield after a serious examination of the terms of the gospel in thy most solemn thoughts. God forbid any thing should now hinder the completing of so great a work.

CHAPTER VIII.

NONE RECEIVE CHRIST UNTIL HIS SPIRITUAL QUICKENING VOICE IS HEARD.

"IF ANY MAN *HEAR MY VOICE* AND OPEN THE DOOR, I WILL COME IN TO HIM." REV. 3:20.

IN the former chapters, Christ's general invitation to sinners has been considered: we are now to consider the principal instrument by which the heart of a sinner is opened to receive Christ; and that is not by the power of his own will, nor merely by the efficacy of the gospel preached, but by *the voice of Jesus Christ*, which opens the will, and makes the persuasions of the gospel effectual. "If any man hear my voice."

Hearing is either external or internal; for the soul has its ear as well as the body. "He that hath an ear, let him hear what the Spirit saith unto the churches," Rev. 2:17; that is, he that hath a spiritual ear, by which to perceive and judge the voice of the Spirit. It is a sore judgment when God denies such an ear to the soul. "Go and tell this people, hear ye indeed, but understand not." Isa. 6:9. Spiritual hearing is the work of the inner man. And though we have many auditors, yet, in this sense, we have no more hearers than believers. Words of sense in Scripture describe affections. This hearing of Christ's voice implies not only the receiving the sound of the gospel into the external organ, but the work of the understanding, which by the ear trieth words as the mouth tasteth meat, Job 12:11; and the work of the affections, which receive the truth in love. 2 Thess. 2:10. It also implies the obedience of the soul to what we hear. We cannot be said, in this sense, to hear what we obey not. Our minds may be delighted with the pleasant melody of the gospel, and yet it is as if we heard it not, when obedience does not follow hearing. "Thou art unto them as a very lovely song of one that hath a pleasant voice, and can play well on an instrument; for they hear thy words, but they do them not." Ezek. 33 : 32. But in this place it signifies the *vital sound of Christ's efficacious voice*, which is the principle of spiritual life to the souls of dead sinners; according to his expression, "Verily, verily, I say unto you, the hour is coming, and now is, when the dead shall hear the voice of the Son of God : and they that hear shall live." John 5 : 25.

From hence the eighth doctrine will be,

No man's will savingly and effectually opens to receive Christ until the spiritual and quickening voice of Christ be heard by the soul.

Now, concerning this almighty spiritual voice of Christ, by which the hearts of sinners are effectually opened, six things must be explained in order : the divers sorts and kinds of Christ's voices; the general nature of this internal voice; the innate characters and special properties of it; the objects to whom it is directed; the motives inducing Christ to speak to one, and not to another; and the special effects wrought and sealed by it upon every soul that hears it.

I. We will speak of THE DIVERS SORTS AND KINDS OF CHRIST'S VOICES.

1. There is an *external* voice of Christ, which we may call his voice in the preaching of the gospel. The Scriptures are his word, and ministers his mouth. Jer. 15 : 19. He that heareth them, heareth Christ.

2. There is also an *internal* voice of Christ, consisting not in sound, but in power; and between these there are two remarkable differences. First, the external or ministerial voice of Christ is but the organ or instrument of conveying his internal and efficacious voice to the soul : in the former he speaks to the ear, and by that sound conveys his spiritual

voice to the heart. Second, the external voice is ineffectual when it is not animated by the internal spiritual voice. It was marvellous to see the walls of Jericho falling to the ground at the sound of ram's horns, Josh. 6 : 20; there was certainly more than the force of an external blast to produce such an effect: but more marvellous it is, to see at the sound of the gospel not only the weapons of iniquity falling out of sinners' hands, but the very enmity itself out of their hearts. Here you see is a voice in a voice, an internal efficacy in the external sound, without which the gospel makes no saving impression.

II. This spiritual voice of Christ must be considered IN ITS GENERAL NATURE, which implies,

1. *Almighty efficacy*, to quicken and open the heart with a word. O what manner of voice is this, which carries such a vital power with it! In all the mighty works of Christ, his power was put forth in some voice, as at the resurrection of Lazarus. "He cried with a loud voice, Lazarus, come forth. And he that was dead came forth." John 11 : 43, 44. So in curing the deaf man, Mark 7 : 34, "He saith unto him, Ephphatha, that is, Be opened; and straightway his ears were opened." Thus, in exerting his almighty power in quickening a soul spiritually dead, and opening the heart locked up by ignorance and unbelief, an internal almighty efficacy passes from Christ, along with the voice of the gospel, to effect this glorious work upon the soul; an emblem of which we have in Ezek. 37 : 9, 10 : "Then said he unto me, Prophesy unto the wind, prophesy, son of man, and say to the wind, Thus saith the Lord God; Come from the four winds, O breath, and breathe upon these slain, that they may live. So I prophesied as he commanded me, and the breath came into them, and they lived, and stood up upon their feet, an exceeding great army." The animating vital breath which quickened the dead came with the four winds of heaven, as this almighty

power of Christ does with the sound of the gospel; and before it the heart opens, and the will bows. Psalm 110:3. Man can no longer oppose God; the power of man can repel that of a fellow-creature, but when the power of Christ comes with the voice of man, there is no more power to resist. This voice of Christ, of which the text speaks, is an impression made on the soul of a sinner from heaven, which is to that soul instead of a voice, and as fully expressive of God's mind concerning it as any articulate voice can be. It is a beam of light shining immediately from the Spirit into the soul of a sinner, as plainly revealing both its danger and duty as if a voice from heaven had declared them. Thus it is said, Isa. 8:11, the Lord spake to Isaiah with a strong hand, that is, by a mighty impression upon his spirit, which was as a voice to him. Thus the Lord not only directs a suitable word to a sinner's condition, but impresses it with such a strong hand upon his heart, as leaves no doubt but that it was the Lord himself that spoke to his soul. This is Christ's way of speaking by his Spirit to the ear of the soul: not by audible voices, which I take to be but the imaginings of an overtroubled fancy, but by an efficacious impression upon the heart. In audible voices we may sooner meet satanical delusions than divine illuminations. The learned Gerson speaks of a good man who, being in prayer, seemed to hear such a voice as this: "I am come in person to visit thee, for thou art worthy." But he justly suspecting a delusion of Satan, shut his eyes and said, "I will not see Christ here, it shall suffice me to see him in glory." Christ's voice in the written word is more sure than a voice from heaven. 2 Pet. 1:19. This spiritual impression is Christ's effectual call from heaven, and is a voice without sound or syllable.

2. As this voice of Christ implies almighty efficacy, so it implies, in like manner, the *facility* of conversion unto Christ: he can do it easily with a word of his mouth, as

in the bodily cures performed by him in the days of his flesh; how suddenly and easily did he effect them. "Speak the word only," said the centurion, "and my servant shall be healed." Thus, let the Spirit but speak to the dead soul and it lives. Elijah did but cast his mantle on Elisha, as he was ploughing in the field, and he entreated the prophet to give him leave to go home and bid his friends farewell, and he would follow him. Thus it is here: let a beam of saving light shine from the Spirit into a man's heart; let an effectual impression be made upon his soul, and he is at once made willing to quit and give up his dearest lusts and interests, and to embrace Christ upon the terms of the gospel. Conversion is too difficult a work for angels or men to effect, but Christ can do it with a word.

III. I shall endeavor to show THE SPECIAL PROPERTIES of this spiritual voice of Christ, which must be heard, or there can be no opening the door of the heart to receive him.

1. It is a *secret and still* voice, whereby somewhat is communicated to the soul, making a particular application of what is spoken to the ear, much like that of Nathan to David, "Thou art the man." 2 Sam. 12 : 7. This still voice sounds through the whole soul, yet none hear it but the soul concerned in it. It is said, "The Lord had told Samuel in his ear, a day before," 1 Sam. 9 : 15, that is, he whispered the secret into the prophet's mind. So the Spirit of Christ whispers a word into the ear of a sinner, which makes his heart tremble, after this manner: "This is thy very condition; this is thy sin, which is now opened by the gospel in thine ears." This is a voice without sound to others, but very intelligible to the soul to whom it is spoken. You read in 1 Kings, 19 : 11, 12, that when Elijah stood upon the mount before the Lord, "a great and strong wind rent the mountains, and brake in pieces the rocks before the Lord; but the Lord was not in the wind: and after the

wind an earthquake; but the Lord was not in the earthquake: and after the earthquake a fire; but the Lord was not in the fire: and after the fire a still small voice. And it was so, when Elijah heard it, that he wrapped his face in his mantle." So it is here: dreadful things are thundered against men by the voice of the law; the terrors of the Lord are made known, hell is set before the eyes of sinners; but until the Lord come in the still voice of his Spirit, and apply these things to the conscience, the sinner never covers his face with shame and confusion, nor goes aside to mourn and lament his misery. This voice of God sounds to the very centre of the soul. As for the outward voice of the gospel alone, it signifies little; in hearing, men hear not. Matt. 13 : 13. They hear the voice of man, but not the voice of God; they hear the sound, but feel not the power of the word. What is spoken externally dies in the ear that hears it, but this still voice of the Spirit makes its way to the heart, and none knows what God speaks but the soul itself.

2. The spiritual voice of Christ is *personal*, speaking distinctly and particularly to the state of the soul, as if by name. Ministers must speak in general; they draw the bow of the gospel at a venture, not knowing to whom God will direct the arrow; but the Spirit guides it to the mark. He applies truth to particular persons, so that the soul to whom he directs it is fully convinced that the Lord intends and means him, in such a threatening expression. Oh, says the soul, has the Lord singled me out in particular? this is my very case. You read that Christ calleth his sheep by name. John 10:3. How does he do this, but by speaking directly and particularly to their condition, as if he called them by their particular names? He does not now in an extraordinary way, as of old, call, "Samuel, Samuel," or, "Saul, Saul," but he sends a beam of convincing light into the conscience, plainly showing this or that to be our sin, danger, or duty;

and as to the effect, it is all one as if God named him. And truly, until it comes to this the word has no saving operation upon the soul. A man may hear ten thousand general truths and assent to them, and yet be no better for them. How quiet was David's conscience, until Nathan struck the nail upon the head by a home personal application, and then his conscience startled. Thus God singles out one from a thousand in the congregation, speaks to the heart, and disturbs the secure conscience: the rest hear the same words, but feel not the same efficacy. And truly it is a choice mercy when God pleases thus to single out one person after this manner, to speak to his heart. As Christ said, in Luke 4:25, 26, many widows were in Israel in the days of Elias, but to none of them was Elias sent, save unto Sarepta, a city of Sidon, unto a woman that was a widow. So here, multitudes sat with you under the same prayer or sermon, but to none of them, at that time, was the Spirit sent to make a particular application thereof, but to thee. In this the peculiar goodness of God shines out, and should for ever be admired by that soul.

3. This spiritual voice of Christ is *distinguishable* by the soul that hears it from all other voices. The sheep know his voice. John 10:4. As in the style of the Scriptures there is a weight and majesty which distinguish them from all human compositions, so in this voice of Christ there is a peculiar efficacy, a divine authority, by which the soul distinguishes it from all human voices. It was said of Christ in the days of his flesh, "Never man spake like this man." John 7:46. The same may be said of his spiritual voice: the soul never heard such a voice before; it seals the truth upon the heart so firmly that no objections are left against it.

There are two things in this inward voice of Christ, which distinguish it from all human voices. First, a marvellous light comes into the soul with it, which discovers all the secrets of the heart. God shines into the heart at the same time he speaks to it, 2 Cor. 4 : 6 ; and now the secrets of the heart are manifest, and God is acknowledged to be in the word of truth. 1 Cor. 14 : 25. Second, a marvellous power accompanies this voice, to make a deep and firm impression of what is spoken on the soul ; and this power is a character of the voice of God, whereby the soul receives it as his, with much assurance, as the apostle speaks in 1 Thess. 1 : 5 : " Our gospel came not unto you in word only, but also in power, and in the Holy Ghost, and in much assurance." They could not be more certain of any thing, than they were that it was the Lord who spoke to them in that word. It is true, at the first instant the soul may be amazed and at a loss, as Peter, when he was delivered out of prison, thought at first he had seen a vision ; but when he was come to himself, he said, " Now, I know of a surety that the Lord hath sent his angel, and hath delivered me." Acts 12 : 11. Thus it is with the soul : it is amazed, and doubts what manner of call or power this is ; it never heard such a voice, nor felt any thing like this before. But the matter is quickly cleared up when the soul has reflected upon it, and finds such a wonderful change of the temper of the heart following upon it. I now speak not of those into whom grace is distilled in the way of godly education in their tender years, but of adult persons, and especially such as have been gross sinners.

4. This spiritual voice of Christ is a *surprising* voice, altogether unexpected by the soul that hears it : " I am found of them that sought me not." Isa. 65 : 1. Little do we foresee the designs God has in bringing us to such a place, and under such a sermon, at such a time ; even as little as Saul thought of a kingdom when he was seeking his father's asses. It is much with us as it was with the apostles when Christ called them : little did Matthew think when he sat at the receipt of customs, or Saul when hasting to Damas-

cus upon the devil's errand, that Christ and salvation were so near them. Some have come to deride the messengers and truths of God; others to gratify their curiosity; and many not knowing where else, with peace or reputation, to spend that hour. But God's thoughts were not theirs; the time of mercy was now come, and whatever sinful ends brought them thither, the Lord's design was then and there to manifest himself to them. It is with such souls, in some respects, as it was with the spouse, Sol. Song, 6:12: "Or ever I was aware, my soul made me like the chariots of Ammi-nadib." I went to the congregation for company; I was sitting under the word with a careless wandering heart, as at other times; when lo, an arrow of conviction was suddenly shot into my conscience, which so wounded and disquieted it, that it is now beyond the power of any but Christ to settle and satisfy it.

5. This spiritual internal voice of Christ is *energetical;* mighty in power, piercing the heart, cleaving, as it were, the very reins; full of efficacy to the soul that hears it. The power of God comes along with his voice. "The word of God is quick and powerful, and sharper than any two-edged sword, piercing even to the dividing asunder of soul and spirit, and of the joints and marrow." Heb. 4:12.

Now this efficacy is not inherent in the word itself, or all would feel this power who come within the sound of it. No, this comes from the Spirit of Christ, speaking in it to the sinner's conscience; when it is the administration of the Spirit, it becomes efficacious. You read, in Psalm 29:4–9, of the wonderful efficacy of God's voice: The voice of the Lord is powerful; the voice of the Lord is full of majesty; it breaketh the cedars, divideth the flames of fire, shaketh the wilderness, maketh the hinds to calve. This the providential voice of God, in the winds, thunders, and lightnings, can do; but what is this to the efficacy of his spiritual voice? What is the breaking of the cedars of

Lebanon to the breaking of the heart of a sinner? What is the shaking of the trees in the wilderness to the fears of wrath to come, which shake the souls of convinced sinners, and make their hearts tremble? Acts 16:29. What is the dividing of flames of fire, to the dividing a soul from its beloved lusts? "The weapons of our warfare are not carnal, but mighty through God, to the pulling down of strong holds, casting down imaginations, and every high thing that exalteth itself against the knowledge of God, and bringing into captivity every thought to the obedience of Christ." 2 Cor. 10:4, 5. Here are the glorious effects of this voice, which plainly show from whom it comes. The voice of God is no less to be admired in its effects in the new creation, than in the first creation, with which the apostle compares it. "God, who commanded the light to shine out of darkness, hath shined in our hearts." 2 Cor. 4:6. It was marvellous to see, at the word of Christ, Lazarus, who was dead in his grave, come forth bound in his grave-clothes, John 11:44; and no less to see a soul dead in sin, at a word of Christ, come forth with spiritual life. "The dead shall hear the voice of the Son of God; and they that hear shall live." John 5:25.

6. This spiritual voice of Christ is *convictive* to the conscience of a sinner, so that it puts a final end to all evasions. While man only spoke, the soul had a thousand means to evade what was spoken; but now all debates are at an end—no more subterfuges and cunning evasions now. The Spirit, when he cometh, shall convince the world of sin. John 16:8. The word signifies to convince by demonstration, and to show that a thing cannot possibly be otherwise than we represent it to be. Formerly, when the terrors of God were threatened against sin, the heart was wont to say, This concerns me no more than another; if it go ill with me, it will go ill with thousands as well as me. It is true, this is my evil; and who is without sin? I

have some evils in me, but I have some good too. But no sooner does the Spirit speak conviction to the conscience, than all these pleas are dismissed. It may be, the state of the sinner's soul was doubtful to him before; but it is not so now. It had some fears of hell, but they were balanced with some vain hopes of heaven; but now the great question is determined. Whatever I am or have, whatever duties I have done, and whatever sins I have avoided, I see I am not regenerated, I am in my natural, Christless state; and except I am changed, I must be lost. This was the effect of Christ's voice to Paul: "I was alive without the law once; but when the commandment came, sin revived, and I died." Rom. 7:9. He had read the law many a time, and had the literal knowledge of it; but his vain hopes lived and flourished, until the spiritual sense of the law came home to his heart by the voice of the Spirit, and then his vain hopes died, and his guilt stared in the face of his conscience.

7. The voice of Christ is generally conveyed to the souls of men through the *word preached*, which is the chosen instrument of its conveyance. We cannot affirm that Christ always speaks to men in this way; but certainly this is his ordinary course: "Our gospel came not unto you in word only, but also in power and in the Holy Ghost." 1 Thess. 1:5. Our gospel, because preached by us; but had that been all, it had come to you in word only, as it does to many thousands of others, who feel nothing in it more than what is human. But unto you it came in power and in the Holy Ghost; that is, our words were the vehicle through which the vital power of the Spirit was conveyed into your souls. Providences have their voice as well as the word; and sometimes the voice of Christ has accompanied the voice of providence, to the conversion of men's souls; but this is unusual. The established way of Christ's speaking to the hearts of sinners is by the word, and especially the word preached, which

on that account is called "the power of God unto salvation." Rom. 1 : 16. This instrument the Lord generally honors for the conveyance of spiritual life into the souls of men, though it is despised and contemned in the world. "The preaching of the cross is to them that perish, foolishness; but unto us which are saved, it is the power of God," 1 Cor. 1 : 18; that is, the instrument by which the saving power of God communicates itself to the souls of men. And although God may exert his saving power through providences, we seldom find he does so where the word may be had, but is neglected. Herein God consults our peace and satisfaction; for if he should make use of another medium, as a voice from heaven, and after calling, which is an usual case, the called soul should question, How do I know but all this may be a delusion? may not Satan impose upon mortals, and this voice be a counterfeit? my eternal estate depends upon it, and I need to be sure it was the voice of God himself: in such a case, it would be hard to give such distinguishing characters as might be to the satisfaction of the soul. But when God makes the word his instrument in this matter, it yields abundantly more satisfaction. We have a more sure word of prophecy, surer than a voice from heaven. 2 Pet. 1 : 19. And though Paul was converted by a voice from heaven, yet the Lord sends him to Ananias, who should preach the gospel to him. Acts 9 : 17. The Lord will honor his word. Providence may prepare the heart, but the word is the instrument by which the Lord ordinarily puts forth his power to salvation.

8. The voice of Christ leaves *abiding effects* on the soul that hears it. The words of men are scattered to the wind, but the effects of Christ's voice are durable: "I will never forget thy precepts; for with them thou hast quickened me." Psa. 119 : 93. How many hundred sermons have we heard, and all vanished away as a dream! Oh, but if ever thou heardst Christ speaking to thy heart in any ser-

mon or prayer, that will remain with thee for ever. His words are sealed upon the soul for ever; they are written in the heart. Jer. 31:33. What Job wished concerning his word, is really performed in the words of Christ: "They are written as in the rock for ever." Job 19:23. We have slippery memories, but the weakest memory must retain the words of Christ, spoken to the heart by his Spirit; for "He openeth the ears of men, and sealeth their instruction." Job 33:16.

IV. I shall next speak of THE PERSON TO WHOM CHRIST ORDINARILY DIRECTS his efficacious and saving voice. And though it be true that the Spirit of Christ is a free agent, and calls whom he will, according to John 3:8, "The wind bloweth where it listeth;" and it is true, in fact, that Christ has made some of all ranks of men to hear his voice; it is seldom that he directs this saving voice to the great and wise of this world: "Ye see your calling, brethren, how that not many wise men after the flesh, not many mighty, not many noble are called." 1 Cor. 1:26. He saith not *any*, but *many*. Christ does call some, "lest," as one says, "the world should think that Christians were deceived through their simplicity and weakness." One rich Joseph of Arimathea; one honorable Nicodemus, but not many. Men of the greatest renown in the world have been the fiercest enemies against Christ: Galen, the chief physician; Porphyry, the chief Aristotelian; Plotinus, the chief Platonist; Libanius and Lucian, the chief orators, were all professed enemies of Christ. Two things make a man great in the eyes of the world: the external endowments of Providence, heaping riches and honors upon him; and endowments of the mind, as strong reason, sharpness of wit, etc. When both these meet in the same person, they make him great in the eyes of the world, and usually in his own; yea, too great to stoop to the simplicity of the gospel, and its humbling, self-denying terms. These the Lord usually passes by, and directs his voice to the poor; the poor receive the gospel; God hath chosen the poor of this world rich in faith, and heirs of the kingdom. James 2 : 5. And this choice of God Christ blesses him for: "I thank thee, O Father, Lord of heaven and earth, because thou hast hid these things from the wise and prudent, and hast revealed them unto babes; even so, Father, for so it seemed good in thy sight." Matt. 11 : 25, 26. And indeed, the wisdom of God deserves our admiration in this dispensation : For

1. Hereby *the freeness of his grace is vindicated.* None can pretend that any earthly excellence commends any man to God, or that the favor of heaven is secured by the same means that the respects of the world are. For you see the truth of that scripture before your eyes, Job 34:19: He "accepteth not the persons of princes, nor regardeth the rich more than the poor; for they are all the work of his hands." Earthly riches and honors, empty as they are, are yet much idolized by men: what would they be, could they procure our favor and acceptance with the Lord?

2. By such a choice as this, the Lord plainly shows that *religion needs not worldly props to support it.* As at first it was spread by the power of God in the world, by poor and despised men, so it is still upheld without human policy or riches. The church is called the congregation of the poor. Psa. 74 : 19. The Lord will have us know, that he is able to maintain and carry on his counsels in the world without the wealth of rich men, the authority of great men, or the policies of wise men; he needs them not.

3. By this choice he *pours contempt upon the things most admired among men.* So he tells us: "God hath chosen the foolish things of the world to confound the wise; and God hath chosen the weak things of the world to confound the things which are mighty." 1 Cor. 1 : 27. And certainly, shame and confusion of face will cover the great ones of this world, when they shall see the poor Christians

whom they scorned on earth, as not worthy to come into their presence, so infinitely preferred before them in the favor of God. In a word, this efficacious spiritual voice of Christ is directed but to a few, even of the many that sit within the call of the gospel: "Many are called, but few are chosen." Matt. 22:14. Christ's flock is a little flock. There are many birds of prey to one bird of paradise—many common pebbles to one sapphire or diamond. It is not for us to dispute as to the reason, but to adore the sovereignty of God in this matter. And of those few whom he calls, the greatest part is of the humbler classes of men. The glitter and dazzle of this world blind the eyes of the greatest; extremity of want diverts the mind of the lowest; but between these two extremes there is a third sort of persons whom the Lord most usually calls.

V. If it be inquired WHY THE VOICE AND CALL OF CHRIST SHOULD BE DIRECTED TO THIS PERSON RATHER THAN TO THAT, certainly it is not from any excellence that Christ sees in one rather than another; for all are shut up under the common sin and misery of the fall; and therefore the apostle told the Ephesians, who had heard and answered the voice of Christ, that they "were by nature the children of wrath, even as others." Eph. 2:3. If it were not so, man would have something to glory in before God; but Christ resolves this whole dispensation into its proper cause, the good pleasure of the divine will: "Even so, Father, for so it seemed good in thy sight." Matt. 11:26. This good pleasure of the will of God sometimes causes those to hear the voice of his Son who seem to stand at a far greater distance and improbability to hear it than others do. It is said of the Ephesians, that they were far off, Eph. 2:13; yet they heard the voice of Christ when that discreet scribe who was not far from the kingdom of God, Mark 12:34, and Agrippa, who was almost persuaded to be a Christian, Acts 26:28, never heard it; therefore it is said, "Many shall come from the east and west, and shall sit down with Abraham and Isaac and Jacob in the kingdom of heaven; but the children of the kingdom shall be cast out into outer darkness." Matt. 8 : 11, 12. O marvellous dispensation! many a soul under the greatest disadvantages, a poor servant who has but little time and many incumbrances, is called effectually by this voice of Christ; when those who enjoy multitudes of opportunities, and have abundance of time on their hands which they know not what to do with, and who have the choicest books at command, amidst all these advantages hear and feel nothing to any purpose: all this is to be resolved into the good pleasure of the will of God.

VI. Let us now view THE EFFECTS of this voice of Christ upon the souls of men, and we shall find divers remarkable effects wrought upon the heart by it.

1. The first effect of the voice of Christ is *conviction* on the conscience—conviction both of sin and misery. John 16 : 8. The Spirit when he cometh shall convince the world of sin. This is a voice of terror, and strikes dead the vain hopes of a sinner. Rom. 7 : 9. The soul that was before secure becomes the seat of anxiety. There was a general conviction of sin before; he knew that all are sinners, he denied not that. But alas, this general conviction is quite another thing from what the soul feels now; now it can waive the matter no longer. This voice of Christ " showeth them their work and their trangressions, that they have exceeded," Job 36 : 9—exceeded in number, and exceeded in heinousness of aggravation. A general conviction of sin affects a man no more than the sight of a painted lion on a sign-post; but when a particular conviction is set home on the conscience by this special voice of Christ, sin is like a living lion, meeting a man in the way and roaring dreadfully upon him. This first effect of Christ's voice is introductory to,

2. *Humiliation* and contrition of heart for sin. Those

threats of Scripture against sin and sinners which were wont to be slighted, are now trembled at; those Jews to whose hearts Christ spoke in Peter's sermon, as soon as they heard his voice sounding conviction in their consciences, were pricked at the heart, Acts 2 : 37 : no sword can make such a wound, and put a man into such pain, as a sight of sin will; therefore they are said to mourn for Christ as for an only son. Zech. 12 : 10. Now this is the glorious prerogative of Jesus Christ, to reach and wound the heart with a word. The voice of man cannot do it; but the spirit of a man lies open both to be wounded and healed by a word from the mouth of Christ. No sooner has a sinner heard the awful voice of conviction spoken to his conscience by the Lord Jesus, but he feels himself sick at heart; he goes home from that sermon by which Christ spoke effectual conviction to him, crying, My soul is distressed because of sin. There is a great difference in the degrees of this contrition and humiliation; it penetrates deeper into some hearts than others, and holds them longer under it; but whoever has heard the convincing voice of Christ, feels so much sorrow for sin as for ever separates him from the love of it.

3. This voice of Christ *awakens the careless mind* to solicitude for deliverance from the danger that hangs over it. Trembling and astonished, the jailer cried out, " Sirs, what must I do to be saved?" Acts 16 : 29, 30. All the powers of the soul are engaged for deliverance. You generally observe, in convinced and humbled sinners, three signs of extraordinary solicitude about salvation. First, there is a strong intentness of their minds and thoughts, they stand night and day like a bow at its full bent; their thoughts are ever poring upon this matter, their sleep departs, for their sin and danger are ever before them. Second, it appears by their searching inquisitiveness about the way of escape; the question they carry with them wherever they meet with any whom they judge able to direct them is, What course

shall I take? What shall I do? Is there any hope for such a one as I? Did you ever know a soul in my condition? Third, it appears by the little notice they take of their outward afflictions, which, it may be, are strong and sharp enough to overwhelm them at another time; but now they take little notice of them. Sin lies so heavy that it makes heavy afflictions lie light.

4. A fourth effect of the voice of Christ is *encouragement and hope*, putting the soul on the use of means in order to the attainment of Christ and salvation; for it is an inviting as well as a convicting voice: and this is a remarkable difference between the voice of Christ and the voice of Satan, with respect to sin. Satan labors to cut off all hope and strike the soul dead under despair of mercy; well knowing, that if he can cut off hope, all endeavors of the soul after Christ are effectually stopped. But how much terror soever there may be in the voice of Christ, there is always something left behind it on the heart to breed and support hope. And truly the soul, amidst these sad circumstances, has great need of some encouragement; but the Lord usually, after sharp convictions, sets home upon the soul such a word as this: "Him that cometh to me I will in no wise cast out: for I came down from heaven, not to do mine own will, but the will of him that sent me." John 6: 37, 38. Here Christ offers the most rational satisfaction, and greatest encouragement that a convinced sinner, if he be willing, shall certainly find a hearty welcome with Christ. For mark how he argues it on purpose for the satisfaction of such souls: "I came down from heaven, not to do mine own will, but the will of him that sent me." The force of the encouragement lies here, "I and my Father are one," John 10: 30—one in will and one in design; our wills never can jar one with the other, on account of the perfect unity that is between us. Now, saith he, I came down from heaven, not only to do mine own will, which must necessarily

be supposed to be strongly inclined to receive and save all convinced and willing sinners, this being the very end of my incarnation and death, but also to do the will of my Father, who hath sent me to bind up the broken-hearted and anointed me to preach good tidings to the meek. Isa. 61 : 1. And therefore no such soul can rationally doubt of a welcome reception with me. And because the fears of a convinced conscience are great and many, and Satan seeks to aggravate them beyond the hope of mercy, it is usual with the Lord to direct the trembling sinner to such a scripture as that in Heb. 7 : 25, "Wherefore he is able also to save them to the uttermost, that come unto God by him;" making the fulness of Christ's saving power shine with a cheerful beam into the dark and distressed soul of a sinner, from such a word as that.

5. A fifth effect of Christ's powerful voice is an *attractive efficacy or sweet alluring* of the soul to Christ by that power which it communicates to the soul. "No man can come to me, except the Father which hath sent me draw him." "Every man, therefore, that hath heard and hath learned of the Father, cometh unto me." John 6 : 44, 45. Mark it, this voice speedily puts the soul into motion after Christ; coming follows hearing : when once the soul has heard the voice of God, away it comes from all sinful engagements in the world ; all ties between the soul and sin break asunder and give way; nothing can hold it from Christ. There is a strange restlessness in the spirit of man, and none but Christ can quiet it.

6. And then the effect of Christ's voice is *rest and consolation to the inner man.* When once the soul is come home to Christ by the efficacy of his heavenly call or voice, it enters into peace. "We which have believed, do enter into rest," Heb. 4 : 3—not only *shall*, but *do* enter into rest. As the first effect of Christ's voice was terror to the soul, so the last effect is peace ; it puts the soul into the most excel-

lent position for comfort and joy; it never stood upon such ground before; for this vocation stands between predestination and glorification: "Moreover, whom he did predestinate, them he also called; and whom he called, them he also justified; and whom he justified, them he also glorified." Rom. 8:30. See here into what a blessed mount of vision the voice of Christ calls the souls of sinners. Let the soul look backward or forward from eternity to eternity, there is nothing but a vision of peace before its eyes. This call of God points backward to God's eternal choice, which by this very call it is now manifest he made of that soul before the world was; and it points forward to that eternal glory unto which God is leading it. These are the effects of this almighty voice of Christ, and these the special instructions sealed by it upon the hearts of men.

But this voice of Christ is not heard at all times, but in some special hour—as Christ calls it, "The hour when the dead shall hear the voice of the Son of God." John 5:25. And elsewhere, by the apostle, it is called the accepted time, the day of salvation. 2 Cor. 6:2. The conjunction of the Spirit of Christ with the word, ordinances, or providences of God, but especially the word, makes this blessed hour. The word alone, though never so well preached, conduces no more to the conviction and salvation of a sinner, than the waters of Bethesda did to healing when the angel came not down to trouble them. John 5:4. But when the Lord pours out his Spirit with the word, according to the promise, "I will pour out my Spirit unto you, I will make known my words unto you," Prov. 1:23, then Christ speaks to the heart; this great conjunction of the word and Spirit makes that blessed season of salvation the time of love and of life. Now the voice of Christ is heard with effect, and the ordinances have a convincing and converting efficacy. There was an abundant effusion of the Spirit in the first age of Christianity, and then the voice of Christ was heard by multitudes of souls at once. There has since been a restraint of the Spirit, comparatively speaking; whereas three thousand souls were then converted at one sermon, possibly three thousand sermons have since been preached, and not one soul effectually called. This has made the church like a wilderness, a land of drought; and so it is likely to remain, "until the Spirit be poured upon us from on high, and the wilderness be a fruitful field," according to the promise, Isa. 32 : 15. And such a time we expect; Lord, hasten it, when the waters of the ordinances shall be healed, and "every thing that liveth, which moveth whithersoever the river shall come, shall live. And fishers shall stand upon it, from En-gedi even unto En-eglaim; they shall be a place to spread forth nets; their fish shall be according to their kinds, as the fish of the great sea, exceeding many." Ezek. 47 : 9, 10. Then ministers shall no longer fish with angles, catching now one and then another; but shall spread forth their nets and inclose multitudes of converts.

There are some happy seasons wherein Christ utters his almighty voice in the word, but their time is unknown to man; we cannot say when it will come, but are to wait for it as the man did at the pool of Bethesda. Ministers must preach in hope, and wait in hope, if at any time God will give the people repentance. 2 Tim. 2 : 25. We are often mistaken in our conjectures: when we have made the best preparations, and have a more than ordinary enlargement of spirit, we are apt to conclude this is the blessed hour wherein Christ will speak to the heart as we do to the ear; but we often find ourselves mistaken; yet we must wait in hope, and so must our people. Such a happy time may come, and when it doth it will be a day for ever to be remembered, because then the first actual application of Christ will be made to your souls; without which all that the Father has done in election, and the Son in his redemption, would be of no advantage to your souls. And therefore you shall find that this work of the Spirit stands between those works, and makes them effectual to our salvation. 1 Pet. 1 : 2. This is the hour upon which our eternal blessedness depends; it will be celebrated for ever in your praises, in the world to come. O what an influence has this hour to all eternity! The hearing of this voice of Christ opens the councils of heaven, and brings to light the eternal counsels of God concerning you: "Knowing, brethren beloved, your election of God. For our gospel came not unto you in word only, but also in power, and in the Holy Ghost." 1 Thess. 1 : 4, 5. This gives greater assurance of the eternal love of God to a man's soul, than the sweetest smile of providence or any voice from heaven could do. This is the day of our spiritual resurrection, John 5 : 25—a greater and more glorious resurrection by far than that of your bodies at the last day; so much greater, as the value of your souls is above that of your bodies: as also, because the blessedness of your bodily resurrection depends on this your spiritual resurrection by the voice of Christ. Dreadful will the voice of Christ be at the resurrection of your bodies, except you first hear this vital voice of Christ quickening your souls with spiritual life. To conclude, this is the great era from which you are to date all your spiritual mercies; for as the Lord said unto the Jews, "From this day will I bless you," Hag. 2 : 19; so saith the Lord to you, From this hour wherein you have heard and obeyed the voice of Christ, will I bless you for ever with all spiritual blessings in heavenly places in him.

INFERENCE 1. This point presents us with abundant matter of *lamentation over multitudes* who sit under the sound of the gospel, yet, as Christ speaks of the Jews, John 5 : 37, have not heard the voice of God at any time. The ministerial voice of Christ they hear daily; but this efficacious internal voice, which makes the ministerial voice the word of life and power, they have not heard. The gospel, to most of our hearers, is but an empty sound : this is a sad symptom. "If our gospel be hid, it is hid to them that are lost ; in whom the god of this world hath blinded the minds of them that believe not." 2 Cor. 4 : 3, 4. This hiding of the gospel is not opposed to the external ministration of it, nor to the understanding of the true sense and meaning of the truths delivered by it ; but to that internal efficacy which is here called hearing Christ's voice. Our hearers are generally satisfied when they have heard a sermon, much more if they can remember something of it, though the Lord has not spoken one truth they have heard home to their hearts. This is a sad case, and God grant it be not that very judgment threatened, Isa. 6 : 9, "Hear ye indeed, but understand not ; and see ye indeed, but perceive not." Hearing the voice of man without feeling the power of God, is all one as if we heard not. Reflect upon this, you that are as unconcerned under the word as the seats you sit upon. God speaketh once, yea, twice, but man perceiveth it not. The eternal decrees and counsels of God are now executing upon the souls of men under the gospel. As many as are ordained to eternal life shall believe and feel the power of God's truth upon their hearts. Acts 13 : 48. And methinks it should be of startling consideration, when you see others struck to the heart, cast into fear and tremblings by the same word that does not in the least touch your hearts. It may be you think this is but fancy and melancholy, but that very thought is an artifice of Satan to blind your eyes. Christ made another use of it when he told the secure and self-righteous Jews, "John came unto you in the way of righteousness, and ye believed him not ; but the publicans and the harlots believed him : and ye, when ye had seen it, repented not afterward that ye might believe him." Matt. 21 : 32. As though he had said, What did you do to quiet your consciences, when you saw other sinners humbled and brought to faith under John's ministry ? It is strange there should be no reflections in your consciences upon your own state and condition; but thus it must be, one shall be taken and another left; to some the gospel shall be the savor of life unto life, and to others the savor of death unto death. Who can look over so great a part of a congregation without tender compassion, considering that unto this day the Lord has not given them eyes to see, nor ears to hear? They have heard multitudes of sermons; and they have also heard what effects these have had upon other men's hearts; but they have none upon theirs. O that such souls would cry to the Lord Jesus in such language as that in Sol. Song 13:13: "The companions hearken to thy voice: cause me to hear it." Lord, let me not sit under the word any longer deaf to the voice of thy Spirit in it. Open the ears of my soul, that I may hear thy voice and feel thy power; otherwise the voice of the ministry will be ineffectual to my salvation; it will but quiet my conscience for a little while, and prove a dreadful aggravation of my misery in the end.

2. It also follows from the subject, that we have this day before our eyes *a great confirmation of the truth of the Scriptures.* No miracles can seal it firmer than the events which are visible to all that will observe them. What you read in the word you may see every day fulfilled before your eyes. "We are unto God a sweet savor of Christ, in them that are saved, and in them that perish: to the one we are the savor of death unto death, and to the other the savor of life unto life." 2 Cor. 2:15, 16. And again, Acts 28:24, when Paul in his lodgings had expounded and testified the kingdom of God to the people, and persuaded them to believe from morning till evening, it is observed, that "some believed the things which were spoken, and some believed not." Here you see the contrary effects of the preaching of the gospel, according to the scripture account of it: it quickens some and kills others; brings some to faith, and leaves others still in unbelief. Compare this account with

what is daily before you: do you not see souls influenced to contrary effects under the same word; one melting and tender, another hardened and wholly unconcerned? Tell me, you that are apt to ascribe all to nature, how comes it to pass in men exercising reason alike, men that have the same inbred fears and hopes of things eternal, who have the same passions and affections, and are in the selfsame condition with others; yet one man's heart is wounded, and goes away trembling from under the selfsame word which affects the other no more than if it had been preached among the tombs to the dead that lie there? Say not that some have more courage than others, or clearer understandings; for the word has convinced as rational and courageous persons as those upon whom it has had no such effect. I doubt not but that the jailer who was filled with such trembling and astonishment, Acts 16 : 27–30, was as stout and rugged a person as any to whom Paul usually preached; his very office bespoke him such a man. Wonder not what it is that makes men alarmed at such a sound, which you hear as well as they, but it affects you not. The Lord speaks in that voice to their hearts, but not to yours; and so it must be, according to the account the Scriptures give us of the contrary effects of the gospel on them that hear it; which is, I say, a firm seal of the truth of the Scriptures, and highly worth the observation of all.

3. *What dignity has God stamped on gospel ordinances*, in making them the medium through which Christ speaks life to dead souls. This greatly exalts the dignity of the gospel, and deservedly endears it to our souls. I deny not but God can convey spiritual life without them; but though he hath not restricted himself, yet he hath enjoined on us a diligent attendance upon them, and that with the deepest respect and reverence. "He that heareth you, heareth me; and he that despiseth you, despiseth me; and he that despiseth me, despiseth him that sent me." Luke 10 : 16.

Behold how this sin is aggravated to the height of sinfulness. The contempt of the gospel runs much higher than men are aware of. We think it no great matter to neglect and contemn a messenger of Jesus Christ; but that contempt flies in the very face and authority of Christ, who gave them their commissions—yea, in the very face of God the Father, who gave Christ his commission. Christ speaks by his ministers, they are his mouth. Jer. 15:19. Moreover, the sin strikes at our own souls, and we injure them as well as Christ. For the word preached is his appointed instrument to convey spiritual life, the best of blessings, to our souls. Upon which account it is called "the word of life," and "the power of God unto salvation." We militate against our life and salvation when we despise and neglect the ordinances of God. It is good for men continually to wait on them; who knows when the Spirit of God will breathe life to your souls through them? What if you have yet found no such benefit from them? The very next opportunity may be the appointed season of your salvation. Bring your ungodly relatives with you, as men did their diseased friends when Christ was on earth, laying them in the way he was to pass. Christ will honor his ordinances; see that you do not despise them.

4. *What a fearful judgment is the loss of the gospel*, seeing that by it Christ speaketh life to the souls of men. The Spirit and the word of God usually come and go together; when therefore these are gone, no more conversions are to be expected: dreadful is the case of that people. "Where there is no vision, the people perish." Prov. 29:18. Those are direful menaces in Isaiah 8:16, "Bind up the testimony, seal the law among my disciples;" and Rev. 2:5, "I will remove thy candlestick out of his place." Better the sun were taken out of heaven than the gospel out of the church. Think not God has made such a settlement of the gospel that it shall never be removed, however you use it.

Your Advocate in heaven has obtained it for you for a time upon trial; if you bring forth fruit, well; you and the generations to come shall be happy in it; if not, this blessed tree, which has brought forth so many mercies to you and yours, must and will be cut down. Yea, and even now is the axe laid at the root of the tree. Matt. 3 : 10. It is an allusion to a carpenter that throws down the axe and the saw at the root of the tree he intends to cut down. The only ground of hope which remains with us is, that there are some buds appearing, some fruits putting forth; and if there be a blessing in the bud, the Lord will spare it, according to Isa. 65 : 8. But these hopes are balanced with many sad symptoms, which may make us tremble to think what God is about to do with such a sinful people.

5. *Those who have heard Christ's voice in the gospel have no reason to be discouraged from going to Christ in faith.* Christ's call is a sufficient warrant to believe. Many are staggered in their work of faith by the fear of presumption, an objection which they know not how to clear themselves of; but certainly this, above all other considerations, destroys the objection of presumption. Men presume when they act without a call or warrant; but if Christ has spoken to our hearts by the voice of his Spirit, you have the best warrant in the world to go to him. What though you know not the issue, your obedience is due to his call. "By faith Abraham, when he was called to go out into a place which he should after receive for an inheritance, obeyed; and he went out, not knowing whither he went." Heb. 11 : 8. So must you. It is not necessary to your going to Christ, that you must know beforehand what the result thereof shall be. Your believing is an act of obedience to Christ who calls you. When therefore Satan shall object, What, such a wretched soul as thou go to Christ? Canst thou imagine to find favor with him, whom thou hast so deeply wronged? Thy answer should be, It is true, I have been a vile wretch,

and deeply wronged the Lord Jesus; but he has spoken to my heart, he hath called me, and therefore it can be no presumption in me to go at his call; but contrariwise, it would be flat rebellion against his sovereign command to refuse to believe, and come unto him; yea, it would be a greater sin than any of my former sins have been. Besides, had the Lord Jesus no intention of mercy towards my soul, he would never have spoken to my heart by conviction and persuasion, as he has done.

6. If no soul opens to Christ until it hear his powerful, spiritual voice, then *the change made in men by conversion is supernatural.* The rise of faith is from this power of Christ, not from the nature of man. John 1 : 13. Proud nature arrogates this honor to itself, but without any ground; for though some things may be done by men in their natural state, which have a remote tendency to conversion and spiritual life, yet the soul never opens to Christ savingly, without a power communicated from himself. Nature produces no such effect as this. The Scriptures speak plainly : " The natural man receiveth not the things of the Spirit of God ; for they are foolishness unto him : neither can he know them, because they are spiritually discerned." 1 Cor. 2 : 14. " By grace are ye saved, through faith ; and that not of yourselves, it is the gift of God." Eph. 2 : 8. " The carnal mind is enmity against God ; for it is not subject to the law of God, neither indeed can be." Rom. 8 : 7. " How can ye, being evil, speak good things." Matt. 12 : 34. " Not that we are sufficient of ourselves to think any thing as of ourselves; but our sufficiency is of God." 2 Cor. 3 : 5. How fallen then is man, who can neither believe nor obey, speak a good word nor think a good thought, without power from on high.

Say not it is against reason for God to require men to do what they cannot do, and then eternally punish them for not doing it. For, first, though man has lost his ability to obey,

God has not lost his right to command. For then any man might shake off the yoke of God's sovereignty by disabling himself through his own sin for the duties of obedience. Second, though man has not sufficient power, yet there is in him an intolerable pride, which fills him with a conceit that he has what he has not, and can do what he cannot. The command is therefore of great use to check this pride, and to convince man of his weakness. Rev. 3 : 17. Third, every man can do more than he does towards his conversion. And therefore it is good for men to be urged by commands to all the duties in the use of which Christ comes into the soul by a supernatural power.

7. This doctrine furnishes a powerful incentive to all within the sound of the gospel, especially to such as feel some power accompanying the word to their hearts, *diligently to hearken to the voice of Christ, and obey his call without further delay.* "He that hath an ear to hear, let him hear." Rev. 2 : 7. It is a dreadful and dangerous thing to turn away the ear from him that speaks from heaven : "See that ye refuse not him that speaketh. For if they escaped not who refused him that spake on earth, much more shall not we escape, if we turn away from him that speaketh from heaven." Heb. 12 : 25. See that ye refuse not. The caution implies the matter to be very weighty, and a neglect or refusal to be highly dangerous. Turn not away your ear, be not guilty of neglect in so important a concern.

Truly this caution is no more than is needful; for Satan is never more busy with the souls of men than when Christ first effectually calls them to himself. O what a thick succession of discouragements impetuously assault the soul at this time ! Art thou young ? then he insinuates that it is too soon for thee to mind the serious things of religion ; that this will extinguish all thy pleasure in a dull melancholy; that thou mayest have time enough hereafter to mind these matiers. This temptation Augustine confesses kept him off many years from Christ. But certainly, if thou art old enough to be lost, thou art not too young to receive Christ and salvation. There are graves just of thy length, and young as well as old are found in eternal perdition. Besides, all those godly youth who turned to the Lord betimes, as Josiah, Abijah, Timothy, and many more, will be your judges, and condemn you in the great day. None ever repented that they opened to Christ too soon: thousands have repented that they kept him out so long. Art thou old? then he alarms thee with the manifold sins of thy youth, and places them as obstructions in thy way to Christ. And whether young or old, he will present the sufferings and persecutions of godliness, to discourage thee from hearkening to the voice of Christ. But what are the sufferings for Christ here, to the sufferings from Christ hereafter? What are the pains of mortification to the pains of damnation? Besides, all the promises of Christ, promises of strength, comfort, and success, go with the command of Christ to believe, and shall surely be performed to the obedient soul. See, therefore, that thou refuse not his voice.

But you will say, All that hear this voice of Christ are said to live. John 5:25. Now I am much in the dark whether this vital voice of Christ has sounded into my soul. Alas, I feel little, if any thing, of the spiritual life in my soul. I am dead and dark. Let us then improve the doctrine by way of TRIAL.

QUESTION. *By what signs does the life of Christ show itself in the souls of men?*

ANSWER. There are diverse signs of spiritual life, and blessed is the soul that finds them.

(1.) There is a spiritual *feeling* accompanying the spiritual life. I speak not only of the sense of comfort, for many a soul in Christ feels little of that; but there is a sense and feeling of the burden of sin. Rom. 7 : 24. And it is well that we can feel that; for there are multitudes in the world that are past feeling. Isa. 6 : 9, 10. It is a sign Christ has spoken to thy heart, if sorrow for sin begins to load it.

(2.) Spiritual *motions towards Christ* are a sign of spiritual life; at least, that God is about that quickening work of faith upon thy soul: "Every man therefore that hath heard, and hath learned of the Father, cometh unto me." John 6 : 45. The effectual voice of God sets the soul in motion towards Christ; the will is moving after him; the desires are panting for him. The voice of God makes the soul that hears it restless. As for others, their wills are fixed, there is no moving them. John 5 : 40. Now consider how it is with thee, reader. Art thou weighing and pondering the terms of the gospel, struggling through discouragements and temptations to come to Christ upon his own terms, lifting up thy heart to him for power to believe, crying with the spouse, Draw me, we will run after thee? Sol. Song 1 : 4. This is a comfortable sign that Christ has spoken to thy heart.

(3.) A spirit of *prayer* is an evidence of spiritual life, as the effect of Christ's voice to thy soul. As soon as Christ had spoken effectually to Paul's heart, the first effect that appeared in him as a sign of spiritual life, was the breath of prayer. Behold, he prayeth! Acts 9 : 11. God has no still-born children. Measure thyself by this rule; time was when thou couldst say a prayer, and wast very well satisfied with it, whether thou hadst any communion with God in it or no; but is it so still? Is there not a holy restlessness of spirit after God, since the time that his word came home to thy heart? Surely thou canst remember when it was not with thee as it is now.

(4.) There is a spiritual *relish* resulting from the spiritual life, which is also an evidence of it. If God has spoken life to thy soul, there will be in it an agreeable pleasure and delight in spiritual things: "My soul shall be satisfied as with marrow and fatness." Psa. 63 : 5. Now thy thoughts can feed with pleasure upon spiritual things which they disliked before.

(5.) Spiritual *aversions* as well as spiritual *inclinations* indicate a spiritual life. Every creature has an aversion to what is destructive to it. Now there is nothing so destructive to spiritual life as sin; that is the deadly poison which the renewed soul dreads. "Keep back thy servant also from presumptuous sins." Psa. 19 : 13. It cries out as a man who finds himself upon the brink of a pit, or the edge of a precipice: "Keep back thy servant." Such aversion to sin, and trembling under temptations tending to sin, are comfortable signs that Christ has spoken life to thy soul.

(6.) *Heavenly tendencies* and longings after God are excellent signs that thy soul has heard his voice, and been quickened with spiritual life by it. Sanctification is a well of water springing up into everlasting life. John 4 : 14. If thou hast seen the beauty, felt the power, and heard the voice of Christ, thy soul, like a body which has lost its centre, will still be gravitating and inclining Christward. When thou hast once heard the effectual call, Come unto me, Matt. 11 : 28, thy soul will continually echo the voice of holy love: "And the Spirit and the bride say, Come. And let him that heareth say, Come." Rev. 22 : 17. Thou wilt say in reply, "Come, Lord Jesus." Rev. 22 : 20. A sweeter sign of hearing Christ's voice can hardly be found in a soul, than a longing to be with Christ in the state of perfect freedom from sin, and full fruition of the beloved and blessed Jesus.

CHAPTER IX.

THE OPENING OF THE HEART TO CHRIST BY FAITH THE GREAT DESIGN OF THE GOSPEL.

"IF ANY MAN HEAR MY VOICE *AND OPEN THE DOOR*, I WILL COME IN TO HIM." Rev. 3:20.

The powerful voice of Christ is the key that opens the door of the soul to receive him. The opening of the heart to receive Christ is the main design in all the external and internal administrations of the gospel and the Holy Spirit.

The gospel has two great designs. One is, to open the heart of God to men, and to show them the everlasting counsels of grace and peace which were hid in God from ages and generations past; that all men may now see what God has been designing and contriving for their happiness in Christ before the world was: "To make all men see what is the fellowship of the mystery which from the beginning of the world hath been hid in God, who created all things by Jesus Christ; to the intent that now unto the principalities and powers in heavenly places might be known by the church the manifold wisdom of God." Ephes. 3:9, 10. The other intention of the gospel is, to open the hearts of men to receive Jesus Christ, without which all the glorious discoveries of the eternal counsels and gracious contrivances of God for us, would signify nothing to our real advantage. Christ's standing, knocking, and speaking by his Spirit, of which we have before treated, receive their success, and attain their end, when the heart opens itself by faith to receive him, and not till then. Hence we see our ninth doctrine is,

The opening of the heart to receive Christ by faith, is the great design of the gospel.

This is the mark to which all the arrows in the gospel-quiver are levelled—the centre into which those blessed lines are drawn. "These are written that ye might believe that Jesus is the Christ, the Son of God; and that believing, ye might have life through his name." John 20:31. All the precious truths that are written in the Scriptures are to bring you to faith. The great design of the Spirit in his illuminations, convictions, and humiliations is the same thing: "This is the work of God, that ye believe." John 6:29. It is not only a work worthy of such an author, but that on which God's eye is fixed in his workings upon us—the end and aim of his work.

Great persons have great designs. This is the glorious project of the great God, and each person in the Godhead is engaged in it. 1. The Father's hand is in this work, and without it no heart could ever open or move towards Christ: "No man can come to me, except the Father which hath sent me draw him." John 6:44. None but he that raised up Christ from the dead, can raise up a dead heart to saving faith in him. 2. The Son's hand is in this work; he is not only the *object*, but the *author* of our faith. "We know that the Son of God is come, and hath given us an understanding, that we may know him that is true; and we are in him that is true, even in his Son Jesus Christ. This is the true God, and eternal life." 1 John, 5:20. 3. And then the Holy Spirit comes from heaven expressly to convince sinners of their need of Christ, and beget faith in them. John 16:9. So that this appears to be the great design of heaven, the drift and level both of the word and works of God. Touching this design of the gospel I shall here speak, endeavoring to illustrate this great and glorious project of heaven in its greatness; its difficulty; the Agent and instrument employed in it; and its scope and aim. And,

I. Of the GREATNESS of this design of God. We little understand what a marvellous thing is done on the earth when the heart of a sinner is brought to close with Christ by faith. It would transport us with admiration, did we

11*

thoroughly consider it. Well may the apostle place it in the first rank of the wonderful works of God : "Great is the mystery of godliness : God was manifest in the flesh, justified in the Spirit, seen of angels, preached unto the Gentiles, believed on in the world." 1 Tim. 3 : 16. Observe with what works of wonder faith is here associated. It is an astonishing work of God, that ever God should be manifested in the flesh—that he who thunders in the clouds should cry in a cradle—that he who is over all, God blessed for ever, should become a man. It is astonishing, that when he was taken down dead from the cross, laid in the sepulchre, and the stone sealed upon it, he should rise on the third day from the dead by his own power. That the gospel should be preached to such miserable people as the Gentiles were, the scorn and contempt of the Jews. And no less marvellous is it, to see the hearts of such poor creatures, which were glued fast to idolatry and dead in sin, open to Christ upon such self-denying terms as to let go all they had in the world for a blessed inheritance which they never saw. Were not this a marvellous work of God indeed, there would not be such joy and triumph in heaven among the holy angels, as there is on the opening of every sinner's heart to Christ. Luke 15 : 7. The whole city of God is moved with it. Heaven rings with the joyful tidings. As soon as the will begins to bow and open to Christ, the news is quickly in heaven, and all the angels of God rejoice at the tidings. As when a young prince is born, there is joy in every city throughout the kingdom ; so also there is in heaven, when Christ hath gotten a new habitation in the soul of any sinner upon earth. Moreover, the greatness of this design appears from the great rewards promised by the Lord to every servant of his who in the least degree helps it on. God would never reward the instruments so richly, if the success of the work were not of great value in his eyes. The ministers of Christ may be ill-rewarded by men, persecuted and reproached for their labor, but God will bountifully repay their pains and faithfulness. "They that be wise shall shine as the brightness of the firmament; and they that turn many to righteousness, as the stars for ever and ever." Dan. 12 : 3. All these things show it to be a great and important design, upon which the heart of God is much set.

II. As it is an exceeding great and important work of God, so it is a very HARD AND DIFFICULT WORK in itself—a work whose difficulties surmount the ability of angels. It is certainly a work carried on by the mighty power of God, through the greatest opposition; and therefore it is said that it is the peculiar prerogative of Jesus Christ, who only hath the key of the house of David, to open the heart of a sinner by faith. Rev. 3 : 7. Men think it is an easy thing to believe; but if you consult the Scriptures, you will quickly be informed how greatly you mistake the nature of this work. The believing soul is said to be risen with Christ, through the faith of the operation of God, who raised him from the dead. Cor. 2 : 12. In the resurrection of Christ there was a glorious operation of the power of God indeed! you know it astonished the world to hear of it. The very same power that wrought that, must also be put forth to work this, or it would never be wrought. So again, "By grace are ye saved, through faith : and that not of yourselves; it is the gift of God." Eph. 2 : 8. Not of yourselves : you are no more able to come to Christ by faith, in your own power, than Lazarus was able to unbind himself in the grave, and come forth. Yea, in Eph. 1 : 19, the work of believing is ascribed unto the exceeding greatness of the power of God. No other but the almighty power of God can do it : it exceeds the power of ministers, yea, of angels. Three things will evince the difficulty of this work.

1. *The nature* of the work of faith, which is wholly

supernatural. It is no less than gaining over the hearty and full consent of the will to take Jesus Christ with his yoke of obedience, Matt. 11 : 29, and with his cross of sufferings, Matt. 16 : 24. And how far these will carry a man into dangers, losses, and sufferings, who can tell? and all this upon the account of an unseen happiness and glory. Lusts and corruptions must be mortified, pleasures and profits in the world abandoned; reproaches, losses, pains, and all that the devil and the world can lay upon us for Christ's sake, must be embraced and welcomed. And can it be supposed that any power beneath the almighty power of the Lord, any voice except the efficacious voice of Christ, can prevail with the will to give its firm, explicit consent to such difficult and self-denying terms as these?

2. Consider the *subject* wrought upon: the hard, obstinate heart of a perverse sinner—a heart harder by nature than the nether mill-stone. It is as easy to melt the most obdurate rock into a sweet syrup, as it is to melt the heart of a sinner into penitential sorrows for sin. What, to bring a dead heart to life; to make a man bitterly bewail the sins that were his delight, more than he ever bewailed the death of his dearest relation in the world; to make a proud heart renounce its own self-righteousness, which it dotes upon, and take all shame and reproach to itself upon account of sin: this is wonderful. You would think it a strange thing to see the course of the tide stopped with the breath of a man; but O what a marvellous thing is here, that at the preaching of the gospel by a poor worm, the Lord should turn the tide of the will, and thus bring the soul to a ready compliance with his most self-denying terms and proposals!

3. That which further increases the difficulty of believing is the fierce *opposition made by the enemies of faith*. All the powers of hell and earth without us are in league with the corruptions within us, to resist and hinder this work

of believing. Never is the devil more busy than when Christ and the soul are treating about union. O the discouragements, objections, and difficulties that are rolled into the way of faith! one while it is the highest presumption; another while it is impossible, and utterly too late: sometimes blasphemous injections, like fiery darts, are shot into the soul; at other times the invincible difficulties of religion are objected, and losses and torments are opposed to this work The tempter presents himself in a thousand shapes to hinder the soul's passing out of nature to Christ; sometimes objecting the greatness of sin, and sometimes the loss of the proper season and opportunity of mercy, together with the want of due qualifications to come to Christ. Thus, and many other ways, he endeavors to prevent sinners from taking hold of Christ: and as every devil in hell opposes this work, so every carnal interest we have in the world is an enemy to faith. We have enemies enough within us, as well as without us, conspiring together to obstruct this work; all things increase the difficulty of believing.

III. We are next to speak of the AGENT AND INSTRUMENT employed in this great design.

1. The *Agent* by whose efficacy the heart is opened is *the Spirit of God*, without whom it is impossible the design should ever prosper: neither ordinances, providences, or ministers can be successful without him. If the Lord make use of any man for the conversion and salvation of another's soul, he may rejoice in it; but withal must say, as Peter to the Jews, "Why look ye so earnestly on us, as though by our own power or holiness we had made this man to walk?" Acts 3:12 So may the ablest minister in the world say, when God blesses his labors to the conversion of any soul, Look not upon me, as though by the strength of my reason, or the power of my gifts, I had opened thy soul to Christ: this is the work of God's Spirit, in whose hand I am an instrument. 1 Cor. 3:7. He that plants is nothing, and he

that waters is nothing—nothing in himself; the very first stroke of conviction, which is introductive to the whole work of conversion, is justly ascribed to the Spirit. John 16:9. The Spirit when he cometh shall convince the world of sin. He is the Lord of all sanctifying and gracious influences. Ordinances are but as the sails of a ship, ministers as the seamen that manage those sails; the anchor may be weighed, the sails spread, but when all this is done, there is no sailing till a wind come. We preach and pray, and you hear; but there is no motion Christward, until the Spirit of God, compared to the wind, John 3:8, blow upon them. Until he illuminates the understanding with divine light, and bows the will by an almighty power, there can be no spiritual motion heavenward. Now the Spirit of the Lord is a free agent, not tied to means, times, or instruments; but, as at a certain time an angel came down upon the waters of Bethesda, and put a healing virtue into them, so it is here: therefore never come to any gospel ordinance without an eye to the Spirit, on whom all the blessings and efficacy depend. O lift up your hearts for his blessing upon the means, as ever you expect saving benefits from them.

2. The *instrument* by which this blessed design is accomplished in the world, is *the gospel ministry*. "Who then is Paul, and who is Apollos, but ministers by whom ye believed?" 1 Cor. 3:5. This is the ordinary method of producing faith; and though God has not bound himself to this or that minister, time, or place, he has bound us to a diligent and constant attendance upon the means of grace: "How then shall they call on him in whom they have not believed? and how shall they believe in him of whom they have not heard? and how shall they hear without a preacher?" Rom. 10:14. I confess, it seems a very unlikely means, a weak and foolish method, according to human wisdom; yet by the foolishness of preaching, it

pleases God to save them that believe. 1 Cor. 1 : 21. That which the wisdom of men derides, God makes effectual unto salvation. And O how many are there that will have cause to bless God to all eternity, for gifting and sending ministers among them, whose doctrine the Lord blessed to the conversion of their souls.

IV. Consider THE GREAT DESIGN for which these instruments are employed; there are no great designs in the world but aim at some end to be accomplished by them. Now there are two things in this design which are worthy of it.

1. The *exaltation of divine grace* and the riches of his goodness before angels and men to all eternity. The name of God is never made so glorious in this world, as it is by bringing the hearts of men to believe. God reaps more glory from the faith of a sinner that comes to Christ empty and weary, than from all other works of his hands. He has not like glory from the sun, moon, and stars as from creatures whose hearts open to Jesus Christ under the gospel call. Thus they are fitted to manifest the glory of his grace. Eph. 1 : 5, 6. God will have his rich and glorious grace praised and admired by angels and men for evermore; and every converted soul is a monument erected unto the praise of his grace. Heaven will ring with praises for ever, that the great God would humble himself to come into the heart of a vile sinner, and dwell and walk therein, as the expression is, 2 Cor. 6 : 16. This is admirable, that the high and lofty One, who inhabits eternity, will take up his dwelling-place in a poor contrite sinner, that trembles at his word. Isa. 57 : 15.

2. The *eternal salvation* and blessedness of the soul so opened to Christ, is also the design of this work of opening the heart. When the soul of Zaccheus was opened by faith, Christ said, "This day is salvation come to this house." Luke 19 : 9. You do not only believe to the glory of God, but to the salvation of your own soul. Heb. 10 : 39. The

opening of our hearts to Christ now, is in order to the opening of heaven to us hereafter; this is both the end of the work and the intention of the worker. "It pleased God by the foolishness of preaching to save them that believe." 1 Cor. 1:21. It at once puts them into a state of salvation, though they be not yet actually and completely saved. There is a necessary connection between conversion and salvation. Though between conversion and complete salvation there may be many groaning hours and sad days and nights, yet full deliverance from sin and misery is secured to the soul in the work of faith. Christ in you is the hope of glory. Col. 1:27.

Thus you see this great design projected and accomplished; and that this is the very scope, aim, and intention of the whole gospel, even the opening the hearts of sinners unto Christ by faith, will evidently appear by considering the several parts of the gospel which have a direct aspect upon this design, and the declared intention of the Spirit, who is sent forth to make it effectual to this very purpose.

(1.) To this the *commands* of the gospel look; it lies full in the eye of the preceptive part of the gospel. "And this is his commandment, that we should believe on the name of his Son Jesus Christ. 1 John, 3:23. It is a very great encouragement, if rightly considered, that faith is constituted a duty by a plain gospel precept; for this cuts off the pretence and plea of presumption. What, such a vile wretch as thou, saith Satan, presume to believe in Christ? But here is a command from the highest Sovereign, the contempt of which men shall answer at their peril.

(2.) This also is the declared intention of the gospel *promises and threatenings*, whereby the souls of sinners are assaulted on both sides. As for *promises*, how are all the sacred pages of the Bible adorned with them as the firmament with radiant stars. Among which that in the text seems to excel in glory. "If any man open to me, I will come in to him." Like unto which is this: "I am the bread of life: he that cometh to me shall never hunger; and he that believeth on me shall never thirst; him that cometh to me I will in no wise cast out." John 6:35, 37. Such rich encouragements to faith had never been put into the *promises*, but for faith's sake. And then for gospel *threatenings*, though they have a dreadful sound, yet they have a gracious design. What a terrible thunder-clap is this: "He that believeth not the Son, shall not see life; but the wrath of God abideth on him." John 3:36. To which another threatening echoes with a like terrible voice: "He that believeth not, shall be damned." Mark 16:16. There are dreadful things, you see, threatened in the gospel against unbelievers; but what is the design of those threatenings, but to rouse men by fear out of their unbelief and security, and guide them to Christ? Thus both the promises and the threatenings, though of far different natures, conspire and meet in the selfsame design, even to open the heart to Christ by faith.

(3.) For the sake of this design, all gospel *ordinances and officers* are instituted and continued in the world to this day. Why did Christ at his triumphant ascension shed forth such a variety of gifts upon men, but that God might dwell among them? "Thou hast ascended on high, thou hast led captivity captive: thou hast received gifts for men; yea, for the rebellious also, that the Lord God might dwell among them." Psalm 68:18. The whole frame of gospel ordinances is set up to bring men to Christ, and build them up in him. Eph. 4:12.

(4.) All the *scripture records of converted sinners*, whose hearts God hath in any age opened, were made to encourage other souls by their example to believe in or open unto Christ as they did. For this purpose the memorable conversion of Paul was graciously recorded. "Howbeit, for this cause I obtained mercy, that in me first Jesus Christ might show forth all long-suffering, for a pattern to them that should hereafter believe on him to life everlasting." 1 Tim. 1:16. Never was any man's heart bolted and made fast with stronger prejudices against Christ than this man's was; yet the Spirit of the Lord opened it. O how flexible became his will: "Lord, what wilt thou have me to do?" Acts 9:6. This gives great encouragement to other sinners to come to Christ as he did; and therefore when men see other sinners receiving Christ, and themselves continue unbelieving, the examples which God has set before their eyes are a dreadful aggravation of their unbelief. "John came unto you in the way of righteousness, and ye believed him not: but the publicans and the harlots believed him; and ye, when ye had seen it, repented not afterwards, that ye might believe him." Matt. 21:32. Though you saw publicans, reputed the worst of men, and harlots, the worst of women, convinced, humbled, and brought to faith, these sights affected not your souls; you never had one such reflection as this: Lord, have not I as much need to flee from the wrath to come, and seek the salvation of my soul, as these? Will it not be a dreadful aggravation of my misery, that such as these should obtain Christ and heaven, and I be shut out?

(5.) The opening of the heart to Christ is *the very end and errand of the Spirit of God*, upon whose concurrence and blessing the success of all ordinances depends; upon this design he is sent expressly from heaven to open the understanding and consciences of sinners by conviction. John 16:9. For it is not in the power of the word alone to produce this effect; thousands of excellent sermons may be preached, and not one heart opened by conviction.

What remains is the application of this doctrine.

INFERENCE 1. If the opening of the heart to Christ be the direct intention of the gospel, *how are they deceived who are satisfied in the attainment of some lesser end, while the effectual persuasion of the will to Christ is not at all effected in them.* There are some collateral effects, as I may call them, which the gospel has upon men. It would pain a considerate man to see how sinners fill themselves with a false happiness in these lesser things, while they still remain in the state of unregeneracy. I would fain undeceive such mistaken souls who bow down under the power of self-deceit, and that in a point in which their eternal salvation is concerned. There are two things which are apt to deceive men in this matter; these are, partial convictions on the understanding, and transient motions on the affections. In these things multitudes deceive themselves, as if the whole design of the gospel were accomplished upon them therein.

(1.) Partial convictions of *the understanding*—light and knowledge breaking into the mind, producing orthodoxy of judgment: this seems to some the effectual opening of the understanding to Christ, though alas, to this day they never saw sin in its vileness, much less their own special sin; nor Christ in his suitableness and necessity. People who live under the gospel can hardly avoid the improvement of their understandings by the light that shines upon them; knowledge grows, their faculties expand, and they can talk well on religion and ably defend it. Perhaps they can even pray with commendable variety and largeness of expression: these things gain applause from men, and excite confidence in themselves, while no saving influences are shed down to quicken, change, and spiritualize the heart.

(2.) There are transient motions and touches of the gospel upon *the affections,* which give some men melting pangs and moods now and then under the word, though it never settles into a spiritual frame, an habitual heavenliness of temper; of such the apostle speaks, Heb. 6:5. And this is the more dangerous, because they now seem to have attained all that is essential to religion, or necessary to salvation. For when to the light of their understandings there are added melting affections, a man seems to himself complete in all that the gospel requires to the being and constitution of a Christian, as a great divine, Mr. Burgess, speaks. Thus men are apt to reason : If I had only light in my mind, and never found any meltings of my affections, I might justly suspect myself to be a hypocrite ; but there are times when my affections, as well as my understanding, seem to feel the power of the gospel. And yet these things may be where the heart never effectually opens to Christ ; all this may be but a morning dew, or an early cloud that vanisheth away ; as is plain in John's hearers, John 5 : 35, and in Paul's hearers, Gal. 4 : 14, 15. For except the convictions of the understanding are effectual, and the motions upon the affections settled to a heavenly habit and temper, the man is but where he was before as to the real condition of his soul. Were thy understanding so convinced of the evil nature and dreadful consequences of sin, and thy affections and will thereupon so effectually determined to embrace the Lord Jesus, upon a considerate and thorough examination of his terms propounded in the gospel, then thou mightest conclude the great design of it was accomplished upon thy soul ; but to rest in general convictions and transient affections without this, is but to mock and deceive thy own soul. Alas, this comes not home to the main end of the gospel.

2. *Learn from hence the prodigious stubbornness and hardness of the hearts of men living under the gospel, which still resist it.* You have heard how all its commands, promises, threatenings, and examples bear directly and jointly upon the hearts of sinners to open the will to Christ ; yet how few comparatively obey and answer this great design of it. All these are like heaven's great artillery planted against the unbelief and stubbornness of men, to batter down their carnal reasonings, overthrow their vain hopes, and open a fair passage for Christ into their souls.

"For the weapons of our warfare are not carnal, but mighty through God to the pulling down of strongholds; casting down imaginations, and every thing that exalteth itself against the knowledge of God, and bringing into captivity every thought to the obedience of Christ." 2 Cor. 10:4, 5. If a mound be raised, and many cannon planted thereon, and all are played against the wall of a fort, thousands of shots made and yet no breach, not one stone moved out of its place, you will say that is a strong wall indeed. Beloved, God hath, as I may say, raised a mound in the gospel, planted the great ordnance of heaven upon it, discharged many dreadful volleys of threatenings; nay, he hath, as it were, come under the walls of the unbelieving soul with terms of mercy, and yet there is no opening. O prodigious obstinacy. "We have piped unto you, and ye have not danced; we have mourned unto you, and ye have not lamented." Matt. 11:17. Neither the sweet airs of gospel grace, nor the dreadful thunders of the law, make any impression upon you. O what an obdurate rock is the heart by nature. Certainly, every Christian may see enough in others, and find enough in himself, without the help of other books, to confute the doctrine which extols and flatters the nature of man. It is as easy to make an impression with your finger upon a wall of brass, as for the best sermon in the world, in its own strength, to make a saving impression upon a sinner's will.

3. Is it the great design of the gospel to open the hearts of men to Christ? *Then wonder not that it meets with such strong and fierce opposition from Satan, wherever it is sincerely and powerfully preached.* As for general and formal preaching, which comes not to the quick, Satan is not so much concerned about it; he knows it will do him no great damage; nay, it secures his interests in the souls of men. But wherever the gospel comes with power, laying the axe to the root, showing men the vanity of their

ungrounded hopes, pressing the necessity of regeneration and faith, this preaching quickly gives alarm to hell, and raises all manner of opposition against it. "What is it to preach the gospel," saith Luther, "but to drive the rage and fury of the whole world upon us?" Satan is the god of this world, all men by nature are his subjects: no prince is more jealous of the revolt of his subjects than he; and it is time for him to bestir himself, when the gospel comes to dethrone him, as it does in the faithful preaching of it. "Now is the judgment of this world; now shall the prince of this world be cast out." John 12:31. Now he falls as lightning from heaven. Luke 10:18. Now sinners are made sensible of the cruel tyranny and bondage of Satan's government, and of the glorious liberty offered to them by Jesus Christ. Satan suspecting the issue of these things, bestirs himself to purpose. O what showers of calumnies and storms of persecution does he pour on Christ's faithful ambassadors. Certainly he owes Christ's ministers a spite, and they shall know and feel it, if ever he get them within the compass of his chain. But let this discourage none employed in this glorious design; the Lord is with them to protect their persons and reward their diligence.

4. If the opening of the heart be the main design of the gospel, *Christ and faith ought to be the principal subjects that ministers should insist on among their people.* There are many other useful doctrines which ought to be opened and pressed in their time and place. Moral duties have their excellencies, but Christ and faith are the great things we are to preach. Let men be once brought to Christ, and the rest will follow; but to begin and end with morality, will never make men gospel Christians. Grace teaches morality, Tit. 2:11, 12; but morality without grace saves no man. It has been a grand artifice of the devil to confound grace with morality, and make men believe that nothing more is required for men's salvation, than a civil,

THE HEART OPENED BY FAITH. 263

sober conversation in the world, and so lay aside the principal part of the gospel, which opens and presses the necessity of regeneration, repentance, and faith in the blood of Christ. Such preaching as this answers not the design of Christ in the conversion of souls; such preaching disturbs not the consciences of men: the Lord help all his ambassadors to mind the example and charge of their Redeemer, and laying aside all carnal interest, to apply themselves faithfully unto the souls and consciences of their hearers, not as men-pleasers, but as the servants of Christ. Gal. 1:10.

5. In the next place, this doctrine is of excellent use to *convince men of the damning nature of the sin of unbelief*—a sin which frustrates the main design of the gospel of Christ on the unbeliever's soul. This is the sin that keeps the heart fast shut against him. As faith is the radical grace, so unbelief is the radical sin. It is the traitor's gate, through which those souls pass that are to perish for ever. The gospel can do you no good, the blood of Christ can yield no saving benefit, while your souls remain under the dominion of this sin. When we consider the mighty arguments of the gospel, we may wonder that all who hear them are not immediately persuaded to Christ by them. And on the other hand, when we consider the mighty power of unbelief, how strongly it holds the soul in bondage to sin, we may wonder that any soul is brought over to Christ even by the gospel. It was not without cause that the apostle puts faith in Christ among the great mysteries of the gospel. 1 Tim. 3:16. The intrinsic evil and fearful consequences of this sin of unbelief will appear in these three particulars.

(1.) *It fixes the guilt of all other sins on the person of the unbeliever;* it binds them all fast on his soul: "For if ye believe not that I am he, ye shall die in your sins." John 8:24. It were better for thee to die any other death. What more terrible can God threaten, or man feel? This is the sin that makes the death of Christ of none effect to us. Gal. 5 : 4. There is indeed a sovereign virtue in the blood of Christ to pardon sin, but thy soul cannot have the benefit of it while it remains under the dominion of this sin. As it was said of the inhabitants of Nazareth in their treatment of Christ, "He did not many mighty works there, because of their unbelief," Matt. 13 : 58 ; so none of his spiritual works, no ordinances can do thy soul good, until the Lord break the power of this sin. "The word preached did not profit them, not being mixed with faith in them that heard it." Heb. 4 : 2. If a man were dangerously sick, or wounded, the best medicines could never recover him, unless received and applied. Unbelief pours the most sovereign cordials of the gospel as water upon the ground. The greatest sins ever committed might be pardoned, did not this sin lie in the way; were this gone, all the rest were gone too : but while unbelief remains, they also remain upon thee.

(2.) Of all the sins that are upon the souls of men, *this is the most difficult to be removed.* Other sins lie open to conviction, but this has the most specious pretences to countenance it. Men commit this sin out of a fear of sin. They will not believe, lest they should presume ; they dare not believe, because they are not qualified. The strength of other sins meets in this sin of unbelief: it is the strongest fort wherein Satan trusts. Take an adulterer, or a profane swearer, and you have an open way to convince him of his sin : show him the command he has violated, and he has nothing to say in his own defence ; but the unbeliever has a thousand plausible defences.

(3.) *This is the great damning sin of the world.* All other sins deserve damnation, "for the wages of sin is death," but this is the sin in consequence of which other sins damn and ruin the soul. "This is the condemnation." John 3 : 19. And it is a sin which damns with aggravated ruin. 2 Thess. 1 : 8. O then, let us mourn over and tremble at this dreadful sin, which opposes and so often frustrates the great design of the whole gospel.

6. Is it the main scope of the gospel to bring men to Christ by faith ? *then be persuaded heartily to comply with this great design of the Father, Son, and Spirit, ministers, ordinances, and providences, in opening your hearts to receive Christ this day by faith unfeigned.* O that I could suitably press this great point, which falls in so directly with the main scope of the whole gospel : and O that while I am pressing it, you would lift up a hearty cry to heaven, Lord, give me faith, whatever else thou deniest me ; open my heart to Christ under the gospel calls. I not only press you to a general assent to the truths of the gospel, that Christ is come in the flesh and laid down his life for sinners, but to a hearty consent to receive him upon gospel terms—to close with him in all his offices, subjecting heart and life to his authority, living entirely upon him for righteousness and to him by holiness. The value of such a faith as this is above all estimation. For,

(1.) This is the grace which God has dignified and crowned with glory and honor above all its fellow-graces. Its praises are in all the Scriptures. It is called precious faith, 2 Pet. 1 : 1; soul-enriching faith, Jas. 2 : 5. That is a poor soul indeed that is destitute of it, whatever the gifts of providence have been to him. And he is truly rich to whom God has given faith, whatever he has denied him of the comforts of this life. This Christ calls the work of God : " This is the work of God, that ye believe." John 6 : 29. So are all other things that your eyes behold the works of God ; the earth, the sea, the sun, the moon, and stars, are his handiwork. True, but this is *the work*, the most glorious and admirable work of God, excelling all his other works. And,

(2.) That which exalts it not only above all the works

of God's hands, but even above its fellow-graces the work of his Spirit, is the high office to which it is appointed in the justification of a sinner. God has singled out this from all the other graces, to be the instrument of receiving and applying the righteousness of Christ for the justification of a guilty soul. You are never said to be justified by love, hope, or desire, but by faith. Rom. 5:1. It is true, all other graces are supposed in the person justified; but none apprehends and applies the righteousness of Christ for justification, but this only. And the justifying act of faith being a receiving act, the glory of God is therein secured: "Therefore it is of faith, that it might be by grace." Rom. 4:16.

(3.) The grace of faith which I am now recommending to you, is not only the instrument of your justification, but the bond of your union with Christ: "That Christ may dwell in your hearts by faith." Eph. 3:17. It is the uniting grace; it is that which gives interest in and title to the person and benefits of Christ; the great thing upon which the eyes of all awakened sinners are intently and solicitously fixed. Whatever views you have of an interest in Christ, and whatever his benefits are worth in your eyes, neither himself nor they can ever be obtained without faith. O brethren, there is a day coming when they that now **neglect** this concern of their souls, would gladly part with **ten thousand** worlds for the friendship of Christ, could it be **purchased** therewith; but it is faith that entitles you to Christ and to his benefits.

(4.) That which should yet more endear this grace of faith to you is, that it is the *hand* which receives your pardon from the hand of Christ, the messenger that brings pardon to a trembling sinner. "By him all that believe are justified from all things, from which they could not be justified by the law of Moses." Acts 13:39. They are cleared from all those sins from which the law could never clear them, nor any repentance, restitution, or obedience of their own without faith. O what a welcome messenger is faith, and what joyful tidings does it bring! you will say so if you have felt the efficacy of the law upon your conscience—if you have lain, as some sinners have, with a cold horror on your panting bosoms, under the apprehensions of the wrath of God. This fruit of faith is rather to be admired than expressed. Psa. 32 : 1.

(5.) Faith is not only the messenger that brings you a pardon from heaven, but it is, as I may say, the heavenly herald that publishes peace to the sinner. O *peace*, how sweet a word art thou ; how welcome to a poor condemned sinner! "Beautiful upon the mountains are the feet of him that bringeth good tidings, that publisheth peace." Isa. 52 : 7. It is faith that brings this blessed news and publishes it in the soul, without which all the publishers of peace without us can administer but little support. Rom. 5 : 1. Faith brings the soul out of the storms with which it was tossed, into a sweet rest : "We which have believed do enter into rest." Heb. 4 : 3. Is the quiet harbor welcome to weather-beaten seamen, after they have passed furious storms and many fears on the raging sea ? O how welcome then must peace be to the soul that hath been tossed on the tempestuous ocean of its own fears, blown up and incensed by the terrible blasts of the law and of conscience. It was a comfortable sight to Noah and his family, to see an olive-leaf in the mouth of the dove, by which they knew the waters were abated. But what is it to hear such a voice as this from the mouth of faith: "Fury is not in me, saith the Lord ; his anger is turned away, and he comforteth thee ?" Isa. 12 : 1. Fear not thou, the God of peace is thy God.

(6.) Faith not only brings the soul into a calm, but opens to it a door of access into the gracious presence of God; without it there is no coming to him acceptably : "He that cometh unto God must believe." Heb. 11 : 6. This access to God is indeed the purchase of the blood of Christ ; but faith is the grace that brings the soul actually into the presence of God, and there helps it to ease its griefs, and with holy freedom to make known its grievances, fears, and burdens to the Lord. This world were not worth living in without such a blessed relief to our troubles. The believer only has the key that opens the door of access unto God; if he has sins, wants, burdens, afflictions, or temptations, here he can lay them down. Ah, Christian, the time may come when thy heart may be filled with sorrows, and there may not be found a person of thy acquaintance in all the world to whom thou canst turn to relieve thy sorrows. Blessed be God for faith; O the ease that the act of faith gives to a troubled soul. Well may it be said, "The just shall live by his faith." Hab. 2:4. How can we imagine we should live without it? Our afflictions and temptations would swallow us up, were it not for the sweet assiduous reliefs that come in by faith.

(7.) And yet further to inflame your desires after faith, this is the grace that gives you the soul-reviving sights of the invisible world, without which this world would be a dungeon to us. It is not only the substance of things hoped for, but the evidence of things not seen. Heb. 11:1. O it is a precious eye: how transporting are those visions of faith. "Whom having not seen, ye love; in whom, though now ye see him not, yet believing, ye rejoice with joy unspeakable and full of glory." 1 Pet. 1:8. We who preach of heaven to you, cannot show you the glorious person of Christ there, nor the thrones and crowns that are above; but faith can make these things visible. That is an eye which can penetrate the clouds, and show to you him that is invisible. Heb. 11:27.

(8.) The grace of faith, which I am now recommending to you, is instrumentally the sustenance of your souls in this world: "The just shall live by his faith." Hab. 2:4. When God gives a man faith, he gives it to him to sustain his life, and expects him to live upon it while he lives in this world. He has made plentiful provision for your souls, when he has given them faith, and furnished such a variety of precious promises for it to feed upon. Abraham, Moses, David, and all the saints, lived on no other provision but what faith brought in; and at what an excellent rate did they live. Here man eateth angels' food. It is a storehouse of provision, it is a shop of cordials: " I had fainted unless I had believed." Psa. 27 : 13. A believer lives the highest life of all men on earth; and as his soul is daily fed by faith, so all his other graces are maintained and daily supported by the provision faith brings them in. The other graces, like the young birds in the nest, live upon the provision this grace of faith gathers for them. Take away faith, and you starve the soul of a Christian. Will not all this engage your desire after faith?

(9.) Consider also, that this is the grace whereby we die safely as well as live comfortably: as you cannot live comfortably without faith in this world, so neither can you die safely or comfortably without it, when you go out of the world. " These all died in faith, not having received the promises; but having seen them afar off, and were persuaded of them, and embraced them." Heb. 11 : 13. These excellent persons all died embracing the promises in the arms of their faith. An allusion to two dear friends embracing each other at their parting. O precious promises, says the dying believer; of what unspeakable benefit have you been to me all the days of my pilgrimage. To you I was wont to turn in all my troubles and distresses; but I am now going into the life of immediate vision: farewell blessed promises, scriptures, ordinances, and communion of saints on earth; I shall walk no more by faith, but by sight.

(10.) In a word, this is the grace that saves you: " By grace are ye saved, through faith." Eph. 2 : 8. Your salvation is the fruit of free-grace; but grace itself will not save you in any other method but that of believing. The grace of God runs through the channel of faith; faith is the grace that espouses your soul to Christ here, and accompanies you every step of the way until you come to its full enjoyment in heaven, and then it is lost in vision. It embarks you with Christ, and pilots you through the dangerous seas, till you drop anchor in the haven of everlasting rest and safety; where you receive the "end of your faith, the salvation of your souls." O then, in consideration of the incomparable worth and absolute necessity of this grace, make it your great study, make it your constant cry to heaven, night and day, Lord, give me a believing heart, a heart opening to Jesus Christ. If you fail of this, you come short of the great design of the whole gospel, which is to bring you to faith, and by faith to heaven.

CHAPTER X.

CHRIST BRINGS GREAT BLESSINGS TO THE SOUL THAT OPENS TO HIM.

"IF ANY MAN HEAR MY VOICE AND OPEN THE DOOR, *I WILL COME IN TO HIM, AND WILL SUP WITH HIM, AND HE WITH ME.*" REV. 3:20.

In the former chapters we have considered Christ's suit for a sinner's heart: we now come to the powerful arguments and motives used by him to obtain his suit, which are two: first, union, "I will come in to him, and sup with him;" and second, communion, " and he with me."

These are strong and mighty arguments and encouragements, able, one would think, to open any heart in the world to Christ: and yet considering how the hearts of men are attached to their lusts and riveted in their sins, until the Spirit come upon them with powerful convictions; and when under conviction, what discouragements they labor under from their former sinfulness and present unworthiness, all is little enough to bring them to faith, nay, utterly insufficient, without the almighty power set them home with effect on the heart; for it is not mere moral suasion will do the work. It is true, Christ will not make a forcible entrance into the soul, he will come in by consent of the will; but the will consents not, until it feels the power of God upon it. Psalm 110:3. Almighty power opens the heart and determines the will, but in a way congruous to the nature of the will. " I drew them with cords of a man, with bands of love." Hos. 11:4. When, under the influence of this power, the soul opens to Christ, he will come in, take that soul for his everlasting habitation, refresh and feast it with the sweetest consolations and privileges purchased by his blood; whence the tenth doctrine is,

Christ will certainly come in to the soul that opens to him; and will bring rich entertainment with him. " I will come in to him, and sup with him."

When the prodigal, the emblem of a convert, returned to his father, Luke 15 : 22, his father not only received, but adorned and feasted him. In opening this point, I shall show what Christ's coming into the soul implies; how it appears that Christ will come in to the opening soul; what entertainment he brings with him; and why he thus entertains the soul that opens to him.

I. WHAT CHRIST'S COMING IN TO THE SOUL IMPLIES; and in general I must say this is a great mystery, which will not be fully understood till we come to heaven : "At that day ye shall know that I am in my Father, and ye in me, and I in you." John 14 : 20. Then the essential union of Christ and his Father, and the mystical union between believers and Christ, will be more clearly understood than we are capable of understanding them in this imperfect state; yet for the present so much is discovered, as may justly astonish poor sinners at the marvellous condescension of the Lord Jesus to them. More particularly, the expression, "I will come in to him," imports no less than his uniting such a soul to himself; for he comes in with a design to dwell in that soul by faith, Eph. 3 : 17—to make such a man a mystical member of his body, flesh, and bones, Eph. 5 : 30, which is the highest honor the soul of man is capable of. This coming of Christ into the soul of a sinner does not indeed make him one person with Christ; that is the singular honor to which our nature was advanced by Christ in his uniting the divine nature with it. But this makes a person mystically one with Christ, and is more than a mere federal union. Christ's coming into the soul signifies more than his entering into covenant with it; for it is taking such a person into a mystical union with himself, by imparting his Spirit unto him. As the vital sap of the stock coming into the graft, makes it one with the stock, John 15 : 4, so the coming of Christ's Spirit into the soul makes it a member of his mystical body; and this is a glorious supernatural work of God, 1 Cor. 1 : 30, most honorable, most comfortable, and for ever sure and indissoluble; as I have more fully showed in THE METHOD OF GRACE.*

II. I shall show THE CERTAINTY *that Christ will come in with refreshments and comforts to every soul that opens to him.* No former rebellions or present unworthiness shall bar out Christ, or obstruct his entrance into such a soul. Whatever thou hast been or done, Christ will come in to thee and dwell with thee, and make thy soul a habitation for himself through the Spirit. Eph. 2 : 22. Let thy heart be open to him, and he will both fill and feast thee, notwithstanding all thy former sins.

I know it is a common discouragement that multitudes of convinced sinners lie under, that seeing so much vileness in their nature and practice, they cannot be persuaded that the Lord Jesus will cast an eye of favor on them, much less take up his abode in them. What, dwell in such a heart as mine, which has been a habitation of devils, a sink of sin from my beginning? this is hard to be believed. But, sinner, thou hast the word of a King from heaven for it, a word whose credit has never failed from the first moment it was spoken, that whatever thy former or present unworthiness has been, or is, he will not withhold himself from such a soul as thou art, if thou be but willing to open to him. Thy great unworthiness shall be no bar to his union with thee. "If any man open, I will come in to him." For,

1. If personal unworthiness were sufficient to bar Christ out of thy soul, it would equally bar him out of *all other souls*, for all are unworthy as well as thyself. Wherever Christ finds sinfulness, he finds unworthiness; and to be sure he finds this wherever he comes. Christ never expect-

* Published by the American Tract Society.

ed to find worthiness in thee, but it highly pleases him to find thee under a becoming sense of thy unworthiness. "Only acknowledge thine iniquity, that thou hast transgressed against the Lord thy God." Jer. 3 : 13. The returning prodigal acknowledged to his father, I am not worthy to be called thy son. Luke 15 : 18, 19. But this did not hinder his acceptance by his father. All that come to God to be justified, must see and confess their own vileness, and come to him as one that justifieth the ungodly. Rom. 4 : 5.

2. Thy former vileness and present unworthiness can be no bar to Christ's entrance, because it can be no *surprise* to him. He knew thou wast unworthy when he made the first overture of grace and reconciliation to thee; and if thy unworthiness hindered not the beginning of his treaty with thee, it shall not hinder the closing act in his union with thee. "I knew that thou wouldest deal very treacherously, and wast called a transgressor from the womb." Isa. 48 : 8.

3. *Christ never came into a soul where Satan had not the possession before him.* Every soul in which Christ now dwells was once in Satan's possession. "To turn them from darkness to light, and from the power of Satan unto God." Acts 26 : 18. "When a strong man armed keepeth his palace, his goods are in peace; but when a stronger than he shall come upon him and overcome him, he taketh from him all his armor wherein he trusted, and divideth his spoil." Luke 11 : 21, 22.

4. Thy present unworthiness can be no bar to Christ's entrance into thy soul, because Christ never objected to any man his *unworthiness*, but only his *unwillingness* to come to him. "Ye will not come unto me, that ye might have life." John 5 : 40. And again, "How often would I have gathered thy children together, even as a hen gathereth her chickens under her wings, and ye would not." Matt.

23 : 37. You find something like a repulse from Christ to the poor Canaanitess : " Have mercy on me, O Lord," said that distressed soul ; " but he answered and said, it is not meet to take the children's bread and to cast it to dogs." Matt. 15 : 22, 26. However harshly these words sound, it was not Christ's intention to discourage her faith, but to draw it forth to a more intense degree ; which effect was produced. Verse 27.

5. Neither would Christ have made *the tenders of mercy so large and indefinite*, had he intended to shut out any soul on account of its personal unworthiness, provided it be but willing to come to him. Cast thine eye, discouraged soul, on Christ's invitations and proclamations of mercy in the gospel, and see if thou canst find any thing besides unwillingness as a bar between thee and mercy ; hearken to that voice of mercy: " Ho, every one that thirsteth, come ye to the waters, and he that hath no money ; come ye, buy and eat ; yea, come, buy wine and milk without money and without price ;" that is, without personal desert or worthiness. Isa. 55 : 1. So again, " The Spirit and the bride say, Come ; and let him that heareth say, Come ; and let him that is athirst come ; and whosoever will, let him take the water of life freely." Rev. 22 : 17. Here you see personal unworthiness is no obstacle in the way of Christ. Once more, " In the last day, that great day of the feast, Jesus stood and cried, saying, If any man thirst, let him come unto me and drink." John 7 : 37. Thus you see what Christ's coming in to the soul is, and what evidences there are that when the soul is made truly willing, Christ will certainly come into it ; and no former vileness or present unworthiness shall be a bar to obstruct his entrance.

III. I shall show that WHEN CHRIST COMES IN TO THE SOUL, HE WILL NOT COME EMPTY-HANDED. It is Christ's marriage-day, and he will make it a good day, a festival day ; bringing such comforts with him as the soul never tasted before. He spreads a table and furnishes it with the delicacies of heaven. "I will sup with him," saith the text. What those spiritual mercies are which Christ brings with him to the opening soul, comes next in order to be spoken of. And,

1. When Christ comes in to the soul of a sinner, he brings a *pardon* with him—a full, free, and final pardon of all the sins which that soul has ever committed. This is a feast of itself, good cheer indeed; Christ thought it to be so when he told the poor palsied man, "Son, be of good cheer; thy sins be forgiven thee." Matt. 9:2. He does not say, Be of good cheer, thy palsy is cured, and thy body recovered from the grave; but, "be of good cheer, thy sins are forgiven." O how sweetly may the pardoned soul feed upon this. And this is not a mercy designed for some special favorites, but what is common to all believers. "By him all that believe are justified from all things." Acts 13:39. Christ and pardon come together; and without a pardon no mercy would relish: neither feast nor music, neither money nor honor bring any comfort to a condemned man; but the comfort of a pardon reaches to the very heart. "Comfort ye, comfort ye my people, saith your God. Speak ye comfortably to Jerusalem," Isa. 40:1, 2; or, as in the Hebrew, "speak to the heart of Jerusalem." But what are the ingredients of that cordial that will comfort Jerusalem's heart? "Cry unto her, that her iniquity is pardoned." That carries with it the spirit of all consolation.

There are three things in the pardon of sin which make it the sweetest mercy the soul ever tasted; comfort which is impossible to be communicated to another as the pardoned soul has it. Rev. 2:17.

(1.) One thing which makes the pardon of sin sweet, is the *trouble* that went before it. The laborings and restless tossings of the troubled soul, before his pardon, make the ease and peace that follow it incomparably sweet. As the bitterness of hell was tasted in the sorrows of sin, so the sweetness of heaven is tasted in the pardon of it.

(2.) *The nature of the mercy itself* is incomparably sweet, for it is a mercy of the first rank. Pardon is a mercy which admits no comfort before it, nor can any just cause of discouragement follow it. If God has not spoken pardon to the soul, it can have no settled ground for joy. Ezek. 33 : 10. And if he has, there can be no just ground for dejection, whatever troubles lie upon it. "The inhabitant shall not say, I am sick; the people that dwell therein shall be forgiven their iniquities." Isa. 33 : 24.

(3.) This mercy is made sweet to the soul by the properties of it, which are four: first, God writes upon thy pardon, *free;* it is mercy which costs thee nothing: "Being justified freely by his grace." Rom. 3 : 24. "Thou hast bought me no sweet cane with money, neither hast thou filled me with the fat of thy sacrifices; but thou hast made me to serve with thy sins, thou hast wearied me with thine iniquities." But, "I, even I, am he that blotteth out thy transgressions, for mine own sake, and will not remember thy sins." Isa. 43 : 24, 25. Second, God writes upon thy pardon, *full*, as well as free; the pardon extends to all the sins thou hast ever committed: "By him all that believe are justified from all things." Acts 13 : 39. The sins of thy nature and practice; the sins of thy youth and riper age; great sins and lesser, are all comprehended within thy pardon. Thou art acquitted not from one only, but from all. Certainly, the joy of heaven must come down in the mercy of remission. What a feast of fat things with marrow is this single mercy, a pardon free without price, full without exception. And then, third, it is *final*, without revocation; the pardoned soul never more comes into condemnation. Thine iniquities are removed from thee as far as the east is from the west. As those two opposite points can never meet, so the pardoned soul and its pardoned sins can never more meet unto condemnation. Psalm 103 : 12. Fourth, God writes upon the pardon another word, as sweet as any of the rest, and that is, *sure*. It is a standing mercy, never to be recalled or annulled. Rom. 8 : 33–35. The challenge is sent to earth and hell, men and devils : "Who shall lay any thing to the charge of God's elect ? It is God that justifieth. Who is he that condemneth ? It is Christ that died." Who can arrest when the creditor discharges ? Who can sue the bond when the debt is paid ? " It is Christ that died." The table is spread, and the first mercy served in is the pardon of sin. " Eat, O friends ; drink, yea, drink abundantly, O beloved." Sol. Song 5 : 2. Now the laboring conscience that rolled and tossed upon the waves of a thousand fears, may drop anchor, and ride quiet in the pacific sea of a pardoned state. What joy must flow through the conscience when the sweetness of that scripture, "There is therefore now no condemnation to them which are in Christ Jesus," Rom. 8 : 1, shall be pressed into thy cup of consolation. The pardoned soul may think of death and judgment without consternation ; yea, may look upon them as a time of refreshing from the presence of the Lord. Acts 3 : 19. This is heavenly manna, the sweetness of it exceeds all expression ; no words, no thoughts can comprehend the riches of this mercy.

2. And yet this is not all ; behold another mercy brought in to cheer the consenting soul, and that is *peace with God*. Pardon and peace go together : " Being justified by faith, we have peace with God." Rom. 5 : 1. Peace is a word of vast comprehension : in the language of the Old Testament, it comprehends all temporal good things, 1 Sam. 25 : 6 ; and peace in the New Testament comprehends all spiritual mercies, 2 Thess. 3 : 16 : the blessings of heaven and earth are wrapt up in this word. The soul that opens to Christ has the peace of reconciliation with heaven ; the enmity that was between God and that soul is taken away

through Jesus Christ. "O Lord, I will praise thee: though thou wast angry with me, thine anger is turned away, and thou comfortedst me." Isa. 12:1. This must be an invaluable mercy, for the purchase of it cost the blood of Christ: "The chastisement of our peace was upon him." Isa. 53:5. He made peace by the blood of his cross, Col. 1:20; and this peace of reconciliation is settled by Christ upon a firm foundation. His blood gives it a more firm foundation than that of the hills and mountains. Isa. 54:10. And that which makes it so firm and sure, is the advocateship of Jesus Christ in heaven: "If any man sin, we have an Advocate with the Father." 1 John, 2:1. There is also peace in the believer's conscience—peace as it were by proclamation from heaven; and this is built upon the peace of reconciliation. We cannot have the sense of peace till we are brought into a state of peace; the one is the result of the other. And this is a part of the supper Christ provides to entertain the soul that receives it. How sweet this is, is better felt than spoken. A dreadful sound was lately in the ears of the law-condemned sinner; but now his heart is the seat of peace. This peace is,

(1.) The *soul's guard* against all inward and outward terrors. The peace of God shall keep, or, as the original word is, guard your hearts and minds. Phil. 4:7. The persons of princes are secured by guards of armed men, who watch while they sleep. Thus Solomon had his royal guard, because of fear in the night. Sol. Song 3:7, 8. This peace of God, Christian, is thy life-guard, and secures thee better than Solomon's threescore valiant men about him. Time was when thou wast afraid to sleep, lest thou shouldst awake in hell. Now thou mayest say with David, "I will both lay me down in peace, and sleep; for thou, Lord, only makest me to dwell in safety." Psa. 5:8. Now, come life, come death, the soul is safe; the peace of God is its royal guard.

(2.) This peace is *ease* as well as safety to the soul; it is heart's-ease. No sooner does God speak peace to the conscience, than the soul finds itself at ease and rest: "We which have believed, do enter into rest." Heb. 4:3. It is with such a soul as it was with the dove Noah sent out of the ark: that poor creature wandered in the air as long as her wings could carry her; had her strength failed, there was nothing but the waters to receive her. O how sweet was rest in the ark!

(3.) This peace is *news from heaven*, and the sweetest tidings that ever blessed the sinner's ear, next to Christ. The blood of Christ speaketh better things than that of Abel, Heb. 12:24; and you are come to this blood of sprinkling, as soon as Christ comes into your soul. This is the voice of that blood: "Thou hast sinned, I have satisfied; thou hast kindled the wrath of God, and I have quenched it." The angels of heaven cannot fare better: their joys are not more sweet than those prepared for believers are, whereof this is a foretaste. Whatever trouble a man may be in, this effectually relieves him. Paul and Silas were in sad circumstances, shut up in the inner prison, their feet made fast in the stocks, their cruel keepers at the door, and their execution expected in a few days: God did but set this dish upon the table before the prisoners, and they could not forbear to sing at the feast. Acts 16:25.

3. After *pardon and peace*, a third blessing will come, namely, *joy in the Holy Ghost*. This is somewhat beyond peace, it is the very quintessence and spirit of all consolation. The kingdom of God is said to consist in it, Rom. 14:17; it is somewhat like the joy of the glorified, 1 Pet. 1:8; it is heaven upon earth. All believers do not immediately attain it, but one time or other God usually gives them a taste of it; and when he does, it is as it were a realization of full salvation. O, who can tell what that is which the apostle calls, the shedding abroad of the love of God in the heart by the Holy Ghost, which is given to us?

Rom. 5 : 5. It is a joy that wants an epithet to express its full sweetness: "Joy unspeakable, and full of glory." 1 Pet. 1 : 8. It has the very taste of heaven in it, and there is but a difference of degrees between it and the joy of heaven. This joy of the Holy Ghost is a spiritual cheerfulness streaming through the soul of a believer from the Spirit's testimony, which proves his interest in Christ and glory. No sooner doth the Spirit shed forth the love of God into the believer's heart, than it overflows with joy.

This will appear, if you consider the matter of it: it arises from the light of God's countenance, Psa. 4 : 6, 7, the heavenly glory : "Whom having not seen, we love." 1 Pet. 1 : 8. The soul is transported with joy, ravished with the glory and excellency of Christ. Didst thou ever see Christ with whom thy soul is so delighted? No, I have not seen him; yet my soul is transported with love to him, "whom having not seen, we love." But if thou never sawest him, how comes thy soul to be so delighted with him? Why, though.I never saw him by the eye of sense, I do see him by the eye of faith; and by that sight my soul is flooded with spiritual joy: "Believing, we rejoice." But what manner of joy is it which you taste? No tongue can express that, for it is joy unspeakable. But how are Christ and heaven turned into such joys to the soul? The Spirit of the Lord gives the believer a sight to discern not only the transcendent excellency of these spiritual objects, but his interest in them also. This is my Saviour, and this the glory prepared for me. Without appropriation, heaven itself cannot be turned into joy. My soul rejoices in God my Saviour. Luke 1 : 47. We read of some who shall have a sight of Abraham, and Isaac, and Jacob, and all the prophets in the kingdom of God, and yet shall be without joy, Luke 13 : 28; a dreadful sight to such, for want of a joint interest with them in that glory. They shall see, and yet weep and gnash their teeth. But an interest sealed gives joy unspeakable.

As to the excellency of this joy, it will prove the pleasant light of the soul. Light and joy are synonymous terms in Scripture. Psa. 97 : 11. It is as the cheerful light of the morning, after a sad and dismal night. You who have sat in darkness and the shadow of death, who have sat mourning in the dark without one glimpse of a promise, who have conversed with nothing but dismal thoughts of hell and wrath—O, I shall be cast away for ever ; what will you say, when after all this darkness, the day-star shall arise in your hearts, and the joy of heaven shall beam upon your souls ? Will not this be a glorious reward for all your self-denial for Christ, and fully recompense the frowns of ungodly relations for giving entertainment to Christ ? This joy of the Lord, if there were no other heaven, is an abundant recompense. This joy of the Lord shall be your strength. Neh. 8 : 10. Let God but give a person a little of this joy into his heart, and he shall presently feel himself strengthened by it, either to do or to suffer the will of God. Now he can pray with enlargement, hear with comfort, meditate with delight ; and if God call him to suffer, this joy shall strengthen him to bear it. This it was that made the martyrs go singing to the stake. This therefore transcends all the joys of the world. There are sinful pleasures which men find in fulfilling their lusts ; there are sensitive joys that men find in the good creatures of God, filling their hearts with food and gladness; there are also delusive joys, that hypocrites find in their ungrounded hopes of heaven. The joys of the sensualist are brutish, the joys of the hypocrite are ensnaring and vanishing ; but the joys of the Holy Ghost are solid, sweet, and leading to the fulness of everlasting joy.

4. We read in Scripture of *the sealing of the Spirit*, a blessed privilege of believers, consequent upon believing : " In whom also, after that ye believed, ye were sealed with that Holy Spirit of promise." Eph. 1 : 13. This may be expected by every soul that opens to Christ, how rich soever

the comforts of it be. The Spirit indeed seals not before faith, for then would he set his seal to a blank; but he usually seals after believing, and that as the Spirit of promise. Notice here the agent or person sealing, "the Spirit;" he knows the counsels and purposes of God. 1 Cor. 2: 10, 11. He also is authorized to this work; and being the Spirit of truth, he cannot deceive us. There is a twofold seal spoken of in Scripture; one referring to God's eternal foreknowledge and choice of men: "Nevertheless the foundation of God standeth sure, having this seal, the Lord knoweth them that are his," 2 Tim. 2: 19; he perfectly knows every soul that belongs to him throughout the world. But the believer has more than this. There is another sealing of the Spirit, as his act on believers, to make them know that they are his. The first is general, The Lord knoweth who are his; but this is particular, The Lord knoweth thee to be his. This is joyful news indeed. The former makes it sure in itself, the latter makes it sure to us. Now this is a glorious privilege, a work of the Spirit, which has a most delightful sweetness in it; for,

(1) *The weightiness* of the matter sealed, which is no less than Christ, and the eternal inheritance purchased by his blood. This seal secures our title to Christ, and to the eternal glory. We are sealed to the day of redemption. The sealed believer can say, Christ, how great, how glorious soever he be, is my Saviour; and the covenant of grace, and all the invaluable promises contained in it, are mine.

(2.) The *rest* which follows it, makes it an invaluable mercy. This brings the anxious conscience to peace. O what a mercy is it to have all those knots untied, those objections answered, those fears banished, under which the doubting soul so long labored, and which kept it so many nights waking and restless. God only knows how some poor creatures live, under their alarms of conscience and frequent fears of hell. And what an inconceivable mercy would it be to them to be delivered at once from their dangers and fears, which hold them under a spirit of bondage! Open to Christ, and thou art in the way to such a deliverance : Come unto me and I will give you rest, saith Christ, Matt. 11 : 28, 29.

(3.) This sealing of the Spirit which follows believing, will *establish the soul in Christ,* and settle it in the ways of God, which is an unspeakable privilege : " Now he which establisheth us with you in Christ, is God; who hath also sealed us." 2 Cor. 1 : 21, 22. Mark how establishment follows sealing. Temptations may come, great persecutions and sore afflictions may come, but how well is that soul provided for them all, that has the sealing of the Spirit unto the day of redemption. Yea, though that soul should for the present be under new darkness, temptations, and fears, the former sealing will give establishment and relief, when the thoughts go back to the sealing day, and the man remembers how clear God once made his title to Christ. Well then, open to Christ, if ever you expect to be sealed to salvation. If you continue to reject the tenders of Christ in the gospel, while others who embrace him are sealed to the day of redemption, your unbelief and final rejection of Christ will seal you to the day of damnation.

5. We read in the Scriptures of the *earnest of the Spirit ;* this is three times mentioned : " Which is the earnest of our inheritance until the redemption of the purchased possession." Eph. 1 : 14. The apostle Paul joins it with the former privilege of sealing : " Who hath also sealed us, and given the earnest of the Spirit in our hearts," 2 Cor. 1 : 22 ; and again, " He that hath wrought us for the self-same thing is God, who also hath given unto us the earnest of the Spirit " 2 Cor. 5 : 5. The word is originally Syriac ; the Greeks are supposed to have got it from the Phœnician merchants with whom they traded, and it denotes a part paid in hand to confirm a bargain for the whole. An

earnest is part of the sum, or inheritance: if it were a contract for a sum of money, it was a small part of a greater amount; if for an inheritance, the earnest is taking a twig, or turf, as a part of the whole. The Spirit of God chooses this word to signify two great things to his people.

(1.) That the comforts communicated by the Spirit to believers, *are of the same kind with the joys of heaven*, though in a far inferior degree. They are called, "Joy unspeakable, and full of glory," 1 Pet. 1:8; and, "The first-fruits of the Spirit." Rom. 8:23. The first-fruits, and the harvest, are one in kind; there is something of heaven, as well as hell, tasted by men in this world: hell is begun here in the terrors of some men's consciences, and heaven is begun here in the peace and comfort of other men's consciences.

(2.) As an earnest is part of the sum or inheritance, so the use of it is *confirmation and security;* as much as to say, take this in part till the whole be paid—take it for thy security that the whole shall be paid. Believers have a double pledge or earnest for heaven: one in the person of Christ, who is entered into that glory for them, John 14:2, 3; the other in the joys and comforts of the Spirit, which they feel and taste in themselves. These are two great securities, and the design of God in giving us these earnests and foretastes of heaven, is not only to settle our minds, but to increase our industry, that we may long more earnestly and labor more diligently for the full possession. The Lord sees how apt we are to flag in the pursuit of heaven, and therefore gives his people a taste, or earnest of it, to excite their diligence in its pursuit. God deals with his people in this case, as with Israel: they had been forty years in the wilderness; many sore temptations had they there encountered; at last they came upon the very borders of Canaan, but then their hearts began to faint; there were Anakims, giants in the land, and Israel feared they should not stand before them: but Joshua sent spies into the land, who brought the first fruits of Canaan to them, whereby they saw what a goodly country it was; and then the fear of the Anakims began to vanish, and a spirit of courage to revive in the people. Thus it is even with the borderers upon heaven: though we are near that blessed land of promise, our hearts are apt to faint on a prospect of the sufferings without us, and the conflicts with corruptions within us; but one taste of the first-fruits of heaven, like the grapes of Eschol, revives our spirits, rouses our zeal, and quickens our pursuit of blessedness. For these reasons, God will not have all heaven reserved till we come thither. And now tell me, you that have tasted these first-fruits of the Spirit,

Is there not something of that *glorified eye*, in faith, by which the pure in heart see God in heaven? Matt. 5:8. O that eye of faith—that precious eye, which comes as near to the glorified eye as any thing in this imperfect state can do: "Whom having not seen, ye love; in whom, though now ye see him not, yet believing, ye rejoice with joy unspeakable and full of glory." 1 Pet. 1:8.

Is there not something of that glorified *love* felt in an inferior degree by the saints in this world? What else can we make of that transport of the spouse: "Stay me with flagons, comfort me with apples; for I am sick of love?" Sol. Song 2:5. Our love to God in heaven will be much more fervent, pure, and constant; yet these high-raised acts of spiritual love have a taste and relish of it.

Is there not something here of that *heavenly delight* wherewith the glorified rejoice in God? As the visions of God are begun on earth, so heavenly delights are begun here also. Some drops of that delight are let fall here: "In the multitude of my thoughts within me thy comforts delight my soul." Psa. 94:19. David's heart had been full of sorrow; a sea of gall and wormwood had overflowed his soul: God lets fall but a drop or two of heavenly delight, and all is turned into sweetness and comfort.

Is there not something here of that *transformation of the soul* into the image of God, which is complete in heaven, and a part of the glory thereof? It is said, "We shall be like him; for we shall see him as he is." 1 John, 3:2. This is heaven, to have the soul moulded into full conformity with God: something thereof is experienced in this world; O that we had more! "But we all, with open face beholding as in a glass the glory of the Lord, are changed into the same image from glory to glory, as by the Spirit of the Lord." 2 Cor. 3:18.

Is there not something felt here of the *sweetness of God's presence* in ordinances and duties, which is a faint shadow, at least, of the joys of his glorious presence in heaven? There is certainly a felt presence of God, a sensible nearness to God at some times and in some duties of religion, wherein his name is as ointment poured forth, Sol. Song 1:3—something that is felt above all the comforts of this world.

In a word, the joys of heaven are *unspeakable joys;* no words can make known what they are. When Paul was caught up into paradise he heard unspeakable words, 2 Cor. 12:4; and are there not times, even in this life, wherein the saints do feel that which no words can express? 1 Pet. 1:8; Rev. 2:17.

Now, if such earnests of the Spirit come with believing, if opening the soul to Christ bring it unto these suburbs of heaven, who would not receive Christ into his soul, and such a heaven upon earth with him? Thus I have showed you what are some of those heavenly joys which Christ gives to believers upon earth, the fulness of which is reserved for heaven, and hereby secured to the opening or believing soul.

IV. We shall show THE REASONS why Christ thus feasts and refreshes the soul that receives him.

1. This he does *to express the great joy he has in the*

faith and obedience of sinners. We read of the travail of Christ's soul, and the satisfaction he has in the fruit and issue thereof: " He shall see of the travail of his soul, and shall be satisfied." Isa. 53 : 11. O what pleasure and satisfaction doth it give him to behold the eternal counsels of God and the travails of his soul brought to such a result; there is no pleasure like it to the soul of Christ in this world. As it is satisfaction to a man to see a design upon which he has laid out many thoughts and much cost, at last happily finished ; or as it is to a woman to behold the fruit of her womb, to embrace and smile upon the child she travailed for ; so, and much more, it is to Christ : and therefore, as the Father of the prodigal manifested the joy of his heart for the return of his son by a feast and music, so does Christ here manifest the satisfaction of his soul by entertaining the believer with these foretastes of heaven ; it is the soul's welcome home to Christ.

2. This Christ does *to relieve distressed souls* who have endured so many fears and sorrows from the time of their first conviction until the day of their union with Christ by faith. The way of faith is a very humble way ; there is much painful work in previous convictions and humiliations, sad nights and days with many poor souls ; and these things bring them low : they see the law broken by sin, wrath hanging over them in the threatenings, the bitterness thereof they have in their consciences ; they have dealt with fears and horrors a long time, and they need support, which the Lord Jesus now gives them, lest the spirit fail before him. Isa. 57 : 16. He delights to comfort them that are cast down. 2 Cor. 7 : 6. Christ is of a compassionate nature ; he is as ready as able to succor them that are tempted. Heb. 2 : 18. The word which we render *succor*, signifies to run in by way of help at the cry of one in distress. Many emphatical cries have gone up to heaven from the distressed soul ; these the compassionate Jesus hears, and now comes

in to succor and refresh it; he has rich cordials for fainting hours; the soul hath had a bitter breakfast, and therefore Christ will give it a comfortable supper: "I will come in to him, and sup with him."

3. *Those that open their hearts to Christ must expect to meet with great troubles and temptations* in the new course on which they have entered: their way to heaven lies through much tribulation; all our troubles are not over when we are once in Christ; nay, then commonly our greatest outward troubles begin: "After ye were illuminated, ye endured a great fight of afflictions." Heb. 10:32. Carnal relations scoff, frown, and cast us off; the world hates us and marks us out for persecution. Now, that Christians may not utterly be discouraged when they meet with troubles in the way of duty, Christ will cheer them by these spiritual refreshments. Christ himself had a voice from heaven, "This is my beloved Son," Matt. 17:5, a little before his great combat; much more do his people need such consolations, to support and encourage them. God foresees and by this provision prepares for the troubles they are to meet with; an hour of sealing fortifies the soul for an hour of suffering. It has been the observation of some Christians when they have felt more than ordinary comforts of the Spirit, that some great trial has been near them; and the event has confirmed it. Whatever comforts Christ gives his people at their first entrance into his service, they will have need enough of them all before they finish their course. To these first sealings they will need to have frequent recourse, and all will be little enough to support them in after-trials.

4. Christ comes in to the opening soul with such divine refreshments to defeat the plot of Satan, who has so often discouraged them by representing the ways of Christ as melancholy; telling them they shall never laugh more, never be merry more, after they have espoused the ways of

holiness. Their own experience shall confute it, for they now taste that pleasure in Christ, in faith and obedience, which they never tasted in the ways of sin; thus that scandalous libel of Satan is confuted. They find they were never truly merry till now; for all true mirth commences from our closing with Christ: "And they began to be merry." Luke 15 : 24.

These spiritual refreshments are here called *a supper*, because the supper among the Jews was their best meal, Luke 14 : 17, and because it is the last meal. This is not only the best enjoyment that a believer ever had, but upon these spiritual comforts, though much more refined and perfected, he is to feed for ever in heaven. O Christian, well mayest thou be contented with thine outward lot of providence, however it shall fall in this world with respect to thy outward man. Will the King of heaven come and sup with thee? Does he feed thy soul with pardon, peace, and joy in the Holy Ghost, and seal an earnest of future glory? Then thou livest at a higher and nobler rate than any of thy carnal neighbors do. "Blessed be the God and Father of our Lord Jesus Christ, who hath blessed us with all spiritual blessings in heavenly places in Christ." Eph. 1 : 3. The same person who thus blesses God with a heart overflowing with joy and comfort, endured as many persecutions, felt as many wants and straits as any man. What if Providence do but meanly clothe your bodies, so that you cannot ruffle it in the splendor that others do? Yet mayest thou say with the church, "I will greatly rejoice in the Lord, my soul shall be joyful in my God; for he hath clothed me with the garments of salvation, he hath covered me with the robe of righteousness, as a bridegroom decketh himself with ornaments, and as a bride adorneth herself with her jewels." Isa. 61 : 10. What if thou fare not so deliciously as the great ones of this world do? Yet, if Christ will give thee to eat of the hidden manna which he promiseth, Rev. 2 : 17, art thou not better clothed and fed than any of the nobles of the world? This takes away all grounds of complaint. It may be you will say, O, but we have bodies as well as souls; if God had created us angels, so that we could live without material food, it were another case. I reply, Christ never thus intended to feast thy soul and starve thy body; he that feeds thy soul with bread from heaven, will take care for all necessary provisions on earth. Isa. 41 : 17. You have sought and found the kingdom of God and his righteousness; fear not but all other things shall be added to you.

The doctrine before us is full of instruction : I shall begin with the following.

INFERENCE 1. *It is a vile and groundless slander upon religion, to say or insinuate that it deprives men of the comfort and joy of life.* The devil, in design to discourage men from the ways of God, puts a frightful mask on the beautiful face of religion, pretending there is no pleasure to be expected therein ; but this is abundantly confuted in the text : "I will come in to him, and sup with him." Solomon tells us, " A feast is made for laughter." Eccl. 10 : 19. I am sure the soul that sits with Christ at such a feast as has been described above, has the best reason of any man in the world to be merry. Religion indeed denies us all sinful pleasure, but it abounds with spiritual pleasure. No rational, solid mirth can come before Christ : the unsanctified rejoice in things of naught, and their joy will be soon ended; they are hastening to the place where they will find that to be verified of the wages of sin, which they now falsely impute to the wages of holiness ; they shall never rejoice more, never be merry more : but believers shall find this scripture attested by their daily experience : "Her ways are ways of pleasantness, and all her paths are peace," Prov. 3 : 17 ; and that there are such pleasures in the ways of God, as they never experienced in the ways of sin. Is it a solid ground of comfort to a man to be out of debt and all fears of arrest; and is it not much greater to have our debts paid to God by Christ our surety? "Be of good cheer; thy sins be forgiven thee." Matt. 9 : 2. Is it matter of joy to have a sufficiency of all things for the supply of every want? He that is in Christ has this: "All are yours; and ye are Christ's." 1 Cor. 3 : 22, 23. Is it a joyful life to border upon heaven, to be on the confines of blessedness itself? Then it is joyful to be in Christ; for they that are so may rejoice in the hope of glory. Rom. 5 : 2. Is it matter of joy to have the Comforter himself, who is the Spirit of all consolation, taking up his residence in thy heart, comforting and refreshing it with cordials unknown in all the unbelieving world? Then certainly the life of a Christian and the ways of holiness must be most comfortable. Let none therefore, that are looking towards Christ, be discouraged in their way by the slanderous reproaches designedly cast upon religion. Christ and comfort dwell together.

2. Hence, in like manner it follows, *that Christians usually meet the greatest difficulties at their first entrance into religion.* The first work of religion is wounding and weeping work. Thus religion usually begins. Acts 2 : 37; 16 : 29. The soul seems to be struck dead, in the giving up of all its former vain hopes: "When the commandment came, sin revived, and I died," Rom. 7 : 9; but afterwards come pardon, peace, and joy in the Holy Ghost. They that go forth weeping, bearing precious seed, now come back rejoicing, bringing their sheaves with them. Psa. 126 : 6. Now the blessing is realized: "Blessed are they that mourn, for they shall be comforted." Matt. 5 : 4. "Light is sown for the righteous, and gladness for the upright in heart." Psa. 97 : 11. It is quite contrary in the ways of sin; all the pleasures of sin come first, the terrors of conscience come after. Sin comes with smiles in its beginning, but a sting in its end. Pleasures lead the van, hell and

destruction bring up the rear. "Though wickedness be sweet in his mouth, though he hide it under his tongue; though he spare it, and forsake it not, but keep it still within his mouth; yet his meat in his bowels is turned, it is the gall of asps within him." Job 20 : 12–14. But here conviction and humiliation come first, these prepare the way for Christ; and with him come rest and peace. Their sorrow is turned into joy. John 16 : 20.

OBJECTION. *But is this always true? Do not the worst things of religion many times come last? How many Christians go out of the world in an unhappy manner.*

ANSWER. Whatever the after-sufferings of Christians may be, the worst is past when they are in Christ. Great and sharp sufferings they may endure, but the Lord sweetens them with answerable consolations: "I am filled with comfort, I am exceeding joyful in all our tribulation." 2 Cor. 7 : 4. The lowest ebbs are followed by the highest tides; the greatest troubles need not give interruption to peace.

3. Hence it follows, that *no man can be truly happy till he be in Christ.* Comfort and refreshment in the natural order follow faith; it is the vainest imagination in the world to expect solid, spiritual comfort before union with Christ; you may as well expect a harvest before a seed-time. I do confess there are two sorts of comforts found in the world without Christ. First, men may have *sensitive* and *sinful* comforts without Christ; these are common in the unregenerate world, where you may daily see rich men taking comfort in their riches, and voluptuous men in their pleasures: "Ye have lived in pleasure on the earth." James 5: 5. But these are pleasures common to brutes, and beneath the immortal spirit of a man. Second, hypocrites have their delights and comforts in an *imaginary happiness*, which they fancy to themselves; but this is a vanishing shadow. They take comfort from their groundless

hope of heaven, whither they shall never come; it is a feast in a dream. Isa. 29:8. Thus they make a bridge of their own shadow, and are drowned in the waters. Such sensitive and false comforts and pleasures men may have, but no true, solid, spiritual joy enters any man's heart before Christ come into it.

4. *See from hence what heaven is, if there be such a feast to the soul in the very foretastes of it.* If a relish, a taste of heaven as the earnest of it, be so transporting and ravishing, what is the full fruition of God? If these are unutterable, what must that be? Whatever the comforts and joys of any believer in this world may be, yet heaven will be a surprise to him when he comes thither. The joys of God's presence are not to be measured by our present comforts; though these are of the same kind with them, they are far inferior in degree. There is a sixfold difference between the spiritual comforts of believers on earth, and the joys that are above.

(1.) They differ in *quantity*. Here, " we know in part; but when that which is perfect is come, then that which is in part shall be done away." 1 Cor. 13:9, 10. When the Scripture speaks of the comforts communicated to saints on earth, it usually expresses them in some diminutive term or other, calling them first-fruits, earnests, and the like; and indeed it is necessary we should receive them here in small degrees, because the weakness of our present state will not bear them in their plenitude and perfection. Here the joy of the Lord enters into us, but there we are said to enter into that joy. Matt. 25:21. It is too great to enter into us; therefore we enter into, and are swallowed up in it.

(2.) They differ in *constancy*. The best comforts on earth are intermitting: a sun-blast and a cloud; a good day and a bad. You know we feed on two sorts of meat, daily bread and dainties; rarities come not every day to the table. The daily bread on which believers live, is the repose and reliance of faith; as for assurance and joy, these come but now and then.

(3.) They differ in *purity*. Here we have the comforts of the Spirit, but we mingle sin with them, and especially the sin of spiritual pride, which spoils all. Yea, many times the Lord suffers Satan to mingle his temptations with them, lest we should be unduly exalted. 2 Cor. 12:7. But in heaven the comforts of the saints are as the pure water of life, clear as crystal. Rev. 22:1.

(4.) They differ in *efficacy*. The highest comforts of the Spirit here do not perfectly transform our souls into the image of God, as they will be in heaven. "We shall be like him, for we shall see him as he is." 1 John, 3:2. Here, after we are comforted by him, we grieve the Comforter by sin. Neither do the comforts of the Spirit, in this state, produce the fruits of obedience in their maturity, as they do above; there is the same difference in point of efficacy, as there is between the influence of the sunbeams in the winter months, and those in May and June.

(5.) There is a great difference in respect to *society*. Here, the believer for the most part eats his pleasant morsels alone: one Christian eats, and another hungers; but in heaven they all feast together at one table. They shall sit down with Abraham, Isaac, and Jacob, in the kingdom of God. Matt. 8:11. O what must it be to rejoice in the fellowship of patriarchs, prophets, and apostles, where the joy of one is the joy of all?

(6.) They differ also in *durability*. Sin here puts a stop to our comforts, but in heaven there shall never be an end: "Everlasting joy shall be upon their heads." Isa. 35:10. There is an eternal feast. It is everlasting consolation: "We shall be ever with the Lord." 2 Thess. 2:16.

5. This doctrine puts serious matter of EXHORTATION into my mouth. The Lord direct it to the hearts of all, whether they be in Christ or out of Christ.

(1.) To those who are *out of Christ*, and will not be persuaded to open their hearts and consent to his terms. O what a spiritual infatuation is here. What, shut the door of thy heart against Christ, and all the delights of this and the coming world? What madness is this. Hear me, thou poor deluded sinner, who wilt not be persuaded to part with thy sinful, sensual delights in exchange for Christ, and the peace, comfort, and joy that follow him. I have a few things to speak on Christ's behalf at this time. O that they may prevail; O that by them the Spirit of the Lord may persuade thy spirit. Let me offer four or five *pleas* on Christ's behalf, if haply they may prevail and make way for his entertainment in thy soul. And,

PLEA 1. Let me plead thine own *necessity:* a mighty argument, which in other cases makes its way through all oppositions, and makes all difficulties fly before it. Thou art a poor, necessitous, pining, famishing soul; however thy body be accommodated, thou hast not one morsel of spiritual bread for thy famishing soul to live upon. Christ is the bread that cometh down from heaven. The starving prodigal is the lively emblem of thy soul; he feeds upon husks, Luke 15:16, 17, and thou feedest upon that which is not bread. Isa. 55:2. "Thou art wretched, and miserable, and poor, and blind, and naked." Rev. 3:17. Thy body has often been filled and refreshed with the good creatures of God, but thy soul never tasted one morsel of spiritual bread since it came into thy body; it never relished the sweetness of a pardon, the deliciousness of a promise, or the joy and comfort of Christ: the choicest food thou hast ever tasted, was such as thy soul cannot live upon.

PLEA 2. *Christ is at the door of thy soul* with plenty and variety of heavenly comforts purchased by his blood; if thou wilt but open to him, thou shalt be abundantly satisfied with the fatness of his house, and drink of the rivers of his pleasure. Psalm 36:8. "He that believeth on me, as the scripture hath said, out of his belly shall flow rivers of living water," John 7:38; meaning the graces and comforts of the Spirit.

PLEA 3. *If Christ be refused now, you may never taste those invaluable mercies for ever.* "For I say unto you, that none of those men which were bidden shall taste of my supper." Luke 14:24. They were invited to this feast, and so are you; they refused to come, God grant that you may not; for methinks this sentence of Christ, "Those men which were bidden shall not taste of my supper," is like a sentence on a malefactor that is to be hanged in chains, whom the law permits none to relieve. O, it will be dreadful to see the saints sitting at the royal feast in heaven, and yourselves shut out like starving beggars standing in the streets and about the doors where the marriage-supper is kept: they see the lights, they behold the rich dishes carried up, they hear the mirth and music of the guests, but not a bit comes to their share.

PLEA 4. *The refusal of Christ's invitation*, as it is the greatest of all sins, *will be avenged with the greatest punishment.* It is said of those guests that were bidden, that they made light of it, Matt. 22:5; but it fell heavy upon them: "He was wroth, and he sent forth his armies and destroyed those murderers, and burned up their city." Ver. 7. Beware of making light of Christ.

PLEA 5. *What vain things are all those pleasures of sin,* for the sake of which you deprive your souls of the everlasting comforts Jesus Christ can give. Deluded soul, it is not the intent of Christ to rob thee of comfort, but to exchange thy sinful for spiritual delights, to thy unspeakable advantage. True, you can have no more pleasure in sin; but instead of that, you shall have peace with God, joy in the Holy Ghost, and solid comforts for evermore. What are the sensitive or sinful pleasures of the world? You have the total sum of them in 1 John, 2:16, 17: "All that is in

13*

the world, the lust of the flesh, the lust of the eyes, and the pride of life, is not of the Father, but is of the world. And the world passeth away, and the lusts thereof; but he that doeth the will of God, abideth for ever."

QUESTION. *But how may a poor unregenerate soul be prevailed upon to make such a blessed exchange as to part with the pleasures of sin for the blessings of Jesus Christ?*

ANSWER. Besides all that has been offered before, let me briefly add three counsels to such a soul.

Labor to feel thy need of Christ, and then thou wilt quickly be willing to give up all the pleasures of sin for the enjoyment of him. What makes men so tenacious of their lusts, so hard to be persuaded to give up their sinful pleasures, but this, that they never felt the need of a Saviour? O, sinner, didst thou but feel thy need of Christ, wert thou but hungry and thirsty for him, thou wouldst never stand upon such trifles for the enjoyment of him. We read, in the famine of Jerusalem, how they parted with their pleasant things for bread to relieve their souls; jewels, rings, bracelets, things which cost dear and were highly valued at another time, were now willingly parted with for bread. Christ is more necessary to thee than thy necessary food.

Consider *the spiritual and immortal nature of thy soul*, which cannot live upon material things, and must outlive all temporal things. If thy soul cannot live upon them, and must certainly outlive them, what a miserable condition will it unavoidably fall into, when all these sensual and sinful enjoyments are vanished and gone, as thou knowest they shortly will be. These things pass away, 1 John, 2:17, and then has thy soul nothing to live upon to all eternity.

Hearken to the experiences of the saints, who have tried both sorts of pleasure, which you never did. They have tried the pleasures of sin, and they have tasted the pleasures of Christ, and so are able to give a true judgment on both; and they have accordingly determined, that one glimpse of the light of God's countenance puts more gladness into their hearts, than in the time that their corn and wine increased. Psalm 4 : 6, 7. Nay, the wisest Christians, on trial of both, have rightly determined, that the worst things in religion are infinitely to be preferred to the best things belonging to sin ; the very sufferings and afflictions of the people of God have been pronounced better than the pleasures of sin for a season. Heb. 11 : 25. Could you but see with their eyes, and were you capable of making a right judgment as they did, there would not need a word more to persuade you to deny your most pleasant lusts, in exchange for Christ and his beneficial sufferings.

(2.) The doctrine also affords various exhortations *to the regenerate*, who have opened their hearts to Christ, and are thereupon admitted into this comfortable state. It is found in experience a difficult thing, for souls after conversion to bear their own comforts, as it was to rightly manage their troubles at conversion. My business here is to advise souls under the first operations of the Spirit, how to improve their spiritual comforts, that they may abide with them and be growing continually in their souls.

ADVICE 1. *See that you humbly admire and adore the condescending goodness of God to you, in all the comforts of the Spirit which refresh you.* O that God should comfort such a soul as thine, that has so often grieved him— that Christ should be a joy to thee, who hast been a sorrow to him. In Paul's epistle to the Ephesians you will find the spirit of the apostle filled with admiration of this mercy, which breaks forth into this rapturous expression : " Blessed be the God and Father of our Lord Jesus Christ, who hath blessed us with all spiritual blessings in heavenly places in Christ." Eph. 1 : 3. Some never enjoy an ordinary degree of earthly comforts, Job 30 : 3–5 ; others enjoy abundance of earthly, but no spiritual comforts. Psalm 17 : 14. There are others for whom God intends everlasting consolation in the world to come, who are kept low as to spiritual comforts in this world. Psalm 88 : 15. What cause have you to admire the bounty of God to you, for whom there is not only fulness of joy prepared in heaven, but such precious foretastes and earnests of it communicated in the way thither.

Advice 2. *Cleave fast to Christ and those duties of religion in which you have found the best comforts that ever your souls knew.* This is one thing God intends in the communication of these spiritual refreshments, to attach your souls fast to the ways of holiness. The Lord knows that temptations will befall you; discouragements enough you will be sure to meet with; but the enjoyments of God, which you have met with in prayer and hearing, in meditation and sacraments, should engage your hearts for ever to the ways of obedience. You never found that sweetness in the ways of sin which you have found in repentance and faith. When a temptation comes baited with sinful pleasures, think of Jotham's parable of the trees, and of the answer of the olive, the fig-tree, and the vine, Judges 9 : 8–13, and say, in reference to thy spiritual enjoyments, Shall I leave such soul-refreshing comforts as these for the pleasures of sin? God forbid.

Advice 3. *Communicate the spiritual comforts you enjoy, for the benefit and refreshment of others.* The Lord never intended you should engross the comforts of his Spirit to yourselves, nor eat your pleasant morsels alone. He comforts us, that we may be able to comfort them that are in any trouble, by the comfort wherewith we ourselves are comforted of God. 2 Cor. 1 : 4. It is true, religion lays not all open; nor yet does it conceal all. There needs a great deal of wisdom, humility, and caution to secure us from pride and vanity in spirit, while we communicate our comforts to others. Both ostentation and self-appropriation of our comforts are against scripture law; he may be justly suspected that opens all, and so may he too that conceals all. Spiritual comforts are not diminished, but improved by a wise and humble communication.

ADVICE 4. *Be frequent in renewing the acts and exercises of faith.* Your first faith brought in your first comfort; your renewing and repeating those precious acts of faith, will bring you in greater stores of comfort than you yet enjoy. We are not to look upon faith as a single, but a continued act: "To whom *coming* as unto a living stone." 1 Pet. 2 : 4. Thy soul, Christian, is to be in a continual motion towards Christ; the more you believe, the more you will rejoice. You see the door through which comfort comes into your soul. Joy is the daughter of faith, Rom. 15 : 13; your present comfort is the first offspring of faith; but there are many comforts more which will yet be born to your souls, if unbelief prevent it not.

ADVICE 5. *Take heed that you be not a grief to Christ, who hath already brought so much comfort to you.* It will be a sad requital if, after he hath given you the joys of heaven to drink, you shall give him that which is as wormwood and gall; the Lord write that caution upon thy soul: "Grieve not the Holy Spirit of God, whereby ye are sealed unto the day of redemption." Eph. 4 : 30. The argument of the apostle in this place strongly infers *caution* from *comfort*. Christ hath been all joy, all peace, rest, and comfort to you; take heed you be not a grief and shame to him. The intermission of thy duties, the falling of thy affections in duties, thy rash adventures upon sin, will be a grief to the heart of Christ, who hath filled thy heart with so much comfort; and if you grieve him, you cannot expect he should comfort you. A little sin may rob you of a great deal of comfort.

ADVICE 6. *Be not dejected if the first comforts Christ gives you should afterwards abate, or be taken away for a time.* This is a common thing in the experience of most

Christians. You must not think your first comforts are such fixed, settled things, that there is no hazard of losing them; alas, nothing is more liable to change than the joys of a Christian. You will be apt to lose your first love, Rev. 2:4; and if you lose your first love, no wonder that you lose your first comforts. Yet if it should so fall out, be not cast down and discouraged; Christ is not gone, though comfort be gone; and though comfort be gone, it is not gone for ever; renew thy repentance, faith, and obedience, and try if God will not renew thy comfort. There is a former and a latter spring of joy; God will make thy comforts spring again. Besides, thy justification is steadfast, though thy consolation is not so. There are two things which belong to a Christian: one to his being, namely, union with Christ; another to his well-being, namely, comfort from Christ. The latter is contingent, the former fixed and steadfast.

ADVICE 7. *Be filled with compassion to others who lack the comforts you enjoy, especially such as God has united to you as natural relations.* Art thou a father or mother, to whom God has given the comforts and soul-refreshments that have been opened in this discourse? And hast thou no compassion for thy children, who never yet tasted one drop of these spiritual consolations? It will do a man little good to be feasted abroad, while his wife and children are starving at home. Say to them as Paul, in another case, "I would to God, that not only thou, but also all that hear me this day, were both almost and altogether such as I am, except these bonds." Acts 26:29. Religion creates bowels of compassion. O tell them what sweetness there is in the ways of godliness; counsel, plead, and pray that those who are yours may also be Christ's.

ADVICE 8. *As ever you expect the continuance and enlargement of your comforts, see that you walk circumspectly.* It is as much as all your comfort is worth to give way to a little carelessness. That is a remarkable expression of the psalmist, "I will hear what God the Lord will speak; for he will speak peace unto his people, and to his saints: but let them not turn again to folly." Psalm 85:8. Sin, in this text, is fitly called folly; for indeed it is the greatest folly and madness in the world to divest ourselves of such sweet peace and comfort by returning to sin, which has cost us so much sorrow before. Are you willing to be in your former darkness and troubles—to exchange the pleasant light you now enjoy for the horrors you formerly felt? This you must do, if you return again to folly.

ADVICE 9. *Long for heaven, where is the fulness of those joys of which these you now taste are but the earnest and first-fruits.* One design of God in giving them, is to set us a longing after heaven, to help our conceptions, and raise our affections: if these be so sweet, what must those be? "Ourselves also, which have the first-fruits of the Spirit, even we ourselves groan within ourselves, waiting for the adoption, to wit, the redemption of our body." Rom. 8:23. We are not to sit down satisfied, and say we have enough of these first-fruits; they are given to make us long after the fulness of those enjoyments. This answers God's end in giving.

ADVICE 10. *Improve every spiritual comfort you have from Christ to greater cheerfulness in the paths of obedience to Christ.* This is another end for which God communicates them, that our souls being refreshed by them, we might move the more nimbly in the paths of duty. "I will run the way of thy commandments, when thou shalt enlarge my heart." Psalm 119:32. God expects that you pray more frequently, meditate more delightfully, and perform every duty more cheerfully; this is the way to perpetuate your comforts. How many Christians go on droopingly in the ways of duty for want of the encouragements you enjoy.

CHAPTER XI.

COMMUNION BETWEEN CHRIST AND BELIEVERS ON EARTH

"I WILL COME IN TO HIM, *AND WILL SUP WITH HIM, AND HE WITH ME.*" Rev. 3:20.

We have heard the first argument of Christ to persuade the hearts of sinners to open to him, that he will come in to them, and that not empty-handed; he will also sup with them. And, to make the encouragement complete and full, he here adds, "and he with me." This last clause sets forth that spiritual, soul-refreshing communion which is between Christ and believers, begun in this world, completed and perfected in the world to come. Hence our eleventh doctrine is,

There is a mutual, sweet, and intimate communion between Jesus Christ and believers in this world.

Communion with Christ is frequent in the lips of many men, but a hidden mystery to the souls of most men. This atheistical age scoffs at and ridicules it as enthusiasm and fanaticism; but the saints find such a reality and incomparable sweetness in it, that they would not part with it for ten thousand worlds. When the Roman soldiers entered the temple at Jerusalem, and found no image there, as they used to have in their own idolatrous temples, they gave out in a jeer that the Jews worshipped the clouds. Thus ungodly men scoff at the most solemn and sweetest part of internal religion as a mere fancy; but the thing is real, sure, and sensible. If there be truth in any thing, there is truth in this, that there is real intercourse between the visible and invisible world, between Christ and the souls of believers, which we here call communion. " Truly our fellowship is with the Father, and with his Son Jesus Christ." 1 John,

1:3. It is really and truly so; we impose not upon the world, we tell you no more than we have felt. The life of Enoch is called his walking with God. Gen. 5:24. O sweet and pleasant walk; all pleasures, all joys are in that walk with God. "Blessed is the people that know the joyful sound; they shall walk, O Lord, in the light of thy countenance." Psalm 89:15. The joyful sound there spoken of was the sound of the trumpet which called the people to the solemn assemblies, where they walked in the light of God's countenance, the sweet manifestations of his favor; and because the world is so apt to suspect the reality and certainty of this doctrine, the apostle again asserts it: "Our conversation is in heaven." Phil. 3:20. We breathe below, but we live above; we walk on earth, but our conversation is in heaven. To understand this doctrine, three things must come under consideration: what communion with Christ is; that there is such a communion between him and believers; and the excellency of this communion.

I. WHAT COMMUNION WITH CHRIST IS, in the general nature of it. To open this, it must be considered that there is a twofold communion: a state of communion, and actual communion. The first is essential to the second; we can have no actual communion with the Father, Son, or Spirit, till we be first brought into a state of communion. This state of communion is in Scripture called our *fellowship* or partnership with Christ: such a fellowship as merchants have in the same ship and cargo, where one has more and another less, but still a joint though unequal interest; one lives in one kingdom, another in some other kingdom, but they are jointly interested in the same goods. This comparison must not be stretched beyond its intention, which is to show nothing but this, that Christ and believers are coheirs in the same inheritance. Hence they are called his fellows or equals: "God, thy God, hath anointed thee with the oil of gladness above thy fellows." Psalm 45 : 7. And again, "If children, then heirs; heirs of God, and joint-heirs with Christ." Rom. 8 : 17. Christ endows his people, gives them a title not only to himself, but to those good things purchased by him, yea, and the very glory he enjoys in heaven. "The glory which thou gavest me, I have given them." John 17 : 22.

It is true, there are some things in Christ which are peculiar to himself, and incommunicable to any creature, as his eternity, equality with his Father, etc.: neither have we fellowship in his mediatorial work; we have the fruits and benefits of it, but no partnership with him in the glory and honor of it; that is peculiarly his own: and though it is said in the Scriptures, that believers are "righteous as he is righteous," 1 John, 3 : 7, yet the meaning is not that they can justify others as Christ doth; no, they are justified by him, but cannot communicate righteousness to others. But there are other things wherein there is a partnership between Christ and his people: they partake with him in the spirit of sanctification on earth, and glory in heaven; the same spirit of holiness which dwells in Christ without measure, is communicated by him to the saints in measure: "He hath given us of his Spirit." 1 John, 4 : 13. And as Christ communicates his Spirit to the saints, so he communicates the glory of heaven to them: not that they shall be as glorious in heaven as Christ is; no, he will be known among the saints in glory, as the sun is known from the stars. Thus briefly of the state of communion, which is called in Scripture our "being made nigh," Eph. 2 : 13, and indeed we must be made nigh before we can actually draw nigh. We must be put into a state of fellowship before we can have actual communion with God.

Besides this state of communion, there is also *an actual communion* which the saints have in this world with the Father and the Son in the duties of religion. This is our supping with Christ, and he with us: and, for clearness' sake, I shall consider,

Negatively, what it is not; for I find persons are apt greatly to mistake in this matter, taking that for communion with God which is not so; and here let it be noted:

Communion with God does not consist in the bare performance of religious duties. I do not say that men may have communion with God in this world without duties; it is a delusion of Satan to think so; but I say, that communion with God consists not in the mere performance of duties. Communion and duties of religion are two things, separable one from the other. Men may multiply duties and yet be strangers to communion with God in them; even days of humiliation and fasting may be kept by souls that are estranged from communion with the Lord: "Speak unto all the people of the land, and to the priests, saying, When ye fasted and mourned in the fifth and seventh month, even those seventy years, did ye at all fast unto me, even to me?" Zech. 7:5; that is, Had your souls pure intentions and respect in those duties to my glory? Had you communion with me, or I with you, in those duties? Did you ever feel your souls in those days wounded for sin? Or did you not fast out of custom? God may be in men's mouths and at the same time far from their hearts. Jer. 12:2. Religious words may flow out of men's lips when no religion touches their hearts, the inward powers of their souls; you cannot therefore safely depend upon outward duties, Christ rejects this plea. Matt. 7:22. Get a better evidence of communion with God than this, or you will certainly come short of your expectation. I know you not, saith Christ; there was never any spiritual acquaintance between your souls and me; I know you not in a way of approbation.

Neither do all stirrings and workings of the affections in duties prove communion between Christ and the soul; for it is possible, yea, common, to have the affections raised by external motives in the duties of religion: this you see in that example, Ezek. 33:32: "Lo, thou art unto them as a very lovely song of one that hath a pleasant voice, and can play well on an instrument; for they hear thy words, but they do them not." The sweet modulation of the prophet's voice was like the skilful touch of a rare musical instrument, which in a natural way moved and excited their affections. Thus John's hearers rejoiced in his ministry for a season. This is very apt to lead souls into a mistake as to their condition. They distinguish not between the influences that come upon their affections from without, and those that are inward, divine, and spiritual.

But to show, *positively, what communion with God is*, we must consider what things it presupposes in us; and in what the nature of it consists.

There are various things *prerequired and presupposed* to all actual communion with God in duties; and where these things are wanting, men have no communion with him. They may have communion with his people and his ordinances, but not with God and Christ in them.

(1.) *Union with Christ* is fundamentally necessary to all communion with him. All communion is founded in union; and where there is no union, there can be no communion. The member receives nothing from the head unless it be united to it; nor the branch from the root. "All are yours; and ye are Christ's." 1 Cor. 3:22, 23. Here is a vast possession, but all founded upon union; union terminates in communion; and the closer the union, the fuller is the communion.

Before our union with Christ we are strangers to God, we live without God in the world, Eph. 2:12: it is in Christ that we are made nigh; it is in the Beloved that we are accepted. While we are in the state of alienation from Christ, we have no more to do with the communications of joy and peace, with the seals and earnests of the Spirit, than an Indian hath with the privileges of London. "If any man open to me, I will come in to him and sup with him, and he with me."

(2.) Communion with God presupposes the *habits of grace implanted in the soul by regeneration;* a sound change of heart. No regeneration, no communion: "If we say that we have fellowship with him, and walk in darkness, we lie, and do not the truth." 1 John, 1 : 6. The apostle gives the lie to such pretenders. "The Lord is nigh unto all that call upon him, to all that call upon him in truth," Psa. 145 : 18; the latter clause restrains all spiritual communion to upright souls: "For a hypocrite shall not come before him." Job 13 : 16.

(3.) Communion with God not only supposes grace implanted, but also implanted grace *excited,* grace in action. A man may have the habits of faith, love, and delight in him, and yet be without actual communion with God. A believer when he is asleep, and performs no acts of grace, is in a state of communion with God; but if he will have actual communion, his faith, love, and delight must be awakened; they must not lie asleep in the habit. "When thou saidst, Seek ye my face; my heart said unto thee, Thy face, Lord, will I seek." Psa. 27 : 8. It is in order to actual communion with Christ that the church so earnestly begs fresh influences of the Spirit to excite her graces into action: "Awake, O north wind; and come, thou south; blow upon my garden, that the spices thereof may flow out. Let my beloved come into his garden, and eat his pleasant fruits." Sol. Song 4 : 16. And though believers are not so to wait for the influences of the Spirit as to neglect the outward means of engaging their hearts to approach unto God, Jer. 30 : 21, yet certainly it is the work of God's Spirit, and without him we can do nothing to any purpose. The seamen may trim the sails, weigh the anchor, and put all into sailing order; but till a gale come from heaven there is little or no motion.

The same Spirit that plants the habits, excites the acts of grace. These three things therefore are prerequisites to all communion with God.

Now let us more directly consider IN WHAT THIS HEAVENLY PRIVILEGE OF COMMUNION WITH GOD CONSISTS; and generally it will be found to lie in a spiritual correspondence between Christ and the soul. God sends forth influences upon our souls, and we, by the assistance of his Spirit, make returns again unto God. Communion is a mutual action; so in the text, "I will sup with him, and he with me." We cry to God, and God answers that cry by the incomes of spiritual grace upon the soul: "In the day when I cried thou answeredst me, and strengthenedst me with strength in my soul." Psa. 138:3. More particularly, there are many ways wherein men have this spiritual correspondence or communion with God, as in the contemplation of his attributes, in the exercises of our graces in religious duties, and in his various providences. In all these the saints have communion with him.

1. There is a sweet communion between God and his people, *in the contemplation of the divine attributes*, and the impressions God makes by them upon our souls while we meditate on them.

(1.) Sometimes the Lord manifests to the souls of his people his *immense greatness;* the manifestation of which attribute makes an humbling impression upon the soul, and saints seem as nothing to themselves. Thus when Abraham, that great believer, considered the greatness of the God with whom he had to do, that sight of God seemed to reduce him as it were into dust and ashes: "Behold now, I have taken upon me to speak unto the Lord, which am but dust and ashes." Gen. 18:27. He looks upon himself as a heap of vileness and unworthiness; so David, "When I consider thy heavens, the work of thy fingers; the moon and the stars, which thou hast ordained; Lord, what is man, that thou art mindful of him?" Psa. 8 : 3, 4 ; that is, When I consider what a great God the Creator of the world is, I am astonished that he should set his heart upon so vile a thing as man. When men compare themselves among themselves, and measure themselves by themselves, their spirits are apt to swell with pride ; but would they look up to God, as these holy men did, they would admire his condescension. And this is communion with God in the meditation of his immense greatness.

(2.) The representation of the *purity and holiness of God*, working shame and deep abasement in the soul for the pollutions and sin that are in it, this is communion with God, and an excellent way of fellowship with him. Thus, when a representation of God in his holiness was made to the prophet, there were the seraphim, covering their faces with their wings and crying one to another, saying, "Holy, holy, holy is the Lord of hosts ; the whole earth is full of his glory." The effect this produced, or the return made by the prophet to this manifestation of God in his holiness, was deep abasement of soul for his unsuitableness to meet so holy a God : " Then said I, Woe is me ! for I am undone ; because I am a man of unclean lips." Isa. 6 : 3–5. This is communion with God in his holiness. Thus Job, who had stiffly defended his own integrity against men, when God enters the lists with him and he saw with what a great and holy God he had to do, cried out, Job 40 : 4, 5, " Behold, I am vile ; what shall I answer thee ? I will lay my hand upon my mouth. Once have I spoken, but I will not answer ; yea, twice, but I will proceed no further." That is, I am silent ; Lord, I have done : I could answer men, but I cannot answer thee ; thou art holy, but I am vile.

(3.) There are sometimes representations of the *goodness and mercy of God* made to the souls of his people. When these produce an ingenuous melting of the heart into an humble, thankful admiration, and a corresponding care of pleasing him in the ways of obedience, then have men communion with God in his goodness. The goodness of God runs down to men in a double channel: to their bodies, in external providences; and to their souls, in spiritual mercies. When the goodness of God, either way, draws forth the love and gratitude of the soul to the God of our mercies, then have we real communion with him. Thus Jacob: "And Jacob said, O God of my father Abraham, and God of my father Isaac, the Lord which saidst unto me, Return unto thy country and to thy kindred, and I will deal well with thee: I am not worthy of the least of all the mercies, and of all the truth which thou hast showed unto thy servant; for with my staff I passed over this Jordan, and now I am become two bands." Gen. 32:9, 10. Ah, Lord, I see a multitude of mercies round about me, and the least of them is greater than I. So "David the king came and sat before the Lord, and said, Who am I, O Lord God, and what is my house, that thou hast brought me hitherto? And yet this was a small thing in thine eyes, O God; for thou hast also spoken of thy servant's house for a great while to come, and hast regarded me according to the estate of a man of high degree. What can David speak more to thee?" 1 Chron. 17:16–18. You see in these instances, what effects the goodness of God, even in inferior, outward mercies, produces in sanctified hearts. But, if you come to spiritual mercies, and ponder the goodness of God to your souls, in pardoning, accepting, and saving such sinful creatures as you have been; this much more affects the heart, and overwhelms it with holy astonishment; as you see in Paul: I "was before a blasphemer, and a persecutor, and injurious; but I obtained mercy, because I did it ignorantly in unbelief: and the grace of our Lord Jesus was exceeding abundant." 1 Tim. 1:13, 14. So when pardoning grace appeared to Mary, that notorious sinner, into what a flood of tears, into what transports of love did the sight of mercy cast her soul! She wept and washed her Saviour's feet with tears of joy and thankfulness. Luke 7:44. No terrors of the law, no frights of hell melt the heart like the apprehensions of pardoning mercy.

(4.) Sometimes special representations of the *veracity and faithfulness of God* are made to his people, begetting trust and holy confidence in their souls; then have men communion with God in his faithfulness. Thus, Hebrews 13:5, 6, "I will never leave thee, nor forsake thee." There is a discovery of the faithfulness of God; and what follows upon this? " So that we may boldly say, the Lord is my helper, and I will not fear what man shall do unto me." Here is faithfulness in God, producing trust and confidence in the believer; this is that reciprocation, that sweet fellowship and communion between God and a believer with respect to his fidelity. "Behold, God is my salvation; I will trust and not be afraid." Isa. 12:2. And truly, friend, this is what the Lord justly expects from thee, even trust and confidence in him, thy steady dependence on him, in return for all the manifestations of his faithfulness to thee both in his word and providence.

(5.) There are manifestations of the *displeasure of God* by the hiding of his face and the frowns of his providence: when these produce repentance and deep humiliation for sin, an unquietness, a restlessness of spirit till he restore his favor and manifest his reconciliation to the soul, even here also is a real communion between God and the soul. "Thou didst hide thy face, and I was troubled." Psa. 30:7. Nor will a gracious soul rest there, but will take pains to sue out a fresh pardon. "Make me to hear joy and gladness, that the bones which thou hast broken may rejoice. Restore unto me the joys of thy salvation." Psa. 51:8, 12.

I cannot here omit to point out a great mistake even among God's own people: many of them understand not what communion there should be with God under the manifestations of his displeasure for sin. They know the affectionate meltings of their souls into love and praise to be communion with God; but that in the shame, grief, and sorrow produced in them by the manifestations of God's displeasure—that even in these things there may be communion with God, they understand not. But let me tell thee, that even such things as these are the choice fruits of the spirit of adoption, and that in them thy soul hath as real and beneficial communion with God, as in the greatest transports of spiritual joy. O it is blessed to be before the Lord as Ezra was, after conviction of carelessness, and spiritual defilements; saying with him, "O my God, I am ashamed and blush to lift up my face to thee, my God." Ezra 9 : 6. Shame and blushing are as excellent signs of communion with God as the sweetest smiles.

(6.) There are special contemplations of the *omniscience of God*, producing sincerity, comfort in appeals, and recourse to it in doubts of our own uprightness; and this also is an excellent method of communion with God. First, when the omniscience of God strongly obliges the soul to sincerity and uprightness, as it did David : " If I say, Surely the darkness shall cover me; even the night shall be light about me; yea, the darkness hideth not from thee; but the night shineth as the day : the darkness and the light are both alike to thee," Psa. 139 : 11, 12, compared with Psa. 18 : 23, " I was also upright before him." The consideration that he was always before the eye of God was his preservative from iniquity, yea, from his own iniquity. Second, when it produces comforts in appeals to it, as it did to Hezekiah : " I beseech thee, O Lord, remember now how I have walked before thee in truth, and with a perfect heart, and have done that which is good in thy sight." 2 Kings, 20 : 3. So Job also appeals to this attribute : " Thou knowest that I am not wicked." Job 10 : 7. So did Jeremiah : " But thou, O Lord, knowest me; thou hast seen me, and tried my heart toward thee." Jer. 12 : 3. Third, when we have recourse to it under doubts and fears as to our own uprightness. Thus did David: "Search me, O God, and know my heart; try me, and know my thoughts; and see if there be any wicked way in me." Psa. 139 : 23, 24. In all these attributes of God, Christians have real and sweet communion with him.

2. The next method of communion with God is *in the exercise of our graces in the duties of religion*, such as prayer, hearing, and the sacraments; in all which the Spirit of the Lord influences the graces of his people, and they return the fruits thereof in some measure to him. As God hath planted various graces in regenerate souls, so he hath appointed various duties to exercise and draw forth those graces; and when they do so, then have his people sweet communion with him. And,

(1.) To begin with the first grace that shows itself in the soul of a Christian, to wit, *repentance*, or sorrow for sin. In the exercise of this grace of repentance, the soul pours out itself before the Lord with much bitterness and brokenness of heart, and spreads forth its sorrows, which are as so much seed sown; and in return thereto the Lord usually sends an answer of peace. "I said, I will confess my transgression unto the Lord; and thou forgavest the iniquity of my sin." Psa. 32 : 5. Here is a voice of sorrow sent up, and a voice of peace coming down, which is real communion between God and man in the exercise of repentance.

(2.) As there are seasons in duty wherein the saints exercise their repentance, and the Lord returns peace; so likewise the Lord helps them in their duties to act *faith*, in return whereunto they find from the Lord inward support, rest, and refreshment. "I had fainted, unless I had believed." Psa. 27 : 13. And ofttimes an assurance is given them of the mercies they have acted their faith about. 1 John, 5 : 14.

(3.) The Lord many times draws forth eminent degrees of our *love* to him in the course of our duties; the heart is filled with love to Christ. The strength of the soul is drawn forth to Christ in love, and this the Lord repays in kind, love for love : " He that loveth me shall be loved of my Father, and I will love him, and will manifest myself to him. My Father will love him, and we will come unto him, and make our abode with him." John 14 : 21, 23. Here is sweet communion with God in the exercise of love. O what enjoyment do Christians thus gain in their duties and exercise of graces!

(4.) To mention no more, in the duties of passive obedience Christians are enabled to exercise their *patience, meekness, and long-suffering* for Christ; in return to which the Lord gives them the special consolations of his Spirit, double returns of joy: "The Spirit of glory and of God resteth upon them." 1 Pet. 4 : 14. The Lord strengthens them with fortitude, and with all might in the inner man, unto all long-suffering; and the reward of that long-suffering is joyfulness. Col. 1 : 11.

3. Besides communion with God in the contemplation of his attributes, and graces exercised in the course of duties, there is another method of communion with God in the way of his *providences;* for therein also his people walk with him. To give a view of this, let us consider providence in a fourfold aspect towards the people of God.

(1.) There are *afflictive providences* and rebukes wherewith the Lord chastens his children; this is the discipline of his house : in answer whereunto, gracious souls return meek and childlike submission, a fruit of the Spirit of adoption; they are brought to accept the punishment of their iniquities. And herein lies communion with God under the rod. This answer to the rod may not be made at once, for there is much stubbornness unmortified in the best hearts, Heb. 12 : 7, but this is the fruit it shall yield; and when it doth, there is real communion between God and the afflicted soul. Let not Christians mistake themselves: if when God is smiting, they are humbled, search their hearts, and bless God for the discoveries of sin made by their afflictions; if they admire his wisdom in timing, moderating, and choosing the rod; if they kiss it with childlike submission, and say, It is good for me that I have been afflicted, they have real communion with God, though it may be for a time without joy.

(2.) There are times when *providence straitens* the people of God, when their waters of comfort ebb and run very low, and their wants pinch; the soul then exercises in return filial dependence upon fatherly care, saying with David, "The Lord is my shepherd; I shall not want," Psa. 23 : 1 : it belongs to him to provide, and to me to depend; I will trust my Father's care and love. Here now is sweet communion with God under pinching wants. The wants of the body enrich the soul; outward straits are the occasion of inward enlargements. See, from hence, how good it is to have an interest in God as a Father, whatever changes of providences may come upon you.

(3.) There are seasons wherein the Lord *exposes his people to imminent dangers*, when to the eye of sense there is no way of escape. When this produces trust in God, and resignation to the pleasure of his will, there is communion with God in times of distress and difficulty. Thus David, Psa. 56 : 3 : "What time I am afraid, I will trust in thee:" Father, I see a storm rising, thy poor child comes under his Father's roof for shelter; for whither should a distressed child go but to his Father?

(4.) And then, as to the events of *doubtful* providences, when the soul resigns and leaves itself to the wise disposal of the will of God, as David in 2 Sam. 15 : 26 : "Here am I ; let him do to me as seemeth good in his sight :" this is real and sweet communion with God in his providences. So much for the nature of communion with God.

II. I shall show the REALITY of communion with God, and prove it to be no fancy. I confess it grieves me to be put upon the proof of this, but the atheism and profaneness of the age we live in seem to make it necessary ; for many men will allow nothing for certain but what falls under the cognizance of sense. O that they had their spiritual senses exercised; then they would sensibly discern the reality of these things. But to put the matter out of question, I shall show the truth and reality of the saints' communion with God in divers ways.

EVIDENCE 1. From *the saints' union with Christ*. If there be a union between Christ and believers, then of necessity there must be communion between them also. Now the whole word of God which you profess to be the rule of your faith, plainly asserts this union between Christ and believers ; an union like that between the branches and the root, John 15 : 4, 5, or that between the head and the members, Eph. 4 : 16. Now, if Christ be to believers as the root to the branches, and as the head to the members, then of necessity there must be a communion between them ; for if there were not a communion, there could be no communications ; and if no communications, no life. It is by the communication of vital sap from the root and from the head, that the branches and members subsist and live.

EVIDENCE 2. There is a *cohabitation* of Christ with believers ; he dwells with them, yea, he dwells in them : " I will dwell in them, and walk in them." 2 Cor. 6 : 16. The soul of a believer is the temple of Christ ; yea, his living temple. 1 Pet. 2 : 5. And if Christ dwell in them and walk in them, then certainly there must be communion between him and them ; if they live together, they must converse together. A man indeed may dwell in his house, and yet cannot be said to have communion with it ; but the saints are a living house, they are the living temples of Christ ; and he cannot dwell in such temples capable of communion with him, and yet have no communion with them.

EVIDENCE 3. The reality of communion between God and the saints is undeniably evinced by *the spiritual relations* into which God has taken them. Every believer is the child of God and the spouse of Christ. God is the believer's Father, and the church is the Lamb's wife. Christ calls the believer not only his servant, but his friend. "Henceforth I call you not servants; for the servant knoweth not what his Lord doeth: but I have called you friends." John 15:15. Now, if God be the believer's Father, and the believer be God's own child, certainly there must be communion between them. If Christ be the believer's husband, and the believer be Christ's spouse, there must be communion between them. What, no communion between the Father and his children, the husband and the wife? We must either renounce and deny all such relation to him, and therein renounce our Bibles; or else yield the conclusion that there is a real communion between Christ and believers.

EVIDENCE 4. The reality of communion with God appears *from the institution of the ordinances and duties of religion*, to maintain daily communion between Christ and his people. As to instance but one institution, that of prayer—a duty appointed on purpose for the soul's meeting with God, and communion with him: "Draw nigh to God, and he will draw nigh to you." James 4:8. Now, to what purpose can such an ordinance be appointed for the soul's drawing nigh to God, and God to it, if there be no such thing as communion to be enjoyed with him? If communion with God were a mere phantom, as the carnal world thinks it to be, what encouragement have the saints to bow their knees to the God and Father of our Lord Jesus Christ? But surely there is an access to God in prayer: "In whom we have boldness, and access with confidence." Eph. 3 : 12. Access to what ? If God be not there, and there can be no communion with him, what means that access ? "And there I will meet with thee, and I will commune with thee from above the mercy-seat." Exod. 25 : 22. Duties had never been appointed, but for the sake of God's communing with us, and we with him.

EVIDENCE 5. This is yet further proved from *the mutual desires both of Christ and his people to be in sweet and intimate communion one with the other.* The Scripture speaks much of the saints' vehement desires after communion with Christ, and of Christ's desires after communion with the saints, and of both jointly. The saints' desires after communion with him are frequent in the Scriptures; see Psa. 63 : 1–3 ; 42 : 1 ; 119 : 20, and the like throughout the New Testament. And Christ is no less desirous, yea, he is much more desirous of communion with us than we are with him. Consider that expression of his to the spouse, in Sol. Song 8 : 13 : "Thou that dwellest in the gardens, the companions hearken to thy voice ; cause me to hear it." As if he had said, O my people, you frequently converse one with another, you talk daily together; why shall not you and I converse with each other ? You speak often to men ; O that you would speak more frequently to me! "Let me see thy countenance, let me hear thy voice ; for sweet is thy voice, and thy countenance is comely." Sol. Song 2 : 14. And then these desires are mutually expressed one to another. Christ has said, "Surely I come quickly." And the church replies, "Amen. Even so, come, Lord Jesus." Rev. 22 : 20. Now, if there be such vehement mutual desires after communion between Christ and his people in this world, then certainly there is such a thing as real communion between them, or else both must live a very restless and dissatisfied life.

EVIDENCE 6. *The mutual complaints of the interruption of communion* plainly prove there is such a thing. If God complain of his people for their estrangements from him, and the saints complain to God of his silence to them, and the hidings of his face from them, surely there must be a communion between them, else there could be no ground of complaints for the interruptions of it. But God does complain of his people for their estrangements from him. "Thus saith the Lord, I remember thee, the kindness of thy youth, the love of thine espousals. What iniquity have your fathers found in me, that they are gone far from me?" Jer. 2 : 2, 5. As if he should say, You and I have been better acquainted in days past; what cause have I given for your estrangements from me? And thus Christ complains of the church of Ephesus; after he had commended many things in her, one thing grieves him: "Nevertheless, I have somewhat against thee, because thou hast left thy first love." Rev. 2 : 4. And then on the other side, when the Lord hides his face and seems to estrange himself from his people, what sad lamentations and moans do they make about it, as an affliction they know not how to bear. Thus the Psalmist: "Lord, why castest thou off my soul; why hidest thou thy face from me?" Psa. 88 : 14. "Hide not thy face far from me; put not thy servant away in anger." Psa. 27 : 9. This is what they cannot bear.

EVIDENCE 7. The reality of communion with God is made visible to others, *in the effects of it upon the saints who enjoy it.* There are visible signs and tokens of it appearing to the conviction of others. Thus that marvellous change which appeared on the very countenance of Hannah, after she had poured out her heart in prayer, and the Lord had answered her: it is said, "The woman went her way, and her countenance was no more sad." 1 Sam. 1 : 18. You might have read in her face that God had spoken peace and satisfaction to her heart. Thus, when the disciples had been with Christ, the mark of communion with him was visible to others: "Now, when they saw the boldness of Peter and John, and perceived that they were unlearned and ignorant men, they marvelled; and they took knowledge of them that they had been with Jesus." Acts 4:13. It is sweet, Christian, when the cheerfulness and spirituality of thy conversation with men shall convince others that thou hast been with Jesus.

EVIDENCE 8. We may prove the reality of communion with God, from *the impossibility of sustaining the troubles which the saints have without it.* If prayers did not go up and answers come down, there were no living for a Christian in this world. Prayer is the outlet of the saints' sorrows, and the inlet of their supports and comforts. Rom. 8:26. Say not that other men have their troubles as well as the saints, and yet bear them without the help of communion with God. It is true that carnal men have their troubles, and those troubles are often too heavy for them. The sorrows of the world work death; but carnal men have no such troubles as the saints have, for they have their inward, spiritual troubles, as well as their outward troubles. And inward troubles are the sinking troubles; but thus the strength of God comes to succor them: and except they had a God to go to, and draw comfort from, they could never bear them. "I had fainted, unless I had believed." Psa. 27:13. Paul had sunk under the buffetings of Satan, unless he had gone once and again to his God, and received the answer, "My grace is sufficient for thee." 2 Cor. 12:9.

EVIDENCE 9. We argue the reality of communion with God from *the end of the saints' vocation.* We read frequently in Scripture of effectual calling; and what is that to which God calls his people, out of the state of nature, but unto fellowship and communion with Jesus Christ? "God is faithful, by whom ye were called unto the fellowship of his Son Jesus Christ our Lord." 1 Cor. 1:9. They are called, you see, into a life of communion with Christ: therefore there is such a communion, else the saints are called to the enjoyment of a fancy, instead of a privilege;

which is the greatest reproach that can be cast upon the faithful God that called them.

EVIDENCE 10. *The characters and description given of the saints in Scripture*, evidently show their life of communion with God. The men of this world are, in Scripture, manifestly distinguished from the people of God; they are called, the children of this world; but the saints, the children of light. Luke 16 : 8. They are said to be after the flesh, but saints to be after the Spirit. Rom. 8 : 5. They mind earthly things, but the conversation of the saints is in heaven. Phil. 3 : 19, 20. By all which it undeniably appears that there is a reality in the doctrine of communion between Christ and his people. We are not imposed upon; it is no cunningly devised fable, but a thing whose foundation is as sure as its nature is sweet.

CHAPTER XII.

COMMUNION BETWEEN CHRIST AND BELIEVERS ON EARTH—CONTINUED.

"I WILL COME IN TO HIM, AND WILL SUP WITH HIM, *AND HE WITH ME.*" REV. 3:20.

I shall now proceed to show you,

III. The transcendent excellency of this life of communion with God: it is the life of our life, the joy of our hearts; a heaven upon earth—as will appear by these twenty excellencies thereof.

Excellency 1. It is the *assimilating instrument whereby the soul is moulded after the image of God.* This is the excellency of communion with God, to make the soul like him. There is a twofold assimilation or conformity of the soul to God, the one perfect and complete, the other imperfect and in part. Perfect assimilation is the privilege of the perfect state, resulting from the immediate vision and perfect communion the soul has with God in glory: "When he shall appear, we shall be like him, for we shall see him as he is." 1 John, 3:2. Perfect vision produces perfect assimilation; but the soul's assimilation or imperfect conformity to God in this world, is wrought and gradually carried on by daily communion with him. And as our communion with God here grows up more and more into spirituality and power, so in an answerable degree does our conformity to him advance: "But we all, with open face beholding as in a glass the glory of the Lord, are changed into the same image from glory to glory, as by the Spirit of the Lord." 2 Corinth. 3:18. All sorts of communion among men have an assimilating efficacy: he that walks in vain company is vainer than he was before; and he that walks in spiritual, heavenly company, will be more serious than before. But nothing so transforms the spirit of a man as communion with God. Those are most like God that converse most frequently with him. The beauty of the Lord is upon those souls; it changes the spirit of a man after the divine pattern.

EXCELLENCY 2. It is the *beauty of the soul*, in the eyes of God and all good men; it makes the face to shine. No outward splendor attracts like this; it makes a man the most desirable companion in the whole world: "That which we have seen and heard declare we unto you, that ye also may have fellowship with us; and truly our fellowship is with the Father, and with his Son Jesus Christ." 1 John, 1:3. This is the great inducement the apostle makes use of to draw the world into fellowship with the saints, that their fellowship is with God. And if there were ten thousand other inducements, there could be none like this. You read of a blessed time, when the earth shall be full of holiness; when the Jews, now as a lost generation, shall be called, and an eminent degree of sanctification shall be visible in them; and then see the effect of this: "In those days it shall come to pass, that ten men shall take hold, out of all languages of the nations, even shall take hold of the skirts of him that is a Jew, saying, We will go with you; for we have heard that God is with you." Zech. 8:23. This is the powerful attractive, the Lord is with you; it is the effect of communion with God, which makes the righteous more excellent than his neighbor. Prov. 12:26. What a visible difference does this make between one man and another. How heavenly, sweet, and desirable are the conversation and company of some men; how frothy, burdensome, and unprofitable is the company of others; and what makes the difference but only this, the one walks in communion with God, the other is alienated from the life of God?

EXCELLENCY 3. It is *the centre on which rests the weary soul*—the rest and refreshment of a man's spirit: "Return unto thy rest, O my soul." Psa. 116:7. When we attain perfect communion with God in heaven, we attain to perfect rest; and all the rest the spirit of man finds on earth, is in communion with God. Take a sanctified person who has intermitted for some time his communion with the Lord, and ask him, Is your soul at rest and ease? He will tell you, No. The motions of his soul are like those of a member of his body out of joint, neither comely nor easy. Let him recover his spiritual frame again, and with it he recovers his rest and comfort. Christians, you meet with a variety of troubles in this world; many a sweet comfort is cut off, many a hopeful project dashed by the hand of Providence; and what, think you, is the meaning of these blasting, disappointing providences? Surely this is their design and errand, to disturb your false rest in the bosom of the creature; to pluck away the pillows you were laying your heads upon, that you may be led back to God, recover your lost communion with him, and say with David, "Return unto thy rest, O my soul." Sometimes we are settling ourselves to rest in an estate, in a child, or the like: at such a time it is usual for God to say, Go, losses, smite such a man's estate; go, death, and take away the desire of his eyes with a stroke, that my child may find rest nowhere but in me. God is the ark; the soul, like the dove Noah sent forth, let it fly where it will, shall find no rest till it come back to God.

EXCELLENCY 4. *It is the desire of all gracious souls throughout the world.* Wherever there is a gracious soul, its desires work after communion with God. As Christ was called, "The Desire of all nations," Hag. 2:7, so communion with him is the desire of all nations; and this speaks the excellency of it: "One thing have I desired of the Lord, that will I seek after; that I may dwell in the house of the Lord all the days of my life, to behold the beauty of the Lord, and to inquire in his temple." Psa. 27:4. That is to enjoy communion with him in the public duties of his worship. One thing have I desired, that is, one thing above all others; such an one, that if God shall give it me, I can comfortably bear the want of other things. Let him deny me what he will, if he will not deny me this one thing; this shall richly recompense the want of all other things. Hence the desires of the saints are so intense after this one thing: "As the hart panteth after the water-brooks, so panteth my soul after thee, O God;" and, "My soul fainteth for thy salvation;" "When wilt thou come unto me?" Psalm 42:1; 119:81; 101:2. No duties can satisfy without it, the soul cannot bear the delay, much less the denial of this communion. Christians reckon their lives worth nothing without it. Ministers may come, ordinances and sabbaths may come; but there is no satisfaction to the desires of a gracious heart, till God comes too: "O when wilt thou come unto me?"

EXCELLENCY 5. As it is the desire, so it is the *delight* of all the children of God, both in heaven and earth. As communion with the saints is the delight of Christ, "Let me hear thy voice;" and again, "The companions hearken to thy voice; cause me to hear it;" so communion with Christ is the delight of his people: "I sat down under his shadow with great delight, and his fruit was sweet to my taste." Sol. Song 2:14; 8:13; 2:3. It is the pleasure of Christ to see the earnest countenances, the blushing cheeks, the weeping eyes of his people on their knees; and it is the delight of the saints to see a smile upon his face, and to hear a voice of pardon and peace from his lips. I must tell you, Christians, you must look for no such delights as these in any earthly enjoyment; there are none better than these, till you come home to glory. Communion with God then appears most excellent, inasmuch as it is the desire and delight of all gracious souls.

EXCELLENCY 6. It is the *envy of Satan*, that which mortifies and disappoints that wicked spirit. O how it grates and galls that proud and envious spirit, to see men enjoying the pleasure of communion with God, from which he himself is fallen and cut off for ever; to see the saints in delightful communion with Christ, while he feels the pangs of horror and despair: this he cannot endure to behold. And therefore you find in your experience, that times of communion with God are usually busy times of temptation from the devil. "And he showed me Joshua the high-priest standing before the angel of the Lord, and Satan standing at his right hand to resist him." Zech. 3 : 1. It is well for thee, Christian, that thou hast an Advocate standing at God's right hand to resist and frustrate his attempts upon thee; otherwise Satan would thus destroy your communion with God, and make that which is now your delight, your terror. Many ways doth the devil oppose the saints' communion with God : sometimes he labors to divert them from it; this business shall fall in, or that occasion fall out, on purpose to divert thy soul's approach to God ; but if he cannot prevail in this, then he labors to distract your thoughts into a thousand vanities; or if he succeed not there, he attacks you in your return from duty, with spiritual pride and security. These fierce oppositions of hell show the worth and excellency of communion with God.

EXCELLENCY 7. It is the *design of all the ordinances and duties of religion.* God has instituted every ordinance and duty, whether public or private, to beget and maintain communion between himself and our souls. What are ordinances, duties, and graces, but perspective-glasses to give us a sight of God and help us to communion with him ? God never intended his ordinances to be our rest, but mediums of communion with himself, who is our true rest. When we go into a boat, it is not with an intention to dwell there, but to be ferried over the water where our business lies. If a man miss of communion with God in the best ordinance or duty, it yields him little comfort. He comes back from it, like a man that hath travelled many miles to meet a dear friend on special business, but met with disappointment, and returns sad and dissatisfied. God appoints ordinances to be meeting-places with himself in this world: "Thou shalt put the mercy-seat above upon the ark; and in the ark thou shalt put the testimony that I shall give thee. And there I will meet with thee, and I will commune with thee from above the mercy-seat, from between the two cherubims." Exodus 25: 21, 22. It was not the sight of the golden cherubims, or of the ark overlaid with pure gold, which could have satisfied Moses, had not the special presence of God been there, and had he not held communion with him. "O God, thou art my God; early will I seek thee: my soul thirsteth for thee, my flesh longeth for thee in a dry and thirsty land, where no water is; to see thy power and thy glory, so as I have seen thee in the sanctuary." Psalm 63: 1, 2. Magnificent structures, or artificial ornaments of places of worship, are of little account with a gracious soul; it is the presence of God and communion with him which is the beauty and glory the saints desire to behold.

EXCELLENCY 8. It is the *evidence of our union with Christ* and interest in him. All union with Christ must evidence itself by a life of communion with him, or our pretensions to it are vain and groundless. There are many—I wish there were more—inquiring after evidences and signs of their union with Christ; here is an evidence that can never fail you: Do you live in communion with him? May your life be called a walking with God, as Enoch's was? Then you may be sure you have union with him; and this is so sure a sign, as that death itself, which usually discovers the vanity of false signs, will never be able to destroy it. Hezekiah could say, "I beseech thee, O Lord, remember now how I have walked before thee in truth and with a perfect heart, and have done that which is good in thy sight." 2 Kings, 20: 3. O, professors, it will be a dreadful thing, whatever ungrounded hopes and false comforts you now have, to find them shrinking away from you, as certainly they will at death; and all on this account: "I have been a man of knowledge, have been frequent in the external duties of religion, but my heart was not in them; I had no communion with the Lord in them, and now God is a terror to my soul. I am going to his awful bar, and have not one sound evidence to carry with me." That is a remarkable text in Gal. 5:25, "If we live in the Spirit, let us also walk in the Spirit;" that is, let us evidence the life of grace in us by exercising that grace in a life of communion with God. When all is said, this is the surest evidence of our union with Christ; and no gifts or performances whatever can amount to evidence of union with Christ without it.

Excellency 9. It is *ease* in all pains, sweet and sensible ease to a troubled soul. As the bleeding of a vein cools, eases, and refreshes a feverish body; so the opening of the soul by acts of communion with God, gives ease to a burdened soul: griefs are eased by groans heavenward. Many souls are deeply laden with their own fears, cares, and distresses; no refreshment for such a soul, no anodyne in the whole world like communion with God. Psa. 32:1, 2. How did troubles afflict David's soul; night and day God's hand was heavy on him; his soul, as Elihu speaks, was like bottles full of new wine: he must speak to God; and so he did, and was refreshed by it: "I said, I will confess my transgressions unto the Lord; and thou forgavest the iniquity of my sin." Ver. 5. It would grieve one to see how many distressed souls carry their troubles up and down the world, making their complaints to one and another; but obtain no ease. Away to thy God, poor Christian; get thee into thy closet, pour out thy soul before him; and that ease which thou seekest in vain elsewhere, will there be found, or nowhere.

Excellency 10. It is *food* to the soul, and the most delicious, pleasant, proper, and satisfying food that ever it tasted; it is hidden manna. Rev. 2:17. "O Lord, by these things men live, and in all these things is the life of my spirit." Isa. 38:16. Regenerate souls cannot live without spiritual food: their bodies can live as well without bread, as their souls without communion with God; it is more than their necessary food. Here they find what they truly call marrow and fatness. Psa. 63:5. O the satisfaction and support they draw from spiritual things by meditations upon them. "To be spiritually minded is life and peace." Rom. 8:6. The delicacies upon princes' tables are husks and chaff to this. Ungodly men may live on the vanities of the world, but a renewed soul cannot subsist long without God. Let such a soul be diverted for a time from its usual refreshments, and he will find his heart aching and pining within him. It is angels' food, that which your souls must live upon throughout eternity.

EXCELLENCY 11. It is the *guard of the soul against the assaults of temptation.* It is like a shield advanced against the fiery darts of the wicked one. Your safety lies in drawing nigh to God. "They that are far from thee shall perish. But it is good for me to draw near to God." Psalm 73:27, 28. It is good indeed; not only the good of comfort, but the good of safety is in it: "The beloved of the Lord shall dwell in safety by him." Deut. 33:12. The gracious presence of God is your shield and safety; and if you would have the Lord thus present with you in all your fears, straits, and dangers, see that you keep near to him in the duties of communion. "The Lord is with you while ye be with him." 2 Chron. 15:2.

EXCELLENCY 12. It is the *honor of the soul,* and the greatest honor God ever conferred on any creature. It is the glory of the holy angels in heaven, to be always beholding the face of God. Matt. 18:10. O that God should admit poor dust and ashes unto such a nearness to himself: to walk with a king, and to have frequent converse with him, puts great honor upon a subject; but the saints walk with God; so did Enoch, so do all the saints. "Truly our fellowship is with the Father, and with his Son Jesus Christ." 1 John, 1:3. They have liberty and access with confidence; the Lord, as it were, delivers to them the golden key of prayer, by which they may come into his presence on all occasions with the freedom of children to a father.

EXCELLENCY 13. It is the *instrument of mortification*, and the most excellent and successful instrument for that purpose. "This I say then, walk in the Spirit, and ye shall not fulfil the works of the flesh." Gal. 5:16. Walking in the Spirit is the same thing as walking in communion with God. Now, says the apostle, if you walk thus in the Spirit, in the actings of faith, love, and obedience, through the course of holy duties, the effect will be, that ye shall not fulfil the lusts of the flesh. He does not say, You shall not feel temptations to sin assaulting you; but, You shall not fulfil the lusts of the flesh, sin shall not have dominion over you; this will free you from the power of sin. A temptation overcome this way is more effectually subdued, than by all the vows, resolutions, and external means in the world. A candle that is blown out with a puff of breath may be rekindled by another puff; but if it is quenched in water, it is not easily lighted again: so you never find such power or success of temptation over you when your hearts are up with God in the exercise of faith and love, as you do when your hearts hang loose from him, and dead towards him. The schoolmen assign this as one reason why no sin can fasten upon the saints in heaven, because they there enjoy the beatific vision of God. This is sure, that the more communion any man has with God on earth, the more free he is from the power of his corruptions.

EXCELLENCY 14. *It is the kernel of all duties and ordinances.* Words and gestures are but the husks and shells of duties. Communion with God is the sweet kernel, the pleasant and nourishing food which lies within them: you see the fruits of the earth are covered and defended by husks, shells, and such-like integuments, within which lie the pleasant kernels and grains; and these are the food. The hypocrite who goes no further than the externals of religion, is said to feed on ashes, Isa. 44 : 20, to spend his money for that which is not bread, and his labor for that which satisfieth not. Isa. 55 : 2. He feeds upon husks, in which there is but little pleasure or nourishment. What a poor house doth a hypocrite keep! Words, gestures, ceremonies of religion, will never fill the soul; but communion with God is substantial nourishment. As David said, "My soul shall be satisfied as with marrow and fatness; and my mouth shall praise thee with joyful lips; when I remember thee upon my bed, and meditate on thee in the night watches." Psa. 63 : 5, 6. It grieves one's heart to think what airy things many souls satisfy themselves with; feeding like Ephraim upon the wind, well contented if they can but perform a few heartless duties; while the saints feeding on hidden manna, are feasted as it were with angels' food.

EXCELLENCY 15. It is the *light of the soul in darkness*, and the pleasantest light that ever shone upon the soul of man. There are many who walk in darkness; some in the darkness of ignorance and unbelief, the most dismal of all darkness, except that in hell. There are others who are children of light in a state of reconciliation, yet walk in the darkness of outward afflictions, and inward desertions and temptations; but as soon as the light of God's countenance shines upon the soul in the duties of communion with him, that darkness is scattered; it is all light within and round about the soul. "They looked unto him and were lightened." Psa. 34 : 5. They *looked*, there is faith acted in duty; and were *enlightened*, there is the sweet effect of faith. The horrors and troubles of gracious souls retire on the rising of this cheerful light. As wild beasts come out of their dens in the darkness of the night, and shrink back again when the sun ariseth, Psa. 104 : 20–22 ; so do the fears and inward troubles of the people of God, when this light shines upon their souls. Nay more, this is a light which scatters the very darkness of death itself. It was the saying of a worthy divine of Germany upon his death-bed, when his eyesight was gone, being asked how it was within : "Why," said he, " though all be dark about me," yet, pointing as well as he could to his breast, " here is light enough."

Excellency 16. It is *liberty* to the imprisoned soul, and the most comfortable and excellent liberty in the whole world. He only walks at liberty who walks with God : " I will walk at liberty ; for I seek thy precepts." Psa. 119 : 45. Wicked men cry out of bands and cords in religion ; they look upon the duties of godliness as the greatest bondage and thraldom. " Let us break their bands asunder, and cast away their cords from us." Psa. 2 : 3. Away with this strictness and preciseness, it extinguishes the joy and pleasure of our lives ; give us our cups instead of Bibles, our jovial songs instead of spiritual psalms, our sports and pastimes instead of prayers and sermons. Alas, poor creatures, how do they dance in their chains, when, in reality, the sweetest liberty is enjoyed in the duties at which they thus scoff. The law of Christ is the law of liberty ; the soul of man never enjoys more freedom than when it is bound with the strictest bonds of duty to God. Here is liberty from enthralling lusts, and from enslaving fears : " The law of the Spirit of life in Christ Jesus hath made me free from the law of sin and death." Rom. 8 : 2. And here is freedom indeed : " If the Son therefore shall make you free, ye shall be free indeed." John 8 : 36. And here is freedom from fears. Luke 1 : 74, 75. Those that will not endure any restraint from their lusts, will have their freedom to sin ; a freedom they shall have, such as it is. " When ye were the servants of sin, ye were free from righteousness." Rom. 6 : 20. Let none therefore be prejudiced against the ways of duty and godliness. The law of Christ is the perfect law of liberty, James 1 : 25—not liberty to sin ; but liberty from sin.

EXCELLENCY 17. It is a *mercy* purchased by the blood of Christ for believers, and one of the principal mercies settled upon them by the new covenant. A peculiar mercy, which none but the redeemed of the Lord partake of—a mercy the purchase of which cost the blood of Christ. I do not deny but there are thousands of other mercies bestowed upon the unregenerate : they have health, wealth, children, honors, pleasures, and all the delights of this life ; but communion with God, and the pleasures which result therefrom, they are incapable of enjoying. There can be no supping with Christ on such excellent privileges and mercies as these, till the heart is opened to him by faith ; you cannot come nigh to God, until you are first made nigh by reconciliation. Eph. 2 : 13 ; Heb. 10 : 19–22. What would your lives, Christians, be worth to you, if this mercy were cut off from you ? There would be little sweetness or savor in all your outward mercies, were it not for this that sweetens them all. And there is this difference, among many others, between this and all outward mercies : you may be cut off from the enjoyment of those, but you cannot from this ; no prison can keep out the Comforter. O bless God for this invaluable mercy.

EXCELLENCY 18. It is *natural* to the new creature ; the inclination of the newly regenerated soul leads to communion with God. It is as natural to him to desire it and work after it, as it is to the new-born babe to seek the breast : " As new-born babes, desire the sincere milk of the word, that ye may grow thereby." 1 Pet. 2 : 2. There is a law upon the regenerate soul, which inwardly and powerfully constrains it to acts of duty, and fellowship with God in them. Communion with God arises out of the principles of grace. You know all creatures act according to the laws of nature: the sun will rise and the sea will flow at their appointed times; and the gracious soul will make towards its God in the times and seasons of communion with him. It is not forced to these duties by the frights of conscience and the fears of hell, so much as by the natural inclination of the new creature. Two things demonstrate communion with God to be conatural to the regenerate soul, the inner-man, the hidden-man of the heart: namely, first, the *restlessness* of a gracious soul without it. The church had sought her Beloved, but found him not. Does she sit down satisfied in his absence? No; "I will rise now, and go about the city; in the streets and in the broad ways I will seek him whom my soul loveth." Sol. Song 3:2. Second, the *satisfaction* and *pleasure* which the soul feels in the enjoyment of communion with God, plainly show it to be agreeable to the new nature: "My soul shall be satisfied as with marrow and fatness; and my mouth shall praise thee with joyful lips; when I remember thee upon my bed." Psa. 63:5, 6. And when it is thus, duties become easy and pleasant to the soul: "His commandments are not grievous." 1 John, 5:3. Yea, such a soul will be constant and assiduous in those duties. That which is natural, is constant as well as pleasant. What is the reason hypocrites renounce the duties of religion in times of difficulty, but because they have not an inward principle agreeable to them? The motives to duty lie without them, not within them.

EXCELLENCY 19. It is *the holy commerce of all sanctified persons*, and the richest trade ever engaged in by men. Thus they grow rich in spiritual treasures; the revenues of it are better than silver and gold. Many of you have traded long for this world, and it comes to little; and had you gained your designs, you had gained but trifles. This is the rich and profitable occupation: "Our conversation is in heaven." Phil. 3 : 20. Our commerce lies that way, so the word signifies. There are few Christians who have engaged in this soul-enriching trade any considerable time, but can show some spiritual treasures which they have gotten by it: "This I had, because I kept thy precepts." Psa. 119 : 56. As merchants can show the gold and silver, the lands and houses, the rich goods and furniture, which they have obtained by their successful adventures abroad ; and tell their friends, so much I got by such a voyage, and so much by another ; so Christians have invaluable treasures, though their humility conceals them, which they have gained by this heavenly commerce of communion with God. Their souls are weak, but by communion with God they have gotten strength : " I cried, and thou answeredst me, and strengthenedst me with strength in my soul." Psa. 138 : 3. They have gained peace by it, a treasure inestimable : " Great peace have they which love thy law ; and nothing shall offend them." Psa. 119 : 165. They have obtained purity by it: "They also do no iniquity : they walk in his ways." Psa. 119 : 3. O what rich returns are here ; nay, they sometimes get full assurance by it. The riches of both the Indies will not purchase from a Christian the least of these mercies. These are the rich rewards of our pains in the duties of religion ; in keeping his commandments there is great reward. Psa. 19 : 11.

EXCELLENCY 20. It is *oil to the wheels of obedience*, which makes the soul go on cheerfully in the ways of the Lord : " I will run the way of thy commandments, when thou shalt enlarge my heart." Psa. 119 : 32. Oiled wheels run freely. How prompt and ready for any act of obedience is a soul under the influence of communion with God. Then it cries, as Isaiah, having gotten a sight of God, " Here am I, send me." Isa. 6 : 8.

Hereby the soul is prepared for the duties of *active obedience*, to which it applies itself with delight : " Then will

I go unto the altar of God, unto God my exceeding joy," Psa. 43 : 4 ; or, as it is in the Hebrew, "the gladness of my joy." The soul goes to prayer as a hungry man to a feast, or a covetous man to his treasures : " I have rejoiced in the way of thy testimonies, as much as in all riches." Psa. 119 : 14.

It prepares the soul for *passive obedience*, and makes a man rejoice in his sufferings. Col. 1 : 24. It will make a Christian stand ready to receive any burden that God may lay on his shoulders, and even be thankful to be so employed : " The joy of the Lord is your strength." Neh. 8 : 10. A Christian under the cheerful influences of near communion with God, can with more cheerfulness lay down his neck for Christ, than other men can lay out a shilling for him. In all these twenty particulars, you have an account of the excellency of this privilege ; but O how short an account have I given of it. What remains, is the application of this doctrine.

INFERENCE 1. *How certain it is, that there is a God, and a state of glory prepared for sanctified souls.* These things are undeniable. God has set them before our spiritual eyes and senses. Besides the revelation of heaven in the gospel, which without any thing more makes it infallible, the Lord, for our abundant satisfaction, has brought these things down to the touch and test of our spiritual senses and experience. You who have had so many sights of God by faith, so many sweet tastes of heaven in the duties of religion, O what a confirmation and seal have you of the reality of invisible things. You may say of heaven, and the joys above, as the apostle did of Him that purchased it, " Which we have heard, which we have seen with our eyes, which we have looked upon, and our hands have handled," 1 John, 1 : 1 ; for God has set these things in some degree before your eyes, and put the first-fruits of them into your hands. The sweet relish of the joy of the Lord is on the very palate of your souls. To this spiritual sense of the believing Hebrews the apostle appealed when he said, ye "took joyfully the spoiling of your goods, knowing in yourselves that ye have in heaven a better, and an enduring substance." Heb. 10 : 34. This knowing in ourselves is more certain and sweet than all the traditional reports we can get from others: "Whom having not seen, ye love; in whom, though now ye see him not, yet believing, ye rejoice with joy unspeakable and full of glory." 1 Peter, 1 : 8. There is more of heaven felt and tasted in this world than men are aware of; it is one thing to hear of such countries as Spain, Italy, and Turkey by the reports we heard of them in our childhood, and another thing to understand them by the rich commodities imported from them, in the way of commerce. O did we but know what other Christians have felt and tasted, we should not have such doubtful thoughts about invisible things. But the secret comforts of religion are, and ought to be for the most part, hidden things. Religion lays not all open ; the Christian life is a hidden life.

2. *If such a height of communion with God be attainable on earth, then most Christians live below the duties and comforts of Christianity.* Alas, the best of us are but at the foot of this pleasant mount Pisgah. As we are but in the infancy of our graces, so we are but in the infancy of our comforts. What a poor table is kept by many of God's own children ; living between hopes and fears, seldom tasting the riches and joys of assurance. And would you know the reasons of it? There are five things which usually keep them poor and low as to spiritual joys. First, the incumbrances of the world, which divert them from, or distract them in their duties of communion with God, and so keep them low in their spiritual comforts. They have so much to do on earth, that they have little time for heavenly employments. O what a noise and din do the trifles of this world make in the heads and hearts of many Christians.

How dear do we pay for such trifles as these. Second, a spirit of formality creeping into the duties of religion impoverishes its vital spirit, like the embraces of the ivy, which binds and starves the tree it clasps about. Religion cannot thrive under formality, which it is difficult to keep out of a settled course of duty, and much more when duties are intermitted. Third, frequent temptations annoy the minds of many Christians, especially such as are of melancholy temperament. How importunate and restless are these temptations with some Christians. They can gain little comfort or advantage in duty, by reason of them. Fourth, heart-apostasy, the inward decay of our first love, is another reason why our duties prosper so little. "Thou hast left thy first love." Rev. 2:4. You were not wont to serve God with such coldness. Fifth, in a word, spiritual pride impoverishes our comforts; the joys of the Spirit, like brisk wines, are too strong for our weak heads. For these causes, many Christians are kept low in spiritual comforts.

3. *How sweet and desirable is the society of the saints.* It must needs be desirable to walk with them who walk with God. 1 John, 1:3. There are no such companions as the saints. What benefit or pleasure can we find in converse with sensual worldlings? All we can carry away out of such company is guilt or grief. David speaks of his delight as being with the saints, the excellent of the earth. Psalm 16:3. And their society would certainly be much more sweet and desirable than it is, did they live more in communion with God than they do. There was a time when the communion of the saints was exceedingly lovely, Mal. 3:16; Acts 2:46, 47; the Lord restore it to its primitive glory and sweetness.

4. *What an unspeakable mercy is conversion, which lets the soul into such a state of spiritual pleasure.* Here is the beginning of your acquaintance with God—the first spiritual pleasures, of which there shall never be an end.

All the time men have spent in an unconverted state, has been a time of estrangement and alienation from God; when the Lord brings a man to Christ, in the way of conversion, he begins his first acquaintance with God. "Acquaint now thyself with him, and be at peace; thereby good shall come unto thee." Job 22:21. This your first acquaintance with the Lord, will grow; every visit you give him in prayer increases intimacy, and humble, holy familiarity between him and you. And O what a paradise of pleasure does this let the soul into; the life of religion abounds with pleasures. Psalm 16:11. "Her ways are ways of pleasantness, and all her paths are peace." Prov. 3:17. Now you know where to go for relief from any trouble that presses your hearts; whatever prejudices and scandal Satan and his instruments cast on religion, this I will affirm of it, that that man must necessarily be a stranger to true pleasure, and empty of real comfort, who is a stranger to Christ and communion with him. True, here is no allowance for sinful pleasures; nor is there any lack of spiritual pleasures. Bless God, therefore, for converting grace, you that have it; and lift up a cry to heaven for it, you that want it.

5. If there be so much delight in our imperfect, and often interrupted communion with God here, *then what is heaven; what are the immediate visions of his face in the perfect state?* "Eye hath not seen, nor ear heard, neither have entered into the heart of man, the things which God hath prepared for them that love him." 1 Cor. 2:9. You have heard glorious and ravishing reports in the gospel of that blessed future state, things which the angels desire to look into. You have felt and tasted joys unspeakable and full of glory, in the actings of your faith and love upon Christ; yet all you have heard, and all you have felt and tasted in the way to glory, falls so short of the perfection and blessedness of that state, that heaven will and must be a great surprise to them who have now the best acquaintance with it.

Though the present comforts of the saints are sometimes as much as they can bear, for they say, "Stay me with flagons, comfort me with apples; for I am sick of love," Sol. Song 2:5; yet these high tides of joy are but shallows, compared with the joys of his immediate presence. 1 Cor. 13:12. And as they run not so deep, so they are not constant and continued, as they shall be above: "So shall we ever be with the Lord." 1 Thess. 4:17.

6. Is this the privileged state into which all *believers* are admitted by conversion? then strive *for the highest attainment* of communion with God in this world: be not contented with just so much grace as will secure you from hell, but labor after such a height of grace and communion with God as may bring you into the suburbs of heaven on earth. Forget the things that are behind you, as to satisfaction in them, and press towards the mark for the prize of your high calling. It is greatly to your loss that you live at such a distance from God, and are so seldom with him. Think not that the ablest ministers or the choicest books will ever be able to satisfy your doubts or comfort your hearts, while you let down your communion with God to so low a degree. O that you may be persuaded now to hearken obediently to three or four necessary words of counsel.

(1.) *Make communion with God the very level and aim of your soul* in all your approaches to him in the ordinances and duties of religion. Set it upon the point of your compass, let it be the very thing your soul designs; let the desire and hope of communion with God be the thing that draws you to every sermon and prayer: "One thing have I desired of the Lord, that will I seek after, that I may dwell in the house of the Lord all the days of my life, to behold the beauty of the Lord, and to inquire in his temple." Psa. 27:4. That was the mark David aimed at; and men's success in duties is usually according to the spiritual aims and intentions of their hearts in them: both sincerity and comfort lie much in men's aims.

(2.) In all your approaches to God, *plead hard with him for the manifestation of his love,* and further communications of his grace: "Hear, O Lord, when I cry with my voice: have mercy also upon me, and answer me. When thou saidst, Seek ye my face; my heart said unto thee, Thy face, Lord, will I seek. Hide not thy face far from me; put not thy servant away in anger." Psalm 27 : 7–9. How full of pleas and arguments for communion with God was this prayer of David. Lord, I am come, in obedience to thy command; thou saidst, "Seek ye my face," thou badest me come to thee, and wilt thou put away thy servant in anger? Thou hast been my help, I have had sweet experience of thy goodness, thou dost not use to put me off and turn me away empty.

(3.) *Desire not comfort for its own sake,* but comforts and refreshments for service and obedience' sake; that thereby you may be strengthened to go on in the ways of your duty with more cheerfulness. " I will run the way of thy commandments, when thou shalt enlarge my heart." Psa. 119 : 32. As if he should say, O Lord, the comforts thou shalt give me, shall be returned again in cheerful services to thee. I desire them as oil to the wheels of obedience, not as food for my pride.

(4.) As ever you expect much comfort in the way of communion with God, *see that you are strict and circumspect in your conversation.* It is the looseness and carelessness of our hearts and lives which impoverishes our spiritual comforts. A little pride, a little carelessness frustrates a great deal of comfort which was very near us, almost in our hands. "When I would have healed Israel, then the iniquity of Ephraim was discovered." Hosea 7 : 1. So, just when the desire of thy heart was at the door, some sin stept in the way of it. "Your iniquities have separated between you and your God, and your sins have hid his face from you." Isa. 59 : 2. The Comforter, the Holy Spirit, is tender, and hath quick sensibility to your unkindnesses and offences. As ever, therefore, you expect comfort from him, be careful in your conduct towards him, and grieve him not.

7. This point speaks needful counsel to *unbelievers*—to all that live estranged from the life of God, and have done so from the womb. Psalm 58 : 3. To you the voice of the Redeemer sounds a summons once more: "Behold, I stand at the door and knock." O that at last you may be prevailed with to comply with the merciful terms propounded by him. Will you shut out a Saviour bringing salvation, pardon, and peace with him ? Christ is thy rightful owner, and demands possession of thy soul; if thou wilt now hear his voice, thy former refusals shall never be objected. If thou still reject his gracious offers, mercy may never more be tendered to thee ; there is a call of Christ which will be the last call, and after that no more. Take heed what you do; if you still demur and delay, your damnation is just, inevitable, and inexcusable. Hear me, therefore, ye unregenerate souls, in what rank or condition soever Providence has placed you in this world, whether you be rich or poor, young or old, masters or servants, whether there be any stirrings of conviction in your consciences or not ; for however your conditions in this world differ from each other at present, there is one common misery hanging over you all, if you continue in that state of unbelief in which you now are.

(1.) Hearken to the voice and call of Christ, *you that are exalted by Providence above your poorer neighbors*—who have your heads, hands, and hearts full of the world: men of trade and business, I have a few solemn questions to ask you this day.

You have made many gainful *bargains* in your time, but what will all profit you if the agreement be not made between Christ and your souls? Christ is the only treasure which can enrich you. Matt. 13:44. Thou art poor and miserable, whatever thou hast gained of this world, if thou hast not gained Christ; thou hast heaped up guilt with thy riches, which will more torment thy conscience hereafter, than thy estate can yield thee comfort here.

You have made many insurances to secure your estates, which you call *policies;* but what insurance have you made for your souls? Are not they exposed to eternal hazards? O impolitic man, to be so provident to secure trifles, and so negligent in securing the richest treasure.

You have adjusted many *accounts* with men, but who shall make up your accounts with God if you are Christless? "What is a man profited, if he shall gain the whole world and lose his own soul?" Matt. 16:26. Say not, you have much business on your hands, and cannot afford time; you will have space enough hereafter to reflect upon your folly.

(2.) *You who are poor in the world*, what say you; will you have two hells, one here and another hereafter? No comfort in this world, nor hope for the next? Your expectations here laid in the dust, and your hopes for heaven built upon the sand? O if you were once in Christ, how happy were you, though you knew not where to obtain your next bread. Poor in the world, but rich in faith; and heirs of the kingdom which God has promised. James 2:5. O blessed state. If you had Christ, you would have a right to all things, 1 Cor. 3:22, 23; you would then have a Father to take care for you. But to be poor and Christless, no comfort from this world nor hopes from the next, this is to be miserable indeed. Your very straits and wants should prompt you to the great duty I am now pressing on you; and methinks it should be matter of encouragement that the greatest number of Christ's friends and followers come out of that rank of men to which you belong.

(3.) You who are *seamen*, floating often on the great deep, you are reckoned a third sort of persons between the living and the dead; you belong not to the dead, because you breathe, and scarcely to the living, because you are continually so near to death. What think you, friends, have you no need of a Saviour? Do you live so secure from the reach and danger of death? Have your lives been so pure, righteous, and innocent, who have been in the midst of temptations in the world abroad? Ponder that scripture, 1 Cor. 6 : 9, 10 : "Be not deceived; neither fornicators, nor idolaters, nor adulterers, nor effeminate, nor abusers of themselves with mankind, nor thieves, nor covetous, nor drunkards, nor revilers, nor extortioners, shall inherit the kingdom of God;" ponder it, I say, and think whether you have not as great and pressing a necessity of Jesus Christ as any poor souls under heaven. You have had from God many temporal salvations, great and eminent deliverances; and will these satisfy you? Is it enough that your bodies are delivered from the danger of the sea, though your souls sink and perish in the ocean of God's wrath for ever? If you will yet accept Christ upon his terms, all that you have done shall be forgiven. Isa. 55 : 1, 2. The Lord now calls to you in a still voice : if you hear his voice, well; if not, you may shortly hear his voice in the tempestuous storms without you, and a roaring conscience within you. Poor man, think what an interest in Christ will be worth, wert thou now, as shortly thou mayest be, floating on a piece of wreck, or shivering on a cold and desolate rock, crying, Mercy, Lord, mercy. Mercy is now offered thee, but in vain wilt thou expect to find it, if thou continue thus to despise and reject it.

(4.) You who are *aged and full of days*, hearken to the voice of Christ; God has called on you a long time. When you were young you said, it is time enough yet, we will mind these things when we are old, and come nearer to the borders of eternity. Well, now you are old, and just on the borders of it; will you indeed mind it now? You have left the great concerns of your souls to this time, this short, very short time; and do the temptations of your youth take hold upon your age? What, delay and put off Christ still, as you were wont to do? Poor creatures, you are almost gone out of time, you have but a short space to deliberate; what you do must be done quickly, or it can never be done. Your night is even come upon you, when no man can work.

(5.) You who are *young*, in the bud or flower of your time, Christ is a suitor for your first love; he desires the kindness of your youth; your spirits are vigorous, your hearts tender, your affections flowing and impressible; you are not yet entered into the incumbrances and distracting cares of the world. Hereafter a crowd and thick succession of earthly employments and engagements will come on; sin will harden you by custom and continuance. Now is your time; you are in the convertible age; few that pass the season of youth are brought to Christ afterwards. It is the wonder of an age to hear of the conversion of aged sinners. Besides, you are the hope of the next generation. Should you neglect and despise Christ, how bad soever the present age is, the next will be worse. Say not, we have time enough before us, we will not quench the sprightly vigor of our youth in melancholy thoughts. Remember, there are skulls of all sizes and graves of all lengths in the churchyard. You may die before those that seem to stand nearer the grave than you. O you cannot be happy too soon. As young as you are, did you but taste the comforts that are in Christ, nothing would grieve you more than that you knew him no sooner. Behold, he standeth at thy door in the morning of thy age, knocking this day for admission into thy heart.

(6.) *To you who have had some slight, ineffectual, and vanishing convictions formerly,* the Lord Jesus once more renews his call. Will you now at last hear his voice? It is an infinite mercy to have a second call. I doubt not but many among you, while you have sat under the word, have had such thoughts as these in your hearts: "Sure my condition is not right, nor safe; there must another manner of work pass upon my soul, or I am lost for ever. External duties of religion I do perform, but I am a stranger to regeneration." Such inward convictions as these were the knocks and calls of Christ, but they passed away and were forgotten: your convictions are dead, and your hearts the more hardened; for it is with a soul under conviction as in putting iron into the fire, and quenching it again; this hardens it the more. You have been near the kingdom of God, but will be the more miserable for that, if you are shut out at last. The quickening of your convictions is the right way to the saving of your souls. The Lord make you this day to hear his voice.

(7.) *Such as go to hear the gospel on vain accounts*, for mere novelty or worse ends—to catch advantages, or to reproach the truths of God—scoffing at the most solemn voice of Christ: the word that you have slighted and reproached, the same shall judge you in that great day, except the Lord give you repentance unto life, and make the heart tremble under it that hath scoffed at it. "Be ye not mockers, lest your bands be made strong." Isa. 28:22.

(8.) Let *all whose hearts the Lord has opened* this day, for the enjoyment of the gospel, the blessed instrument of their salvation, bless the Lord that has made it a key by regeneration to open the door of salvation to your souls: "And as ye have therefore received Christ Jesus the Lord, so walk ye in him." Col. 2:6.

CHAPTER XIII.

THE TRUTH HELD IN UNRIGHTEOUSNESS.

" THE WRATH OF GOD IS REVEALED FROM HEAVEN AGAINST ALL UNGODLINESS, AND UNRIGHTEOUSNESS OF MEN, WHO HOLD THE TRUTH IN UNRIGHTEOUSNESS." Rom. 1:18.

IN all the foregoing discourses, I have been pleading and wooing for Christ. And as Abraham's servant, to win Rebekah's consent, told her what treasures his master's son had, so I have labored to show you some part of the unsearchable riches of Christ, if by any means I might allure your hearts, and be instrumental to close the happy union between him and you; and, as the apostle speaks, espouse you to one husband, even to Christ. 2 Cor. 11 : 2.

But alas, how few move towards him. The most seem to be immovably fixed in their natural state and sinful course. All our arguments and entreaties return to us again, and effect nothing. It is amazing to think that souls which have in them the hopes and fears of the world to come, and self-reflecting powers, cannot be prevailed upon to quit the way of sin and to embrace the way of holiness, though their consciences meanwhile stand convinced that eternal damnation is the result of the one, and life, peace, and eternal joys of the other.

This has put me upon a serious search what may be the cause of this fixed and unreasonable obstinacy; and it seems evident that most who live in an unregenerate state under the gospel, put a force upon their own consciences, and imprison and hold the truth in unrighteousness, though the wrath of God be revealed from heaven against all that do so

If by this discourse I can but set truth at liberty, and loose the Lord's prisoners which lie bound in your souls, I shall not doubt that the estimate of the value of Christ will quickly rise among you, and free convictions will make the work of your ministers more easy and successful than they now find it. It is hardly imaginable but that the things you have heard must leave your souls under convictions; but if you suppress and stifle them, they produce nothing but aggravations of sin and misery. Now, in order to the effectual working of your convictions, and awakening the reverence which is due to them from every soul, as to the voice of God, I have chosen this scripture, the scope and sense whereof I shall endeavor to give you.

The true scope and aim of this context is to prove the justification of sinners to be only by the imputed righteousness of Christ in the way of faith. To make this evident, he divides the whole world into Gentiles and Jews: the one seeking righteousness by the dim light of nature, or the law written in their hearts; the other, the Jews, by the works of the law, or external conformity to the law of Moses. But that neither can find what they seek, he distinctly and fully proves. He proves it first upon the Gentiles from this verse to the seventeenth of the second chapter; and then he proves it upon the Jews also, from thence to the end of the third chapter. As for the Gentiles, he acknowledges that they had some notions of God imprinted in their nature; they had also the book of creation, giving them knowledge enough to leave them without excuse. But this knowledge of God, and of good and evil, they did not obey and put in practice, but acted against the dictates of their consciences. For which cause the wrath of God was revealed from heaven against them, as the text speaks. Wherein we notice,

1. Here is *a clear and dreadful revelation of divine wrath*, "the wrath of God is revealed from heaven;" ὀργη Θεου, the indignation or vengeance of God. It is a word of deep and dreadful signification; the damned who feel its weight, have the fullest sense of it. It is said, Psa. 90:11, "Who knoweth the power of thine anger? even according to thy fear, so is thy wrath." That is, the fears of an

incensed Deity are no vain imaginings, nor the effects of ignorance and superstition, as atheists fancy; but let men's fears of it be what they will, they shall find, except they repent, the wrath of God to be according to, yea, far above their fears of it. If the wrath of a king be as the messenger of death, what is the wrath of the great and terrible God? This wrath is here said to be revealed, discovered, or made manifest; and so it is in various ways. It was revealed to them by the light of nature, their own consciences gave them notice and warning of it. Thus it was revealed to them by an internal testimony, a witness within them; and it was also revealed to them by the instances of punishment of sin in all ages by the immediate hand of a justly incensed God. They came not by chance, but divine direction; therefore it is added, "from heaven," or from God in heaven.

2. Here is *the cause of this revealed and inflicted wrath:* it "is revealed from heaven against all ungodliness and unrighteousness of men." The former word, *ungodliness*, comprises all sins against the first table of the law; the irreligious lives and practices of men, living in the neglect of the duties of religion: the other word, *unrighteousness*, comprises all sins against the second table, such as acts of fraud, uncleanness, lying, and other sins, against men. And because these two comprehensive words are branched out into many particulars, therefore the apostle says, "The wrath of God is revealed against *all* ungodliness and unrighteousness." There is not one of the many sins into which ungodliness and unrighteousness are branched out, but incenses the Lord's wrath; and though he only mentions the sins, we are to understand them as put for the sinners that commit them, or God's punishing these sins upon the persons of the sinners.

3. We have here before us *the special aggravation of these sins*, or that which made them more provoking to God than otherwise they had been. And it was this: that while

they committed these sins, or omitted those duties, they "held the truth in unrighteousness:" the word signifies to *detain* or *hinder* the truth of God, or the knowledge they had of his being, power, goodness, and truth, as also of his worship, and the difference between good and evil. These truths acted on their consciences; conscience labored to excite them to duty, and restrain them from sin; but all in vain, they overbore their own consciences, and kept those sentiments and convictions prisoners, though they struggled for liberty to break forth into practice and obedience. Their convictions were kept down under the dominion of corruption, as a prisoner is shut up by his keeper. Their lusts were too hard for their light. Thus you have both the scope and sense of the text. The doctrine taught by it is this,

The wrath of God is dreadfully incensed against all those who live in any course of sin, against the light and dictates of their own consciences.

Sins of ignorance provoke the wrath of God; yet they are not of so heinous a nature as sins against light and convictions are, nor will they be punished so severely. "That servant which knew his Lord's will, and prepared not himself, neither did according to his will, shall be beaten with many stripes." Luke 12:47. It excuses a man in some measure, when he can say, Lord, had I known this to be a sin, I would not have done it. But when the conscience is convinced, and strives to keep us from such an act or course of sinful actions, and we stop our ears against its voice and warnings, here is a high and horrid contempt of God and his law, and it gives the sin a scarlet dye. Sins of ignorance cannot compare with such sins as these. John 3:19; 15:22. To open this point, let me show what conscience is; what the light of conscience is; and how this light binds the conscience and makes it strive in us; then instance some cases wherein it doth so; and lastly show how and

THE SIN OF STIFLING CONVICTION.

why the imprisoning of these convictions so dreadfully incenses the wrath of God.

I. It will be needful to speak of THE NATURE OF CONSCIENCE in general. Conscience is the judgment of man upon himself, as he is subject to the judgment of God. A judgment it is, and a practical judgment too; it belongs to the understanding. "If we would judge ourselves, we should not be judged." 1 Cor. 11:31. This self-judgment is the proper office of the conscience, and to enable it to fulfil its office, there are three things belonging to every man's conscience.

1. A knowledge of the rule or law according to which it is to judge; without which conscience can no more do its work, than an artificer without his square or level can do his.

2. Knowledge of the facts or matters to be judged. The conscience of every man keeps a register of his actions, thoughts, and the very secrets of the heart.

3. An ability or delegated authority to pass judgment on ourselves and actions according to the rule and law of God. Here it sits upon the bench as God's vicegerent, absolving or condemning, as it finds the sincerity or hypocrisy of the heart upon trial. 1 John, 3:20, 21.

Conscience, therefore, is a high and awful power; it is next to and immediately under God our Judge. Concerning conscience, God says to every man, as he once did to Moses with respect to Pharaoh, "See, I have made thee a god to Pharaoh." Exod. 7:1. The voice of enlightened conscience is the voice of God. What it binds or looses on earth, is bound or loosed in heaven, 1 John, 3:20; the greatest deference and precise obedience is due to its command. Its consolations are of all the most sweet, and its condemnations, excepting those by the mouth of Christ in the last judgment, most terrible. Zuingle spoke not without ground, when he said, "What death would I not rather choose; what punishment would I not rather bear; yea, into what a profound abyss of hell would I not rather enter, than to witness against my conscience?" It is likely he had felt the terrors of it to be more bitter than death. How many have chosen strangling, rather than life, under the terrors of conscience. Wherever you go, conscience accompanies you; whatever you say, do, or but think, it records, in order to the day of account. When all friends forsake thee, yea, when thy soul forsakes thy body, conscience will not, cannot forsake thee. When thy body is most weak, thy conscience is most vigorous and active. Never is there more life in the conscience than when death makes its nearest approach to the body. When it smiles, acquits, and comforts, O what a heaven does it create within a man. And when it frowns, condemns, and terrifies, how does it becloud, yea, benight all the pleasures and delights of this world. O conscience, how glad would the damned be to have taken their last farewell of thee, when they bade this world and its inhabitants farewell at death. And what had become of all the martyrs, when shut up from friends in dungeons, had it not been for the cheering cordials and comforts thou didst administer to support them? It is certainly the best friend or the worst enemy in the whole creation. This is conscience, these are its powers and offices.

II. Our next inquiry must be into the LIGHT OF CONSCIENCE, and the various kinds of that light. The Lord did not frame such an excellent structure as the soul of man, without windows to let in light, nor does he deny the benefit of light to any soul; but there is a twofold light which men have to inform and guide their consciences.

1. There is *the common light of natural reason*, called by Solomon, the candle of the Lord: "The spirit of man is the candle of the Lord." Prov. 20 : 27. This is affirmed by him who had an extraordinary portion of intellect, a brighter lamp of reason and wisdom than other men; and

this is not only true of the soul in general, but of that special power of it which is called *conscience*, which is God's witness, and man's overseer. The heathen had this light shining in their minds and consciences; some of them, by the help of this natural light, made wonderful discoveries of the mysteries of nature; yea, they found its efficacy and power great in their consciences, to raise their hopes or fears, according to the good or evil they had done. Ovid says, "As is every man's conscience, so are his hopes and fears." And to the shame of many who are called Christians, some among the heathen paid great reverence to their own consciences. "Principally revere thyself," says one; "tempted to any base action, dread thyself, even when there is no other witness." The generality of the heathen, however, did not so, and are charged with this in the text; besides, this light can make no discoveries of Christ, and of the way of salvation by him. The most eagle-eyed philosophers among them were in the dark here. And therefore,

2. *God has afforded men a more clear and excellent light to shine into their minds and consciences, even the light of the gospel,* which compared with the light of natural reason, is as the light of the sun to the dim moonlight. "He showeth his word unto Jacob, his statutes and his judgments unto Israel. He hath not dealt so with any nation; and as for his judgments, they have not known them. Praise ye the Lord." Psa. 147 : 19, 20. Every creature has the name of God engraven on it, but he has magnified his word above all his name. Psa. 138 : 2. God, who best knows the value of his own mercies, accounts this a singular favor and privilege to any nation. Without revelation we could never have known the cause of our misery, the fall of Adam, or the only way of our recovery by Christ: by this a people are lifted up to heaven, Matthew 11 : 23, in respect to the means of salvation; and consequently, the neglect of such light and love will plunge the guilty into

proportionable misery. "This is the condemnation, that light is come into the world, and men loved darkness rather than light." John 3 : 19.

Moreover, God not only affords the light of reason and gospel revelation to some men in an eminent degree, but to these he adds the internal illumination of his Spirit, the clearest and most glorious light in the world. He shineth into their hearts to give the light of the knowledge of the glory of God in the face of Jesus Christ. 2 Cor. 4 : 6. These are the three sorts of light God makes to shine into the souls and consciences of men to guide them; the first a common and general light, the two last the most clear and transcendent in excellency, especially that of the Spirit with the gospel. For though the sun be risen, yet men may draw the curtains about them, and lie in darkness; but the Spirit enlightens the soul.

III. How this light shining into the consciences of men LEADS THEM TO OBEDIENCE, and how men's lusts struggle against the obligations of an enlightened conscience, is the next thing to be considered.

It is beyond all controversy, that an enlightened conscience lays strong and indispensable obligations on the soul to obedience; for the will of God is the supreme law; it is the will of "the only Potentate, the King of kings, and Lord of lords." 1 Tim. 6 : 15. And the promulgation and manifestation of it binds the conscience to obedience, so that no authority on earth can loose the bands. For conscience, as God's vicegerent, in his name requires obedience, and the man that hears the voice of God from the mouth of his own conscience thereupon becomes a debtor, Rom. 1 : 14, and is put under a necessity. 1 Cor. 9 : 16.

Now conscience, by reason of the light that shines into it, feeling itself under such strong bands and necessities, stimulates and urges the soul to obedience, warns, commands, and presses the soul to its duty against the contrary inclinations of the flesh; and hence arise those conflicts in the bosoms of men. Sometimes conscience prevails, and sometimes lusts and corruptions prevail, and that with great difficulty; for it is not alike easy to all men to shake off or burst the bands of their consciences. What a hard task had Saul to conquer his conscience. "I forced myself," saith he, 1 Sam. 13 : 12; he knew it belonged not to him to offer sacrifice, his conscience plainly told him it would be sin; but the fear of the Philistines being stronger than the fear of God, he ventured upon it against the plain dictates of his conscience. Thus Herod gave sentence to put John to death : " The king was sorry; nevertheless, for the oath's sake, and them which sat with him at meat, he commanded it to be given her." Matt. 14 : 9. His honor weighed more than his fear of sin, his own word more than God's word. No man is so perplexed between two vices, but he may find an issue without falling into a third.

Pilate's conscience was convinced of Christ's innocence, Matt. 27 : 18, 19, yet the fear of Cesar hurried him on to the greatest wickedness, even to give sentence against innocent blood, yea, the blood of the Son of God. Darius, in like manner, knew that Daniel was not only an excellent person, but that he was entrapped by the nobles merely for his conscience, and that to put him to death was to sacrifice him to their malice. This he and his conscience debated, and many encounters he had with it; for the record saith, he "was sore displeased with himself, and set his heart on Daniel to deliver him; and he labored till the going down of the sun to deliver him," Dan. 6 : 14 ; but after a day's contest between him and conscience, sin prevailed against light and returned victor in the evening. So it was with poor Spira, a sad apostate; he seemed to hear, as it were, an inward voice, Do not write, Spira, do not write. But the love of his estate, wife, and children, drew his hand to the paper, though conscience struggled hard to hold it back.

Thus, as the restless sea strives to beat down or break over its bounds, so do impetuous lusts strive to overbear light and conviction. As the Roman poet has said,

> . . . "Video meliora proboque,
> Deteriora sequor."
>
> . . . "I see the right and must approve; and yet
> The wrong pursue."

They know this or that to be sin, and that they hazard their souls by it; yet they venture on it, and rush into sin as the horse into the battle.

IV. I promised to give SOME INSTANCES OF THE CONFLICT BETWEEN MEN'S CONSCIENCES AND THEIR CORRUPTIONS, wherein conscience is vanquished and overborne, and by what weapons the victory over conscience is obtained. The convictions of men are twofold: general, respecting their state; and particular, respecting this or that action.

1. There are *general convictions* given to some men by their consciences, that their state of soul is neither right nor safe—that they want the main thing which constitutes a Christian, namely, regeneration, or a gracious change of heart. They hear and read the signs and effects of this change, but their consciences plainly tell them that these evidences are not to be found in them—that they enjoy the external privileges of the saints, but belong not to them—that something is still wanting, and that the main thing too. "O my soul, thou art not right; thou hast gifts, thou hast a name to live, but for all that thou art dead; some further work must be done upon thee, or thou art undone to eternity: thou passest for a good Christian among men, but woe to thee if thou die in the state thou art." These, and such as these, are the whispers of some men's consciences in their ears; and yet they cannot so yield themselves up into the hands of their convictions, as to confess and bewail their hypocrisy and gross mistake, and seek for a better foundation to build their hope on. Felix's conscience gave him such a

terrible monition as this, and made him tremble while Paul reasoned with him of righteousness, temperance, and judgment to come. Acts 24:25. It whispered in his ear such language as this: "O poor soul, how shall such an oppressor, such an intemperate wretch as thou art, stand before God in this day of judgment, which Paul proves is certainly to come?" For, as Tacitus says of him, he was an insatiable gulf of covetousness. So it was with Agrippa; he stood unresolved what to do: he saw the heavenly doctrine of Christianity evidently confirmed by doctrines and miracles, his conscience pleaded hard with him to embrace it, and had almost prevailed; almost, or within a little as the word is, thou persuadest me to be a Christian. Acts 24:27. But Agrippa had too much wealth and honor to forsake for Christ; the love of the present world overbore both the hopes and fears of the world to come. And thus that excellent fisher for souls, who had thoroughly converted so many to Christ, came short of securing Agrippa: *almost* is a great deal for so great a person. The gospel is a net, and encloses all sorts, whole Christians and half Christians. The conscience is caught, and the will begins to incline; but O the power and prevalence of sin, which, like the rudder, commands all to a contrary course.

Let us come a little nearer, and inquire what are those hinderances that stop conscience in its course, bind and imprison, stifle and suppress its convictions; so that although a man strongly suspect his foundation to be but sand, and his hopes for heaven a strong delusion, yet will he not throw up his vain hopes, confess his self-deceits, and begin all anew. What is it which overbears conscience in this case? Let men impartially examine their hearts, and it will be found that three things bind and imprison these convictions of conscience, and hold the truth in unrighteousness.

(1.) *Shame.* Men who have been professors, and of good esteem in the world, are ashamed the world should know the mistakes and errors of all their life past, and what deluded fools and self-deceivers they have been: this is a powerful restraint upon conviction; how shall they look their acquaintances in the face? what will men think and say of them? "How can ye believe, which receive honor one of another?" saith Christ. John 5:44. What, you Christians, and yet not able to endure a censure or a scoff upon your names! you who stand more upon your reputation than your salvation, how can you believe?

O what madness and folly appear in this case! men will choose rather to go on, though conscience tells them the end of that way will be death, than make a just and necessary retraction, which is not their shame, but their duty and glory. You who are so tender of the shame of men, how will you be able to endure the contempt and shame that shall be cast on you from God, angels, and men, in the great day? Luke 9:26. It is no shame to acknowledge your mistake; but to persist in it, after conviction, is shameful madness.

I knew an excellent minister, who proved an eminent instrument in the church of God, who, in the beginning of his ministerial course, was not upon the right foundation of regeneration. He had excellent natural and acquired gifts, and could preach of regeneration, faith, and heavenly-mindedness, though he felt nothing of these things in his own experience. His life was unblamable, and he had no mean esteem among good men. It pleased the Lord, while he was studying an excellent spiritual point to preach to others, that his conscience first preached it in his study to himself, and that with such a close and rousing application, as made him tremble; telling him, that though he had gifts above many, and sobriety in his conversation, yet one thing, and that the main thing, sanctifying grace, was wanting. Hereupon the pangs of the new birth seized his soul, and the Lord made him a most searching, experimental minister, and crowned his labors with unusual success. This minister, to his dying day, was not ashamed in all companies to acknowledge his mistake, and bless God for his recovery out of it; and in most of his sermons, he would endeavor to convince false professors of the necessity of a second conversion.

(2.) *Fear* is another drawback which withholds men from executing the convictions of conscience, and obeying its calls in this grand concern of the soul. They are easy under the external profession and duties of religion, and are afraid of throwing up their vain hopes, and engaging themselves heartily and thoroughly in religion. There are two things which alarm them.

The troubles of spirit attending the new birth; which they have read and heard of, and seen the effects in others. O it is a dreadful thing to lie under the terrors which many have felt! and thus it is with them as with one that hath a bone ill-set, who, if he have any ease, will rather endure a little daily pain, and be content to halt all his life, than undergo the pain of another fraction or dislocation in order to a perfect cure.

They are afraid of external sufferings. The form of godliness leaves men a liberty to take or leave, according as the times favor or frown upon the ways of religion; but the power of godliness will engage them beyond retreat. They must stand to it, come what will. But, soul, let me tell thee, if the just fears of hell and eternal wrath of God, to which thou art exposed by thy formality, were upon thee, all these fears of inward or outward troubles would vanish the same hour.

(3.) *Pride of heart* suffers not this conviction of conscience to work out its effects, but holds the truth in unrighteousness, to the ruin of many souls. Men that live upon their own duties and self-righteousness, are not easily brought to renounce all this, and live upon the righteousness of Christ alone for justification. Proud nature will rather venture the hazard of damnation than practise such self-denial, Rom. 10 : 3 ; as you see it common among poor people to live on coarse fare of their own, rather than upon the alms and bounty of another.

But if once the day of God's power come, and a man feels the commandment come home to his conscience as Paul did, Rom. 7 : 9, when he comes to realize the world to come, the value of his soul, and the danger it is in, then all these hinderances are as easily swept away, as so many straws by the rapid course of a mighty torrent. Then let men say or think what they please, I must not throw away my own soul to maintain a vain estimation among men. Let inward or outward sufferings be ever so great, it is better for me to feel them, than to suffer the everlasting wrath of the great and terrible God. Let my own righteousness be what it will, all is but dung and dross to the pure and perfect righteousness of Christ.

2. As this general conviction with respect to men's condition is held in unrighteousness, and they go with troubled consciences and frequent inward fears by reason of it ; so there are many *particular convictions* bound and imprisoned in men's souls—particular convictions both as to sins committed and known duties omitted against both tables of the law of God, called in the text *ungodliness* and *unrighteousness*. Conscience labors and strives to bring men to confess, bewail, and reform them, but cannot prevail ; contrary lusts and interests overpower them, and detain them in unrighteousness. What these are, and how they are withheld by those lusts, I shall give in some INSTANCES. And first, for convictions of UNGODLINESS.

INSTANCE 1. There are many who call themselves Christians, whose conscience tells them that *God is to be daily worshipped by them, both in family and closet prayer.* It sets before them Joshua's pious practice : "As for me and my house, we will serve the Lord." Joshua 24 : 15. They know God is the founder, the owner, the master of their families; that all family blessings are from him, and therefore he is to be acknowledged and sought in daily family prayers and praises. It tells them that the curse of God hangs over prayerless families, Jer. 10 : 25; and that they live in the inexcusable neglect of these duties, seldom worshipping God with their families or in their closets, and that therefore they live without God in the world. Dreadful will the reckoning be at the great day for their own souls, which they have starved for want of closet prayer, and for the souls committed to their charge, which perish for want of family duties. This is the case of many who yet pass for professors of Christianity.

Lord, how sad a case is here. How can men live in the neglect of so great, so necessary a duty? Certainly it is not for want of light and conviction; the very light of nature, if we had no Bibles, discovers these duties. But three things hold this truth of God dictated by men's conscience in unrighteousness.

(1.) *The love of the world* chokes this conviction in the souls of some; and they think it enough to plead for their excuse, the want of opportunities and the many encumbrances they have, which will not allow them time for these duties. The world is a severe taskmaster, and fills their heads and hands all the day with cares and toils. And must the mouth of conscience then be stopped with such a plea as this? No; God and conscience will not be answered and put off so. The greatest number of persons in the world from whom God has the most spiritual and excellent worship, are of the poorer class. Psalm 74 : 21 ; James 2 : 5. And it is highly probable your necessities had been less, if your prayers had been more. And what sweeter outlet and relief for all these troubles can you find than prayer? This would sweeten all your labors and sorrows in the world.

(2.) *Consciousness of want of gifts* restrains this conviction in others. Should they attempt such duties before others, they shall but expose their own ignorance and shame. But this is a vain pretence to shake off duty. The neglect of prayer is a principal cause of the inability you complain of; gifts as well as graces grow by exercise. "Unto every one that hath shall be given, and he shall have abundance." Matt. 25 : 29. And besides, it is the fruit of pride, and argues your eye to be more upon your own honor than God's. The Lord regards not oratory in prayer; your broken expressions, yea, your groans and sighs please him more than all the eloquence in the world.

(3.) But the principal thing which restrains men from obeying their convictions as to family and closet prayer, is *a disinclined heart;* that is the root and true cause of these sinful neglects and omissions. You savor not the sweetness of these things; and what a man tastes no sweetness in, or finds no necessity of, is easily omitted.

But woe to you that go from day to day self-condemned for the neglect of so known, so sweet, and so necessary a duty. If our heart condemn us, God is greater than our heart. 1 John, 3 : 20. He who lives without prayer is dead while he lives; and let men say what they please of secret communion with God, I am sure, if religion thrives in the closet, it will never be banished from the family. The time is coming when death will break up your families, separate the wife from the husband, the child from the parent, the servant from the master; and then where you will find relief and comfort who have spent your time together so sinfully and vainly, I cannot tell; nor what account you can give to God in the great day. Think seriously on these things, they are worth thinking of.

INSTANCE 2. A second instance of ungodliness under the convictions of conscience, is *formality* in the external duties of religion and ordinances of God. Have not the consciences of some of you often and plainly told you, that though you are often engaged in the public duties of hearing, prayer, and other ordinances, yet your hearts are not with God in those duties? They do not strive after communion and fellowship with him therein. It is nothing but the force of education, of custom, and the care of reputation which brings you there.

Such a conviction as this, could it do its work thoroughly, would be the salvation of thy soul; were power added to the form, as conscience would have it, thou wouldst then be a real Christian, and out of the danger of hell. The want of this thy conscience sees will be thy ruin, and accordingly gives thee plain warning of it. O what pity is it such a conviction as this should be held in unrighteousness. But so it is in very many souls, and that on several accounts.

(1.) Because hypocrisy is *so odious and abominable a sin* that men are loath to own and acknowledge it, how guilty soever they be of it. What, dissemble with God, and play the hypocrite with him? It is so foul a crime that men cannot easily be brought to charge themselves with it. They may have the infirmities which are common to the best of men, but they are not hypocrites. Thus, pride of heart casts a chain upon conviction, and binds it, that it cannot do its work.

(2.) It is a cheap and easy way to give God the external worship of the body, but *heart-work is hard work.* To sit or kneel an hour or two is no great matter; but to search, humble, and break the heart for sin, to raise earthly affections into a spiritual, heavenly frame, this will cost many a hard effort. It is no severe task to sit before God as his people, while the fancy and thoughts are left at liberty to wander where they please, as the thoughts of hypocrites use to do, Ezek. 33:31; but to set a watch on the heart, to retract every wandering thought with a sigh, and to fix the thoughts on God, this is difficult, and the difficulty overpowers conviction of duty.

(3.) The *atheism* of the heart quenches this conviction in men's souls. Formality is a secret sin, not discernible by man; the outside of religion looks fair to man's eye, and so long it is well enough, as if there was not a God who trieth the hearts and the reins. Thus, when a beam of light and conviction shines into the soul, a cloud of natural atheism overshadows and darkens it.

But, poor self-deceiving hypocrite, these things must not pass so; thy conscience, as well as the word, tells thee it is not the place of worship, but the spirituality of it that God regards, John 4 : 23, 24 ; that they are hypocrites in scripture account who have God in their mouths, while he is far from their reins, Jer. 12 : 2 ; and that hypocrites will have the hottest place in hell. Matt. 24 : 51.

INSTANCE 3. A third instance of convictions of ungodliness held in unrighteousness, is in *declining or denying to confess the known truths of God*, which we ourselves have professed, when the confession of them exposes us to danger. In times of danger, conscience struggles hard with men to appear for the truths of God, and on no account whatever to dissemble or deny them; and enforces its counsels and warnings upon us with such awful scriptures as these: "No man having put his hand to the plough, and looking back, is fit for the kingdom of God." Luke 9 : 62. "But whosoever shall deny me before men, him will I also deny before my Father which is in heaven." Matt. 10 : 33. In this case conscience useth to struggle hard with men, yet is many times overborne by the temptations of the flesh. As,

(1.) *By carnal fears.* The fear of suffering gets ascendency over the fear of God; men choose rather to venture their souls upon wrath to come, than the present wrath of incensed enemies. They vainly "hope to find mercy with God," but expect none from men. Thus the fear of man bringeth a snare, Prov. 29 : 25 ; and so the voice of conscience is drowned by the louder clamors and threats of adversaries.

(2.) As the fear of man's threatenings, so the *distrust of God's promises* defeats the design of conscience. If men believed the promises, they would never be afraid of their duties; faith in the promises would make men bold as lions, if such a word was in mind as this: "Of whom hast thou been afraid or feared, that thou hast lied, and hast not remembered me?" Isa. 57:11. Men would say, as Zuingle in the like case, What death would I not rather choose to die; what punishment would I not rather undergo; yea, into what vault of hell would I not rather choose to be cast, than to witness against my own conscience?

(3.) The inordinate *love of the world* overpowers conscience, and drowns its voice in such an hour of temptation. So Demas found it. 2 Tim. 4:10. O what a dangerous conflict is there in an hour of temptation, between an enlightened head and a worldly heart.

(4.) *The examples of others* who embrace the sinful terms of liberty to escape the danger, embolden men to follow, and Satan will not be wanting to improve their examples. "Do not you see such and such men travelling the road before you? Learned and prudent men, who, it may be, have less heart but more wisdom than you. Why will you be singular, and hazard all for that for which others will hazard nothing?"

But certainly such sins as these will cost you dear: it is a dreadful thing to betray the truth and honor of God for base, secular ends; and you will find it so when you and your consciences shall debate it together in a calm hour.

There are also sins of UNRIGHTEOUSNESS against the second table, in which many live against the plain dictates and warnings of their own consciences, though they know the wrath of God is revealed from heaven against all unrighteousness of men who hold the truth in unrighteousness.

INSTANCE 4. And here let me instance the sin of *defrauding* others, in our dealings with them; overreaching and cheating the ignorant or unwary, who, it may be, would not be so unwary as they are, did they not repose confidence in our deceitful words and promises. Conscience cannot but startle at such a sin, the light of nature reveals it, and even the sober heathen abhor it; but we who live under the gospel cannot but feel some terror and trembling in our consciences when we read such an awful prohibition, backed with such a dreadful threatening as that in 1 Thess. 4:6: "That no man go beyond and defraud his brother in any matter; because that the Lord is the avenger of all such." The Greek word imports that no man overtop, that is, by power, or by craft and policy. To this sin a dreadful threatening is annexed, "the Lord is the *avenger* of all such." This word is but once more, that I remember, used in the New Testament, Rom. 13:4, and is there applied to the civil magistrate, who must see execution done upon malefactors; but here the Lord himself says he will be this man's avenger. This rod, or rather this axe, conscience shows to men, and gives warning of the danger, and yet its convictions are overpowered and bound as prisoners by,

(1.) *The excessive love of gain.* "But they that will be rich fall into temptation and a snare, and into many foolish and hurtful lusts, which drown men in destruction and perdition." 1 Tim. 6:9. When a resolution is made for the world, men will be rich by right or wrong; this powerfully arms the temptation. Set gain before such a man, and he will break through the law of God and convictions of conscience, but he will have it; this drowns them in destruction and perdition, that is, it surely, thoroughly, and fully ruins them. He is a dead man who is only drowned; but to be drowned in destruction, yea, in destruction and perdition too, this must needs make his ruin sure; and so all shall surely find who persist in such a course.

(2.) *Necessities and straits* overbear conscience in others; necessity has no ears to attend the voice of the word and conscience. Here conscience and poverty struggle together, and if the fear of God is not exalted in the soul, it now falls a prey to temptation. This danger the wise Agur foresaw, and earnestly entreated the Lord for a competency to avoid the snare of poverty. Prov. 30:8, 9. How much better were it for thee to endure the pains of hunger than those of a guilty conscience. Such gains may be sweet in thy mouth, but bitter in thy bowels.

(3.) *The examples of others* who venture on such sins without scruple, and laugh at tender consciences. This emboldens others to follow them, Psa. 50:18, and thus the voice of conscience is drowned, and convictions buried for a time; but conscience will thunder at last, and thy buried convictions will have a resurrection, and it shall be out of thy power to silence them again.

INSTANCE 5. The truth of God is held in unrighteousness, *when men's lusts will not suffer them to restore what they have unjustly gotten into their hands.* This sin resting on the consciences of some men, makes them very uneasy, and yet they make a hard shift to rub along under these regrets of conscience. Now those things which make a forcible entry into the conscience, take the truths of God prisoners and bind them, that they cannot break forth into the duty of restitution, are,

(1.) The *shame* which attends and follows the duty to which God and conscience call the soul. It is a shame and reproach, they think, to get the name of a cheat; loath, loath they are, that these works of darkness should come to the open light; men will point at them, and say, There goes a thief, a cheat, an oppressor. This keeps many from restitution. But dost thou not here commit a greater cheat than the former? Which is the greatest shame, thinkest thou, to commit sin, or to confess and reform it? To bind the snare upon thy soul by commission, or loose it from thy conscience by repentance and restitution; to be the derision of wicked men, for none else will deride thee for thy duty, or be the contempt and derision of God, angels, and all good men for ever; to attain inward peace at this hazard, or to lie under the continual lashes and wounds of thy own conscience?

(2.) *Poverty* is sometimes pleaded to quiet the troubled conscience; and indeed this is a just, and very frequent blight of God on ill-gotten goods; the curse of God is upon them, and they melt away. O in what a snare have you now entangled your souls. Once you could, but would not restore; a worldly heart would not part with unjust gains: now you would, but cannot. Thus a worldly heart and an empty purse hold you first and last under the guilt of a known sin. A lamentable case.

(3.) *Vain purposes* often suppress and silence convictions. My condition may alter; I may be in a situation hereafter when I can better spare it than at present; or I will do it in my last will, and charge my executors with it. Thus do men bribe their consciences to get a little quiet, while they continue under known guilt, and cannot tell how soon death shall summon them to the awful bar of a just and terrible God.

Sirs, as you value your peace, and which is more, your souls, release the Lord's prisoner which lies bound within you with cords and chains of Satan's making; do it, I say, as you hope to see the face of God in peace. You know that without repentance there can be no salvation, and without restitution no repentance; for how can you repent of a sin you still knowingly continue in? Repentance is the soul's turning from sin, as well as its sorrow for sin. You cannot therefore repent of sin and still continue in it: "How shall we that are dead to sin, live any longer therein?" Rom. 6 : 2. Trust Providence for the supply of your wants and the wants of those dependent on you in the way of duty and righteousness. "A little that a righteous man hath is better than the riches of many wicked." Psa. 37 : 16. You will have more comfort in bread and water with peace of conscience, than in full tables with God's curse. You will lie more at ease on a bed of straw, than on a bed of down with an accusing conscience.

INSTANCE 6. *How many lie under the condemnation of their consciences, for the lusts of uncleanness in which they live.* They read, and their consciences apply to them such scripture as 1 Cor. 6 : 9, 10 : "Be not deceived ; neither fornicators, nor idolaters, nor adulterers, nor effeminate, nor abusers of themselves with mankind, nor thieves, nor covetous, nor drunkards, nor revilers, nor extortioners, shall inherit the kingdom of God." A dreadful sentence! And this, "Whoremongers and adulterers God will judge." Heb. 13 : 4. Yet convictions are overborne and stifled by,

(1.) *The impetuous violence of carnal lusts*, which permit not calm debates, but hurry them on to the sin, and leave them to consider the evil and dangerous consequences afterward. Thus they go, "as an ox to the slaughter, or as a fool to the correction of the stocks." Prov. 7 : 22. Lust besots them. To give counsel now is but to give medicine in a paroxysm, or counsel to him who is running a race. Lust answers conscience as Antipater did one that presented him a book treating of happiness, I have no leisure to read such discourses.

(2.) Others would fain solve their scruples with *the failings of good men*, as David, Solomon, and others ; not considering what brokenness of heart it cost David, Psa. 51, and Solomon sorrow more bitter than death, Eccl. 7 : 26. This is a presumptuous way of sinning, and how dreadful that is, see in Num. 15 : 30.

INSTANCE 7. Truth is often held in unrighteousness by sinful silence, *in not reproving other men's sins;* thereby making them our own. We are sometimes cast into the company of ungodly men, where we hear the name of God blasphemed, or the truth, worship, or servants of God reproached; and have not so much courage to appear for God, as others have to appear against him: in such cases conscience is wont to stir up men to their duty, and charge it home upon them in the authority of such a scripture as this: "Thou shalt not hate thy brother in thine heart; thou shalt in any wise rebuke thy neighbor, and not suffer sin upon him." Lev. 19: 17. O, says conscience, thy silence now will be thy sin; this man may perish for want of a seasonable, plain, and faithful rebuke; thy silence will harden him in his wickedness. No sooner does such a conviction stir in the conscience, but many things are ready to lay hold on it. As,

(1.) *A spirit of cowardice* which makes us afraid to displease men, and chooses rather that the wrath of God should fall on them, than their wrath fall on us. We dare not take as much liberty to reprove sin as others do to commit it. They glory in their shame, and we are ashamed of what is both our glory and our duty.

(2.) *Dependence on, or near relation to the person sinning.* It is a father, a husband, a superior, on whose favor I depend, and should I displease him I may ruin myself; this is the voice of the flesh. Hence duty is neglected, and the soul of a friend basely betrayed; our interest is preferred to God's, and thereby frequently lost; for there is no better way to secure our own interest in any man's heart, than to fasten it in his conscience by our faithfulness and by being willing to hazard it for God's glory. The Lord blesses men's faithfulness above all their sinful, carnal policy. "He that rebuketh a man, afterwards shall find more favor than he that flattereth with his lips." Prov. 28: 23.

(3.) *Men's own guilt* silences them. They are ashamed and afraid to reprove other men's sins, lest they should hear of their own. Fear of retort keeps them from the duty of reprehension. Thus we fall into a new sin for fear of reviving an old one. "He that reproveth a scorner, getteth to himself shame; and he that rebuketh a wicked man, getteth himself a blot." Prov. 9 : 7. But this is the fruit of our pride and ignorance. What we fear, might turn to our benefit. The reproof given is duty discharged; and the retort in return is a fresh call to repentance for sin past, and a caution against sin to come.

INSTANCE 8. Another instance of conviction of unrighteousness imprisoned in men's souls is, *not distributing to the necessities of others*, especially such as fear God, when it is in the power of our hands to do it, and conscience as well as Scripture calls us to our duty. Men cannot be ignorant of that text where charity to the saints is by the Lord Jesus Christ put for the whole of obedience, and men's eternal states are fixed according to their observance of this command, Matt. 25 : 40, 41; though I fear few, very few study and believe it as they ought. Thou canst, says conscience, if thou wilt, relieve such or such a poor Christian, and therein express thy love to Christ : do it, God will repay it; if thou refusest, how dwelleth the love of God in thee? 1 John, 3 : 17. This is the voice of God and conscience, but divers lusts are ready to seize and bind this conviction also as soon as it stirs.

(1.) *The excessive love of earthly things.* The world is so deep in men's hearts, that they will rather part with their peace, yea, and their souls too, than part with it. Hence come those churlish answers, like that of Nabal, "Shall I then take my bread, and my water, and my flesh, that I have killed for my shearers, and give it unto men whom I know not whence they be?" 1 Sam. 25 : 11.

(2.) *Unbelief;* which denies honor and due credit to

Christ's bills of exchange drawn upon them in Scripture, and presented to them by the hands of poor saints. They refuse to credit them, though conscience protest against their non-compliance. Christ says, "Whosoever shall give you a cup of water to drink in my name, because ye belong to Christ, verily I say unto you, he shall not lose his reward." Mark 9 : 41. He shall gain that which he cannot lose, by parting with that which he cannot keep.

(3.) *The want of love to Jesus Christ.* Did we love him in sincerity, and were that love fervent as it ought to be, it would make us more ready to lay down our necks for Christ, than we now are to lay down a shilling for him. 1 John, 3 : 16. It is our duty, in some cases, to spend our blood for the saints. So it was in the primitive times: Behold, said the Christian's enemies, how they love one another, and are willing to die one for another. But that spirit is almost extinguished in these degenerate days.

INSTANCE 9. How many stand convinced, by their own consciences, what a sin it is to *spend their precious time so idly* and vainly as they do. When a day is lost in vanity, duties neglected, and no good done or received, at night conscience reckons with them for it, and asks what account they can give of that day to God, how they can satisfy themselves to lie down and sleep under so much guilt. And yet, when the morrow comes, the vanity of their hearts carries them on in the same course again the next day; and while they keep in vain company they are quiet, till conscience finds them at leisure to debate it again with them. Now the things which overpower these convictions are,

(1.) In some men, their *ignorance and insensibility* of the preciousness of time. They know it is a sin to spend their time so vainly, but little consider that eternity itself hangs upon this little moment of time; that the great work of their salvation will require all the time they have; and if it be not finished in this small allotment of time, it can never be finished. John 9 : 4.

(2.) *The examples of vain persons* who are as prodigal of their precious time as themselves, and entice them to spend it as they do.

(3.) The delusive power of *sensual pleasures*. O how pleasantly does time slide away in theatres and taverns, in relating or hearing stories, news, and other such matters.

(4.) *Inconsiderateness* of the sharp and terrible rebukes of conscience for this on a death-bed, or the terrors of the Lord in the day of judgment.

In all these instances you see how common is this dreadful evil of holding the truth in unrighteousness; yet these are but a few selected from many.

CHAPTER XIV.

THE TRUTH HELD IN UNRIGHTEOUSNESS—CONTINUED.

"THE WRATH OF GOD IS REVEALED FROM HEAVEN AGAINST ALL UNGODLINESS AND UNRIGHTEOUSNESS OF MEN, WHO HOLD THE TRUTH IN UNRIGHTEOUSNESS." ROM. 1:18.

V. I now proceed to show how and why the imprisonment of convictions, or holding the truths of God in unrighteousness, SO DREADFULLY INCENSES HIS WRATH. And this it does on several accounts.

1. *Knowledge of sin is a choice help to preserve men from falling into it.* There are thousands of sins committed in the world, which had never been committed if men had known them to be sins before they committed them. Every sinner durst not make so bold with his conscience as you have done. The apostle tells us, the reason why the princes of this world crucified the Lord of glory was, because they knew him not, 1 Cor. 2:8; had they known him they would not have dared to do as they did. And so, in multitudes of lesser sins, Satan blinds the eyes of men with ignorance, then uses their hands and tongues in wickedness; he is the ruler of the darkness of this world. Eph. 6:12. But when men know this or that to be sin, and yet venture on it, an excellent antidote against sin is turned into a dreadful aggravation of it, which highly incenses the wrath of God.

(2.) Knowledge and conviction going before, *add presumption to the sin* that follows after it; and presumptuous sin is the most provoking and daring sin: from this way of sinning David earnestly besought God to keep him: "Keep back thy servant also from presumptuous sins." Psa. 19:13. When a man sees sin and yet ventures on it, in such sinning there is a despising of the law of God: a man may break the law while he approves, reverences, and honors it in his heart, Rom. 7 : 12, 13; but here the commandment is despised, as God told David, 2 Sam. 12 : 9. It is as if a man should say, I see the command of God armed with threatening in my way, but I will go on for all that.

3. Knowledge and conviction *leave the conscience of a sinner wholly without excuse* for his sin. In this case there is no plea left to extenuate the offence: " Now they have no cloak for their sin." John 15 : 22. If a man sins ignorantly, his ignorance is some excuse for his sin; it excuses it in a measure, as Paul tells us, 1 Tim. 1 : 13, "I did it ignorantly:" here is a cloak or covering, an extenuation of the sin; but knowledge takes away this cloak, and makes the sin appear naked in all its odious deformity.

4. Light or knowledge of the law and will of God, is a very choice and excellent mercy; it is a choice and singular favor, for God to make the light of knowledge shine into a man's understanding; it is a mercy withheld from multitudes, Psa. 147 : 19, and those who enjoy it are *under special engagements to bless God for it*, and to improve it diligently and thankfully to his service and glory: but for a man to arm such a mercy as this against God, to fight against him with one of his choicest mercies, this must be highly provoking to the Lord; it is therefore mentioned as a high aggravation of Solomon's sin, that he sinned against the Lord, after the Lord had appeared unto him twice. 1 Kings, 11 : 9.

5. This way of sinning argues an extraordinary degree of *hardness of heart;* it is a sign of but little tenderness, or sense of the evil of sin. Some men, when God shows them the evil of sin in the glass of the law, tremble at the sight of it; so did Paul: "When the commandment came, sin revived, and I died," Rom. 7 : 9, he sunk down at the sight of it. But God shows thee the evil of sin in the glass of his law, and thou makest nothing of it: O obdurate

heart! When the rod was turned into a serpent Moses fled from it, being afraid to touch it; but though God turn the rod into a serpent, and discover the venomous nature of sin in his word, thou canst handle and play with that serpent, and put it into thy bosom: this shows thy heart to be awfully infatuated.

6. To go against this convincing, warning voice, *wounds a man's conscience* more than any other way of sinning doth; and when conscience is so wounded, who or what shall then comfort thee? It is a true rule, the more any sin violates a man's conscience, the greater that sin is. The sin of devils is the most dreadful sin; and what makes it so, but the horrid violation of their consciences, and their malicious rebellion against clear knowledge? They know and sin, they believe and tremble, Jas. 2:19; they roar under the tortures of conscience like the roar of the sea, or the noise of the rocks before a storm.

O then, if there be any degree of tenderness left in you, if any fear of God or regard for salvation, let go all God's prisoners which lie bound and imprisoned in the souls of any of you this day. Blessed be God, some have done so, and are at rest in their spirits by so doing; they could have no ease till they unbound and yielded obedience to them. It is said, Acts 16:38, that when the magistrates at Philippi understood that the men whom they had bound and imprisoned were Romans, they feared; and well they might, for the punishment was great for any man who injured a citizen or freeman of Rome; but every conviction you imprison is a messenger of heaven, a commissioned officer of God, and woe to him that binds or abuses it. Do you know what you do? Are you aware of the danger? Wast thou not afraid, asked David of the Amalekite, to stretch forth thine hand to destroy the Lord's anointed? 2 Sam. 1:14. So say I, Art thou not afraid to destroy the immediate messenger of God, sent to thy soul for good? Conviction is a kind of embryo of conversion; the conversion and salvation of thy soul would be the result, were it obeyed: thy striving with it renders it abortive, and thy life must go for it, except. God revive it again. Loose then every man the Lord's prisoners—I mean, your restrained, stifled convictions—stifle them no longer; you see what a dreadful aggravation of sin it is, and that "the wrath of God is revealed from heaven against all ungodliness and unrighteousness of men, who hold the truth in unrighteousness."

INFERENCE 1. This will prove a fruitful doctrine to inform us, first, *that knowledge in itself is not enough to secure the soul of any man from hell.* No gifts, no knowledge but that only which is influential upon the heart and life, and to which we pay obedience, can secure any man from wrath: "If ye know these things, happy are ye if ye do them." John. 13:17. The greatest sins may be found in conjunction with the greatest knowledge, as you see in the fallen angels: light is then only a blessing when it guides the soul into the way of duty and obedience: there is many a knowing head in hell. Yet let no man indulge himself in ignorance, or shun the means of knowledge, that he may sin with less danger; for you must account to God for all the knowledge you might have had, as well as for that you possessed—for the means of knowledge he gave you, as well as for the knowledge you actually attained.

2. *What a choice mercy is a tender conscience*—a conscience yielding obedience to conviction. A drop of such tenderness in the conscience is better than a sea of speculative knowledge in the head. 1 Cor. 12:31. Many Christians are ashamed to see themselves excelled by others in gifts, and are apt to be discouraged; but if God has blessed thee with a tender heart, obedient to his will, so far as he is pleased to manifest it to thee, thou hast no reason to be discouraged for want of those gifts which others enjoy. You

cannot discourse floridly or dispute subtlely, but do you obey conscientiously, and comply with the manifested will of God tenderly? Then happy art thou. O, it is far better to feel a truth than merely to know it. It was the high commendation of the Romans, that they obeyed from the heart the form of gospel doctrine which was delivered them, Rom. 6:17, or rather into which they were delivered, as melted metals into moulds. Two learned divines travelling to the council of Constance were affected even to tears at the sight of a shepherd in the fields, mourning and melting at the sight of a toad, and blessing God that he had not made him such a loathsome creature; whereupon they applied Augustine's words to themselves: "The unlearned will rise and take heaven from the learned." Thy little knowledge made effectual by obedience, is more sanctified, more sweet, and more saving than other men's, and therefore of much greater value. It is more sanctified; for the blessing of God is upon it. Gal. 6:16. It is more sweet; for you relish the goodness, as well as discern the truth of gospel doctrines. Psa. 119:103. It is not an insipid, dry speculation. And then it is more saving, being one of those better things that accompany salvation. Heb. 6:9.

3. Learn hence *what an uncomfortable life intelligent, but unregenerate men live:* they are frequently at war with their own consciences. "There is no peace, saith the Lord, to the wicked." Isa. 48:22. They and their consciences are ever and anon at daggers; they have little pleasure in sin, and none at all in religion: they have none in religion, because they obey not its rules; and little in sin, because their consciences are still galling and terrifying them for imprisoning their convictions.

It is true, some men's consciences are seared as with a hot iron, 1 Tim. 4:2; but most have grumbling, and some have raging and roaring consciences: they seldom come under the word or rod, but their consciences lash them;

and when death approaches, the terrors of the Almighty do shake and terrify them. Altogether to neglect duty they dare not, and how to escape a lash from their consciences they know not. Fain they would have the pleasures of sin, but, like Balaam, they meet a sword in the way; they plunge themselves into diversions like Cain, to be rid of a fury within them; but all will not do. Is this a life for thee, reader, to live? No peace with God nor with thyself? Expect no peace while thy convictions lie bound and imprisoned in thy conscience. Sin for a moment is sweet in thy mouth, but it is presently turned into the gall of asps within thee. Job 20 : 14. O that you did but know the pleasures of a pure, peaceable conscience, and how much it excels all the delights of sense and sin.

4. *Ministers had need often to repeat and inculcate the same truths to their hearers; for the work is not half done, when truth is got into the minds and consciences of men.* Our work sticks at the heart more than at the head; the understanding is many times opened, when the heart and will are locked and fast barred against it. To open the passages between the head and heart is the greatest difficulty; this is the work of almighty power. There is knowledge enough in some men's heads to save them, but it has not its liberty; restrained truth cannot do its office. It is much easier to convince the mind than to change the heart or bow the will. The hardest part of the ministerial work is to preach truth into the hearts and lives of men. This makes the frequent inculcation of the same truths necessary to the people's souls. "To write the same things to you, to me indeed is not grievous, but for you it is safe." Phil. 3 : 1.

5. *How wonderful is the strength of sin, which can hold men fast after their eyes are opened to see the misery and danger it has involved them in.* One would think if a man's eyes were but once opened to see the moral evil that is in sin, and the everlasting train of penal evils that follow

it, together with a way of escape from both, it would be impossible to hold that sinner a day longer in such a state of bondage: the work were then as good as done. But alas, we are mistaken; sin can hold those fast who see all this. They know it is a horrid violation of God's just and holy laws; they know it brings them under his wrath and curse, and will damn them to all eternity if they continue in it; they know Christ is able to save them to the uttermost that come unto God by him, and that he is as willing as he is able; and yet no arguments can prevail with them to part with sin. Show but a beast a flame of fire, and you cannot drive him into it if he see any way of escape. Tell a man this is rank poison and will kill him, and you cannot make him swallow it though wrapt up in sugar, or put into the most pleasant sweetmeats. But let a sinner see death and destruction before him, and sin can make him rush on, as a horse into the battle. Jer. 8:6. He goes as an ox to the slaughter; his heart is fully set in him to do evil, Eccl. 8:11; as one, when his physician told him if he followed such a course of sin he would in a little time lose his eyes, said, Farewell, then, sweet light: I cannot part with this practice. So with sinners: rather than forego their pleasures and break their customs in sin, farewell heaven, Christ, and all. O the bewitching power of sin. "And they said, there is no hope, but we will walk after our own devices." Jer. 18:12. When a man considers what visions of misery and wrath convictions give men, he may wonder that all convinced men are not converted; and on the other hand, when he considers the strong hold sin has upon the hearts of sinners, it may justly seem a wonder that any are converted.

6. *How dreadful is the state of apostates who have had their eyes opened, their consciences awakened, their resolutions for Christ seemingly fixed; and yet, after all this, return to their former course of sin.* You see, brethren, sin has not only power to hold men in bondage to its lusts after

their eyes have been opened, but it has power to entice back those who seemed to have clean escaped out of its hands. 2 Pet. 2 : 18, 19. The unclean spirit may depart for a time, and make his reëntry into the same soul with seven spirits worse than himself. Matt. 12 : 43–45. Restraints by conviction and formality do not wholly dispossess Satan, he still keeps his property in the soul, for he calls it "my house;" and that property which he keeps under all these convictions and partial reformations, opens to him and all his hellish retinue a door for his return. But O how awful will the end of such men be; and how just is that law of heaven which dooms the apostate to eternal wrath! Heb. 10 : 38. Such are twice dead, and will be plucked up by the roots. Jude 12.

7. *How sure and dreadful will be the condemnation of all those, in the day of the Lord, who obstinately continue in sin, under the convictions and condemnations of their own consciences.* Unhappy men, you are condemned already, John 3 : 18; condemned by the law of God and by the sentence of your own consciences. What your own conscience says according to God's law, he will confirm and make good. "If our heart condemn us, God is greater than our heart, and knoweth all things." 1 John, 3 : 20. His sentence will be as clear as it will be terrible; for in the last day the books will be opened—the book of God's omniscience, and the book of thine own conscience. The book of conscience is as it were a transcript or counterpart of God's book for thee to keep in thine own bosom. When God's book and thy own shall be compared and found exactly to agree, there can be no further dispute of the equity of the account. Then God shall charge thee, saying, "Thou knewest this and that to be sin, and yet thy lusts hurried thee on to commit it; is it not so? look, sinner, into thine own book, and see if thy conscience has not so charged it to thy account. Thou knewest prayer was thy duty when thou neglectedst it; and over-

reaching the ignorant, credulous, and unwary was thy sin when the love of gain tempted thee to it. You knew I had plainly told you that theft, uncleanness, drunkenness, and extortion would bar you out of the kingdom of Christ and of God, 1 Cor. 6 : 9, 10; and yet, putting that to the venture, you have lived in those sins; is it not so? Examine the book in your own bosom, and see." The Lord make men sensible of coming wrath for the sins they live in under light; for the wrath of God is revealed from heaven against them.

Is the wrath of God revealed from heaven against all who hold the truth in unrighteousness? Then let me exhort and persuade you by all the regard and love you have for your souls, by all the fears you have of the incensed wrath of the great and terrible God, that you forthwith set your convictions at liberty, and loose all the Lord's prisoners that lie bound within you: "Because there is wrath, beware." Job 36 : 18. O stifle the voice of your conscience no more, slight not the softest whisper or least intimation of conscience; reverence and obey its voice. MOTIVES pressing and persuading this, are many; yet estimate them by weight rather than by number.

MOTIVE 1. The wrath of God is revealed from heaven against them who hold the truth in unrighteousness; and *because there is wrath, beware.* Are you truly informed what the wrath of God is? "Who knoweth the power of thine anger? even according to thy fear, so is thy wrath." Psalm 90 : 11. O, if the wrath of a king, who in all his glory is but a worm, be as the roaring of a lion, and as the messengers of death, Prov. 20 : 2; 16 : 14; what then is the power of *His* wrath, at whose frowns the kings of the earth tremble, and the captains and the mighty men shrink away? If the lesser executions of it by providence in this world be so dreadful that even good men have desired a hiding-place in the grave till it be past, Job 14 : 13; then what is the full execution thereof upon the ungodly in the place of torment? If the threats and denunciations of it against others made Habakkuk, though assured of personal safety, to quiver with his lips and tremble in his bowels, Hab. 3 : 16 ; how much more should those tremble and quiver who are to be the subject of it, and not the mere heralds of it as he was? And, which is more than all, if Jesus Christ, who was to feel it but a few hours, and had the power of the Godhead to support him under it, did, notwithstanding, sweat as it were great drops of blood, and was sore amazed ; think with thyself, poor man, how shall thy heart endure, or thy hands be strong, when thou hast to do with an incensed God?

MOTIVE 2. *Till you set free your convictions, Satan will not let you go;* he binds you while you bind them. Here is the command of God and the command of Satan in competition. Let my truths go free, which thou holdest in unrighteousness, says Jehovah ; bind and suppress them, says Satan, or they will deprive thee of the liberty and pleasure of thy life. While thou slightest the voice of God and conscience, dost thou not avowedly declare thyself the bondslave of Satan ? "His servants ye are to whom ye obey." Rom. 6 : 16. Dare not to take one step further in the way of known sin, says conscience ; continue not at thy peril in such a dangerous state, after I have so clearly convinced and warned thee of it. Fear not, says Satan, if it be ill with thee, it will be as ill with millions. God will wound the heads of such as go on in their trespasses, says the Scripture. Psalm 68 : 21. Tush, others do so, and escape as well as the most scrupulous, says Satan. Now, I say, thy obedience to Satan's commands plainly declares thee, all this while, to be a poor enslaved captive to him, acted on and carried according to the prince of the power of the air, the spirit that now worketh in the children of disobedience.

MOTIVE 3. *Until you obey your convictions, you are confederates with Satan* in a desperate plot against your own souls; you join with Christ's great and avowed enemy to dishonor him and destroy yourselves. Two things make you confederates with Satan against your own souls. First, your *consent* to this project for your damnation; for so your own conscience out of the Scriptures informs you it is: consent makes you a party. Second, your *concealment* of this plot brings you in as a party with him. Confess thy sin, and bewail it, says conscience: not so, says pride and shame; how shall I look men in the face if I do so? Do not you, in all this, believe Satan and make God a liar? Do not you act as men that hate their own souls, and love death? Prov. 8:36. O it is a dreadful thing for men to be accessory to their own eternal ruin, and that after fair warning and notice given them by their own conscience. Satan, be his power what it will, cannot destroy you without your own consent.

MOTIVE 4. *While you go on stifling convictions, and turning away your ears from calls to repentance, you cannot be pardoned;* you are in your sins, and the guilt of them all lies at your door. You see what the terms of remission are: "Let the wicked forsake his way, and the unrighteous man his thoughts: and let him return unto the Lord, and he will have mercy upon him; and to our God, for he will abundantly pardon." Isa. 55:7. So again, "He that covereth his sins shall not prosper: but whoso confesseth and forsaketh them, shall have mercy." Prov. 28:13. You see by these, and many more plain scripture testimonies, that there can be no hope of remission while you go on in this path of rebellion; concealing, yea, and persisting in your known wickedness. There is a necessary and inseparable connection between repentance and remission, Acts 5:31, and Luke 24:47; and can you endure to have guilt your companion during life and for ever?

MOTIVE 5. *You can never have peace with conscience while you keep convictions prisoners.* A man's conscience is his best friend or his worst enemy; thence are the sweetest comforts, and thence are the bitterest sorrows. It is a dreadful thing for a man to lie with a cold sweating horror upon his panting bosom. And this, or which is worse, obduracy and stupidity must be the case of them who hold the truth in unrighteousness. There can be no sounding a retreat to these terrors till Sheba's head be thrown over the walls; I mean, till that sin which your conscience convinces you of, be delivered up. As Israel could have no peace till Achan was destroyed; so thou shalt have no peace while thy sin is covered and hid. Men may cry peace, peace, to themselves while they continue in sin, Deut. 29 : 19, but the sharpest troubles of conscience are better than such peace. Deliver up thyself, if thou love peace, into the hands of thy own convictions, and thou art in the true way to peace. Thy rejoicing must be in the testimony of thy conscience, as the apostle speaks, 2 Cor. 1 : 12, or thou rejoicest in a dream, in a delusion, in a thing of naught.

MOTIVE 6. *What dreadful charges are you likely to meet with on your death-beds on account of the sins you have lived in, against knowledge and conviction.* Conscience is never more active and vigorous than in the last hours and moments of life. Now it will be stifled and overruled no longer. It whispered before, but now it thunders. If a man has a clear and quiet conscience, his evening is clear and his sun sets without clouds: "The end of that man is peace." Psalm 37 : 37. In contemplation of this felicity, Balaam uttered that wish, "Let my last end be like his." Num. 23 : 10. This peace is the result of a man's obedience to the voice of conscience, this being the evidence we can most safely rely upon of our interest in Christ; but the result of such violations and abuses of thy conscience cannot be peace to thy soul. It is true, some wicked men die in seeming peace, and some good men in trouble, but both the one and the other are mistaken: the first, as to the good estate he fancies himself in, and the other as to his bad estate; and a few moments will clear up the mistake of each.

Motive 7. Obedience to conviction will not only produce peace at death, but *will give you present ease and refreshment*. No sooner did David resolve to obey the voice of conscience in confessing his sin, but he had ease in his spirit. Psa. 32 : 5. "The work of righteousness shall be peace; and the effect of righteousness, quietness and assurance for ever." Isa. 32 : 17. On the contrary, you find wicked men have no rest in their conscience, Job 20 : 20; for guilt lies working there as a thorn in the flesh. And what is life worth without ease? To live ever in pain, to live upon the rack, is not to live. If, then, you love ease and quietness, obey your conscience; pull out that thorn—I mean, the sin that sticks fast in thy soul, and pains thy conscience. Who would endure so much anguish for all the flattering pleasures of sin?

Motive 8. *Convictions obeyed are the inlets to Christ and eternal salvation by him;* they are the leading of the Spirit, in order to union with Christ. John 16 : 14. Till you obey and yield up yourselves to them, Christ is shut out of your souls; he knocks, but finds no entrance. At your peril, therefore, be obedient to their calls. While you parley with your convictions, and demur to their demands, Christ stands without, offering himself graciously to you, but is not admitted; so that no less than your eternal happiness or misery depends on your obedience or disobedience to the calls of your convictions.

Motive 9. Obey your convictions, honor their voice, and restrain them not; *then shall your conscience give a fair testimony for you at the judgment-seat of Christ.* You read of the answer of a good conscience toward God, 1 Pet. 3 ; 21 ; than which nothing can be more comfortable. This gives a man boldness in the day of judgment. 1 John, 4 : 17

Believe it, sirs, it is not your baptism, your church privileges, or the opinion men have of you, but the testimony of your conscience, that must be your comfort. I know men are not justified at God's bar by their own obedience, nor by any exactness of life; it is only Christ's righteousness that is the sinner's plea; but your obedience to the calls of God and conscience is the evidence that you are in Christ.

MOTIVE 10. *Consider what a choice mercy it is, to be under such calls and convictions of conscience as may yet be obeyed:* it is not so with convictions after death. Conscience convinces in hell as well as here, but all its convictions there are for torment, not recovery. O it is a choice mercy that your convictions are yet remedial, not purely penal—that you are not fixed in the state of sin and misery as the damned are, but yet enjoy the benefit of your convictions; but this you will not enjoy long; therefore I beseech you, by all that is dear and valuable in your eyes, reverence your conscience, and set free the Lord's prisoners which lie bound within you.

I now come to expostulate the matter with your consciences, and propound a few convictive queries to your souls. I am afraid there are many in this wretched case, who hold the truths of God in unrighteousness, though the wrath of God be revealed from heaven against all them that do so. Let me set before you some of GOD'S DEMANDS.

DEMAND 1. *Do not some of you stand convinced by your own consciences this day, that your hearts and practices are vastly different from those of the people of God* among whom you live, and whose character you read in Scripture? Do not your consciences tell you, that you never took the pains for your salvation you see them take; that there are some in your families, nay, possibly in your bosoms, who are serious and heavenly, while you are vain and earthly—who are on their knees wrestling with God, while you are about the things of the world? And does not conscience sometimes whisper thus into thine ear: Soul, thou art not right; something is wanting to make thee a Christian; thou wantest that which others have; and except something further be done within thee, thou wilt be undone for ever? If it be so, let me advise thee to hearken diligently to this voice of conscience; do not venture to the judgment-seat of God in such a case: ponder that text, Matt. 21 : 32, "For John came unto you in the way of righteousness, and ye believed him not: but the publicans and the harlots believed him; and ye, when ye had seen it, repented not afterward, that ye might believe him;" and let the disparity your conscience shows you between your own course and that of others, awaken you to more diligence and seriousness about your own salvation. How canst thou come from the tavern, or thy vain recreations, and find a wife or child in prayer, and thy conscience not smite thee? It may be, they have been mourning for thy sins while thou hast been committing them. Perhaps there lives not far from thee a godly poor man, who out of his hard and pressing labors redeems more time for his soul in a week, than ever thou didst in thy life. O hearken to the voice of thy conscience, else thou art he that holdest truth in unrighteousness.

DEMAND 2. *Did thy conscience never meet thee in the way of sin*, as the angel of the Lord met Balaam with a drawn sword, brandishing the threatenings of God against thee? Did it not say to thee, as a captain once said to his soldiers about to retreat, casting himself down in their way, "If you go this way you shall go over your captain, you shall trample him first under your feet?" "Stop, soul, stop!" said thy conscience; "this and that word of God is against thee; if thou proceed, thou must trample upon the sovereign authority of God, in this or that command." Yet thy impetuous lusts have hurried thee forward: thou wouldst not fairly debate the case with thy conscience; and then did not thy conscience say to thee, as Reuben did to his brethren, "Spake I not unto you, saying, Do not sin against the child; and ye would not hear? therefore behold also his blood is required." Gen. 42:22. If this has been your course of sinning, verily you are the persons that have held the truth of God in unrighteousness, and against you the wrath of God is revealed from heaven.

DEMAND 3. Have you not seen the wrath of God revealed from heaven *against other sinners who have gone before you* in the same course of sin in which you now go? and yet you persist in it, notwithstanding such dreadful warnings. Thus did Belshazzar, though he saw all that the God of heaven had done to his father. Dan. 5:20–22. You have seen great estates scattered, and their owners that got them by fraud and oppression reduced to beggary; yet when a temptation is before you, you cannot forbear to take the advantage, as you call it, to get the gain of oppression. You have seen drunkards clothed with rags, and brought to miserable ends—adulterers severely punished, their names and estates, souls and bodies blasted, and wasted by a secret, but just stroke of God. Have you taken warning by these strokes of God, and hearkened to the monitions and cautions your consciences have thereupon given you? If not, thou art the man who holdest the truth of God in unrighteousness.

DEMAND 4. *Do not your hearts rise against necessary and due reproofs given you by those who love your souls better than you do?* If you hate a faithful reprover, though you know you are guilty of the sin he reproves—if you recriminate or deny in such cases, you are certainly so far confederate with Satan against your own soul, and imprison your own convictions.

DEMAND 5. *Have not some of you apostatized from your first profession*, and are not those hopeful blossoms which once appeared upon your souls blighted and gone?

You had lively convictions and melting affections, tenderness in your conscience and zeal for duties; but all is now vanished; your affections are cold and your duties are omitted, though conscience often bids you remember from whence you are fallen, and do your first works. You are the persons guilty of this sin.

DEMAND 6. *Do none of you presume upon future repentance,* and make bold with your conscience for the present, thinking thus to compound with it? This argues thee to be a self-condemned man, and one holding truth in unrighteousness: thy sin is present and certain, thy repentance but a peradventure. 2 Tim. 2:25. This is a daring way of presumptuous sinning.

DEMAND 7. *Have none of you taken the vows of God upon you* to break off your iniquities by repentance, when you have been in dangerous sickness on shore, or dreadful tempests at sea? Have you not said, Lord, if thou wilt but spare me this once, I will never live in the way I have lived any more: try me, O Lord, this once; and yet, when that affliction has vanished, your purposes and promises to God have vanished with it: you are the persons that hold the known truths of God prisoners in your souls. And to all these seven sorts of sinners, this text may justly be as the handwriting upon the wall once was, even a *mene tekel* that may make thy very loins to shake. Dan. 5:25–31.

This doctrine furnishes important DIRECTIONS for the prevention of such presumptuous sins in men, that truth may have its free course through their souls.

DIRECTION 1. And to this end my first direction is, that you *fail not to put every conviction into speedy execution.* Do not delay; it is a critical hour, and delays are exceedingly hazardous. Convictions are fixed and secured in men's souls four ways. First, by deep and serious consideration: "I thought on my ways, and turned my feet unto thy testimonies." Psalm 119 : 59. Secondly, by earnest prayer: thus Saul, under his first convictions, fell on his knees: "Behold, he prayeth." Acts 9 : 11. The breath of prayer foments and nourishes the sparks of conviction, that they be not extinct. Thirdly, by diligent attendance on the word. The word begets conviction, and the word can through God's blessing preserve it. Fourthly, by performing, without delay, the duty thou art convinced of. "If any be a hearer of the word, and not a doer, he is like unto a man beholding his natural face in a glass; for he beholdeth himself, and goeth his way, and straightway forgetteth what manner of man he was." James 1 : 23, 24. Take the sense thus: a man looks into the glass in the morning, and perhaps he sees a spot on his face, or a disorder in his hair or clothes, and thinks with himself, I will rectify it anon; but being gone from the place, one thing or other diverts his mind, he forgets what he saw, and goes all the day with the spot on his face, never thinking of it more. O brethren, delays are dangerous, sin is deceitful, Heb. 3 : 13; Satan is subtle, 2 Cor. 11 : 3, and in this way he gains his point. This motto may be written on the tomb of most that perish: "Here lies one that was destroyed by delays." Your life is uncertain, so are the strivings of the Spirit. Besides, there is a mighty advantage in the first impulse of the soul. When thy heart is once up in warm affections and resolutions, the work may be easily done; as a bell, if once up, goes easily, but is hard to raise when down. See, in 2 Chron. 29 : 36, what advantage there is in a present warm frame. Besides, the nature of these things is too serious and weighty to be postponed and delayed. You cannot get out of the danger of hell, or into Christ too soon. Moreover, every repetition of sin after conviction greatly aggravates it. For it is in sinning as in numbering, if the first be one, the second is ten, the third a hundred, and the fourth a thousand. And to conclude, think what you will, you can never have a fitter season than the present: the same difficulties you have to-day, you will have to-morrow, and it may be greater. Begin at once, therefore, to execute your convictions.

DIRECTION 2. If you would be clear from this great wickedness of holding the truth in unrighteousness, see that you reverence *the voice and authority of your conscience;* and resolve with Job, "My heart shall not reproach me so long as I live." Job 27:6. There are two considerations fitted to beget reverence in men to the voice of their consciences.

(1.) *Conscience obeyed and kept pure and inviolate, is thy best friend on earth.* "Our rejoicing is this, the testimony of our conscience." 2 Cor. 1:12. The very heathen could say, "A good conscience is a wall of brass." What comforted Hezekiah on his supposed death-bed, but the testimony his conscience gave of his integrity? 2 Kings, 20:3. Solomon says, "The backslider in heart shall be filled with his own ways; and a good man shall be satisfied from himself." Prov. 14:14. Mark the opposition; conscience gives the backslider a heart full of sorrow, while the heart of the upright man is full of peace. He is satisfied from himself, that is, from his own conscience, which though it be not the original spring, yet is the conduit at which he drinks peace, joy, and encouragement.

(2.) *Conscience wounded and abused will be our worst enemy;* no poniards are so mortal as the wounds of conscience. "A wounded spirit who can bear?" Prov. 18:14. Could Judas bear it, or could Spira bear it? What is the torment of hell, but the worm that dies not; and what is that worm, but the remorse of conscience? Mark 9:44. Oh, what is that fearful expectation mentioned by the apostle, Heb. 10:27; and what sorrows are those described, Deut. 28:65, 66. The primitive Christians chose rather to be cast to the lions than into the power of an enraged conscience. Every little trouble will be insupportable to a sick and wounded conscience, as a quart of water would be to your shoulder in a great vessel of lead.

Oh, if men did but fear their own consciences, if they reverenced themselves, as the moralist speaks, if they exercised themselves to have always a conscience void of offence, as Paul did, Acts 24:16, then would they be clear of this great sin of holding the truth in unrighteousness.

DIRECTION 3. If you would escape the guilt and danger of holding God's truth in unrighteousness, *keep your hearts under the awful sense of the day of judgment*, when every secret thing must come into judgment, and conscience like a register-book is to be opened and examined. The consideration of that day gives your conscience a seven-fold defence against sin. First, it incites every man to get real, solid grace, and not rest in an empty profession, and this secures us from formal hypocrisy, that we be not found foolish virgins. Matt. 25:3. Second, it excites us to the diligent improvement of our talents, that we be not found slothful servants, neglecting any duty to which God and conscience call us. Matt. 25:21. Third, it confirms and establishes us in the ways of God, that we wound not conscience by apostasy. 1 John, 2:28. Fourth, it is a loud call to every man to repent, and not to lie stupid and senseless, under guilt. Acts 17:30, 31. Fifth, it is a powerful antidote against formality in religion, the general and dangerous disease of professors. Matt. 7:22, 23. Sixth, it excites holy fear and watchfulness in the whole course of life. 1 Peter, 1:17. Seventh, it puts us not only on our watch, but on our knees in fervent prayer. 1 Peter, 4:7.

And he who feels such effects as these from the consideration of that day, is fortified against the sin my text warns us of, and dares not hold the truth of God in unrighteousness. It is our indifference as to a judgment to come, and ignorance of the nature of it, which embolden us to neglect known duties and commit known sins. Amos 6:3; 2 Pet.

3 : 3, 4. If our thoughts and meditations were engaged more frequently and seriously on such an awful subject, we should rather choose to die than to do violence to our consciences.

DIRECTION 4. *Get true apprehensions of the moral evil that is in sin, and of the penal evil that follows;* then no temptation shall prevail with you to commit sin that you may escape a present trouble, or neglect a known duty to accommodate any earthly interest, and consequently to hold no truth of God in unrighteousness. It is fear of loss and sufferings that so often overbears conscience; but if men were thoroughly sensible that the least sin is worse than the greatest affliction or suffering, the peace of conscience would be well secured. That this is really so, appears thus: first, afflictions do not make a man vile in the sight of God. A man may be under manifold afflictions, and yet very precious in God's account, Heb. 11 : 36–38; but sin makes man vile in the sight of God. Dan. 9 : 14. Second, afflictions do not put men under the curse of God; blessings and afflictions may go together, Psa. 94 : 12, but sin brings the soul under the curse. Gal. 3 : 10. Third, afflictions make men more like God, Heb. 12 : 10; but sin makes us more like Satan. 1 John, 3 : 8; John 8 : 34. Fourth, afflictions for conscience' sake are but the creature's wrath inflamed against us; but sin is the inflamer of God's wrath against us, as in the text. Fifth, afflictions are but outward evils on the body; but sin is an internal evil on the soul. Prov. 8 : 36. Sixth, afflictions for duty's sake have many sweet promises annexed to them, Matt. 5 : 10; but sin has none. Seventh, the effects of sufferings for Christ are sweet to the soul, 2 Cor. 7 : 4, but the fruits of sin are bitter; it yields nothing but shame and fear. Eighth, afflictions for Christ are the way to heaven, but sin is the broad way to hell. Rom. 6 : 23. Ninth, sufferings for duty are but for a moment, 2 Cor. 4 : 17; but sufferings for sin will be eternal. Mark 9 : 44.

If such thoughts might be suffered to dwell with us, how would they guard the conscience against temptations, and secure our peace and purity.

DIRECTION 5. Be thoroughly persuaded of this great truth, that *God takes great pleasure in uprightness*, and will own and honor integrity amidst all the dangers which befall it. Psa. 11 : 7 ; Prov. 11 : 20. When he would encourage Abraham to a life of integrity, he engages his almighty power for his protection in that way : " I am the Almighty God ; walk before me, and be thou perfect." Gen. 17 : 1. " The Lord God is a sun and shield ; the Lord will give grace and glory ; no good thing will he withhold from them that walk uprightly." Psa. 84 : 11. An upright man is the boast of heaven, Job 1 : 8, because he bears the image of God. " The righteous Lord loveth righteousness." Psa. 11 : 7. And if integrity brings men into trouble, they may be sure the Lord will bring them out. " Many are the afflictions of the righteous, but the Lord delivereth him out of them all." Psa. 34 : 19. How safely then may they leave themselves in the hands of his infinite wisdom, power, and fatherly care. Nay, God is not only the *protector*, but also the *rewarder* of conscientious integrity, Psa. 18 : 20 ; and that in four ways. First, in the inward peace it yields : " The work of righteousness shall be peace ; and the effect of righteousness, quietness and assurance for ever." Isa. 32 : 17. But the effect of sinful and carnal policy is shame and sorrow. Second, in the success and issue of it ; it not only turns to God's glory, but it answers and accommodates our own designs and ends far better than our sinful projects can do. Prov. 28 : 23. Third, great is the joy resulting from it in the day of death. 2 Kings, 20 : 3 ; Psalm 37 : 37. Fourth, in the world to come. Psalm 49 : 14. Were this duly considered and believed, men would choose rather to part with life than with the purity and peace of their consciences. They would suffer all wrongs and injuries rather than do conscience the least injury.

DIRECTION 6. *Do not idolize the world,* nor overvalue the trifles of this life: it is the love of the world which makes men violate the rules of their own conscience, 2 Tim. 4 : 10 ; it is this that makes men strain hard to get loose from the ties of conscience. The young man was convinced, but the world was too hard for his convictions, Luke 18 : 23 ; the degree of his sorrow was according to the degree of his love of the world. It is not having, but overloving the world that ruins us ; it is a worldly heart which makes men turn and dissemble at the rate they do, in time of temptation. Could you once dethrone this idol, how safe would your conscience be. The church is described as clothed with the sun, and the moon under her feet, Rev. 12 : 1 ; the most zealous age of the church was the age of poverty. Try then these considerations upon your hearts, to loose them from the inordinate love of the world. First, what good will the world do when you have lost your integrity for its sake, and peace is taken away from the inner man? What joy of the world had Judas, and what comfort had Spira? If you part with your integrity for it, God will blast it and it shall yield you no joy. Second, except you renounce the world, you are renounced by Christ : disclaim it, or he will disclaim you. Luke 14 : 33. No man can be admitted into Christ's service, but by sealing this covenant with him. Third, whatever loss you shall sustain for Christ and conscience, he stands pledged to repair it to you, and that with an infinite overplus. Mark 10 : 29, 30. Fourth, in a word all the riches, pleasures, and honors in the world are not able to give you such joy and heart-refreshing comfort as the acquitting and cheering voice of your own consciences can do. Settle these things in your hearts as defences against this danger.

DIRECTION 7. *Beg of God, and labor to get more Chris-*

tian courage and magnanimity; for want of this, conscience is often overborne against its own light and conviction: Christian magnanimity is the security of conscience. It is excellent and becoming a Christian to be able to face any thing but the frowns of God and his own conscience. All the famous champions of truth and witnesses for God who came victorious out of the field of temptation, with safe and unwounded consciences, were men of courage and resolution. Dan. 3 : 16; Heb. 11 : 27; Acts 21 : 13. And what is this Christian courage but the fixed resolution of the soul to encounter all dangers, all sufferings, all reproaches, pains, and losses, in the strength of assisting grace, which shall assault us in the way of our duty? and so it stands opposed in Scripture to the spirit of fear, Heb. 11 : 27 ; to shame, Mark 8 : 38 ; to apostasy, Heb. 10 : 39. He must neither be afraid nor ashamed, nor lose one inch of ground for the sake of whatsoever dangers he meets with, and that because he has embraced Christianity upon those terms, and was told of all this before, John 16 : 1 ; because there is no retreating, but to our own ruin, Heb. 10 : 38 ; because he owes all this, and much more than this, to Christ, Phil. 1 : 29 ; because he understands the value of his soul above his body, and of eternal things beyond all temporal concerns, Matt. 10 : 28 ; and, in a word, because he believes the promises of God's assistance and reward, Heb. 11 : 25–27.

O my friends, were our fears thus subdued, and our faith thus exalted, how free and safe would truth be in our consciences! He who owns any truth for the sake of a living, or to promote worldly interest by it, will disown that truth when it comes to live upon him, let conscience plead what it will; but he that has agreed with Christ upon these terms, and is content to be miserable for ever if there be not enough in Christ to make him happy, this man will be a steady Christian, and will rather lie in the worst prison, than imprison God's known truths in unrighteousness.

CONCLUSION.

I HAVE now delivered my message. I have set before you the Lord Jesus in the glory of his free-grace and condescending love to sinners. O that I had had skill and ability to do it better! I have wooed and expostulated with you on Christ's behalf; I have labored according to my little measure of strength, to cast up and prepare the way by removing the stumbling-blocks and discouragements out of it. This has been a time of conviction to many of you, some have no longer held their convictions under restraint, but many, I fear, do so; and therefore I have in the close of all handled this awakening scripture, to show you what a horrid evil it is to detain God's truths in unrighteousness. I have also, in the name and by the authority of God, demanded all the Lord's prisoners, his suppressed and restrained truths, at your hands: if you will unbind your convictions this day, and cut asunder the bonds of carnal fear and shame with which you restrain them, those truths you make free will make you free indeed; if not, but you will still go on stifling and suppressing them in your own bosoms, remember they are so many witnesses prepared to give evidence against you in the great day. And O that while you delay this duty, the sound of this text may never be out of your ears, nor suffer you to rest: "The wrath of God is revealed from heaven against all ungodliness and unrighteousness of men, who hold the truth in unrighteousness."

www.ingramcontent.com/pod-product-compliance
Lightning Source LLC
Chambersburg PA
CBHW051247300426
44114CB00011B/924